AMERICAN

Traveling with Tocqueville

RICHARD REEVES

JOURNEY

in Search of

Democracy in America

SIMON AND SCHUSTER / NEW YORK

10   9   8   7   6   5   4   3   2   1

Library of Congress Cataloging in Publication Data

Reeves, Richard.
  American Journey.

  Bibliography: p.
  Includes index.
    1. United States—Politics and govern-
ment—1945- . 2. United States—Social
conditions—1960- . 3. United States—
Description and travel—1960- . 4. Tocqueville, Alexis de, 1805–1859. 5. Reeves, Richard I. Title.
E839.5.R38   973.92   82-710
ISBN 0-671-24746-8   AACR2

All illustrations are courtesy of the Beinecke
Rare Book and Manuscript Library, Yale University. The American sketches are taken from
the sketchbooks of Gustave de Beaumont.

Scattered extracts from Democracy in America
by Alexis de Tocqueville, translated by George
Lawrence, edited by J. P. Mayer and Max
Lerner. English language translation copyright
1966 by Harper & Row, Publishers, Inc. Reprinted by permission of the publisher.

The excerpt on pages 64–65, copyright © 1976
by Harrison Salisbury, is reprinted by permission of Curtis Brown, Ltd.

This book is for Catherine O'Neill

Contents

DE LA

DÉMOCRATIE

EN AMÉRIQUE,

PAR

ALEXIS DE TOCQUEVILLE,

AVOCAT A LA COUR ROYALE DE PARIS,

L'un des auteurs du livre intitulé :

DU SYSTÈME PÉNITENTIAIRE AUX ÉTATS-UNIS.

Orné d'une carte d'Amérique.

—

TOME PREMIER.

PARIS,

LIBRAIRIE DE CHARLES GOSSELIN

RUE SAINT-GERMAIN-DES-PRÉS, 9.

M DCCC XXXV.

The title page of the original edition of *De la Démocratie en Amérique*

Preface

One hundred and fifty years ago a young Frenchman named Alexis de Tocqueville, a minor nobleman and a minor official in his country's government, came to the United States and traveled here for nine months. The reason for his trip, officially, was an assignment to report on the American prison system, which was then quite different from those in Europe. But, really, he hoped to write a grand work, a book that would reveal the mysteries and wonders of the great experiment in democracy in the New World. A book, perhaps, that would make his name.

"I shall go see there what a great republic is like," he wrote to a friend before he left, speculating on what such a book might mean to the career of an ambitious young man interested in politics. "If the moment is favorable, some publication may let the public know of your existence and focus on you the attention of the parties."

He landed in Newport, Rhode Island, in May of 1831, and his journey took him through New York City, Philadelphia, and Boston, west across the Great Lakes to a frontier fort that would become Green Bay, Wisconsin, then south down the Ohio and Mississippi valleys to New Orleans, and north again through the Old South to Washington, D. C. He filled fourteen notebooks with his observations and thoughts, and with interviews with more than two hundred people he met along the way. The book he wrote, *De la Démocratie en Amérique—Democracy in*

America—fixed on him the attention of much of the world, from 1835, when the first of his two volumes was published, to 1981, when I was finishing this book.

Like many Americans, I first heard of *Democracy in America* in high school. Someone at Lincoln High School, in Jersey City, New Jersey, tried valiantly to explain to us what America might have been like in the 1830s, when Andrew Jackson and his frontiersmen came out of the hills of Tennessee to give democracy new meaning by tracking mud through the White House. I read some of the book in college. I became a newspaper reporter and began writing about politics and government, and about how Americans lived, about what kind of people we are. When I read about those things, someone always seemed to be quoting Tocqueville; when I wrote about them, I began quoting Tocqueville. "As Alexis de Tocqueville said . . ." There could be a single key that punches out those words on the typewriter of anyone who writes about the United States.

Well, Tocqueville did say much of what there was to be said about us. I discovered that when I finally read, really read, and then reread his work. One day, several years ago, a friend gave me a small volume of Tocqueville's travel diaries, his notebooks, translated from French into English for the first time in the 1930s. They were a working reporter's notebooks, complete with questions and answers:

"Q. Is it true that public opinion begins to be against slavery in Kentucky?"

"A. Yes. In the last few years there has been . . ."

I was in awe. I was looking at the notes for what was probably the best book ever written about my country, my people. I decided then that, whatever else I did, I would try to take those notes and recreate Tocqueville's journey: travel the same roads, see the same things or what had replaced them, talk to the modern counterparts of the men and women he questioned.

The little books were more adventure than political science. Tocqueville's notes and his letters home during those nine months tell the stories of Indians in the wilderness of Michigan and duels in Alabama. There was also more adventure, the adventure of discovery—discovering the Americans themselves, their energy, their ideas, their democracy. The words scrawled on the page in French raced as he explored America in his mind in conversations with John Quincy Adams, the embittered ex-

President; with Salmon Portland Chase, the Cincinnati lawyer who was to become Chief Justice of the United States; with Charles Carroll, the last surviving signer of the Declaration of Independence; with Sam Houston, the disgraced former governor of Tennessee who happened to be traveling down the Mississippi when Tocqueville was there.

One hundred and fifty years later, the journey was as thrilling for me. Forgotten streets in Detroit were a modern wilderness. There was gunfire and there were riots in Philadelphia. And my notes were an exploration of our character and our time with Richard Nixon, an ex-President in a sort of exile; with Supreme Court Justice Potter Stewart, a lawyer from Cincinnati; with the descendants of Charles Carroll, who had been the richest man in the United States; with Jerry Brown, the governor of California, who happened to be in New England when I was there.

I, in fact, was living in California, in Los Angeles, when I began following the trail of Tocqueville. I thought then that I would make a separate trip through the modern West, a huge area which had not been part of the United States in 1831. But, soon enough, I learned that the questions and the themes—mine and Tocqueville's—were the same everywhere in the great land. I was also, as a new "Westerner" for those years, traveling extensively in the great new arc of American civilization from Houston, Texas, through California and north to Seattle. I was asking the same questions; so, occasionally, in the book, a thought or a few words in a restaurant in Louisville, Kentucky, might be followed by a shout in the hallways of a high school in East Los Angeles. The words, the ideas, were the same in both places. The vigorous "can do" free enterprise mania of Texas and the sweet narcissistic detachment of California were in sharper focus in those regions but they were visible everywhere, part of the national character of the nomad people settling, resettling and unsettling the continent and nation. We were, I found, one people: Americans. There were no regional answers to questions of war and peace, of equality, of justice. The question was still American democracy: What had it become? Did it work? Could it peacefully translate the will of the people into life, liberty, and the pursuit of happiness for each of those people?

I began looking for my answers with an incomparable guide, Monsieur de Tocqueville, in the same place and in the same way he had.

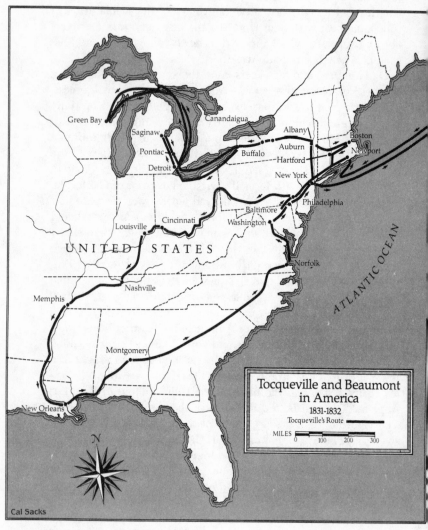

The American travels of Alexis de Tocqueville, May 9, 1831, to February 20, 1832

PART ONE

Newport
to Rochester

1
NEWPORT

"Trading Traffic Lights for Pensions ..."

I arrived in Newport, Rhode Island, on May 9, 1979. It was an old place by American standards, tucked in the northeast corner of the country, where the Europeans had first come. In the spring of 1639, religious refugees from the Massachusetts Bay Colony built a few houses on the south end of Aquidneck Island. The name, in the language of the Algonquin Indians, meant "Isle of Peace." It was a place meant to be a port; the east side of the island confronted the Atlantic Ocean, but the west side curled around a safe harbor.

The port and the town around it thrived for a while as a stop in the "Triangle Trade" of rum, molasses, slaves, and Bibles between New England, the West Indies, and Africa, supporting a population of about 11,000 people in 1776. But the Revolution came that year and 6,000 British troops marched into the little city, smashing and burning it to the ground. It never regained that early importance. By the time I arrived, it was a parody of its three pasts—a struggling resort town of 32,000 people hung with signs directing visitors to lovely areas of homes built in the years after that war, to the huge, late-nineteenth- and early-twentieth-century mansions of rich families who once summered in the air conditioned by the sea breezes that sweep the island's east side, and to the empty docks and buildings of the U.S. Navy, which had moved 45 ships and 23,000 people away from Newport in 1973. In the decades when the Navy supported and ruled the town, Thames Street, along the harbor, was called "Blood Alley" because of the fights inside and outside the bars and taverns on Saturday nights. Now the city's Convention and Visitor's Bureau was trying to persuade people to call the avenue "The Street of the Sea Captains."

It is a pretty place. They say it has the largest collection of eighteenth-century structures in the United States. The little skyline of the old waterfront is dominated by the white spire of Trinity Church, rising from a small hill above Thames Street, as it has been since 1726. It was quiet—the summer tourists had not yet come—too quiet for me. I didn't know exactly what it was I wanted to hear, or to see, but I had come to Newport to begin traveling the United States, to try to see, perhaps to understand, America and Americans in my time. I think I was trying to be a stranger, a foreigner, someone in a strange place. But it was hardly foreign to me. It seemed quite ordinary, a quiet American street.

I changed all that by pressing a button.

I turned on the radio. I pressed the "On" button on the dashboard of my rented automobile. I was, instantaneously, miraculously, swept into, engulfed in storms of facts, of ideas, of information, of opinions, of urgings, of preachments. I was on the unpeopled streets of a corner of America, in this torrent, amazed and confused. I could freely change my perspective and my environment, again and again, back and forth, by touching these buttons.

There were 38 different stations broadcasting on the AM band of the car radio. I had begun idly searching the little dial for the continuous drone of music and news and talk and voices telling me to try, try, try, buy, buy, buy—the sounds of electronic nature that fill American air. Then I began to actually listen.

Revolution was being preached—political, social, and religious—quite openly. A convicted criminal was being interviewed—quite respectfully—about how he judged the performance of the current President of the United States. Men were speaking in a language strange to me, Portuguese, broadcast daily from WRIV in Providence, Rhode Island. From Boston, WILD was broadcasting the voices of black Americans who telephoned the station from their homes and were put on the air—

live, uncensored, unedited—attacking the government, the police, white Americans. Referring to each other as "Brother" and "Sister," the callers I heard offered a consensus opinion that the public policy of the United States was deliberately designed and executed to subjugate 26 million black Americans. The brothers and sisters, who obviously had little formal education, worked out, over an hour, a fairly sophisticated analysis of what they saw as a colonial policy: Ruling whites sought out the most talented and therefore the most dangerous blacks and quickly elevated them into the majority's comfortable financial structure, eliminating the leadership cadre of potential black revolution. And some of the callers were calling for that revolution—for the violent overthrow of the government. From Lexington, Massachusetts, on WROL, a Protestant evangelist named Kathryn Kuhlman, who had been dead fór three years, was on tape that could play until eternity, vigorously attacking all recipients of government welfare. Work, she said, was God's welfare—and woe to the men or government that subverted Divine provisions. From New York City, WOR was broadcasting an interview with a man named John Ehrlichman, who had recently been released from jail for crimes committed while he served in the President's office, the White House. He had written a book, fiction, about Washington and was being asked to criticize the current President—the criminal's judgments being greeted with impressed murmurs of "I see." Four stations were broadcasting nothing but news. One of them, WEAN in Providence, reported with hints of shock and outrage that radio in the Soviet Union had, for 20 hours, withheld news from the Russian people that their government and the United States had completed negotiations on an arms limitation treaty. News withholders would be dealt with sternly, I thought, in this electronic place. Five stations were broadcasting only religious programming—Protestant services and analysis of current events—and as I began thinking about what that might mean, WCBS in New York broadcast a commentary by a man named Forrest Boyd, commenting on the commentary of *Public Opinion* magazine, which had recently commented on polling data:

There have not been any massive changes in formal religious participation in the United States in recent years. The appeal of the churches has continued to weaken somewhat.

Thus, only four Americans in ten now indicate that they have attended a church or synagogue in the last week. And there's been a sharp decline since the mid-1960s among Catholics—just over one in four attend religious services at least weekly. The plurality of the public think religion is losing influence in American life ... But, at the same time, personal religious beliefs and the acceptance of many religious principles seem exceptionally strong. Over 90 percent of Americans state that they believe in God. More than 70 percent believe in life after death ... 85 percent of the populace considered the Bible the word of God.

That was one hour on the AM band of one radio—and I have recorded only a tiny fraction of the information and opinion on concerns from stocks to sex that I heard in that hour.

An American in Newport during that day could choose among 79 radio stations—the 38 I heard plus 41 more on the FM band—and 8 television channels. Six newspapers printed that day were laid out in piles at Brooks Discount Drugstore—the day's papers from Newport, Providence, Boston, and New York. There were 250 different magazines in dazzling display at Lalli's News on Broadway. Down the street, the Christian Action Center, a bookstore, was selling hundreds of titles about one subject, God.

The magazines were more specialized than radio, aimed at much smaller audiences of Americans willing to pay from 75 cents to $5.00 for entertainment or for information on politics, business, religion, sports, science, health, heterosexuality and homosexuality, cooking, wine, automobiles, trucks, trailers, motorcycles, airplanes, movie stars, television stars, home repair, home decorating, camping, dogs, cats, astrology. . . .

Spending $13.25, I suddenly found printed reason to believe or consider that:

> Seldom in any nation's past has a powerless minority moved into politics as fast as American blacks have over the past 25 years. . . .
>
> —*U. S. News & World Report*

In California, a group called Analytical Assessments Corporation (4640 Admiralty Way, Marina del Rey 90291, (213) 822-2571) is trying to find a way, with the right kind of bombing, of bringing about the collapse of the Soviet government that now exists, but without massive destruction of that country.

—*Mother Jones*

Now that living together out of wedlock has become so common, many American institutions have been trying to come up with words that can be used in place of such terms as "husband," "wife," or "married couple." The Ford Foundation has replaced the word "spouse" with "meaningful associate," and the National Academy of Sciences, instead of saying "husband" or "wife," now employs the term "special friend." One maternity hospital in Washington, D.C., asks expectant mothers not for the father's name, but for the identity of the "significant other person."

—*New Age*

Most important, the new communications enlarge the areas in which social action takes place . . . By satellite communication, through television, every part of the world is immediately visible to every other part. The multiplication of interactions and the widening of the social arenas are the major consequences of a shift in the modalities of the infrastructure. This is a problem we shall return to later.

—*Harvard Business Review*

"America is growing at a rate of 10 billion words per minute," read the headline of an advertisement for an NBI computer word processing system that I saw in a national business newspaper, another daily paper, the *Wall Street Journal.* I couldn't vouch for the exact figure, but words and other information were certainly exploding in the air around me. And it was all for sale, all the time. On Broadway, down from Lalli's, there was a place called Store 24—a store open 24 hours a day. I could buy anything I wanted—food, cosmetics, one of more than 100 magazines—at three o'clock in the morning. It was that way, I knew, all over the country. Supermarkets were open around the clock and there was something both liberating and greedily uncivilized about that.

My own greed—and appetite—for information reached its limit at that $13.25, spent in the daylight. I passed up the opportunity to pay $2 for *High Times* magazine, which featured the cover headline, "APHRODISIACS—A Guide to the Sexiest Drugs and Herbs." The story was squeezed between almost a hundred pages of advertisements for complicated devices and chemicals useful in the storage, preparation, and use of various illegal narcotics and drugs—one for a "Bong," a water pipe for smoking marijuana or hashish, said, "Saturate your senses with a Sarah's Family acrylic bong by RIZLA. It cools the smoke, while it conserves your stash. Breathe deeply, and the only thing wasted will be you." Another magazine, the *Progressive,* cost $1.50, but I was not interested in the current issue, preferring to wait for the next one, which promised information on the construction of a hydrogen bomb capable of turning Aquidneck and all its people into vapor. My car radio had informed me several times that the government was trying to prevent distribution of the magazine to 30,000 regular readers, but commentators I heard, withholding nothing, said that no one expected the government to succeed because suppression of the information would violate the country's freedom of the press. The details of the bomb's design, it turned out, were public information. The writer of the article had found what he wanted by walking into government offices and public libraries and asking for it.*

It was there. Everything seemed to be. Americans could know, if not absorb, just about anything. One of the things I wanted to find out traveling the country was how Americans sorted it out. How did one choose what he or she had to know, wanted to know—didn't want to know, didn't care about, couldn't handle? To begin with, it was easier to find out what most of them read. That was the local newspaper and in Newport it was the *Newport Daily News,* delivered to 16,000 homes on the island each day.

How do you decide what information people want and what they should have? I was talking with Albert Sherman, Jr., the

* The government, which had not realized so much information was available to a sophisticated researcher about the design of the weapon, eventually dropped the legal attempt to prevent publication. In the November 1979 issue of the *Progressive,* Howard Morland wrote: "I am telling the secret to make a basic point as forcefully as I can: Secrecy itself, especially the power of a few designated 'experts' to declare some topics off limits, contributes to a political climate in which the nuclear establishment can conduct business as usual, protecting and perpetuating the production of these horror weapons."

general manager of the *Daily News*. "By surveying our readership," he said. "We survey extensively and we take the results
very, very seriously. First we find out who our readers are. We
know they are well educated and relatively affluent—one-third
are college graduates or have gone beyond college and 16 percent make more than $25,000 a year. Then we ask them what
they want and we try to give it to them."

What do they want?

"Fluff, mainly. More features. We are trying to find a feature
writer right now. Help on what to do in their leisure time. They
also say they want 'investigative reporting,' although I'm not
sure they know what they mean by that. They want national,
state, and local news presented in 'briefs,' little one-paragraph
items that summarize what happened someplace. We don't do
much foreign news, because I don't really think we're qualified
to."

There was indeed a lot of "fluff"—or padding—in the *Newport Daily News* that day. It is not a great newspaper—"Rhode
Isalnd" was the spelling at the top of the front page—but it
seemed fairly typical of small American newspapers. Twenty-
two of its 36 pages contained nothing but advertising and of the
14 "news" pages, three were devoted to sports and one to comic
strips. So, judging by their newspaper, the people of Newport
were primarily concerned with commerce and games. The third
concern was government—seven of the eight stories on the front
page dealt with government at the local, state, or federal level.
It was a government that seemed pervasive and overwhelming,
reaching deep into the daily lives of those people. Elected executives and legislatures and appointed judges, boards, councils,
commissions, and managers were reported deciding whether a
fireman named John Daniels could be discharged for missing
work too often, whether teachers at Portsmouth High School
could mention birth control in classes, whether Jeffrey Kolb
could serve hot as well as cold sandwiches at The Corner Store,
whether the actors of The Incredibly Far Off Broadway Theater
could legally produce plays on private property, whether Eric
Alsanger could sell lemonade at the Newport Police Parade, and
whether nineteen-year-old Donald Gomes had the right, under
the United States Constitution, to play volleyball with girls at
Rogers High School.

A page from Tocqueville's original notebooks, containing notes on the federal government

The official groups making those decisions for the people of Newport, Aquidneck Island, Rhode Island, and the United States had a formidable array of titles: Middletown Administrator, Middletown Personnel Review Board, Rhode Island Employment Security Board, Portsmouth School Committee, Newport City Council, and the United States First Circuit Court of Appeals. The Court of Appeals, the second highest court in the land, had the Gomes case. Federal judges, 74 miles away in Boston, would decide whether the young man's civil rights had been violated because the local public high school had a girls' volleyball team but did not have one for boys. The *Daily News* editorial on May 10 complained:

> Some judges continue to push their legal reasoning in such cases beyond the point of common sense, beyond the point of public acceptance.... Ignored by the judge was the fact that as long as Rogers lacked a girls' football team, girls were also deprived of the right to play football if they wished. Also ignored by the judge was the fact that boys— being bigger, faster and stronger than girls—can readily make the girls volleyball team, while girls are extremely unlikely to be able to make the boys' football team. No judge can alter these physical facts.... Respect for the law is of paramount importance in our society. Judges should not test such respect beyond the point of public acceptance.

The editorial did not question the right of government, through the courts, to enforce such strict legal equality among Rogers High students and, by extension, all Americans. What was questioned was the intelligence of the judge in the Gomes case. That question was consistent with Albert Sherman's answers when he was asked about the public officials who were making these decisions every day. "We have real trouble getting anyone of stature to run for office around here," he said. "We vote pretty much straight Democratic and, often, there isn't even a Republican candidate on the ballot. The candidates we do get are second-rate lawyers—the ones who need the prestige and income—and insurance brokers, bartenders. Mediocre people. Our state senator, Charley Thomas, just voted to give a lifetime pension of $41,000 a year to a judge in another part of the state. The judge wasn't supposed to be eligible for the pension for another 10 years. When we asked him why, Thomas said he did it as part of a deal to get a traffic light—the state controls traffic-light placement—at Hillside Avenue and Admiral Kalbfus Road here in Newport. So these people, the politicians, are making us pay more than $400,000 in taxes for the light, and we've got a state senator who was not only stupid enough to go for the deal but so stupid he's proud of it. I don't think that's the way things were supposed to work."

How is it supposed to work and how does it work in Newport, Rhode Island? Did democracy mean that anyone could know anything by turning a dial or walking into a library, or did it mean that you could hardly cross the street in Newport without the permission of government? Did information, the truth, make men free—or were individual thought and freedom of action drowning in tidal waves of facts and ideas? Had 200 years of dreams and energy—American democracy—come down to trading traffic lights for pensions? I went to Newport to look and to talk. There were many more places to go.

2
VERSAILLES
TO NEWPORT

"It Was an Exciting Time . . ."

I had gone to Newport because Alexis de Tocqueville had been there 148 years before, on May 9, 1831. That day, after a 37-day trip across the Atlantic, he began a nine-month journey through the new United States of America. With a companion, Gustave de Beaumont, Tocqueville was on a minor mission for the French government. After returning home in 1832—he never saw America again—he wrote a book, two volumes, titled *De la Démocratie en Amérique. Democracy in America.* It is probably enough to say of that work that it is still being published almost 150 years after the first volume appeared in Paris. Not many people would argue with the judgment of a contemporary reviewer in England, John Stuart Mill, who described *Democracy in America* as "the first philosophical book ever written on democracy as it manifests itself in modern society; a book, the essential doctrines of which it is not likely that any future speculations will subvert, to whatever degree they may modify them; while its spirit, and the general mode in which it treats its subject, constitute the beginning of a new era in the scientific study of politics."

Four days after landing in Newport on a 126-foot American-built sailing ship, the *Havre*—which had been forced away from its intended harbor, New York, by bad weather—Tocqueville wrote a letter to his mother describing the few hours he had spent in the Rhode Island port: "We went to visit the town, which seemed to us very attractive. It's true we weren't diffi- cult. It's a collection of small houses, the size of chicken coops, but distinguished by a cleanness that is a pleasure to see and that we have no conception of in France. Beyond that, the inhabi- tants differ but little superficially from the French. They wear the same clothes, and their physiognomies are so varied that it would be hard to say from what races they have derived their features. I think it must be thus in all the United States."

"This race is entirely commercial," Beaumont wrote to his family. "In the small city of Newport, there are four or five banks; the same is true in all the cities of the Union. . . ."

And today there are 24-hour stores in Newport—and the same is true in all the cities. The two young Frenchmen, in their days, were beginning to fill pages—of letters, of notebooks—with their impressions of this great new land and its people, *les Américains*. Tocqueville, traveling south and west through the most inhabited parts of the North American continent, to the Mississippi River and a bit beyond, to the Gulf of Mexico, filled fourteen notebooks with the words and thoughts of 270 men and women as he moved on by boat and coach, on foot and on horse- back. His first note was written on board the *Havre* after a con- versation with Peter Schermerhorn, a prominent New York busi- nessman returning home after travels in Europe:

CARACTÈRE NATIONAL DES AMÉRICAINS

M. Schermerhorn
(qui cefreudant est fort infatué de son pays) m'a dit que la plus grande bâche de caractère n *al* était l'avidité à l'enri- chir et à la faire vite pal. tous les moyens. il y a aux états unis une multitude de faillité et elles ne font pas assez de tort à ceux qui les font.
24 avril 1831

NATIONAL CHARACTER OF THE AMERICANS

Mr. Schermerhorn (who is however much infatuated with his country) told me that the greatest blot on the national character was the avidity to get rich and to do it by any means whatever. There are in the United States a great number of business failures, and these do not sufficiently in- jure those who are responsible. 24 April 1831.

Trinity Church, Newport

The writer of that note, Alexis Charles Henri Maurice Clérel de Tocqueville, was twenty-five years old at the time. He was born in 1805, the son of the Comte Hervé de Tocqueville, who had been imprisoned during the French Revolution but survived to serve royalty again during the brief Bourbon restoration of Charles X; and he was the great-grandson of Lamoignon de Malesherbes, the great statesman who had not survived, being guillotined after defending Louis XVI before the Convention. He had been trained as a lawyer, and in 1827 his father, a prefect to the King, arranged his appointment as a magistrate at Versailles. Perhaps he was more ambitious than most, but there seemed to be little to distinguish Alexis de Tocqueville from other young men of the *petite noblesse.*

The Bourbons, however, were again falling—and Tocqueville knew that. Restored to the throne in 1814 after the fall of Napoleon, Louis XVIII did not have the talent or the will to permanently establish a constitutional monarchy—and neither did his brother, Charles X, who became king in 1824. In 1830, as before, the King clashed with the Chamber of Deputies, the barricades went up in Paris, and on July 30 of that year, Charles fled to England. Tocqueville, by chance, was standing on a boulevard in Versailles at dawn as the King's carriages left the city for the last time—and the young man wept.

The last of the Bourbons was replaced by a *bourgeois* king, Louis Philippe. Tocqueville, with his friend Beaumont, began scheming to find some way to salvage his young political career under a king and government he despised and in the turmoil he saw ahead. Already the two young men had alienated many of their friends and their class by twice swearing loyalty oaths to Louis Philippe, whose ministers nevertheless demoted both of them to a level that might be described as assistant apprentice magistrate.

Only a month after the fall of Charles, Tocqueville wrote to a friend: "I have long had the greatest desire to visit North America: I shall go see there what a great republic is like; my only fear is lest, during that time, they establish one in France." Three months later, in another letter, he was arguing that becoming an expert on America might just be the making of him, referring this time to himself in the second person: "You know just exactly what a vast republic is like, why it is practicable here, impracticable there! All the points of public administration have been examined successively. On returning to France, you certainly know yourself possessor of a talent that you did not have on leaving. If the moment is favorable, some sort of publication may let the public know of your existence and fix on you the attention of the parties. If that doesn't happen, well and good! Your voyage at least has not injured you ..."

Ah, fame! Ah, survival. The idea that won their escape—in the form of 18-month leaves as magistrates—was Tocqueville's and Beaumont's proposal for an official study of American prisons and the reforms being tested in penal institutions on the other side of the Atlantic. It wasn't a bad idea—French prisons were still medieval, with men, women, and children, murderers, thieves, and debtors thrown together in foul dungeons and courtyards. But it wasn't such a good idea that the government would finance it; the families of the two young aristocrats won their appointments as prison commissioners and agreed to pay all the bills. Early on the morning of April 3, 1831, with 161 other passengers, Tocqueville and Beaumont set sail from the port of Havre bound for New York, for the United States of America.

There were 24 states united then; there were 13 million Americans. They were moving in a new field of extraordinary energy, not all of it controlled. It was an exciting time, the time of a triple frontier—of geography, of industry, of democracy itself. Americans were settling and also moving on from new places, building homes, towns, roads, and canals west of the Appalachians, in the great valley of the Mississippi River, around the Great Lakes. A man who was not from the original 13 colonies, a westerner, Andrew Jackson, was President; mass democracy was beginning to triumph. And the talk was always of *improvement* and of *reform*—what to do about slavery, about education, about God and the churches, about the rich, about women, about alcohol, about prisons.*

That was what Alexis de Tocqueville came to see—all of it. He began Democracy in America by writing as if he had come from the sky:

"North America has striking geographical features which can be appreciated at first glance.

"Land and water, mountains and valleys, seem to have been separated with systematic method, and the simple majesty of this design stands out amid the confusion and immense variety of the scene. . . .

"All things considered, the valley of the Mississippi is the most magnificent habitation ever prepared by God for man, and yet one may say that it is still only a vast wilderness.

"On the eastern slopes of the Alleghenies, between the mountains and the Atlantic, there is a long strip of rock and sand which seems to have been left behind by the retreating ocean. This strip is only forty-eight leagues broad on the average, but three hundred and ninety leagues long.† The soil in this part of

* The phrase "triple frontier" is from an essay, "Tocqueville and America," written by Max Lerner in 1964 and appearing as the introduction to the 1966 edition of *Democracy in America* (see Notes, page 372).

† A French league was the equivalent of 2.88 miles.

the American continent can be cultivated only with difficulty. The vegetation is scanty and uniform.

"It was on this inhospitable shore that the first efforts of human industry were concentrated. That tongue of arid land was the cradle of those English colonies which were one day to become the United States of America. The center of power still remains there, while in the land behind them are assembling, almost in secret, the real elements of the great people to whom the future of the continent doubtless belongs. . . .

"It was there that civilized man was destined to build society on new foundations, and for the first time applying theories till then unknown or deemed unworkable, to present the world with a spectacle for which past history had not prepared it."

That tongue of arid land, the northeastern United States and a little more, was supporting more than 70 million people by 1981, the 150th anniversary of Tocqueville and Beaumont's trip to the great new democracy of America. Tocqueville, however, covered geography and the economics of agriculture in a very few pages when the first volume of his work was published in Paris in 1835. He was interested in the people of the United States, in how they governed themselves and what that new form of governing meant to older societies in Europe. His introduction to that first edition began: "No novelty in the United States struck me more vividly during my stay there than the equality of conditions. It was easy to see the immense influence of this basic fact on the whole course of society. It gives a particular turn to public opinion and a particular twist to the laws, new maxims to those who govern and particular habits to the governed." And he concluded the second volume, ended the work, by writing: "The nations of our day cannot prevent conditions of equality from spreading in their midst. . . ."

That scope, those words were far in the future when Tocqueville and Beaumont finally reached New York City on May 11, 1831, after an 18-hour voyage from Newport on the steamboat *President.* There they were, two young foreigners—Beaumont was three years older—speaking not quite enough English, with a letter saying they represented the government of France. The *President* docked at the foot of Cortlandt Street in Manhattan and the two of them walked to a boarding house on Broadway and went to bed. The next day, to their amazement, the *New York Mercantile Advertiser* reported:

"We understand that two magistrates, Messrs. de Beaumont and de Tonqueville [sic], have arrived here on the ship *Havre,* sent here by order of the Minister of the Interior, to examine the various prisons in our country, and make a report on their return to France. To other countries, especially in Europe, a commission has also been sent, as the French Government have it in contemplation to improve their Penitentiary system, and take this means of obtaining all proper information. In our country, we have no doubt that every facility will be extended to the gentlemen who have arrived."

The same item, word for word, began to appear in newspapers across the country. The Americans were flattered! French commissioners had come across the sea to learn from Americans. Within two days Beaumont was writing to his mother: "Everyone here overwhelms us with courtesy and services . . . We have a thousand letters of introduction we could do without entirely, to such an extent are our wishes anticipated. . . ."

In fact, the Frenchmen had been in New York barely 24 hours when they were presented to the state's chief executive, Governor Enos T. Throop. It was a brief meeting, but Tocqueville, not for the last time, was struck by the informality of the Americans, by the small rituals of equality. Afterward he wrote his first diary note since actually arriving in the United States:

AMERICAN USAGES

The greatest equality seems to reign, even among those who occupy very different positions in society.

The authorities seem extraordinarily approachable.

The thirteenth of May *Mr. Morse,* judge of Cherry Valley, presented us to the governor of New York, who was staying at a *boarding house* and who received us in the parlor without any ceremony whatever. Mr. Morse assured us that anyone could at any time do as we had done.

3
ALBANY

"There Was No Parade in Albany . . ."

A few weeks later Tocqueville and Beaumont took advantage of the great American equality to approach the governor of New York again. They found Throop "a man of very simple manners . . . living on a small country place a league from Auburn."

"He took us for a walk in the woods," Beaumont wrote in a letter home. "While admiring the beauty of the trees we caught sight of a squirrel. At that the governor began to run as fast as his legs would carry him to get his gun at the house. He soon came back, all out of breath, with his murderous weapon. The small animal had had the patience to wait for him, but the big man had the clumsiness to miss him four times in succession.

"The governor is a fine fellow, but undistinguished. . . ."

So undistinguished that neither of the Frenchmen ever recorded a single thought or word of Enos T. Throop. But he did unwittingly confirm one question and answer Tocqueville had written in his first notebook after an interview on June 7, 1831, in Yonkers, with one of the patriarchs of one of New York's first families, the Livingstons:

"I. What kind of men generally fill public office?

"He. Ordinarily the offices are held by men whose capacity and character place them in the second rank. Public positions yield neither enough money nor enough consideration nor enough power to attract the energies of distinguished men. It was not so at the beginning of the Republic. Today we no longer see great statesmen. One's energies and means are employed in other careers."

That complaint seems to go with democracy, particularly when rich and richly educated men like Livingston assess the choices of the people. And Tocqueville, rich and educated, later wrote: "In the United States it is men of moderate pretensions who engage in the twists and turns of politics. Men of parts and vaulting ambition generally avoid power to pursue wealth; the frequent result is that men undertake to direct the fortunes of the state only when they doubt their capacity to manage their private affairs."

The current choice of the people, Throop's latest successor, Hugh Carey, did indeed go into politics after an older brother assumed control over the family business. But, sitting in his office in Albany, Carey did not necessarily disagree with Tocqueville:

"It is true, I guess," he said. "I don't find the same level of people in government that I find in other fields. Young lawyers, young doctors, young financiers, young planners, young engineers and environmentalists—they all seem—they all are more impressive than the people I see in politics and government anymore."

Emphasizing the word "young," the sixty-two-year-old governor presented the idea as a new one, a problem—if that was the right word—that had somehow developed after his generation had succeeded in public life by their "own exertions."

There is, in fact, not much really new under the sunlight of American politics. "By his own exertions" was a phrase Tocqueville used in his notebook five months after he had been in Albany and met the governor of New York for the second time. The Frenchman was still pondering the quality of American politicians on December 27, 1831, on a steamboat churning down the Mississippi River, when he met a former governor of Tennessee, another man he found unimpressive:

"I was again assured today that in the new States of the West the people generally make very bad choices. Full of pride and without enlightenment, the voters wish to be represented by people of their own sort. Moreover, to gain votes, one must descend to maneuvers that disgust men of distinction. One must haunt the taverns, drink and argue with the mob; that is what is called *Electioneering* in America.

". . . This man has been governor of Tennessee. Afterwards he left his wife, having before that, it is said, subjected her to very bad treatment. He took refuge with the Indians, married one of them and became one of their chiefs. I asked what could have commended him to the people's choice. 'That he came from them,' I was told, 'and had risen by his own exertions.' "

"Mr. Houston" was the identification in the notebook. The first name, unrecorded, was "Sam." Sam Houston—whose popular nicknames included "Squaw Man" and "Big Drunk"—was leaving Arkansas and his home among the Creek Indians on the journey that would lead him to military glory in Texas, the presidency of the Republic of Texas, and, when his country became a state, a seat in the U. S. Senate.*

It's a free country. American politicians are self-selected; thus American leaders are self-selected. A century and a half after Tocqueville expressed disgust over the maneuvers of democracy, Governor Carey was saying: "It's not surprising that good people wouldn't want to run. I can't imagine why anyone does it . . . There's less income and less fulfillment than in other careers, and now you have to work with people who don't have any commitment to anything. There's no privacy left at all. The media has become more exotic as it's developed the capacity to

---

* Later on the same trip, Tocqueville talked for a while with Houston and came away more impressed—"his person indicates physical and moral energy." With a couple of other American heroes, the visitor never got that second chance. "Daniel Webster," he said, "like thousands of other statesmen, cares only for power." Tocqueville only heard about another Western politician, who was to die a hero in Texas, but used him as an example of the coarseness of American politics: "When the right of suffrage is *universal,* and when the deputies are paid by the state, it's singular how low and how far wrong the people can go. Two years ago the inhabitants of the district of which Memphis is the capital sent to the House of Representatives in Congress an individual named David Crockett, who has had no education, can read with difficulty, has no property, no fixed residence, but passes his life hunting, selling his game to live, and dwelling continuously in the woods. His competitor, a man of talent and wealth, failed."

track and trace every area of your life and your family. They destroy you for no reason."*

As we talked, the governor was going ahead with plans to run for a third term. Before being elected to state office, he had been a member of Congress for 14 years. A reelection campaign would be his eleventh campaign in 22 years; Carey, in effect, ran for office for a living. The people of New York had hardly called him to duty. No important group, publicly established or secretly conspiring, had selected him as their candidate. He wanted the job and the title—first as congressman then as governor—and there was a way to get it through his own exertions.

The democracy that Tocqueville saw was, politically, a seedling, the acorn of the oak that had shaded Hugh Carey's life. "In the United States," the visitor reported in *Democracy in America*, "except for slaves, servants, and paupers fed by the township, no one is without a vote and, hence, an indirect share in lawmaking." That seemed quite remarkable to him, but since then the right to vote had been extended and expanded again and again—to white male servants and paupers, to black males, to all women, to all Americans eighteen years old and older except convicted criminals. That extension of the franchise made it impossible to electioneer just by haunting the taverns. For better or worse, what Tocqueville called a "mob" became a mass as technologies were developed making it possible for Hugh Carey or anyone else to reach each potential voter individually although not personally. There was instant, pervasive, and persuasive communication throughout the nation—the environment of radio and recording, of television and transmission. The expansion of franchise and communication created a system that fulfilled or perhaps even created a fundamental promise of American democracy: the freedom and opportunity of any citizen to become part of the governing elite. If any evidence of that freedom and opportunity was needed, it was provided in

---

* Carey's view of the press may have been colored by the fact that he had recently been married to a woman who described herself as "a Chicago widow"—and day after day New York newspapers were investigating her background, a past that included three unacknowledged but living ex-husbands in different parts of the world.

1976, when a former governor of Georgia with no established or organizational support and almost no reputation or recognition beyond his own circle of friends and employees was able to win the presidency of the United States through the amplification of his voice articulating a few widely held principles and frustrations.

What the system, the processes of a democracy more democratic than even Tocqueville could imagine, could not necessarily produce, however, was talent. There has been no guarantee of public men and women worthy of the admiration of brilliant French visitors—or, as often as not, of the respect of resident voters. "I despair at the students I see who plan to go into politics," said Stanley Hoffman, a professor of government at Harvard University, as other teachers nodded in agreement during a dinner at the school's faculty club. "They are unbelievably mediocre people. It's very sad."

"I know something about Tocqueville," said Stanley Fink, the Speaker of the New York State Assembly. "One thing I remember, anyway. He's the guy who said American politicians were men of the second rank. Well, I know it's improved dramatically here in the last ten years. You used to have people here who were just feathering their own nests. State government used to be just regulators, arbitrators. But now programs are really initiated by us and really run by us. We're suffering an image problem because of what past generations of politicians did. Now you have better people. I think so, anyway. Maybe I'm just jerking myself off."

Monsieur de Tocqueville would probably be appalled but not surprised by Stanley Fink, the son of a Brooklyn hat salesman who never made more than $150 in any week of his life. This was the leader of one house of the legislature of the second largest of the United States. "I was elected by my colleagues to be their leader because they thought I was the best," he said. "That's where my loyalty is, to them, not to the Governor, not to the leaders of my party, not to 'the people.' 'The people' didn't elect me leader."

"Judgment, integrity, dedication and courage," Speaker Fink pledged as he was inaugurated into his lofty position on January 3, 1979. "These are the four points of the compass which I shall use to keep me on course in the years ahead, and which, my colleagues, with your help, your participation, your energy, your intellect, your friendship, shall guide this Assembly in doing the people's business.

"In conclusion . . . this body, in the days and years ahead, shall be able to boast that it was alive, that it partook in the passions of its times without fear, without favor, with courage and wisdom in the endless effort to advance the interest of all of the people of this great state."

"National prosperity is the prosperity of every individual," Enos Throop had said as he was inaugurated for his second term almost 150 years before. "Not a cent is contributed by way of tax, not a dollar is expended from the public coffers, which is not assented to by the people, and employed to enlarge their means of enjoyment . . .

"Permit me, in conclusion, to assure you of my readiness to cooperate with you in all such measures as tend to strengthen our political institutions, to promote the honor and prosperity of the country, and to add to the happiness of our fellow citizens."

The sounds of democracy! It is not for nothing that for as long as anyone can remember the great Assembly chamber in Albany has been called "The Cave of the Winds." Tocqueville and Beaumont heard a lot of that—once accompanied by cannon fire. They were in Albany on July 4, 1831. The Fourth of July! The fifty-fifth birthday of the Declaration of Independence.

Cannons and church bells rudely woke the young Frenchmen in their room at the Eagle Tavern. Just before nine o'clock, two state officials were at their door, inviting them to join a great parade. The visitors—an ornament in the little capital of 2,500 people—marched near the head of the parade, close behind the local militia. "All fine corps," the local newspaper, the *Argus*, reported, "well disciplined and equipped, and exhibiting on this occasion their usual soldier-like appearance."

"It's the national guard of the country," Tocqueville wrote in a letter home, "but of a country where the military spirit is absolutely unknown. You may judge what kind of *pigeons* these honest citizens made; their martial appearance was really quite comic to see."

The militia and surviving veterans of the Revolution led the parade through the town, up South Market and Ferry streets, then along Pearl Street, paralleling the Hudson River. State officials (and the Frenchmen) came next, followed by trade associations—the Mechanics Benefit Society, the Association of Printers and Albany Typographical Society, the Carpenters' Architectural and Benevolent Association, the Painters' Association, the Apprentices Society and so on.

"In a carriage, at the head of the procession, are three or four old soldiers, who fought with Washington, whom the city preserves like precious relics, and whom all citizens honor," Beaumont wrote. "Nothing would be easier than to ridicule these standards on which one sees written: Association of Butchers, Association of Apprentices, etc., etc. But, when one reflects, these emblems seem very natural among a people which owes its prosperity to commerce and industry."

There was more than enough to make fun of as the day proceeded. The day's orator, a local lawyer named John Van Schaik, apparently spoke for two hours or more, urging common cause with fighters for freedom in Poland. Local singers offered an American version of the "Marseillaise," with verses such as "In this proud land, where freemen cherish/Untrammelled thought and action free." And then the banquets and the endless toasts, including "The Fair Sex—always entitled to our protection."

It was enough, sometimes, to make a twenty-five-year-old French aristocrat gag. And Tocqueville occasionally did. He could not resist writing in *Democracy in America*, "Nothing is more annoying in the ordinary intercourse of life than this irritable patriotism of the Americans. A foreigner will gladly agree to praise much in their country, but he would like to be allowed to criticize something, and that he is absolutely refused."

But the two foreigners did find much to praise that day.

"Once more, however," Beaumont wrote, "it is not good taste and distinction that one must look for in these popular celebrations. Taken all together, this ceremony with its parade *en habit bourgeois*, with its commercial signs and its music with flute *en retournelle*, has made a deeper impression on me than our great celebrations in France ... There is more brilliance in our ceremonies; in those of the United States there is more truth ..."

"That was really a fine spectacle," Tocqueville wrote of a public reading of the Declaration at a Methodist church near the center of town. "A profound silence reigned in the meeting. When in its eloquent plea Congress reviewed the injustices and the tyranny of England we heard a murmur of indignation and anger circulate about us in the auditorium. When it appealed to the justice of its cause and expressed the generous resolution to succumb or free America, it seemed that an electric current made the hearts vibrate.

"This was not, I assure you, a theatrical performance. There was in the reading of these promises of independence so well kept, in this return of an entire people toward the memories of its birth, in this union of the present generation to that which is no longer, sharing for the moment all its generous passions, there was in all that something deeply felt and truly great."

Tocqueville found ceremony but could not find government. "We had wanted to stay several days at Albany because that city is the capital of the state of New York," he wrote to his friend Ernest de Chabrol. "The administration is installed and the legislature holds its sessions there. We wanted to gather there some precious information on whatever central governments there might be in the country. All the bureaus as all the registers were opened to us, but as for the *Government*, we are still seeking it. It really does not exist at all."

On July 4, 1979, there was no ceremony to be found. But the government existed. There was no parade in Albany that day; even the flagpoles in front of the Capitol were bare. The same was pretty much true of the streets where Tocqueville and the workmen of Albany had marched. Many of the attached brick houses that had lined Ferry and South Pearl streets then were still standing, but they were empty, boarded up behind red-white-and-blue signs that read:

Project of Albany Urban Renewal Agency
with Additional Funding from
United States Department of Housing
and Urban Development

Ferry Street, which once went to the river but is blocked now by part of the Federal Interstate Highway System, Route 787, has only a couple of inhabited, working buildings—the Albany County Department of Health and Project REAP, a government-financed "Rehabilitation and Energy Action Project." A few people, most of them black, sat on the steps of the houses along South Pearl. A small corner store was open and four men sat in front of it playing cards. Down the street, a white man wearing a yellow sport shirt and faded brown pants was sitting on a step—a policeman, part of a federal program to test the reaction of poor residents to the removal of symbols of authority (uniforms and marked police cars) from their neighborhoods.

South Market Street begins now as a ramp off Route 787 and becomes a tunnel under the Albany Mall, the gleaming marble cluster of office towers, plazas, and fountains that dominates the skyline of the city, which now has a population of just over 100,-000. The Mall buildings are the headquarters of the state government; they are quite visible, for miles and from every direction. More than 19,000 state employees work in the towers. More than 1.3 million of the 17.5 million residents of New York State work for government—168,400 federal employees, 246,200 state employees, 899,600 employees of local government.

The church where the parade ended in 1831 and where Tocqueville was moved by the reading of America's declaration to the world was demolished fifty or so years later to make room for commercial development. Then, as the suburbs of Albany began growing, many of the stores and shops relocated from the area around Pearl Street and State Street to new shopping centers on what had been farms. So on the July Fourth 203 years after the declaration was written, the center of Albany, too, was deserted. The only sign of the holiday was a red-white-and-blue banner tacked over the State Street offices of the Chase Manhattan Bank, one of the dozens of state banks that maintain offices on the street leading up to the capitol building and the mall. The banks and the government are close.

"Banking and insurance," Stanley Fink answered when I asked what essential functions of the society were controlled by state government. "All the details of social life," Tocqueville had written of the involvement of the states in describing to French readers the American federalism he had studied.

"In a word," he wrote, "there are twenty-four little sovereign nations who together form the United States. . . . Therefore the attributes of the federal government were carefully defined, and it was declared that everything not contained within that definition returned to the jurisdiction of state governments. Hence state authority remained the rule and the federal government the exception . . . the rights and duties of the governments of the states were many and complicated, for such a government was involved in all the details of social life."

"There had to be centralization of authority when there were foreign or domestic threats to the peace," said Governor Carey, discussing the shift of effective authority from the states to the federal government in his lifetime. "Emergency powers became permanent shifts in power to Washington. It was inevitable . . . The states had no resources, no funding sources, to meet greater demands on government. Taxes on real property couldn't do it." That certainly seemed a fair summary of one of the things that had happened between those two July Fourths: threats of war and economic calamity had forced a choice of centralized authority and unified action or dissolution of a union that was an unrealistic compromise from the start. The centralization was facilitated by the federal assumption of the most useful taxing power—income taxes, which were first levied in 1861 to finance a military effort to preserve the union—but unified action and state sovereignty were mutually exclusive from the beginning.

In fact, although he did not necessarily see the ultimate consequences of the contradictions in the American federal form, Tocqueville did spot one of the reasons the central government was destined to prevail and the United States of America would always be something different from what it said it was. "In America," he wrote, "the Union's subjects are not states but private citizens. When it wants to levy a tax, it does not turn to the government of Massachusetts, but to each inhabitant of Massachusetts. . . . It does not borrow its power, but draws it from within. It has its own administrators, courts, officers of justice, and army."

Before 1789, before the Constitution of the United States was written, federal governments—Switzerland and Germany were examples—had been leagues or true confederations in which the central government dealt with regional governments. In the new United States, though, the central authority could deal directly with citizens and had the means to execute the laws it made with or without state cooperation. That was the key to much of American history, and that was one of the things Tocqueville discussed in *Democracy in America:* "Here the central power acts without intermediary on the governed, administering and judging them itself, as do national governments, but it only acts thus within a restricted circle. Clearly here we have not a federal government but an incomplete national government. Hence a form of government has been found which is neither precisely national nor federal; but things have halted there, and the new word to express this new thing does not exist."

The word, so far, has not come into being. "American" will have to do. What happened—and continued to happen even as the United States perpetually debated "New Federalism" or "States' Rights"—was that power and authority gravitated toward the center as the need for—and individuals' demands on—government grew with the growing size and complexity of the nation and its commercial, social, and foreign interaction. The "restricted circle" of the national government became less restricted.

"The balance of power between the federal government and the states changed enormously during my lifetime," G. Mennen Williams, a former governor of Michigan, told me in Detroit, where he sat as a justice of the Michigan Supreme Court. "The federal government had the power of the purse and it used it. . . . Federal taxing power is enormous and the results we've seen were inevitable when Washington began giving conditional aid to local governments. In my life, I saw it after World War II with the highway programs. They gave us, the state government, most of the money to build a highway. But we had to build it where they wanted it and how they wanted it. . . . That was probably the only way the highways could have been built because the states and municipalities, even if they had unlimited income taxes, won't tax themselves enough—there is just too much interstate competition for people and industry. Cities and states are competitive, but the federal government has no competition."

In Massachusetts, the state Tocqueville used as his example of inevitable limits on state power, I asked Barney Frank, a member of the state's House of Representatives from Boston: "Who runs Massachusetts?" "The businesses that threaten to move out of the state," he answered. "They have a chokehold on us. We have to do what they want done, or they'll move someplace else, taking their taxes, taking their jobs, and leaving government to clean up the mess, to take care of the people who are hurt when companies move."*

The legislator was echoing one of Tocqueville's most prophetic thoughts, the idea that an "industrial aristocracy" would inevitably arise in a democracy. "I think that, generally speaking, the manufacturing aristocracy which we see rising before our eyes is one of the hardest that have appeared on earth," he wrote in the second volume of *Democracy in America*, which was published in 1840. "The territorial aristocracy of past ages was obliged by law, or thought itself obliged by custom, to come to the help of its servants and relieve their distress. But the industrial aristocracy of our day, when it has impoverished and brutalized the men it uses, abandons them in time of crisis to public charity to feed them."

Frank, more directly, compared them to rats. "Justice Brandeis on the Supreme Court said the states were laboratories of democracy," he said. "That's not true anymore. The rats have figured out that they can move from lab to lab. The political form doesn't correspond anymore to the economic form. We have fifty political entities, the states, and one giant economic entity, the country. Someday, the world."

So it was the circles of the states that became restricted. In practice, over almost two hundred years, it has become difficult not to conclude that the effect of the Tenth Amendment to the Constitution, the last item of the Bill of Rights adopted in 1791, has been almost the opposite of what the writers of the fundamental law of the land seemed to have in mind when they said: "The powers not delegated to the United States by the Constitution, nor prohibited it by the States, are reserved to the States respectively, or to the people."

What powers did New York State have? Speaker Fink, the state's chief legislator, listed the few that were still inside his circle: the regulation of a few businesses that had resisted federal control, primarily banking and insurance; control of the criminal code; the power to devise formulas for the ritual distribution to municipalities of some revenues from state and federal taxes;

---

* Frank was elected to Congress in 1980, the year after our conversation.

control over many public utility companies; and the power of the employer over a large interest group, the state's own bureaucracy and employees. The circle around Albany was the ring of interstate highways—Routes 87, 90 and 787—lined with red-white-and-blue signs, the symbols of the central power, marking the fact that 90 percent of the funds for the projects was collected by and distributed by "Washington."

"We work with the power we have; we're trying to democratize the balance of power between the state and the banking and insurance industries," Fink said with great pride. "We have made it possible to bring bills to the floor of the Assembly for a vote of all the members. All our committee meetings are now open. Bills can't be killed secretly in committee anymore—that was how the banks and insurance companies controlled a lot of the legislation that affected them. In secret."

So now the people control banking and insurance?

"No," he said. "We don't have the resources to get to the bottom of their operations. We regulate them, but we really don't always know what they are doing."

The regulators, in fact, are dependent on the regulated—for information, for services, for taxes, and, often, under the American system of campaign financing, for the money that fuels the regulators' political careers.

"Hearings," a staple of legislative government at all levels, are as often as not farcical attempts by uninformed legislators to elicit damaging information from the very people that information would be used against in the formulation of new restrictions and regulations. Beyond that, as Barney Frank grumbled, the potentially regulated often have the option of traveling the interstate highways—built essentially to facilitate commercial mobility—to a state less inclined to interfere with the business of business.

In two trips to Albany, following Tocqueville's two journeys up the Hudson, I could hardly avoid seeing the interdependence that inevitably made partners of regulators and regulated, and made the bonds of dependence greater at the state level than the federal level. One time, two international oil companies—Mobil and Texaco—had representatives outside the doors of the Assembly threatening Fink and other legislators with the relocation of offices and employees outside the state if the Assembly approved a gross receipts tax on their companies. Another time, local newspapers routinely reported that 21 state banks and several unions and organizations of state employees were among the contributors helping the state Comptroller, Edward Regan, pay off $842,000 in loans that some of those same banks had made to finance the campaign that got him elected in the first place to an office overseeing the operations of both banks and state employees. When employees of government—teachers in the public schools were a good example—provided significant campaign funding and volunteer campaign workers to help elect legislators, they were essentially trying to hire their own bosses, the men and women who regulate their numbers, salaries, benefits, and working conditions. The speaker was loyal to his colleagues, the people who elected him, and many of those colleagues were just as loyal to the people who elected them, often the membership of public employee associations. For everybody concerned this was business: government was their business.

One of Fink's colleagues, Assemblyman William Hoyt of Buffalo, one of the 86 Democrats who elected him Speaker, described that business this way: "I'm an advocate, a lobbyist for my constituents. Ninety percent of my time is constituent-oriented. I deal with government for them. I get the things for them that they have coming to them, because many of them don't know how to deal with bureaucracy themselves. They don't know how to make the phone calls—I make the calls for them and, because I have a title, my calls are answered and they can get the check or the permit or whatever they want. A tree blows down in front of their house and they don't know how to get the city to remove it so they call me. That's my job."*

What about legislating, making laws?

"I don't worry much about that. There are only eight or ten

---

* Some of that, of course, has always been true. Tocqueville perceived legislators as both lawmakers and advocates. "The electors," he wrote, "see their representative not only as a legislator for the state but also as the natural protector of local interests in the legislature; indeed, they almost seem to think he has the power of attorney to represent each constituent and they trust him to be as eager in their private interests as in those of the country."

votes a year that could possibly affect my reelection. I'm very careful about those. The rest I don't worry about too much."

Hoyt, who used to teach American history, must have seen something in my expression. "Yes, I know," he said. "I know it's not exactly what the writers of the Constitution had in mind."

Why do you do it if that's what you think of it?

"Because it's exciting. I'd like to be a congressman next. It's just a game, but it's fun. It's better than teaching school."

"We work in the margins now," said Barney Frank, the Massachusetts legislator. "We survive by taking care of our districts. It's really the voters' fault. People think wholesale, but they vote retail. We get more credit for bringing a little pork into our district—a new building or something—than we get blame for giving pork to other districts. We are literally irresponsible. No one holds us responsible for anything. Maybe they shouldn't. What are states really responsible for anyway?"

As he spoke, Frank's secretary called and said a television crew from a Boston station was waiting outside. "Oh, yeah," he said. "Some people were hurt by a fireworks display in the city. The station needs someone to say that fireworks can be dangerous. I'm always good for a quote for the evening news.

"Okay," he said, pulling on his coat and striding toward the door. "Let's denounce people getting hurt from fireworks. Your state legislature in action!"

4
ITHACA
AND AUBURN

"Auburn's Riot Was After Cornell's . . ."

"I was saying that the whole country is but a forest," Beaumont wrote to his sister as he and Tocqueville traveled west from Albany. "I might add that everywhere where a clearing is to be seen, which is rare enough, the clearing is a village. They give to these villages the most celebrated names of ancient or modern cities, such as Troy, Rome, Liverpool . . ."

And Ithaca, the ancient home of Ulysses, which became a small city of 28,000 people, many of them the students and faculty of one of the country's best universities, Cornell. It was a place, unlike Albany, where men spoke of ideas, where professors, unlike politicians, coined their own phrases.

"Demonic commerce" were the words used by a professor of American history, Cushing Strout, when I asked him what he thought might be the first thing a modern Tocqueville would take note of in the United States. The phrase struck a chord, it complemented Tocqueville's words for an American trait, "breathless cupidity." The 24-hour market: perhaps it was a national symbol. "Mutual surveillance" was Strout's smiling definition of Puritanism. I laughed at the phrase. Later, I was to take it much more seriously, but even on that day I noticed a newspaper report that Governor Carey had vetoed a bill which would have outlawed the use of two-way mirrors as spying devices in restrooms, hotel rooms, and the dressing rooms in stores.

"Totalitarian democracy" was a phrase casually used by another history professor, L. Pearce Williams. He was discussing, with more than a touch of cynicism, the conformity he saw underneath American celebrations of diversity, individualism, and freedom. It was, I thought, his way of expressing the ideas and concerns that Tocqueville had pessimistically presented about democracy and equality—he often used the two words synonymously—near the end of the second volume of *Democracy in America:*

"Men's main opinions become alike as the conditions of their lives become alike . . . though any one of them could part company with the rest and work out his own beliefs, in the end they all concur, unconsciously and unintentionally, in a certain number of common opinions . . .

"It must, I think, be rare in a democracy for a man suddenly to conceive a system of ideas far different from those accepted by his contemporaries; and I suppose that, even should such an innovator arise, he would have great difficulty in making himself heard to begin with, and even more in convincing people. . . ."

Professor Williams, however, did say that he saw two sets of common opinions at the university and he divided the students into two groups, the "Coastals" and the "Traditionals." "The students from the East Coast and the West Coast seem to have a shared set of assumptions. There seems to be an unwillingness to commit themselves completely to others or to the nation itself. Somehow, part of their assumption seems to be that there is no real responsibility attached to actions they take . . . The students from the Midwest, say, are quite different. Traditional. They have the same values as most Americans 50 years ago—the commitments to country, family and work, often to religion."

Why should there be a difference?

"I'm not sure, of course, but I would call it Jewish sensibility. There is still some Jewish rootlessness, an inability to commit that last ten percent, to say: I am an American," said Williams, who self-consciously added that he was half Jewish himself. "It comes, I think, from the influence of Jews in American intellectual life and in education, particularly in New York and Los Angeles, on the two coasts. There is a triumph of the ideas of the left, that government is the natural place to turn for solutions, and an acceptance of Freud."

"Freud?" I said.

"Perhaps interpretations or perversions of Freud," Williams said. "The idea that the individual is more important than the community."

It was a provocative conversation; the professor was a deliberately provocative man. Perhaps too provocative. The next group of students I met, the editors of Cornell's newspaper, the *Daily Sun*, were all "Coastals" from the suburbs of New York City, and all described government as "worthless" and "ineffective." Andrew Knobel, Thomas Buerkle, and Robert Murray each described himself, simplistically, as "libertarian"—people who believed, theoretically, in the elimination of government and, practically, in substantial reduction of its functions. "Students just don't expect very much from government," summarized Knobel, the editor in chief. Then he added, with only a half-smile, "Except, of course, student loans."

Who did students believe was responsible for the care of their grandparents and parents in old age?

Each of the three said: "The government."

Two older men, professors, were talking about avoiding the power and reach of the government in a conversation I heard in a coffee shop off the campus. Their subjects were money and work. In fact, in more than a year of travel, almost every conversation I overheard in public places—taverns, restaurants, waiting rooms, planes, and trains—tended to end with those two subjects: money, always; work, usually. Sports, for men, and sex (or "relationships"), for women, were opening subjects and were often treated lightly, with humor and with exaggerated frustration. Money and work were serious. With the same allowance for hyperbole, a twentieth-century eavesdropper would not argue with the assessment Beaumont offered in a letter to his sister: "They prefer trade and business in which one makes *more money*. There in two words, you have the American character . . ."

This time, in the Ithaca coffee shop, one professor was telling another about a family plan to make more. "My wife is going into business," he said. "The garage-sale business. She'll hold one big garage sale a month. First she'll go around to all the other garage sales and pick up stuff and then resell it at a profit . . ."

"Isn't that an awful lot of work?"

"Yes, but the whole business is in cash. No taxes. The government doesn't know you're making more money."

So there was an underground economy in western New York; people traded in cash and goods to avoid records and taxation. But there was something similar everywhere I traveled—illegal commerce was booming on both coasts and in between. Outside the grandest stores on New York's richest streets, peddlers were selling gloves, perfumes, and women's bags at a third of the price charged for similar goods inside stores with names like Bloomingdale's, Altman's, Macy's, Gimbels—some of those the names of the street peddlers of earlier American generations. In Los Angeles, three thousand miles to the west, a family who wanted their home painted called in a contractor for an estimate. He arrived at the house with a foreman who spoke only Spanish and measured the walls while the boss asked about colors and the rest. The estimate was $3,500. That night the foreman returned with a friend who spoke English and offered to do the job for $650—in cash. In the same California city, and presumably in other places across the country, a person who knew the right telephone numbers could have an automobile overhauled by the same men who did the work at the dealer's and for half the price. The mechanics—in the classic fashion that the French call *travail au noir*—worked at night or on weekends in the car owner's garage or driveway, or right on the street. In Oregon and Georgia, I saw barter and work-exchange marts complicated enough to have to use computers to keep track of which lawyer was drawing up a will for which plumber in exchange for repairing that sink, or just to bank some time, that is, credit, for the day when he might need an electrician or a baby sitter or some firewood stolen from a nearby national forest.

All of that was illegal if no taxes were paid on those transactions—and the whole point of the underground commerce was to avoid government interference in general and taxes in particular. "Income is income, whether it's cash, goods or services," said Leon Levine, the spokesman of the Internal Revenue Service, the federal government's tax collector, assigned to answer my questions about the "off-the-books" business I had seen going on in many places. We agreed that we were talking about the "straight" underground economy as opposed to traditional criminal activity—garage sales rather than heroin sales. "We are aware of what's going on," Levine said. "Beyond that, I don't know what to say. If you write a couple of advertisements for your next-door neighbor's liquor store and he gives you a case of whiskey, that's awfully hard for us to detect. We're always undecided about publicity on the subject—maybe it will frighten people, maybe it will just give more and more people ideas."

Acknowledged and widespread lawbreaking is not a healthy state of affairs for a country, especially for the United States. But large numbers of Americans have always broken certain laws designed to control personal behavior: liquor laws, drug laws, sex laws. "Every American feels a sort of personal interest in obeying the laws," Tocqueville wrote in *Democracy in America* after pondering what he had seen in the United States, "for a man who is not today one of the majority party may be so tomorrow, and so he may soon be demanding for laws of his own choosing that respect which he now professes for the lawgiver's will. Therefore, however annoying a law may be, the American will submit to it, not only as the work of the majority but also as his own doing; he regards it as a contract to which he is one of the parties."

If those words were ever strictly true, they are not today. But, surely, they were not—Tocqueville saw racial equality laws casually ignored almost every day—and the Frenchman must have been exaggerating to make the point that there were practical as well as philosophical reasons for Americans to obey their own laws. Most of them, anyway. There is no law or system that can't be beaten by resourceful, energetic people. Which laws were obeyed, and which disobeyed, told me something about the American character: Americans, individually, routinely, and guiltlessly violated almost all laws attempting to regulate personal, private behavior or entrepreneurial commerce and labor performed during what has traditionally been defined as personal time. Within bounds defined by history and the energy and effectiveness of government enforcement, Americans did not consider those things lawbreaking or cheating.

The harder the times, the more certain laws would be broken, and times were hard in western New York as I traveled. The legal economy had been sluggish for decades in the cities and towns that developed along the Erie Canal when it was the world's route to the riches of the American West. But the glory days were just about to begin when Tocqueville and Beaumont traveled through on their way to visit the prison at Auburn, one of the most famous in the world. It had been built in 1816 and was considered a model in the country that was then the acknowledged pioneer in penal reform. Auburn, in fact, turned out to be the most important stop in the French commissioners' official travels—Tocqueville's book was *un travail au noir*. There is still a penitentiary there today, the Auburn Correctional Facility.*

"Sweet Auburn! loveliest village of the plain." That line from Oliver Goldsmith inspired the naming of the town in 1803. By 1831, it was, in Tocqueville's words, "a small town of 2,000 souls . . . the center of an immense commerce." Quite a place. It was the home of Harriet Tubman, who was running an underground railroad for escaped slaves. And it was, too, the home of William Henry Seward, who became Abraham Lincoln's Secretary of State and purchased a wasteland called Alaska from Russia. Seward's brick house had been completed a couple of years before with the help of a young mason named Brigham Young, who was to lead the Mormons to Utah. A local farmer, Jethro Wood, invented the cast-iron plow. The area's representative in Albany, Assemblyman Millard Fillmore, was to become President of the United States.

That was a long time ago. Auburn, with a declining population of about 33,000, unemployment of more than 12 percent, and an average annual income (for men) of about $7,200, had become a place to grow up in and leave. The people on the streets were mainly old people, who looked down when they walked, and children and teenagers. The Correctional Facility was the largest employer in the area. The 400 guards and staff had just gone back to work after a 16-day strike and the city of Auburn was petitioning the state for $50,000 to cover the cost of additional local police costs related to the strike. Many of the local people who were neither old nor very young worked in the prison, and in the schools and community colleges, federal and state offices—as in many declining areas, Cayuga County's prin-

* Tocqueville and Beaumont came to Auburn by taking a slightly more northerly route from Albany and passing through Syracuse to talk with the first warden of Auburn Prison, Elam Lynds.

cipal employer was government, which provided about one out of five local jobs.*

The famous "Auburn system" that the Frenchmen had traveled so far to see—and were tremendously impressed with—was based on single cells, silent communal labor, and the whip. There were 600 men in Auburn prison at that time. Each had his own cell and was required to maintain silence and to work in shops at stonecutting, toolmaking, weaving, and other trades of the day. Violations of the rules were punished by whipping— with "an instrument which the Americans call the Cat, and we call the *fouet*," Tocqueville wrote. Elam Lynds, originator of the system and first warden at Auburn, called it "the most effective and at the same time the most humane punishment, for it never injures the health and forces the inmates to live an essentially healthy life."

The system may not sound so healthy now, but it was when compared with communal prisons of Europe in the early nineteenth century, and Lynds also established it at another famous New York prison, Sing Sing. It was also attractive to Tocqueville—and later to French authorities—because it made money. Auburn prison, in those days, ran at a profit, with contractors paying for the work of inmates.

"How much do you pay the prisoner a day?" Tocqueville asked the contractor running the tool shop.

"An average of 30 cents."

"How much do you pay the prisoner a day?" I asked Robert Henderson, the current warden of Auburn.

---

* Most of the newer buildings in Auburn are federal and state government buildings. Old housing, mainly Victorian, was preserved when the city stopped growing as railroads took away the traffic of the canals. The old canal cities and towns are filled with beautiful houses on relatively large properties, homes that would sell for hundreds of thousands, even millions of dollars in more thriving regions of the United States. In central and western New York, those houses were priced from $20,000 to $50,000—bargains if work were available for new residents. One random thought I had walking and driving along impressive blocks of such houses was that if advancing electronics technology—computers and the rest—did at some point allow large numbers of Americans to work in their own homes, some of those Americans would inevitably opt for living in places that had been left behind for decades, places like Auburn.

The prison at Auburn, New York

"Forty-five cents a day to start. That can rise, over time, to $1.25 a day. A year ago we instituted a bonus system, so that it's possible for a man to double his pay for better work. Two men have actually done that and we've had a tremendous increase in productivity and the quality of the things made here: license plates, road signs, furniture for state offices."

"We must understand each other," Lynds said to Tocqueville. "I do not believe in complete reform (except for juvenile delinquents), that is to say that I do not think that one has often seen a mature criminal become a religious and virtuous man. I don't have any faith in the saintliness of those who leave prison, and I don't believe that the exhortations of the chaplain or the private reflections of the inmate ever make a good Christian of him. But my opinion is that a great number of former convicts do not relapse into crime, and they even become useful citizens, having learned a trade in prison and acquired the habit of steady work. There's the only reform that I have ever hoped to produce, and I think it's the only one which society can demand."

"The aim of this prison is to protect society," Warden Henderson said to me 150 years later. "I don't think you can really change people. But there is a better chance of rehabilitation than most people on the outside think. This is a maximum security prison—it's the end of the line—and if someone is convicted again he's coming back here. But the number of repeaters we have is only about 33 percent. This prison is a decidedly unpleasant experience. By the time a guy gets out of here, he really doesn't want to come back."

One day was enough for me. The Correctional Facility covers 32 acres inside its walls—parts of those walls were built in 1817—on State Street, a few blocks from downtown Auburn. A blue-and-gold sign in front of the walls commemorates the first death in the electric chair: the electrocution, inside, of a murderer named William Kemmler on August 6, 1890. The guard searching me before I passed through the same sort of metal detector as the ones at airline gates mentioned that there had never been an escape from Auburn—not one in 173 years. The prisoners—1,580 that day—were locked in cells, six-foot by eight-foot cells, from 8:30 P.M. to 7:20 A.M. each day. There were, on the average, six fights each week between inmates; there were two stabbings the week I visited. All but three of the trees that once provided some shade and a hint of the outside world in the prison's courtyards were long ago cut down to give tower guards a greater field of vision, to prevent knifings and homosexual encounters. In the yards, prisoners segregated themselves by race, then into ethnic, regional, and religious groupings; there were clusters of Black Muslims, "hillbillies"—white prisoners from rural areas—and urban Italians (who had painted a couple of benches red, white, and green). The hospital had six beds and as many "isolation cells." Three naked men were inside those cells, screaming and grimacing through small glass windows in the door. That, I was told, was about the average number since the state began closing hospitals for the criminally insane and distributing their populations through the prison system—to save money.

It cost the Auburn Correctional Facility $9,736 a year to maintain one inmate.* That was one change from the profit-

* The average cost for an inmate in a New York State prison facility was $13,254 per year in 1980. Auburn's relatively low figure can be attributed in large part to its size and structure.

making days of 1831. And, of course, there were no more whips and the electric chair had been dismantled. The silence was a thing of the past, too. In fact, Henderson said, the system has encouraged certain kinds of noise since Auburn prisoners rioted on November 4, 1970. Black prisoners, more than half the population, most of them from New York City, had been refused a request to celebrate Black Solidarity Day on that day. After that, the unofficial holiday was celebrated with official ceremonies in the prison auditorium that included outside speakers invited by the inmates.

"We realized finally that rhetoric doesn't hurt discipline," Henderson said. "A free flow of information inside did not have the impact we thought it would. With things like outside speakers, it probably improved discipline because the prisoners felt an obligation to the outsiders." Auburn inmates were now allowed to subscribe to any newspapers or journals and have more access to television—even if that only meant two sets in the main yard and a set hung in the "honor galleries" that housed the best-behaved of the population.

Honor galleries, work incentives bringing in that little extra money for cigarettes and shaving cream, permission to use recreation facilities like the expensively equipped exercise and weight-lifting rooms—simple rewards and, through withdrawal of those privileges, simple punishments that seemed to serve the same purpose as the whip and Christian instruction. The purpose to Henderson, as to Lynds 150 years before, was control of a potentially dangerous population. "The difference," Warden Henderson said, "is that prison is now a psychological experience, deliberately unpleasant. Then it was a religious experience. Religious people and thinking controlled the prisons then. Psychology substitutes for that Christianity . . . The key to controlling a prison is developing strong leadership among the inmates. Then they accept responsibility for controlling themselves in return for rewards that are almost totally psychological."

There was also demonic commerce inside the prison, an underground economy based on cigarettes and narcotics. Anything, any "swag"—the prison word for goods of any sort—could be bought and sold inside for the right price. That commerce, the freedom of information, the breakdown of the small society into ethnic groups, the tendency to replace religion with psychology—Auburn was not all that different from Cornell. "It's just a little America," an inmate, James Charlton, said when we talked inside his institution, Graterford prison near Philadelphia. "The difference is that there are more wild people here."

When I mentioned some similarities between the university and his penitentiary, Henderson replied: "Yes, any prison is just a reconstruction of the outside society." He then reminded me that Auburn's riot, the prisoner takeover of 1970, happened more than a year after armed Cornell students took over university buildings.

5
CANANDAIGUA

"A Grudging Acceptance of Decent Government ..."

"Canandagua is on the road from Auburn to Buffalo," Beaumont wrote to his parents as he and Tocqueville moved west. He misspelled the name of the town and one of New York's Finger Lakes. It is Canandaigua, the white man's version of "Kanandarque"—"chosen spot" in the language of the first settlers, Seneca Indians. In 1779, Kanandarque was a village of 23 well-built log cabins surrounded by the orchards and farms of the Senecas. That fall, under orders from his commander, George Washington, to disband the Indians, General John Sullivan of the Continental Army marched his troops into the village and burned it to the ground so that the Indians could not shelter British troops. In 1794, Colonel Thomas Pickering, also acting for Washington, who had become President, negotiated a treaty with 1,600 Indians, giving them a reservation near Buffalo, where their descendants still live, in exchange for the land on the lake. White settlers moved in and built a courthouse that year.

When Tocqueville arrived, Canandaigua was a thriving town of 2,000 people, another economic beneficiary of the opening of the Erie Canal in 1825. The young Frenchmen were following the great water trail that opened the western frontier, making cities of Chicago, Detroit, Buffalo, Syracuse, and Rochester and channeling the commerce of the new nation through New York

City. Canandaigua was the county seat of Ontario County, which in 1826 had established a poorhouse, according to a report in the *Ontario Repository*, published in Canandaigua on September 27, 1826:

> In obedience to a law of this state, the Supervisors of this county, at their last annual meeting, made provisions for a County Poor House establishment.
>
> A farm has been purchased, of very good land, containing upwards of 100 acres, and cost—$1,868.84. A substantial brick building has been erected thereupon, which, together with the wood furniture of the kitchen and dining room cost—$8,000. The buildings are nearly completed, and are calculated to accommodate one hundred persons. The farm has been in the possession of the keeper since the 1st of April last, is much improved and is yielding considerable crops for the use of the establishment.
>
> The expense for supporting the poor in this county for the last year, was not less than $5,000. It is estimated that the amount now received for excise, together with the labor of the paupers, and produce of the farm, will be sufficient to support this establishment, and that no tax will be necessary to sustain it.
>
> The benefits that will result to the counties, in which the poor houses may be established, will be soon felt, we believe, in diminishing the expenses of supporting the poor, and in reducing their number; while their confinement will be greatly promoted—thus combining economy and humanity by these institutions.

There were 10,000 people in Canandaigua when I arrived and that population was declining. My notes said: "Pretty town—*old* people." I wrote that walking along Main Street, past side streets of old houses leading down to Lake Canandaigua. Most of the town was pretty anyway—except for a strip of bars and hamburger joints and little amusement parks along the lake.

"It's not fair to just write about the Strip," said George Ewing, publisher and editor of the *Daily Messenger*. The *Messenger* was one of the oldest newspapers in the country, tracing its history to the *Ontario Repository* and beyond, back to 1796. "That's what Harrison Salisbury did. A lot of people here are angry about that."

"That" had happened a while ago, in 1976. Salisbury, a retired assistant managing editor of the *New York Times*, passed
through town while writing a long magazine article about his
own family. His great-great-grandfather, John Salisbury, had
settled in the town in 1802 with his wife Mary and their sons,
Hiram and Amasa. The writer had come back and been dis-
gusted by the Strip and the wreck of the old family house. The
fact that Ewing and other Canandaiguans still remembered the
five-year-old literary slight gave me an idea of how much happened in the town. Not much.

Salisbury's most interesting observations, however, were not
about the desecration of a shoreline by signs advertising Sno-
Kones and Kentucky Fried Chicken. Frightened, I think, by seeing old Americans packed away in new poorhouses, he wrote:

> I know Canandaigua lives by its racetrack, its Veterans
> Hospital, the big Mobil warehouse for plastic meat trays
> and plastic egg cartons . . . I know it lives for its colony of
> senior citizens. It is late afternoon and I see the senior citi-
> zens, the ladies with their too careful makeup, their dresses
> that shrink from their bones, their thin, thin legs and cau-
> tious small steps . . . They begin to move early, sometimes
> before four o'clock. They move out of the rooming houses,
> out of the senior-citizen compounds, the nursing homes, the
> non-nursing homes, the cheap condominiums, the cheap
> flats, the massive citadel of Grove Home for Senior Citi-
> zens, a gray-stone castle of 1855, set back on an oak-shaded
> park, hundreds of them coming out into the open air. They
> begin to move from their cells, those who are able, in the
> late afternoon.
>
> They move carefully and look at the others on the street
> with open anger, the anger of unfulfillment, fear, poverty
> and emptiness. They are angry because they are old and
> they do not know what to do with their lives . . .

This was not the role of those past middle age in Hiram's
time. To be sure there were the infirm. Some had to be
cared for at the poor farm or kept at town expense. Hiram
was overseer of the poor for a while. But the aged, as Hiram
catalogued in letters to his father, usually lived on the
farms. They worked as they could. If they were bound up
with arthritis or what they called sciatica they did little,
sitting by the fire in the winter, sunning themselves on the

bench outside the door on warm days. But there was always something for the elderly to do—minding the baby, carding the wool, weeding the kitchen garden, sorting the beans, whittling dolls. They whittled a lot in those days.

Hiram or John or Amasa could not have imagined a society that systematically segregated able-bodied people, sequestered them in institutions . . . condemned them to idleness, severed their normal relations with families, factories and offices, and set them down on the frayed edges of the real world, there to live out their days in frustration, venting their hostility in alcohol, golf and quarrels . . .

I do not know what we think we are doing. I know that it is wrong. Very wrong.

I did not know about that either.

But I did know that a few days before, at Cornell University, I had asked three young men who they thought should care for their grandparents and parents? They had answered with the same words I had heard in other parts of the country: "The government."

The government, the great employer in Auburn, cared for Canandaigua in different ways. George Ewing took me through his town, a place which had no particular economic purpose anymore, showing me the new 118-unit Senior Citizens Complex, paid for by the State of New York; Baker Park, 75 percent paid by the federal government; the new sewage disposal plant to protect the clear waters of Lake Canandaigua, 90 percent paid by the federal government; the Veterans Administration Hospital, run by the federal government and employing 2,000 local residents.

"Revenue sharing"—a federal program that returned federal taxes to localities in block grants—"is what keeps local taxes down around here," Ewing said.

Would local people do these things? I asked. Would the people of the town spend the money directly if higher levels of government weren't collecting the taxes and then returning them as part of the financing of municipal projects?

"No," Ewing said. "I don't suppose they would. I don't think we'd build a sewer plant. No. I kind of suspect people here would rather keep their taxes down."

"Americans have not come to grips with many things," a for-

mer President, Richard Nixon, told me in New York City.
"There is an acceptance that government should do these things,
but there is a withholding of enthusiasm."

Whatever was being done—cleaning up lakes or taking care
of the old—Americans did seem inclined to separate themselves
from the appearances of dependence on government. That
thought was reinforced by the day's *Daily Messenger.* The local
member of Congress—Representative Gary Lee, a Republican
from Ithaca—had issued a statement proudly announcing that
he had voted for a $2.5-billion reduction in the increased federal
budget proposed by the President. He was demanding that the
President and government "pull the belt tighter." The *Messenger* duly reported Lee's public outrage and that the amendment
he supported would leave the budget at $529.8 billion.

Lee, though, was in a grand tradition. Writing on the politics
of his day, Tocqueville noted that critics of the federal government were in favor—as they usually are—and "it was by promising to weaken it that one won the right to control it."

What Tocqueville had written about, perhaps even then a bit
romantically, was an American instinct and talent for making
government unnecessary:

"Better use has been made of association and this powerful
instrument of action has been applied to more varied aims in
America than anywhere else in the world. . . .

"The inhabitant of the United States learns from birth that he
must rely on himself to combat the ills and trials of life; he is
restless and defiant in his outlook toward the authority of society
and appeals to its power only when he cannot do without it. . . .
If some obstacle blocks the public road halting the circulation of
traffic, the neighbors at once form a deliberative body; this improvised assembly produces an executive authority which remedies the trouble before anyone has thought of the possibility of
some previously constituted authority beyond that of those concerned."

I could not write that, even though I supposed some of that
instinct survived. But not enough—in Canandaigua the oldest
and best examples of what had astonished Tocqueville, the volunteer fire companies and the Canandaigua Emergency Squad,
now received half their support from government funds. Those
exemplary associations, however, I had concluded after working

in many small towns, were the result of a more primal urge than civic betterment: the companies and squads gave the men of a town the chance to get away from their women in a good cause. Most of the time, now, neighbors were more likely to get together to merely petition the government to raise or lower taxes to do or stop doing something; or, maybe, one of them would improvise and telephone an assemblyman to have someone come and remove that tree from the road. The system, not so inspiring or exciting anymore, still seemed to work, though, because there was, basically, a consensus in the sometimes grudging acceptance of what decent government should do— certainly it should clear the roads and educate children and, there came a time when enough people agreed, take care of the old.

But even 150 years ago it was obvious that there had to be some distance between the consensus on the necessary and the good and the actual collection of taxes. Americans, it seemed, agreed on what kind of people they should be and would even pay for government to make them that way—but, Canandaiguan, congressman, and Cornell professor, they wanted the freedom to complain about it and, maybe, cheat on it, too.

"How is your public education organized?" Tocqueville had asked a resident of Canandaigua, John Canfield Spencer.

"The state has a special fund set aside for this use," Spencer answered. "Portions of this fund are accorded to counties which need it, in proportion to the efforts which the latter are willing to make themselves. For it is generally admitted with us that the state should always help and never do the job all itself. It is thought that the individuals, who give their money and who are on the spot, are by interest and situation in a position to give to the application of the fund a watchful attention of which a great administration would be incapable. Besides, we want as far as possible to create local interests. This combination of state and township money attains both objectives admirably. Education awakes here the solicitude of all. The people really being King, everyone feels the need of enlightening it."

In time that financing became a combination of national, state, and township money, but the solicitude remained fundamentally strong. It was a solicitude the young Frenchman found uniquely American. "All of the people I've seen up to now, to whatever rank of society they belong, have seemed incapable of conceiving that the advantages of education might be doubted," he wrote before reaching Canandaigua. "They never fail to smile when told that this opinion is not universal in Europe. . . . Here less than anywhere else is to be feared the disquiet caused a state by the large number of people whom their education raises above their fortune, and whose restlessness torments society. Here the resources presented by nature are still so far beyond the efforts of men to exhaust them that there is no moral energy or intellectual activity which does not find a ready outlet."

That point was made to Tocqueville and Beaumont on one of their first nights in America. They were immediately offered the hospitality of Walter Bowne, the mayor of New York City, who honored them at more than one formal banquet. Part of the entertainment at those affairs, according to the newspapers of the day, was the toasts, thirteen of them, one for each of the original states. The ninth one at a Tammany Society and Columbian Order banquet was: "Education—The extension of our public schools a national blessing—a means afforded whereby the rising generation can properly appreciate our free institutions."

As new generations rose and the nation maintained its solicitude not only for education but for more and more of it, many local governments became more and more grudging in their acceptance of the costs. Local property taxes could not bear the load and the familiar pattern developed: local governments could not or would not do what the American consensus wanted done. "Government had to take over higher education, usually from churches, once the decision was made that education should be universal," said Kristor Stendahl, a Lutheran minister and dean of the School of Divinity at Harvard University. "Education was the American ideal, the key to opportunity. The government, particularly the federal government, may have wanted to stay out of higher education, but it could not because there was no other way to give that education to the poor."*

* The place of education in the American mind may be best demonstrated by the rewards offered soldiers after the War of Independence and World War II. Revolutionary veterans were often given land. The land, of course, was gone by the 1940s and veterans were given an education under the "G.I. Bill of Rights," which provided federal

Tocqueville, reflecting the fears of educated Europeans, took a long time to conclude that the Americans were right about universal education, or, at least, about "useful education," as he called it—that is, instruction in citizenship and vocational skills. More than five years later, in the second volume of *Democracy in America*, he wrote: "The Americans . . . enjoy explaining almost every act of their lives on the principle of self-interest properly understood. It gives them pleasure to point out how an enlightened self-love continually leads them to help one another and disposes them freely to give part of their time and wealth for the good of the state. . . . Every American has the sense to sacrifice some of his private interests to save the rest. We [the French] want to keep, and often lose, the lot. . . . I do not think that the doctrine of self-interest as preached in America is in all respects self-evident. But it does contain many truths so clear that for men to see them it is enough to educate them. Hence it is all-important for them to be educated, for the age of blind sacrifice and instinctive virtues is already long past, and I see a time approaching in which freedom, public peace, and social stability will not be able to last without education."

The theory, which Tocqueville was apparently using to try to persuade his countrymen to practice political moderation, is easier to see than to defend. It struck me as glib, even when Nixon said to me 150 years later, "The secret of American leadership is convincing Americans that what you want to do is in their self-interest." But over two hundred years it explains a lot, particularly the spectacular expansion of what could one day become, for all practical purposes, a complete national government. The people of Canandaigua perhaps know themselves well enough to understand the necessity for a system that does for them or forces them to do things for themselves that they might not do willingly themselves. "I kind of suspect people here would rather keep their taxes down." Who wouldn't? But who, having the political power to prevent it, would violate self-interest by trusting his or her old age to the three students I had talked with at Cornell? Or to that hard industrial aristocracy? And when,

---

grants of up to $565 a month for tuition and expenses. From that time on, universities were still state, local, or private institutions but more and more of their financing began to come from Washington.

along with their peers, their own cohort, will those three educated young men, filled with self-love, recognize that one day they will not be the children but the parents? Who will take care of them? If they have the power, they will take care of themselves—they'll do it by associating with others sharing their self-interest. The sad warrens of the aged in Canandaigua are the beginning of a new kind of nation with new needs and priorities dictated by an aging population. Americans have been generous with their public and private money in seeking cures for the nation's greatest killer, cancer—a surviving mortal disease after so many others have been eliminated—because it is in very few citizens' self-interest to die. But if the cure is found, the nation will inevitably be aged and changed even more—a new nation will continue evolving as life expectancies increase with advances in medicine, as fewer children are born because of innovations in birth control, and as immigration is restricted because there is less need for unskilled labor.

As I traveled, a commission appointed by the President of the United States issued a short report entitled, "A National Agenda for the Eighties." In a chapter called "Dependency," the commission projected that Americans above the age of sixty-five would constitute half the dependent population of the country by the year 2000. Where will they live? They will be the people living in the poorhouses of Canandaigua.

"In the past," said the report of the presidential commission, "the family has assumed primary responsibility for caring for all dependents, young and old. But over the past two decades, the American family has undergone a dramatic transformation. The most significant change affecting children and the elderly has been the increasing disappearance of their traditional caretakers. Women have entered the labor force in large numbers, reducing the time they can spend with children and old people. . . . The numbers of the young and the old will grow, and families—a rapidly increasing number of which will contain working women—will be obligated to seek newer and more flexible means of maintaining care. In this search, private and public institutions must act as vital, sympathetic, and helpful allies."

In fewer words: The commission did not know what to do. But

the vague theory of self-interest properly understood seems to explain what has happened in America and to offer a pretty good idea of what will happen next. "Blind sacrifice and instinctive virtues" are longer gone than when Tocqueville wrote them off in 1831. That is not necessarily because Americans are terrible people. Often, new virtues replaced old. "It seemed like a good idea to raise our children to be independent," said Ellen Goodman, a newspaper columnist in Boston. "But there were enormous implications to that independence. . . . We are a nation of leavers. We left to go West. Now we can't go West anymore so we leave each other. I wonder how much things have really changed. Our ancestors left the old country or they moved West from New England—they left relationships for opportunity. Now people do the same thing personally, psychologically. They leave each other for real or imagined opportunity. Americans are living alone—it's the centrifugal force at the end of individualism."

Old people, parents and grandparents, restricted leaving, were the enemies of independence; the teachers of the old value stood in the way of independence, geographical, financial, and social. Independence and self-interest for each new generation meant freedom—an unhampered ability to relocate, quit jobs, quit marriages and families, to move on. The individual was replacing the family as the basic unit of the society. National statistics shifted significantly—the average number of people in an American household in 1930 was 4.1; in 1950 it was 3.4; in 1980, 2.8.

By then, 23 percent of America's households were one-person homes, according to the Census Bureau. Most of those people living alone were old, most of them were women. They were wandering around Canandaigua—no longer mothers or grandmothers. Someone had to clean up the mess: government tried. The federal government not only took and distributed more and more money to care for those people, it gave them a sad identity, new names: "senior citizens" or just "seniors." They were individuals now, sharing self-interest. And that self-interest was inevitably leading to association around a political agenda—not to do something themselves but to take a larger share of the money collected by the government. The political weight of their numbers would inevitably make the government their vital, sympathetic, and helpful ally. As more and more Americans grew old in relatively good health—and older and older as medical technology advanced—America would inevitably become something it never was: old.

God, it was young when Tocqueville and Beaumont reached the exciting little village of Canandaigua. They walked along the same sloping Main Street, past the small frame building—still there—where a local eighteen-year-old, Stephen Douglas, was studying with a local lawyer before moving west to Illinois, becoming a U.S. Senator, and running for President against his friend Abraham Lincoln. It was because the place was so vital that the Frenchmen had come. They had wanted to meet John Canfield Spencer, the man who told them about the bilevel financing of the public schools. Spencer had already held several state positions and was later to become Secretary of War and then of the Treasury under President John Tyler. "The most distinguished man whom I have yet met in America," Beaumont wrote home. Not surprisingly, Spencer became a major influence in the writing of *Democracy in America*. That influence and Tocqueville's methodology are both demonstrated by comparing the writer's notes of their conversations in Canandaigua with passages from the final work.

"Q. What is the influence of the press on public opinion?"

"A. It has a great influence, but it does not exercise it in the same manner as in France. Thus we attach very little value to the opinions of the journalist. He obtains influence only through the facts which he makes known and the turn he gives them . . ."

"Q. What are the limits that you put on its liberty?"

"A. Our principle in this matter is very simple. Everything in the realm of opinion is perfectly free. In America one could every day print that a monarchy is the best of all governments. But when a journal publishes calumnies, when it gratuitously attributes culpable intentions, then it is sued and ordinarily punished with a heavy fine."

"Q. What is, in your opinion, the way to diminish the influence of the periodical press?"

"A. I am completely convinced that the most effective of all is to multiply the number of newspapers as far as possible and sue them only in extreme cases. Their power diminishes as they be-

come more numerous; our experience has shown this to be unde-
niable ... With us interests are divided in a thousand ways,
there are no great centers of action. It is almost impossible to
agitate public opinion over a large area."

This is, in part, what Tocqueville later wrote about the press:

"... the number of periodical or semiperiodical publications
in the United States surpasses all belief. The most enlightened
Americans attribute the slightness of the power of the press to
this incredible dispersion; it is an axiom of political science there
that the only way to neutralize the effect of newspapers is to
multiply their numbers. ...

"There is hardly a hamlet in America without its newspaper.
Of course, with so many combatants, neither discipline nor unity
of action is possible, and so each fights under its own flag. It is
not the case that all the political newspapers in the Union are
lined up to support or oppose the administration, but they use a
hundred different means to attack or defend it. Therefore
American papers cannot raise those powerful currents of
opinion which sweep away or sweep over the most powerful dikes.

"... the personal views of journalists carry, so to speak, no
weight with the readers. What they look for in a newspaper is
knowledge of facts, and it is only by altering or distorting those
facts that the journalist can gain some influence for his views."

The agitation of public opinion that Spencer talked about
with Tocqueville was not designed to effect a gentle and benevolent uplifting of the democratic mind and spirit. That multitude
of newspapers was, generally, biased and nasty, ignorant and
stupid. But it was lusty: the voice of a young people. Tocqueville
was a bit shocked: these people were conducting the public's
business in public. On landing in Newport, his first day in
America, he picked up a paper at the docks and was impressed
enough with what he read to write out this long note quoting a
front-page story:

"The first newspaper I saw on arrival in America contained
the following article, which I translate faithfully: 'In this whole
affair the language used by Jackson [the President] was that of a
heartless despot exclusively concerned with preserving his own
power. Ambition is his crime, and that will be his punishment.
Intrigue is his vocation, and intrigue will confound his plans and

snatch his power from him. He governs by corruption, and his guilty maneuvers will turn to his shame and confusion. . . .'

"So, where the press is concerned, there is not in reality any middle path between license and servitude. To cull the inestimable benefits assured by freedom of the press, it is necessary to put up with the inevitable evils springing therefrom. . . ."

Two days later, on May 12, 1831, Tocqueville was in New York City, where the thirteenth toast at the Tammany banquet was: "The Press—the channel of public opinion. Who would not submit to its occasional abuse rather than forego the blessings of its freedom?"

"I admit," he would write in *Democracy in America,* "that I do not feel toward freedom of the press that complete and instantaneous love which one accords to things by their nature supremely good. I love it more from considering the evils it prevents than on account of the good it does. The more I observe the main effects of a free press, the more convinced I am that, in the modern world, freedom of the press is the principal and, so to say, the constitutive element in freedom. A nation bent on remaining free is therefore right to insist, at whatever cost, on respect for this freedom."

And, he went on, the evils the press itself might generate were small and many, because the newspapers themselves were small and many. "Starting a paper being easy," he wrote, "anybody may take to it; but competition prevents any newspaper from hoping for large profits, and that discourages anybody with great business ability from bothering with such undertakings."

He should have known better. This was America, the land of breathless cupidity. Someone with great business ability was bound to figure out a way to make large profits in the newspaper business. In fact, Americans did it just thirty miles from Canandaigua; they formed a great national press combine in Rochester.

6
ROCHESTER

"Democratic Commerce and Commercial Democracy ..."

Rochester likes to call itself America's first boom town. And it was just that when Tocqueville passed by; from 1820 to 1830, the population of the town on the Genesee River had grown from about 150 to more than 15,000. When the Erie Canal opened in 1825, Rochester attracted entrepreneurs from New England and England, and from Germany. Hard-working Calvinists, they built and ran mills using the water power of the falls of the Genesee to grind local wheat into flour for shipment down the canal to New York City.

What Rochester did was commercialize American agriculture. Then, beginning in the 1880s, it commercialized photography. George Eastman, a local bank clerk who was an experimenter and a marketing genius, made a fortune by developing cameras and film for the masses. "KODAK" was the trademark; he created it to be understandable in any language. "You press the button—we do the rest" was the slogan. It could have been an American motto.

In the 1950s, it was xerography, a dry-copying process that made it possible to reproduce printed material without ... without printing, without a press of any sort. A device which, like Eastman's cheap camera, "would add new dimensions," in the words of Daniel Boorstin, a historian and, then, Librarian of Congress, "to the repeatability of experience, enabling anyone

75

who had access to a simple machine to destroy the uniqueness or confidentiality of any document." A Rochester businessman, Joseph C. Wilson, developed a huge corporation, Xerox, around the almost-forgotten 1938 experiments of a New York inventor named Chester F. Carlson.

In the 1970s, it was newspapers. Using Rochester's morning paper, the *Democrat and Chronicle,* and a couple of smaller upstate New York papers as his base, Frank E. Gannett and the Gannett Corporation, founded in Elmira, N. Y., in 1906, began the process which eventually mocked Tocqueville's conclusion that competition prevented newspapers from hoping for large profits.

Gannett commercialized newspapering, as Rochester's flour mills had commercialized agriculture. The method was simple: avoiding competition. Gannett swept and reswept the country, picking up small papers in one-newspaper towns, in Wausau, Wisconsin, in Marietta, Georgia, in Coffeyville, Kansas. Usually the owner of a local paper had no children interested in the business or was trying to avoid inheritance taxes. Sometimes Gannett simply offered much more money than the property was worth, knowing it could quickly earn enough to repay itself when costs were cut and advertising rates raised. With managers and editors being moved around the country from headquarters in Rochester, often staying only two or three years in each place, the corporation ran its newspapers from regional centers, one in Rochester, the others in Rockford, Illlinois; Cocoa, Florida; and Reno, Nevada.

Gannett, like most other large companies, had its own geography; its maps were different from the ones used by government. One internal memo to the president of Gannett, Allen Neuharth, that I happened to come across in Rochester said: "El Paso, Santa Fe, Tucson and San Bernardino are viewed as an area that can be grouped together for coverage." The cities, almost 1,000 miles apart and in four different states, apparently looked the same to the senders of the memo, a committee of the corporation's managing editors.

During the 1970s, Gannett's chain grew from 36 to 82 newspapers, total circulation more than doubled to 3,580,000, earnings increased by 486 percent. With Gannett as the model, two-thirds of the country's 1,769 daily newspapers—compared with 2,500 dailies in 1900—were owned and operated by chains.*

When I saw him in 1980, Allen Neuharth had been president of Gannett for ten years; in 1979 he was paid $1,160,000 in salary, benefits, and stock options as both president and chairman of the board. His office was in Rochester, but that did not necessarily mean he was always or even usually there. He used four private jet planes to travel more than 300,000 miles a year, a hundred times across the United States, often looking for or negotiating for new properties. Both the office and the man seemed quite extraordinary to me. The room, starkly modern, was controlled by a console at Neuharth's left hand—doors opened, walls moved back and forth, revealing charts and television monitors. The man himself had, for years, dressed only in black, grays and white—associates called him "The Black Prince"—in suits and shirts that practically shone. Eight pairs of sunglasses in a neat row were the only objects on his huge, semicircular desk as we talked. I could have been interviewing the captain of a space ship.

"Our business is the sale of news and information," he said. "That includes shopping information. Store news. Other than that we provide diversity according to the wants and needs of our readers." He emphasized the word "wants," adding: "Our papers are edited in response to the wishes of our readers."

Do the newspapers educate the public?

"We may have a bit of a role in educating the public," he answered, "but not so much that it gets in the way of the information they want and will pay for."

Very American. Very democratic. "Yes," Neuharth said. "I believe the country is becoming more democratic. You have to give people what they want if you're going to pay the rent. And the newspapers that survive are the ones that pay the rent. We have to give people what they do not get from all those other things they read and watch.

"We are not, however, democratic in business. I would prefer

* If Tocqueville and Beaumont had made their journey to America in 1981 instead of 1831 and read the newspapers in each place they passed through—as they did—they would have seen 28 Gannett papers.

to do a modestly responsible and professional editorial job—our newspapers, I think you'll find, are better than they were under their old owners—but this is, first, a business to make money. We dictate—I hate to use that word—we dictate all things concerning internal business policy, advertising rates, purchasing of equipment, things like that."

"If one of your editors," I asked, "was meeting all business projections, bottom-line profit and the rest, and following all your internal procedures, but was taking an editorial line you found objectionable, what would you do?"

"Fire him. That's not our kind of journalism."

"Our expanding empire" is one of the ways Gannett executives referred to the company in internal memos. Those internal communications, read in the context of the company's success, could make an American cringe at one of Tocqueville's casual dismissals of American attainments: "So the Americans have not yet, properly speaking, got any literature. Only the journalists strike me as truly American. They certainly are not great writers, but they speak their country's language and they make themselves heard."

The very American managing editors of the Gannett empire, in one of those confidential memos to Neuharth, described their goals in overall reportage by using recent copy on travels in China as an example: "Theme was perhaps best exemplified by [coverage of] China. No double-dome copy, but excellent on acupuncture, Chinese food . . ."

The newspapers those people put out—from St. Thomas, Virgin Islands, and Pensacola, Florida, to Oakland, California, and Honolulu, Hawaii—were not, individually, so terrible. It was just that each had so little chance of becoming much better. They were not so much a newspaper company as . . . well, as Neuharth wrote in the Gannett annual report that year: "The nation's premier newspaper growth company . . . reaching out to become the nation's foremost diversified media company . . . new earnings records for the 12th consecutive year and 49th consecutive quarter."

"There is no reason," he said as we talked, "why Gannett can't be the biggest communications company in the world." To what end? He was once asked how to pronounce the name of the company: was the emphasis on the first or the second syllable of Gannett? He replied: "Money!"

Alexis de Tocqueville, the elegant young Frenchman worrying that elegance itself might not survive democracy, had been appalled by American newspapers from the moment he saw that first attack on the "heartless despot" President Jackson. He concluded that "the hallmark of the American journalist . . . [was] a direct and coarse attack, without any subtleties, on the passion of his readers; he disregards principles to seize on people, following them into their private lives and laying bare their weaknesses and their vices."

That passage appeared near the middle of the first volume of *Democracy in America.* Some 300,000 words later, in the final pages of his great work, Tocqueville wrote:

"In times of equality each man is naturally isolated. He can call on no hereditary friends for help nor any class whose sympathy for him is assured. He can easily be set upon alone and trodden underfoot. Nowadays an oppressed citizen has only one means of defense: he can appeal to the nation as a whole, and if it is deaf, to humanity at large. The press provides his only means of doing this. For this reason freedom of the press is infinitely more precious in a democracy than in any other nation. It alone cures most of the ills which equality may engender. Equality isolates and weakens men, but the press puts each man in reach of a very powerful weapon which can be used even by the weakest and most isolated of men. Equality deprives each individual of the help of his neighbors, but the press enables him to call to his aid all his fellow citizens and all mankind. Printing has hastened the progress of equality, but it is also one of its best correctives. . . . I should put no trust in great political assemblies, parliamentary prerogatives, or the proclamation of the sovereignty of the people to secure personal independence.

"All those things can, to some extent, be reconciled with personal servitude. But such servitude cannot be complete if the press is free. The press is, par excellence, the democratic weapon of freedom."

That is the role, the defense, and the glory of a free press. The rest, however annoying, is incidental. The American press shielded by—sometimes hiding behind—the Constitution has been able again and again to prevail over governments determined to mold institutions and individuals to the "national interest"—that interest, of course, being defined by whoever happened to be in power at the time. "We have shown that we can survive as a political institution, that we can meet challenges from governments and courts," said John Siegenthaler, the fifty-one-year-old publisher of an independent newspaper, the *Nashville Tennessean.* "But I think that, in my lifetime, the chains will be challenged as businesses. The key to government control of the press might be antitrust legislation and regulation."

We were two old newspapermen drinking away part of an afternoon in Nashville, where Tocqueville had been for two days. We understood only the outlines, not the details, of the business operations of the corporations taking over our professional world, but we did not believe the business itself—the "corporate side," as reporters refer to it, pretending that, somehow, they're not part of it—could avoid government control. "I can visualize the heads of the chains—Gannett, Newhouse—sitting in a row before a Congressional committee," Siegenthaler said. "How much will they give in to avoid that and to preserve their business interests?"

The *Tennessean,* with a circulation of 132,154, was owned by a local family. On July 5, 1979, six months after Siegenthaler and I talked, the newspaper was sold—to Gannett. Siegenthaler was retained as publisher and named a vice president of Gannett.

The danger Siegenthaler talked about that earlier day was national. As Gannett or any expanding, diversifying billion-dollar corporation went about its businesses—which already included television and radio stations, plus advertising, marketing, and public opinion research companies—its operations would inevitably and increasingly be intertwined with legislation, regulation, inspection, permission, consultation, litigation, and the maze of other intersections of complicated commerce and complex government. Tax benefits, merger approvals, or investigations and prosecutions were becoming more useful tools of government control over information than a blatant and clumsy censorship ever could be. Overt government moves against a rowdy and inconvenient press were greatly inhibited by the First Amendment to the Constitution—"Congress shall make no law . . . abridging the freedom of speech, or of the press"—but as the press became just another business, branching further and further afield from journals of fact and opinion, it was voluntarily moving under the comforting and threatening umbrella of federal power. I got the impression from talking with Neuharth that Gannett was also considering moving its headquarters to the base of the umbrella—from Rochester to Washington, D. C., or its suburbs. That would be a blow to Rochester—not a boom town anymore—whose population had declined from 332,000 to 241,000 from 1950 to 1980. But, I thought, it would also dramatize something about Gannett's links to its cities—and the local dangers of chain journalism.

The old publishers and editors bought out and moved out by Gannett and other chains all across the country were, often, stupid, lazy, biased, or dishonest. Sometimes they were all those things and worse. Neuharth was essentially accurate in saying that his chain "improves" the papers it buys—at least in the sense of making them more professional. But the old-timers had a stake in their communities that would not be shared by upwardly mobile strangers. Gannett's company magazine, the *Gannetteer*, ran a feature story on one of their people—Gary Watson, thirty-five years old, who was becoming publisher of the Rockford, Illinois, *Register Star* after three years as editor of the chain's papers in Springfield, Missouri, and before that, three years as editor in Boise, Idaho. The angle of the inspirational little story on Watson was that he was going home—he had grown up in Rockford and actually once worked for the *Register Star*. But hometown boy or not, Watson would be a failure if he stayed long back in Rockford. The idea was "up or out." If he succeeded in Rockford—success being defined as meeting Gannett's projections for a record 50th straight quarter of record profits—Watson would be moved up in the Gannett empire, perhaps to Cincinnati, Ohio, to Wilmington, Delaware, to San Bernardino or El Paso. It didn't matter where; it's all Gannett.

But what would Watson do if local advertisers threatened to boycott the *Register Star* if it published stories on, say, a pattern of avoiding state taxes on commercial receipts? The old publishers, for all their faults, were a permanent part of a local power structure. One of them might lose some money over an editorial or a journalistic principle, but he knew that in the long run, local businessmen had to come back. In a monopoly market, the merchants had no choice; there are always many local businesses and services that have no other practical advertising medium. A Gannett publisher, on the other hand, would have to think long and hard before alienating any business advertisers. Even a short boycott or shortfall of advertising would destroy his paper's and the company's monthly profit and growth projections—and thus his career.

Of another chain in another city, Jack Davis, city editor of the New Orleans *States-Item*, one of 22 Newhouse Newspapers, said: "Newhouse is only interested in whether or not we meet profit projections. They wouldn't mind if we put out a good newspaper." Both Newhouse and Gannett are, in Neuharth's phrase, in the business of selling information. And the emphasis is on the selling. The information, again relying on Neuharth, will be whatever people "want and will pay for."*

And there were ways of telling what the public wanted. Gannett, in fact, owned a company—Louis Harris and Associates— that could do readership surveys like the one used by Albert Sherman, the manager of the *Daily News* in Newport. Survey numbers, the compilations of the responses of readers to standard questions, could substitute for the traditions and instincts of journalism, good and bad, which had often made the American press the most influential adversary—or the tool of the most influential adversaries—of governors and government. While I was in Rochester, the American Society of Newspaper Editors was sponsoring polling and interviewing that was published as a 51-page booklet called: "Changing Needs of Changing Readers—A Qualitative Study of the New Social Contract Between Newspaper Editors and Readers."†

*I first interviewed Jack Davis on February 7, 1979. On June 2, 1980, Newhouse Newspapers, with headquarters in Syracuse, N. Y., merged the two newspapers it owned in New Orleans—the *States-Item* and the *Times-Picayune*—into a single paper, the *Times-Picayune and States-Item*. Like most American cities, New Orleans was reduced to one daily paper. It had, a long time ago, supported 32.

† The study, based on nine sets of long interviews, was conducted by Yankelovich, Skelly & White, Inc., a New York public research firm, under the direction of Ruth Clark. The cities covered were: Buffalo and Niagara Falls, N. Y.; Chicago and Rockford, Ill.; Boulder and Denver, Colo.; Charlotte, N. C.; Kitchener, Ontario; Minneapolis, Minn.; New Britain, Conn.; New York, N. Y.; and Riverside, Calif.

"Under the impact of rapid social and cultural change," the report stated,

> many readers—especially young readers and occasional readers—have developed different attitudes about newspapers. They expect them to be more attentive to their personal needs, more caring, more warmly human, less anonymous. Instead of faceless editors and reporters—traditional symbols of objectivity—they want real people to relate to . . .
>
> As one reader complained, 'Editors live in one world and I live in another. They're worried about the Middle East, and I'm worried about meeting my bills.'
>
> There are indications in this study and elsewhere that this 'focus on self' will continue, among middle-aged and older readers as well as among the young. And the emphasis is subtly shifting from the earlier goal of self-improvement, to self-fulfillment, to getting ahead, to gratifying one's immediate desires and needs.

The study then reported that readers want more local news and listed some of the specific news people desired: more coverage of schools and school sports; stories on interesting local residents; listings and stories on career opportunities and places to visit; 'Action Line' features committing the paper to handle reader complaints against business and government; more gardening features; and more classified advertising. The words "coping" and "caring" were repeated through the study—and, soon enough, I noticed that some Gannett papers had "Coping" sections along with "News" and "Sports" and "Business."

One editor, Clay Felker of the *Daily News Tonight* in New York City, mentioned the impact of readership studies on the relationship between journalism and government—specifically on a 1980 federal court ruling that government agents had the right to search newspaper offices if they had reason to believe editors or reporters had evidence potentially useful in the prosecution of accused criminals. "Who cares if the government kicks down the doors?" Felker said. "The way things are going, all they're going to find in newsrooms are P.T.A. notices and supermarket advertisements."

"Authors are quick to see in what direction public taste secretly inclines, and they trim their sails accordingly." The quote is not new; it was Tocqueville speaking, disapprovingly, of the American theater. So part of what happened in 150 years was the institutionalization, with the aid of new research methodology, of the inevitable tendencies of democratic commerce in a very commercial democracy. There is a logic to the union of those two words—"democracy" and "commerce"—that affects every phase and minute of life in the United States. American journalism became like American theater—even, within the offices of newspapers, using the word "story" rather than "report" or "article"—or like American politics. Or is that reversed? It was, then and now, very hard to tell, to separate one realm from the other.

"The idea is to find out what the public wants, what it needs. We study the constituency and try to figure out what will sell." That was not Neuharth speaking about newspapers, about the commercialization of information that, through Kodak, Xerox, and Gannett, had replaced the commercialization of agriculture as Rochester's reason for being. This time the words came from the "boss" of Rochester's politics, Laurence Kirwan, chairman of the Monroe County Democratic Committee.

Kirwan's idea, hardly original but very democratic, took him a long way in a short time. About a year after moving to the county, Kirwan, a twenty-nine-year-old insurance underwriter, and three friends who had been active together in a local civil rights organization went to see their local Democratic ward chairman. They said they wanted to become active in partisan politics and were interested in running for one or more of the 48 seats on the party's ward committee.

"You're kidding," the ward leader said, as Kirwan recalled the meeting ten years later. "There are no vacancies on the committee."

Kirwan said he knew that wasn't true. He had bought his house from a committeeman who moved away from Rochester a year before. The ward boss, a very small cog in the party's machinery, threw the four friends out of his office.

Angry, they went to the county courthouse and looked up the list of the Democratic voters registered in the ward. There were only 2,000 of them, and the four friends together knew 141 personally. They called the ones they knew and lined up candidates for all 48 of the committee seats. Then they went door to door urging neighborhood Democrats to vote for their candidates. On election day 1970, the minor results newspapers rarely reported showed that Kirwan and his friends and their candidates won 43 of the 48 seats. The campaign cost them $20.

Two years later, using the same mundane techniques, Kirwan was elected chairman of the Monroe County Democratic Committee. One of the techniques was running women for half the county committee seats—which was considered almost revolutionary in 1970. The title was nice and so was the pay—$24,000 a year—but it wasn't as if the new political boss had many people to boss around. Like many things in Rochester, local politics and government had been an extension of the will of the city's great patron, George Eastman, whose company, Eastman Kodak, employed more than 50,000 people. The city and county, with a population of 750,000, were, by reputation, the most Republican and most conservative urban constituency in the Northeast. Voter registration was more than 70 percent Republican and the party held every countywide office and controlled, by large margins, the county legislature and the Rochester City Council.

Then Kirwan began figuring out what would sell. One state assembly district, for instance, was about evenly divided between Italian working-class families and students, professors, and others associated in one way or another with local colleges. Kirwan found a State University of New York dean with an Italian name. The dean was a winner and so were other candidates, who, Kirwan said, were "handpicked—by my hand." By 1979, the Rochester City Council was 8-to-1 Democratic and the party had also won three state Assembly seats, controlled the Monroe County Legislature, and had elected a state senator, sheriff, district attorney, and three judges. County registration of Democrats increased from less than 30 percent to about 40 percent during the decade.

Neither Kirwan nor Neuharth grew up in Rochester; both came there seeking opportunity, to make their fortunes—and both men's success, like that of Jimmy Carter, the little-known ex-governor of Georgia who became President, could be considered proof of the open, or vulnerable, nature of most American institutions. The political leader was born and raised in Massachusetts and came to upstate New York only because he was assigned to an office there by the Aetna Insurance Company. The publisher was from South Dakota and worked his way up to the head office during a reporting and editing career that took him through Miami and Detroit. "Rochester used to be a tight little island," said Alan Underberg, a prominent attorney who did grow up in the city. "The city was shaped by George Eastman—keep politics Republican, and outsiders out. *Noblesse oblige*—he started the first Community Chest in the country here in 1916. There was one important bank, one important law firm; whatever had to be done in business and politics could be done at the Country Club of Rochester or the Genesee Valley Club. . . . But we can't pretend to be a homegrown city anymore. There are absentee owners now, the Al Neuharths of the world."*

Neuharth and Kirwan had power in Rochester. (Neuharth, of course, had it in many other cities as well.) The publisher, if nothing else, could raise the advertising rates local merchants must pay—many of them had no other way of reaching consumers than through Gannett pages—and that would inevitably raise the price someone paid for an apple or an automobile. The county chairman could pick a sheriff. But that seemed to be about where the use of their power ended: Neuharth was interested in growing, not in educating; Kirwan was interested in electing, not in governing.

One man who lived within their orbit expressed contempt for them and their influence without mentioning their names. Christopher Lasch, a historian on the faculty of the University of Rochester since 1970, had just written a surprising best-seller, *The Culture of Narcissism: American Life in an Age of Diminishing Expectations*, a profoundly depressing book on the "cultural crisis" and the "despair of a society that cannot face the future." Those quotations were from the preface and things got worse after that. Certainly the commercial success of the book indicated that many Americans were deeply concerned about

---

* U. S. Senator Gary Hart of Colorado was one of many successful people who commented on that openness of systems. "A small number of people—ten to 10,000—can elect a governor or a senator in Colorado, if they're willing to work," he said. "That's how I got where I am."

the directions in which the society was moving in a time of rapid, disorienting change—or it indicated that many Americans, true to Puritan roots, could not face the future without being constantly told of a guilty past and present drifting toward aimless, self-indulgent egalitarian frivolity.

"The same historical development that turned the citizen into a client transformed the worker from a producer into a consumer," Lasch wrote in conclusion. "In a dying culture, narcissism appears to embody—in the guise of personal 'growth' and 'awareness'—the highest attainment of spiritual enlightenment. The custodians of culture hope, at bottom, merely to survive its collapse. The will to build a better society, however, survives, along with the tradition of localism, self-help and community action that only need the vision of a new society, a decent society to give them new vigor. The moral discipline formerly associated with the work ethic still retains a value independent of the role it once played in the defense of property rights. That discipline—indispensable to the task of building a new order—endures most of all in those who knew the old order only as a broken promise, yet who took the promise more seriously than those who merely took it for granted."

There seemed to be some hope there at the end, I said to Lasch. What gives you that bit of optimism?

He looked out the window of his home in Pittsford, a suburb of Rochester, at his children and a large dog playing on the grass, and said, "I think people are beginning to realize how bad things really are."

Democracy, Lasch thought, had failed. I was a long way from believing that—what I really wanted were his perceptions of the roles of gifted American opportunists like Neuharth and Kirwan. What did he think of the press? What did he think of politics?

"The press," he said, "doesn't really initiate anything in the society. Television, if that's part of the press, only accents and speeds up movements that begin within the society itself. It has not been the cause."*

* In dismissing television as a fundamental cause for social and cultural change in the United States, Lasch referred to *The Lonely Crowd—A Study of the Changing American Character* by David Riesman, with Nathan Glazer and Reuel Denney, a book that analyzed many aspects of American behavior and character that have

I agreed with that. Certainly in our lifetimes—Lasch and I were about the same age—the ideas that had moved large amounts of Americans had begun within the society, usually with a very small number of people. New movements or new waves of old movements—civil rights for blacks, feminism, anti-militarism, environmentalism, revolts against growing taxes and government, another "return" to fundamental Christianity—all had real trouble attracting reporters and cameras during their beginnings. A few black students, some crazy women, hippy draft dodgers, holy-roller preachers . . . who cared? When they became interesting enough—sometimes violent enough—the people pushing the ideas attracted the press, and soon the whole world was watching. That undoubtedly accelerated the growth and heightened the impact of those movements, but the real test of the power of the press would have been to try to initiate its own waves of change or to try to ignore those building up in colleges or kitchens.

As Tocqueville wrote in that note to himself when he saw his first newspaper attack on Jackson, ". . . the press, so skilled to inflame human passions, can yet not create them all on its own."

It still can't. What had changed since Tocqueville's note—in addition to the fact that the rules of attack were now more tempered—was the speed and reach of the transmission of information. The technology of the press, including television and radio, had changed what people knew and when they knew it—as the printing press did five centuries before in Europe. And what the new technologies—including computers arranging and processing storms of information—were most likely to do was speed up events, trends, movements, in a society in which, in Tocqueville's words, "public opinion is the dominant power."

"The Union," he wrote, in words that, 30 years later, were confirmed as prophetic when the Civil War began, "principally exists in the law that created it. A revolution or a change in public opinion could shatter it forever. The republic has deeper roots.

---

since been attributed to the influence of television and television watching. *The Lonely Crowd*, however, was written between 1947 and 1949, before television was in widespread use in the United States.

"What is meant by 'republic' in the United States is the slow and quiet action of society upon itself. It is an orderly state really founded on the enlightened will of the people. It is a conciliatory government under which resolutions have time to ripen, being discussed with deliberation and executed only when mature."

Using that specific definition of the "republic" for the moment, the danger of the "press" 150 years later—of the technology of communications itself—was its threat to slowness, to deliberation and deliberateness. The republic was indeed designed to be deliberate; the Constitution created a cumbersome system of checks and balances to slow down the processes of governing. The idea of multiple approvals and appeals, of legislatures and courts and bureaus, was, in the simplest terms, to prevent democracy from deteriorating into government by mob. Action was slow; nothing could be done until the mob went home. Now the mob could be at home—people could, electronically, receive political information instantaneously and simultaneously and they could act on it immediately. Democratically.

It was not hard for me to visualize direct democracy or, perhaps, an electronic republic—using the word here in the sense of democracy exercised through elected representatives—based on the developing "interactive" capability of television. Two-way television—in which viewers (citizens) with push-button panels in their homes could register their opinions (votes) in central computers linked to their televisions—was already in use in one city I traveled through, Columbus, Ohio. With the system, called QUBE, viewers watched a drama or a discussion at home, then could punch in their own opinions or thoughts—limited, of course, by the questions flashed on the screen.

Watching QUBE one day as a candidate for President of the United States (George Bush, who later became Vice President) sought viewer opinion on his party's positions, I was struck by two thoughts. Whoever decides which questions are to be asked and how they are to be worded has enormous power. And there was no reason not to think that there could be a similar national system in which Congress would debate the issues of the day, perhaps in a structured evening program, and citizens could then register their views of the issue as arguments ended.

The results of those instant national referenda would then be flashing in front of each legislator. A member of Congress, knowing public opinion in the district or the country, would then have the dubious honor and politically dangerous duty of voting, perhaps testing his or her conscience against the recorded will of the majority.

"My instinct tells me that's unconstitutional," said one member of Congress, Senator Gary Hart of Colorado, when we discussed that kind of electronic republic. "But maybe I'm just thinking of my own job. What would be the function of the elected official under that system?"

What is the function now? asked Christopher Lasch. In his very critical view, modern American politics was without public purpose. "The contagion of unintelligibility spreads through all levels of government," he had written. "It is not merely that propagandists fall victim to their own propaganda; the problem goes deeper. When politicians and administrators have no other aim than to sell their leadership to the public, they deprive themselves of intelligible standards by which to define the goals of specific policies or to evaluate success or failure. . . . Political discussion founded on such principles degenerates into meaningless babble. . . ."

The same kind of point—about the press, this time—had been made to me the day before by the man who publishes the newspaper in the town where Lasch lives.

"Gannett newspapers are not interested in power or influence as you understand it," said Andrew Wolfe, who was an executive of the chain before quitting to become publisher and editor of a string of local weekly papers, including the *Brighton-Pittsford Post.* "They do what readers tell them. If someone proposes two expressways, they'll favor one and oppose one. It doesn't make any sense, but it keeps up appearances."

Selling appearances. Selling leadership. One of the leaders Kirwan picked and sold was Richard Wilson, chairman of the Monroe County Legislature: a good-looking candidate, son of Joseph Wilson, the man who built Xerox, well known, rich enough to be obviously immune from petty corruption, well educated, the kind of candidate who could, and did, win Democratic votes in a Republican area. In three hours of conversation about his goals, his public purposes, Wilson only said over and over again that he believed in "regionalization." He believed that there should be closer cooperation between Rochester and the governments of the 19 smaller communities within the county.*

For example?

He said he would like to see a county-wide "911" system—a single three-digit telephone number that could be used in an emergency to connect any resident of the county with a local police or fire department. "But we won't get it," Wilson said. "There have been five attempts to do it in the last 12 years. They shoot it down because everyone is afraid someone else will control it."

"The central question today," Lasch said, "in a therapeutic-technological society"—the society described both in his book and in the ASNE survey of readers who want "caring" help in coping with a fast, complex world—"is whether you can get the necessary work done. Can you accomplish anything?"

"The central question," Andrew Wolfe said, "is, as it always has been, as Tocqueville saw it: Can you fulfill the majority and still leave room and freedom for the explosively creative?"

Is America doing that?

"America still works," he said. "The systems are sound. People can still get what they want."

There was one more person I wanted to see in Rochester. I had met Eugene Genovese fourteen years earlier, when he was

* Wilson, on the local level, was an example of the candidate with the presold name, a phenomenon that seems to have increased with mass voting and television. With great competition for the public's attention, name recognition is valuable and celebrity seems to have become the coin of the realm of American politics. The U. S. Senate was becoming a reward for people who won fame in or had famous relatives in other fields—astronauts, professional athletes, television personalities, the sons and daughters of tycoons and politicians—and, at the end of my journey, a movie actor was elected President. Tocqueville would not have been surprised. In his notebook, on November 3, 1831, he wrote: "In Massachusetts the governor is Mr. Lionel (Levi) Lincoln and the lieutenant governor Mr. Winthrop, both descended from early governors of the colony. In the state of New York the lieutenant governor is Mr. Livingston, scion of the greatest family of the region. In Maryland the governor is Mr. Howard, son of the famous Colonel Howard and the representative of one of the oldest families. All these gentlemen are very ordinary individuals and evidently owe their elevation simply to their names. The populace is attracted. . . ."

an assistant professor of history at Rutgers University in New Brunswick, N. J. A Marxist, he had triggered a national political controversy by telling a crowd of students that he would welcome a victory by North Vietnamese Communist armies fighting South Vietnamese and American troops in Southeast Asia. Now, like Lasch, he was a professor of history at the University of Rochester and had just stepped down as head of that department.

"It's still working," he said.*

"The American people are not going to kick over a going concern," Genovese said, not, I thought, without a little regret. "The rhetoric of alienation outruns the content. Institutionally, the country is much more democratic than it used to be. Even if people feel a sense of lost participation, the openings for participation, the opportunities, are still there. If things were as bad as they're supposed to be, if the feelings of alienation were as deep as some people say, you'd see some form of real rebellion. Where is it?"

---

* "Americans, looking around the world, see no alternative to this system," Genovese said. "The alternative, socialism, has been sealed off, I think during my lifetime, by socialism's union with political repression in the Soviet Union and Eastern Europe. The American people have come to equate socialism and repression and they will never accept political repression."

PART TWO

Cincinnati
to Baltimore

7

CINCINNATI

"Fairness Was Being Demanded and Enforced . . ."

The damn thing seemed to work!

"There is one thing that America demonstrates invincibly of which I was hitherto doubtful. This is that the middle classes are capable of governing a state," Tocqueville wrote in his notebooks as he traveled by steamboat south to Cincinnati, Ohio. "I don't know if they would come off honorably from really difficult political situations, but they are adequate for the ordinary conduct of society, despite their petty passions, their incomplete education, their vulgar manners. Clearly they can supply practical intelligence, and that is sufficient."

Then the surprised young aristocrat underlined a title and wrote a short essay to himself, "Concerning Equality in America":

"It's not a question now of equality before the law, that kind is complete in America. . . . In France, whatever people say, the prejudice of birth still exercises a very great power. Birth still forms an almost insurmountable barrier between individuals. In France the professions still to a certain degree classify those that follow them. These prejudices are of all the most inimical to equality, because they create distinctions that are permanent and almost ineffaceable, even with the aid of fortune and time. Those prejudices don't exist in America. Birth is a distinction, but it doesn't classify those who have it, it creates neither right nor incapacity, nor obligations toward the world or toward one-self. Classification by professions is likewise almost unknown. It does indeed establish some practical difference between the position of individuals, and in this a difference of fortune is even more effective, but it creates no fundamental inequality, for it does not in any way prevent the intermarriage of families (that's the great touchstone).

"When one wishes to estimate the equality between different classes, one must always come to the question of how marriages are made. That's the bottom of the matter. An equality resulting from necessity, courtesy or politics may exist on the surface and deceive the eye. But when one wishes to practice this equality in the intermarriage of families, then one puts one's finger on the sore."

Tocqueville seemed to equate equality with opportunity for economic and political—and *social*—mobility. In the France he knew "fortune and time" could not overcome lineage—men and women married their own kind, men were generally restricted to the professions of their fathers. In America, a small-farmer's son from a far province, as far as South Dakota, would not only be able to take over the country's largest newspaper chain, but could marry any woman he might persuade.

Tocqueville was impressed, but he was not fooled. "Yet one must not think that in America all the classes of society mingle in the same *salons*," he continued. "Nothing of the kind is true. The people of the same professions, the same ideas, the same education, choose each other by a sort of instinct and gather together, exclusive from the rest. The difference is that no arbitrary and inflexible rule presides at this arrangement. Thus it shocks no one; it is final for nobody. . . . There's what distinguishes American society favorably from ours. And unfavorably.

"In sum then, men in America, as with us, are arranged according to certain categories in the course of social life; common habits, education, and above all wealth establish these classifications. But these rules are neither absolute, nor inflexible, nor permanent."

That settled in his mind, he arrived in Cincinnati.

"A singular spectacle," he wrote of the city of 30,000 that had sprung up in the wilderness along the Ohio River, "a city which

Scene along the Ohio River

seems to want to rise too quickly for people to have any system or plan about it. Great buildings, thatched cottages, streets encumbered with debris, houses under construction, no names on the streets, no numbers on the houses. . . . All that there is of good or of bad in American society is to be found there in such strong relief, that one would be tempted to call it one of those books printed in large letters for teaching children to read; everything there is in violent contrast, exaggerated. . . .

"The Europeans, on coming to America, left behind them, in large part, the traditions of the past, the institutions and customs of their fatherland. . . . In the last forty years, from the midst of that new society has gone out another swarm of emigrants marching west, as once their fathers came to the coasts of New England and Maryland. Like them abandoning the ideas of their fatherland along with the soil that bore them. . . . A people absolutely without precedents, without traditions, without habits, without dominating ideas even, opening for itself without hesitation a new path in civil, political and criminal legislation. . . ."*

The frontier, new laws, new institutions, a new people? Tocqueville may have been driven to enthusiastic exaggeration. But a lot was happening and it was happening very fast. "Is it true," he asked a young lawyer named Timothy Walker, "that a portion of the population of Ohio is already starting to move to the right bank of the Mississippi?"

"Yes," said Walker, who had arrived from Massachusetts earlier that year, "here's what's happening. Those who possess lands generally keep them and remain here. But their sons go to seek their fortunes further west, in the states where the lands are as yet uninhabited. . . ."

In Cincinnati, the Frenchman talked mainly with lawyers, and he chose his subjects remarkably well. Walker, who was twenty-five years old then, was to go on to found Ohio's first law school. Salmon Portland Chase, just entering practice at the age of twenty-four, was to become Chief Justice of the United States. An older man, John McLean, had just been named an associate justice of the U. S. Supreme Court.

One hundred and fifty years later, the senior justice on the Supreme Court was another Cincinnati lawyer, Potter Stewart. "In my lifetime the courts have replaced the frontier," said Stewart, who had been appointed to the high court in 1958. "When this country was new, a nonconformist or someone who just wasn't making it could always go west. There was always space. Now there is no more space and the courts have been called on to protect the rights of these individuals. The courts are trying to provide that space.

"Originally, the courts were established just to resolve dis-

---

* I was struck by the similarity between Tocqueville's and Beaumont's observations on Ohio in 1831 and twentieth-century writings about California, particularly Southern California. "The character of this society is that of having none," Beaumont wrote home. One of the Cincinnatians they interviewed, Timothy Walker, a young lawyer from Massachusetts, talked of laws marked by "boldness in innovation, the scorn of the past and precedents. . . . You run into the same freedom of spirit everywhere," the young man continued, "nothing is fixed, nothing is regulated with us, in civil society or even in religious life. Everything goes forward from an individual impulsion that denotes a total absence of established opinion."

putes. Now there are more rights and new laws. . . . Poverty law and environmental law were never heard of when I began. Now they are needed to provide the economic opportunity that the frontier was. There was no need for environmental law when there was enough water that you could dump anything into it."

Can the courts do all that?

"No," Stewart said. "They are inadequate. Society expects too much now. There are too many larger questions here—moral, social, political, economic. We have been given power beyond the ken of the courts. . . . The courts became strong because of a default of the other branches of government."

"The power of the courts is becoming awesome because they have become the only place the public can find decision making," said J. Vincent Aug, United States Magistrate for the Sixth Circuit of the U. S. Court of Appeals. "You cannot get relief anymore in the executive and legislative branches. Politicians are avoiding decisions on controversial questions. Judges may not want to make those decisions, but they don't shy away from them—especially federal judges who have life tenure. So, increasingly, people who feel they're being pushed around turn to the law or to the press."*

What is "the law"?

"Enforced fairness."

"It is of the essence of judicial power to be concerned with private interests and gladly to pay attention to trivial subjects submitted to its consideration. . . ." Tocqueville wrote in the concluding pages of the second volume of *Democracy in America*. "Such a power is therefore peculiarly adapted to the needs of freedom at a time when the ruler's eye and hand are constantly interfering in the tiniest details of human actions . . . Private rights and interests are, then, always in danger unless the power of the courts grows and extends commensurately with the increase of equality of conditions."

That power was growing and extending in Cincinnati when I arrived on October 17, 1979. Fairness was being demanded and enforced in the city and around the country that day. Local

---

* United States Magistrate is a position that was once known as U. S. Commissioner. The magistrate, appointed by the judges of the Circuit Court for an eight-year term, is sometimes empowered to settle cases before their referral to a panel of judges.

newspapers were filled with stories of decisive, ongoing, or threatened action by courts ordering or preventing action by elected officials from county commissioners to the President of the United States. In Cincinnati, which had a declining population now of about 400,000, Common Pleas Judge Harry T. Klusmeier was reported to be ready to appoint a committee of "receivers" to take over the local jail because elected officials in the city and Hamilton County had not complied with court orders to renovate the building. Those officials, in turn, blamed voters who had turned down special tax levies for the renovation. In Washington, U. S. District Court Judge Oliver Gasch ruled, in a suit filed by 25 senators and congressmen, that the President did not have the authority unilaterally to abrogate a defense treaty with another country, Taiwan. In Chicago, Illinois, a member of the President's Cabinet, Secretary of Health, Education and Welfare Patricia Roberts Harris, announced that she had requested the U. S. Justice Department to file a suit forcing that city's Board of Education to produce a plan, acceptable to her department, to racially desegregate its public school system. In San Francisco, U. S. District Court Judge Robert F. Peckham ruled that California boards of education could not use standardized intelligence tests because such tests had resulted in disproportionate numbers of black children being classified as "mentally retarded."

The courts, state and federal, did not initiate these actions—they were ruling on complaints filed by citizens in prison and in Congress—and some of their decisions would, inevitably, be modified or overruled by negotiation or higher courts. But the day's news was part of an irresistible American movement: individual citizens or groups of citizens had turned to the courts to demand that their own concept of fairness be enforced.

"The miracle, mystery, and authority of the courts in basically political situations is growing because it does not depend on the notion of judges as superhuman," said Professor Laurence Tribe of Harvard Law School. "The authority is rooted in the common and earthy idea that everyone can get in . . . the conception of 'your day in court.' "

The days in court of these citizens had begun a process of decision making that often supplanted representative government. In the three cases where rulings had been handed down, the courts assumed, legally, the power of elected officials—those decisions could be appealed, of course, but the final judgment would still be made by the courts, higher courts. If that was asking too much of the courts, as Stewart said, they were still capable of dealing with it, at least in terms of providing some answer—right or wrong, but usable.

When I left Magistrate Aug's office in Cincinnati's U. S. Courthouse, I stopped by Room 822, a courtroom. Tocqueville had visited a courtroom in the city in 1831. "I went today to view the Court of Common Pleas," he recorded. "The jury appeared to us to be composed of individuals belonging to the lowest class among the people."

There was no jury in Room 822. Three federal judges—Anthony J. Celebrezze, Bailey Brown, and Cornelia G. Kennedy—sat behind a high bench and in front of burgundy-colored velvet drapes. There were fourteen other people in the big room—four clerks, two attorneys and eight spectators. The case number was 77-3452: *Franklin County Welfare Rights Organization, Anna M. Peppers individually and on behalf of all others similarly situated* versus *Ohio Division of Public Assistance and other state agencies.* "Defendants," the brief read, "appeal from the injunction prohibiting the termination of Aid for Dependent Children benefits and Food Stamps without a due process hearing."[*]

Each side was allowed fifteen minutes of argument. The issue: Anna Peppers and others claimed that the state had cut off their welfare benefits without sufficient notice or chance to appeal and the state countered that established procedures had been followed and Anna Peppers and the others were ineligible for the benefits. The state's attorney also said that there was a backlog of thousands of people appealing welfare cut-offs and sepa-

---

[*] The Welfare Rights Organization suit was a "class action." The plaintiffs had been granted legal standing to represent all persons— the "class" of citizens—who might have been damaged financially by the state's procedures. The use—and court acceptance—of class-action suits had expanded almost explosively in the 1960s, when judges began accepting civil rights cases, because they determined that the cases affected all black citizens—a "class"—within a jurisdiction rather than requiring an individual claiming discrimination to prove that he or she had suffered personal damages. In the 1970s suits began being filed in the name of an even larger "class"—"consumers."

rate hearings for each one would mean long delays and, in effect, would mean that no one could be declared ineligible. Celebrezze, the presiding judge, upheld the decision of a lower court that had issued an injunction preventing cut-offs and told the state's attorney: "You go back and tell the state legislature that they're under court order and to hire more hearing officers. Say: 'Hey, you're going to have to allocate more money.' That's it."

That was it. The court simply ordered the elected legislature of the State of Ohio to continue paying benefits and to hire more officers. The three judges in Room 822 had the power of the law and the ability and willingness to act—and that's where Anna Peppers "and all others similarly situated," sensibly, turned for relief.

Two blocks away, in the window of Batsake's Cleaners on Walnut Street, was a poster showing a blank-faced young man holding a telephone. Under his picture were two words: "Luke Listens."

"Luke," it turned out, was Charles Luken, a Democratic candidate for the Cincinnati City Council. He did not need further identification because he was the son of a congressman, Thomas Luken, and local voters presumably had a vague idea of who he was because of the family name. "The sure sign of the decline of politicians is those slogans that say 'So-and-so Cares' or 'So-and-so Listens,' " one of them, Wilson Wyatt, a former mayor of Louisville, told me as I traveled through Kentucky. "That's an absolutely meaningless phrase unless it means that so-and-so doesn't intend to do anything in office." Many professional So-and-sos, in fact, don't intend to do anything—at least anything that might make voters mad. Politicians don't so much try to make friends as they try to avoid making enemies. Making decisions can make enemies. If you just "listen" and "care," you may go unnoticed forever, you may be reelected forever. Decisions are for judges.

But those "So-and-sos," a species of democratic politicians, have been with us for a long time. At least they were in Cincinnati in 1831. "We have yielded too much to 'Democracy' here," another lawyer, Bellamy Storer, told Tocqueville. "We have carried 'Democracy' to its last limits," said John McLean, the Supreme Court justice. The Frenchman by then had heard variations of the same sentence everywhere in the new Republic. "The right of voting is universal," McLean went on. "The result, especially in our towns, is some very bad elections. For instance, the last four members elected for the county of Cincinnati are absolutely unworthy to occupy the position to which they have been elected."

"But how did they get themselves chosen?" Tocqueville asked.

"By flattery, something distinguished men will never do, by mingling with the populace, by base flattery of its passions, by drinking with it."

"Doesn't this excessive development of the 'democratic' principle frighten you at all?" Tocqueville asked Timothy Walker.

"Yes," the young lawyer answered. "I wouldn't say so in public, but between ourselves I admit it. I am frightened by the current that is carrying us on. The United States, it seems to me, are in a crisis; we are at this moment trying out a 'democracy' without limits; everything is going that way. But shall we be able to endure it? As yet no one can say so positively."

"Yet the state enjoys immense prosperity," Dr. Daniel Drake, a medical professor who was classifying the diseases of the Mississippi Valley, replied when Tocqueville asked the same questions. "The enterprises are great and favorable to the general well-being. I have never heard of the slightest resistance to the law."

How can that be?

"If there were but one demagogue in charge of our affairs, things would doubtless go very badly," Dr. Drake answered. "But they control each other, injure one another . . . the ill effects resulting from the elections by the people are not as great as one might believe."

Dr. Drake, it turned out, knew more than medicine. And the answer to Timothy Walker's question was: Yes, we were able to "endure it." "It" and much more. The excess of democracy that concerned the gentlemen of Cincinnati 150 years ago involved less than a third of the adult population of the United States. Only white males could vote in 1831, and one state, Virginia, still maintained financial qualifications for voting. No black men were allowed to vote for another thirty-five years. Women, white and black, had to wait ninety years.

Democracy, even an "excess" of it, though, was not enough for a free people. The very existence of the frontier was a liberating force; moving on became part of being an American. And when the land was gone, there were still frontiers of freedom and power. Timothy Walker was wrong when he thought he was seeing democracy without limits; men and women around him were pushing on to find limits and then pushing those limits. Potter Stewart was right: interpretation of the law and the rhetoric of America were the frontier. "Enforced fairness"—Aug's words—had to go beyond politics and government. "Democracy" defined as political equality was not enough for many Americans. They inevitably moved on to grander frontiers—toward social equality, toward economic equality. They went to court!

Perhaps there had to be limits, but if an individual thought the limit of the day was unfair to him and had the power to push that limit, he could try, and, sometimes, he would succeed. It was in the courts that the individual had that power. Tocqueville considered titling the second volume of his great work "Equality in America." He decided against it. A century and a half later, I don't think he would have hesitated. It would be called *"De l'Egalité en Amérique."*

I asked a twenty-seven-year-old lawyer, Darlene Kamine, a former attorney in the Public Defender's Office of Hamilton County and chairman of the Young Lawyers Section of the Cincinnati Bar Association, this question: Does the majority rule in America?

"No," she answered. "Our system is based on equal access."*

---

* In a letter of January 2, 1981, Darlene Kamine explained what she meant by that phrase:

"It is critical to the success of our society that every person has easy and meaningful access to the legal system and that each person gets an equal 'shake' within the system. These axioms proved themselves daily, much to my surprise, during my years with the Public Defender's Office. I observed hundreds of poor, angry and potentially explosive individuals bring their domestic and neighborhood problems to court, often without the assistance of police or any other official. Rather than finishing off the argument and, undoubtedly, each other on the street, the parties submitted themselves to the judgment of the Court. Even after a passionate recital of the facts supporting his innocence, a defendant would accept a guilty finding. Moreover,

Equal access, she meant, to the levers of power, to the state's power to enforce fairness—not equal access to the voting booth or to Luke and the other so-and-sos who will dutifully listen, but each individual's access, through the courts, to the weight, the leverage of the law. Vincent Aug, the U. S. Magistrate, described the use of that access in talking about two of the cases before him. In the first, a black man was fired when he missed several days of work because he was in jail. But, the man said, white men had gone to jail and kept their jobs. So, he contended, he was really being fired because of his race. In the second, a white professor at a local university who initiated and planned a course on black American history was not allowed to teach that course because administrators believed a black teacher was required. Both men sued—each demanded his own perception of fairness—and the courts were drawn further into areas of competence, into regulating, through legal precedent, what were once the ordinary decisions of everyday life. Now they are public decisions and the courts, as Aug said, cannot shy away from the decision making.

It was a cumbersome system, enormously complicated, reducing political power but increasing the power of each citizen. As Darlene Kamine said, the majority did not necessarily rule, but Anna Peppers had the power to force the State of Ohio to hire new welfare hearing officers.

The way it works is beyond most of us. Darlene Kamine understood it because she was trained to—she was an attorney, licensed to go where most Americans could not. So was Robert Newman, the Legal Aid Service attorney who filed the lawsuit in a prisoner's name that led the Common Pleas Court into jurisdiction over the Cincinnati jail. They did not think of themselves as different or powerful—both are young and frus-

---

the court's final verdict ended the dispute between the parties. The same behavior is evident in the civil system where the 'little' man can go one on one with the faceless corporation.

"As one close to the system, I know that the poor, angry parties in criminal court and the little men in civil court are not really getting equal justice. But the relative ease of access to the system leads them to believe they are part of the system and, therefore, placates them enough to preserve the order."

trated—but Kamine and Newman seemed to me some sort of supercitizens. They had power, more than they knew, because of their specialized ritualistic knowledge. The system of democracy which they understood—perhaps legal egalitarianism is a better phrase—was not visible to Tocqueville but it was apparent to him: "... nothing could be more obscure and out of reach of the common man than a law founded on precedent. Where lawyers are absolutely needed, as in England and the United States, and their professional knowledge is held in high esteem, they become increasingly separated from the people, forming a class apart. A French lawyer is just a man of learning, but an English or an American one is somewhat like the Egyptian priests, being, as they were, the only interpreter of an occult science."*

"There is hardly a political question in the United States which does not sooner or later turn into a judicial one," he wrote, also in *Democracy in America*. And: "It is at the bar or the bench that the American aristocracy is found."

With their own elevated and slightly mysterious rituals and a professional inclination to consider more than one self-interest—since they were always available for hire by clients with opposing self-interests—American lawyers, Tocqueville believed, might make up an aristocracy in the traditional terms he best understood. "Naturally strongly opposed to the revolutionary spirit and to the ill-considered passions of democracy," he wrote of lawyers. And: "The legal body forms the most powerful and, so to say, the only counterbalance to democracy in the country."

It didn't work out exactly that way, partly because the revolutionary spirit faded as the conditions of men's lives became more alike and the passions of democracy were channeled into lust for equality. Lawyers, with a knack for benefiting from any condi-

* This priesthood also appeared to be attracting America's best young minds. Asked where their best students went, most college professors I interviewed answered, "Law school." Michael Mandelbaum, associate professor of government at Harvard University, said: "The A students are going into law, or into medicine if they're scientifically inclined. The B students go into business; the best ones into banking, the others into industry. The C students actually go into jobs in industry, although some of the C students are the people who go into law to get into politics."

tion or changing conditions, certainly became an elite group—
like Egyptian priests—but their role seemed to extend rather
than to counterbalance democracy.

"We dedicated ourselves to a powerful idea—organic law
rather than naked power," said Justice Stewart. "There seems to
be universal acceptance of that idea in the nation."

The Justice waved at the shelves of books behind him—yellow, red, and black volumes recording Supreme Court decisions
back to 1790—and said: "They reflect nothing more than what
was on the mind of contemporary America. Those decisions are
a reflection of American morality with a time lag."

There was one more thing I wanted to know before I left Cincinnati. How had Tocqueville's idea of intermarriage as a test of
equality held up over the years?

A check of the city records and newspaper announcements of
some 400 marriages in Cincinnati over a five-week period at the
end of 1980 indicated that there was at least one strong pattern
of class intermarriage. Young men and women were marrying
people they met in college or while working at rather good jobs,
regardless of how or where each other grew up or what their
parents did for a living. That was, of course, at a certain level of
achievement: the young lawyer whose widowed mother worked
as a receptionist marrying the "urban planner" who attended
the area's best private schools. They were, dozens of them, marriages of education, of ambition, of real and potential achievement. Beyond that, there was significant religious intermarriage,
with Protestants and Catholics more likely to choose partners
outside their faith and upbringing than Jews were—but Jews
were doing it, too. What there was not, judging from addresses
and photographs, was racial intermarriage. Cincinnati was a city
two-thirds white, one-third black, with a racial equality resulting from necessity, courtesy, or politics that by Tocqueville's
standards existed on the surface and deceived the eye.*

* Kathy Lang Guastaferro, associate director of the Cincinnati Bar
Association, researched the marriage records for November and December of 1980. She reported one unexpected finding: "I was surprised that over 50 percent of all the marriage license applications
listed the same home address for both parties. Lots of Cincinnati
mothers' hearts must be broken."

8
LOUISVILLE

"Freedom Was a Lie . . ."

"Just now the vessel is cracking from poop to prow," Tocqueville noted on the morning of December 5, 1831. He and Beaumont were among the travelers trapped on a steamboat that was in danger of being crushed as the Ohio River froze. "The thaw doesn't come. The cold increases," Beaumont took up the story in his notes the next day. "The captain makes up his mind to set us on the shore, which we approach little by little, thus opening a passage for our boat . . .

"Impossible to find either carriage or horses to carry us to Louisville; necessary to make the journey on foot; our luggage thrown into a cart with which we keep pace. We march all day through the woods in a half-foot of snow. America is still nothing but a forest . . ."

After a march of 25 miles, the Frenchmen and ten companions reached Louisville, Kentucky. They were in the great Mississippi Valley, which Tocqueville was one day to call the most magnificent habitation ever prepared by God for man. At the moment, it was also one of the coldest. Caught in the worst local winter in memory, Tocqueville and Beaumont were forced off the Ohio, the major thoroughfare of the day, and began a long detour through Kentucky and Tennessee instead of the river journey they had planned from Cincinnati south to New Orleans.

The weather was not much different in the winter 147 years later. As I traveled from Cincinnati to Louisville, there were six inches of snow on the ground. Worse, the city of Louisville, the largest in Kentucky, was practically immobilized by three- and four-inch layers of ice under the snow, ice that only hardened in day after day of temperatures 30 and 40 Fahrenheit degrees below freezing.

My trip, on a Sunday night, was difficult, but not as dangerous as theirs had been—what had been American forest was now hilly farmland broken up by small villages. I was alone on the slippery roads, but not in the car. The radio again. WHAS, a station in Louisville affiliated with the CBS radio network in New York, first broadcast a National Football League championship game between teams representing Dallas, Texas, and Los Angeles, California, then sent out five straight hours of religious programming. Some of it was quite crazy. "America's Promise"

Tocqueville's steamboat aground in the Mississippi

featured someone called Reverend Emery of Phoenix, Arizona, offering a tirade of complicated conspiracy theories. The man, with a certain manic intensity, interpreted the Bible as revealing a worldwide cabal involving Communists in Russia and American heroes, including a former President, Dwight Eisenhower, and a former Secretary of State, George Marshall. The message was more political than religious. Or perhaps it was financial. Emery asked listeners to send money for tapes and pamphlets of his and God's warnings—and presumably they did, because he had the money to pay WHAS for time on Sunday nights. The rest of the evening's Christian messages were more joyous: old hymns that would have had me clapping my hands if the driving weren't so treacherous. But after the music, those folks asked for money, too.

"There are preachers hawking the word of God from place to place," Tocqueville wrote. He was an intellectual Roman Catholic, troubled at falling away from his faith as a teenager reading agnostic philosophy, but still preferring religion with some grandeur. He had been appalled watching Shakers dance madly about at a service near Albany. He had also met some of the Emerys of his day, Protestant ministers he called "business men of religion."

Impressed that religious teaching of a fundamental morality and the republican organization of Protestant sects obviously helped condition Americans for orderly democratic life, Tocqueville was still quite skeptical about native Protestantism. "Sunday is rigorously observed," he wrote to a friend. "And yet, either I am much mistaken or there is a great depth of doubt and indifference hidden under these external forms . . . One follows a religion as our fathers took medicine in the month of May. If it doesn't do any good, one seems to say, at least it can do no harm."

Coming from a part of the country, New York City, where the old-time religion I was hearing on the radio was less common and less popular than in places like Kentucky, I probably shared Tocqueville's thoughts across the centuries. I wasn't the only one. In Louisville, I met Barry Bingham, chairman of the Louisville Courier-Journal Corporation, which published both of the city's daily newspapers, and I mentioned my evening with Reverend Emery. "It's ridiculous, isn't it?" Bingham said. "I don't know why they allow things like that on the air."

The next day I learned that Bingham's family corporation owned station WHAS—he was "they." And he was indifferent, too. If people chose to define themselves that way—and paid his family to do it—what harm could it do? It was certainly a widespread phenomenon—900 Christian radio and television programs were separately produced each week—but it seemed confined by the spiritual borders of the minds of people who were part of, or identified themselves with, an older South. It went back to a confluence of time and place that extended even into Tocqueville's time, as he wrote in a political context near the end of the first volume of *Democracy in America*: "The South, whose men are ardent and irascible, is getting angry and restless. It turns its melancholy gaze inward and back to the past, perpetually fancying that it may be suffering oppression."

It seemed negative, nostalgic—and harmless. That, at any rate, was what I thought that winter day in Louisville. A couple of months later, in New York, I turned on the television to watch one of the more popular of the religious programs, the PTL Club—Praise the Lord or People That Love—produced in Charlotte, North Carolina, and claiming a weekly audience, with reruns, of 20 million people. A panel of smiling ministers said they thought the time had come for believers to take to the streets to scatter pornographers and, perhaps, chop off the hands of a few of them. "Amen," said the host of the show, a former disc jockey, the Reverend Jim Bakker. "Those powers that are mocking religion: You won't be laughing in a few months."

Louisville struck a chord for Tocqueville—the town on the river was named for Louis XVI. The Frenchman, who had never planned to stop there, still had his notebook ready and started talking on the hike from the wrecked ship. "Mr. McIlvain, one of the greatest merchants of Louisville," was one of the Americans he interviewed in Kentucky.* This is some of what was said:

---

* John Brent McIlvaine, a wholesale grocer and, later, a general merchandiser, from Maysville, Kentucky, was thirty years old when he met Tocqueville, having begun working as a fourteen-year-old clerk in a dry-goods store.

"Q. I am told that the prosperity of Louisville has shown great progress in the last few years?"

"A. Immense. When I came here to settle seven years ago, Louisville had only 3,000 souls; there are 13,000 today ... Louisville is become the emporium of almost all the merchandise coming up the Mississippi to provision the emigrants. I believe Louisville is called to become a very large city."

Settled originally in 1778, it became a city of 390,000 souls. That was in 1960. Since then, with its municipal boundaries fixed around 65 square miles on the Ohio, the city itself has steadily lost population to its own suburbs. By 1980, fewer than 300,000 people lived in Louisville, while the population of the metropolitan area, which reached across the river into Indiana, had reached more than 900,000, an increase of almost 200,000 since 1960.

Falls City. The falls on the river there were the reason for the town and then the city in the early nineteenth century. People and goods moving west and south had to come off the river at the point that became the city's thriving downtown and then the city's declining downtown as the commerce of the area spread to suburban centers—81 separate municipalities with 70 shopping centers surround Louisville just on the Kentucky side of the river—and the commerce of the nation began to drive and fly over the falls of the Ohio.

"Falls City." It was the name of the local beer. For 73 years, since 1906, Falls City beer had been made in Louisville, from the local water. The same thing was true in most American cities; most places had their own beers. In 1950, there were 380 companies brewing beer in the United States. By the end of the 1970s, that number was down to 42—and half the beer brewed in the country was made by two companies, Anheuser-Busch and Miller's. Falls City, the name, was bought out by G. Heilman Brewing Companies of Lacrosse, Wisconsin, the country's fourth-largest beer company; its biggest beer was Blatt's, and it made more than forty "local" beers, including Falls City, saying it could chemically reproduce local formulas and waters. While I was in Louisville, the equipment that was used to make the beer in the old brewery on West Broadway was being dismantled for shipment to the Philippines.

"There really aren't that many substantial local merchants

here anymore," said Barry Bingham, the newspaper publisher. Most of Louisville's large stores and businesses were, like its beer now, branches of national and multinational corporations. "The managers of the stores and factories come and go, to and from other parts of the country. They don't really touch life here . . . Ninety-five percent of the people here are from here, they're Kentuckians. But they're not running the companies."

Well, who would be one of the greatest merchants these days? "Dann Byck," he said. "I'd talk to Dann Byck."

Dann Byck, Jr., was the president of one of the city's last significant locally owned mercantile businesses, Byck's, a chain of four women's clothing stores employing 300 people. He was a handsome, articulate man, forty-one years old, and my first thought was that he would make a good political candidate. In fact, his father had been president of the Louisville City Council.

"Local leadership of the kind there was here during my father's day just doesn't exist anymore," Byck said. "All of that is left to politicians now. That's their business. I have my own."

Q. What kind of people are they?

A. A bunch of garbage. Second-rate people. Bright, aggressive people don't need politics to make it. I've been asked to run for office several times—for mayor, senator—but I don't want to give up everything I have to try to make a contribution. My father could say what he wanted and get away with it. You can't do that anymore. The "little people" won't stand for anyone who disagrees with them. Also we have "sunshine" laws—all government meetings are open to the public, so you can't debate, you can't really talk about what's on your mind.

Q. Do you think about politics? Do you and your friends talk about national affairs, local affairs?

A. About zero-point-six percent of the time. I have access to the people who run this state, but that doesn't do me any good. Politicians have interests of their own, they run things for themselves.

Q. You don't participate at all in civil life or politics?

A. No, I'm very active in theater and I care very much about the cultural life of Louisville. I'm a founder and the president of the Actors Theatre of Louisville, that takes a great deal of my time and energy. I'm also president of the Kentucky Merchants and Manufacturers Association. I'm a lobbyist. What we do is lobby to kill legislation. The general rule, I think—as a citizen and as a businessman—is that there's nothing government can do to help me, it can only hurt me.

Q. How does it hurt you?

A. Here's an example. ERISA. The Employees Retirement Income Security Act of 1974. It was designed to prevent dishonest businessmen from collecting pension money and then not paying it to retired employees. A good thing—but it's totally out of control. At Byck's our pension costs doubled and our retired employees are getting less money than they used to.°

Q. Is your experience typical?

A. Probably not. Thousands of small companies just eliminated their pension plans altogether rather than deal with the regulations and paperwork. We considered dropping the whole thing and just distributing the pension money we had collected among our employees. Forty years from now, a lot of people who would have had pensions just won't. Of course, what will happen before then is that the government will be forced to take over all pensions—that's what ERISA will mean in the end. Many people will get less that way and the costs of administration and regulation will be tremendous, but under democracy we all have to even out.

° In a letter on January 29, 1979, Dann Byck wrote:

"Under our old plan (pre-ERISA) we paid our pensioners one percent of their average wage multiplied by the number of years they worked for us. That plus their Social Security gave them, on retirement, between 85 and 110 percent of their salary.

"Under the new formula, we pay 40 percent of their average wage, less 50 percent of their Social Security.

Example: Retiree worked 35 years at Byck's and averaged $1,000 per month salary. For this purpose assume Social Security benefit of $500 per month: under our old plan, the pensioner received $500 a month in Social Security (Byck's pays half the Social Security costs) plus $350 a month directly from us; under the new plan, Social Security is still $500 a month but the pensioner gets only $150 per month from us. So, the retired employees monthly income has gone from $850 to $650 per month.

"But . . . our contributions to the pension plan averaged $17,600. In 1977, it jumped to $29,000 and in 1978, to $36,685. This does not include the tremendous increase in cost due to paperwork, actuarial and lawyer fees."

It was not a particularly encouraging conversation. Not because of Byck's disdain for the practice and practitioners of his father's avocation. Politics and politicians were obviously in disrepute. "The people" know themselves and their self-interests too well to revere the men and women who clamor and claw to represent them. It wasn't, however, the wants of the governed or the quality of the governors that was disturbing about Byck's perceptions. It was the reach of the government, more specifically the effects of the reach of the federal government, which I saw, which I kept hearing about—and the questions that kept being raised about those effects—everywhere I traveled. The questions were the echoes of one of the most sobering passages in *Democracy in America*:

"I have previously made the distinction between two types of centralization, calling one governmental and the other administrative. Only the first exists in America, the second being almost unknown. If the directing power in American societies had both of these means of government at its disposal and combined the right to command with the faculty and habit to perform everything itself, if having established the general principles of the government, it entered into the details of their application, and having regulated the great interests of the country, it came down to consider even individual interests, then freedom would soon be banished from the New World."

"The federal government is now *the* government," said Wilson Wyatt, who had been mayor of Louisville from 1941 to 1946. "State and local governments just perform housekeeping functions now. Washington collects the taxes and that's where the power is. If you look at the voter turnouts here, you'll see that people understand that. Turnouts are high for federal elections, significant for state elections, and low for local elections."[*]

"The city and the state don't even control their own programs," interjected Barry Bingham, Sr., as the three of us ate lunch at the Louisville Club, literally and figuratively overlooking their city. "They can't cut back programs the federal gov-

---

[*] In the 1976 Presidential election, 69 percent of the eligible voters in Jefferson County, Ky., which includes Louisville, came out to vote. The comparable figure in the 1977 state and local elections was 51.9 percent.

ernment wants without losing the federal aid the city needs. The federal government, Washington, is everywhere here."*

Indeed, one of Bingham's papers, the *Louisville Times*, reported that day in a short article about the federal government and one small suburb:

> The U.S. Department of Housing and Urban Development has begun studying final plans for a proposed eight-story apartment house in Lyndon.
>
> The plans, submitted by the developer and the Jefferson County Housing Authority, must meet Federal guidelines before they are accepted.
>
> The 125-unit apartment house, planned for 3.6 acres at LaGrange and Wood roads, would provide federally subsidized housing to people over 62 or those who are handicapped.
>
> Lyndon's City Council and several community groups have objected to the proposed high-rise, saying it would not fit in with the character of the city, where no buildings are taller than two stories.

The next day's *Courier-Journal* published an Associated Press report that said, in part:

> The U. S. Office of Surface Mining has authorized the spending of up to $150,000 in emergency funds to deal with a mud slide near Phelps in Pike County, Kentucky ... Three homes were evacuated because of the slide ...
>
> [Inspectors] determined that the mud slide had been caused by an abandoned underground coal mine ... Kentucky officials said the Chisholm Coal Co. had stopped mining there in 1975.

Government, the federal government, was cleaning up the mess—this one made by a coal company. The complaints of government intervention and interference went on; so did the de-

---

* Wyatt and Bingham were both men of broad experience, including work on national and international levels. The former mayor was the manager of Adlai Stevenson's 1956 presidential campaign. The newspaper publisher had served in Europe as assistant administrator of the Marshall Plan after World War II.

mands for cleanup crews from Washington. The problem, as Dann Byck saw it, though, was that the federal government itself was making more of the messes. If small companies were eliminating pension plans to avoid dealing with the government, then the same government would one day have to deal with the needs of those retired people without income.

The red-white-and-blue signs were going up in Pike County, just as they had in Albany. In Louisville, they were on West Main Street, outside the Museum of Natural History and Science. "JOBS for your community . . . in partnership with the United States Department of Commerce." The sidewalks there were being put in with federal money. "Those 'JOBS for your community' signs are the signs of tyranny," a New Orleans city councilman named Brod Bagert told me downriver, and he went on angrily: "They even have the sound of 'Relief packages for the poor of China,' as if we were not Americans here. We're the underprivileged being helped by somebody in Washington. The people I've met in this job with the most power are not elected officials. They're the third- and fourth-level bureaucrats who sign applications to get the money on those damned signs."

It was, now, a government of details and applications. It did reach deeply toward individual interests. Dann Byck was the president of three voluntary associations: his company, with its pension plan dictated by law; the merchants and manufacturers association, formed to lobby government; and the civic theater, receiving $236,000 a year in aid from the state and federal governments after meeting their multi-leveled conditions concerning profit, health, safety, and pay. That's what Byck and almost every other American had to live with in a free country—"free" meant they could fight government after they got their share of it.

Eric Alsanger, the man who wanted to sell lemonade at the Police Parade back in Newport, could fight the town council, too. He had the right to go to court—a local court or a state court, perhaps even to the Supreme Court of the United States. He could go to Providence, the state capital, to try to persuade the legislators there to amend the peddling laws to exempt lemonade sales at parades on hot days. He could, as Larry Kirwan had done in Rochester, go to the directing power itself, the people, and try to overthrow the town or state authorities electorally. Or he could try to get away with selling the stuff without a permit.

But he was far more likely—and probably better advised—to stay within the administrative structure, appealing. That was the lever of modern American freedom: appealing; appealing to government; appealing to higher levels of government. Each American could hear or say just about anything he or she pleased, each could initiate or challenge any idea or plan—anyone could also try to stop Alsanger from selling lemonade—but, in the end, the final judgment was almost always going to be made by someone else constituted as "government." A clerk, an inspector, a council, a judge—someone with authority over lemonade. Someone higher up. The freedom of appeal—the mechanisms of fairness—inevitably centralized the governing of the people of the United States. Decision making inexorably rose to the highest levels. The intentions and traditions of eighteenth-century America were inevitably perverted by the momentum of determined democratic institutional fairness.

It's a negative freedom. The freedom of appeal is not the freedom to do anything; the United States is no longer an exuberantly entrepreneurial country where any citizen can legally sell lemonade wherever and whenever he wants. It is, instead, a place where he can always complain that "they" are not allowing him to exercise his right to sell lemonade, and where he can probably stop someone else from selling lemonade.

Or, in Louisville and its suburbs, parents could complain— demonstrate in the streets—and appeal to courts and legislatures that their "freedom" was a lie when their children were being used, against their wishes and to their own detriment, to implement a questionable national experiment in racial equality.

And they did. The city and other parts of Jefferson County had been rocked by weeks of public disorder in 1975 when parents, most of them white, complained about the mandatory busing of 22,600 of their children to comply with federal formulas for the racial mix of children in local schoolrooms. The idea was equality: some disputed sociological analysis indicated that if some Americans, black Americans, were not living as well as the majority of whites, the reason had to be that the education of the blacks must be inferior. The analysis itself, leaving aside the specifics of statistics and studies, was thoroughly American: the quality of people's lives, black and white, was measured by how much money they made each year, and the reason for any discrepancies was assumed to be education. The solution, too, as usual, was education—or an attempt to improve education. In practice, the public remedy adopted, by order of the courts which had received legal appeals from black parents and organizations, was the mixing of white and black students in the same schools at early ages. That meant busing children around the area to create similar racial ratios in most schools—with the goal, eventually, of proving racial equality by showing earning equality.

Whatever the merits of the arguments on both sides, freedom—the freedom of appeal—had run out. The orders or affirmations of the orders were now coming from the last and highest level, the Supreme Court. The parents of Jefferson County, with their elected representatives—impotent ornaments—did not have the power to dispute effectively the judgment of federal courts that they shared in a collective majority guilt for the historical subjection of the minority blacks or the judgment that somehow that was a root cause of the relatively low economic status of modern blacks. They were like the folks in Canandaigua. When local government wouldn't do it—build sewers or integrate schools—sooner or later, someone somewhere very far away was going to do it for them or to them, once a national consensus had been reached on clean water or racial fairness.

The complaints of the local majority, the whites, in 1975, though, were hopeless. That majority had become a minority in a nation where majority rules—the fact was that when the first lawsuits were filed about Jefferson County schools, in 1971 and 1972, they were, for all practical purposes, still racially segregated in violation of the law of the land, and, more important, of the national consensus on what was fair in the last days of the twentieth century. What was done, the busing, might be right or wrong, effective or ineffective, but it would be done because the national majority had agreed *something* must be done.

"People could protest all they wanted. But it didn't matter and, after a while, they just got tired," said Elmer Hall, the city editor who had supervised the *Courier-Journal*'s coverage of school desegregation. "More than 10,000 people would come out to the antibusing rallies, but after a while they just wore themselves out. Some people moved away. But most finally accepted busing with resignation. What could they do? They didn't have the money or jobs to move. They couldn't keep protesting forever, and the government was just there."

Fourteen thousand of the 92,000 white students in the county schools left—they went somewhere else, no one is sure where. Moving away is the American way. "We are a nation of leavers," Ellen Goodman said. The country was founded and built by people moving away, from repression or lack of opportunity in the Old World, from repression and lack of opportunity in Connecticut or Massachusetts or Oklahoma. Tocqueville was surprised to discover that the settlers at the frontier of 1831, Michigan and Ohio, were not from Europe but from Connecticut. They were moving away, seeking more opportunity, a chance, a new beginning.

People were leaving Louisville at the rate of perhaps 75,000 every ten years. Thirty thousand different people were coming in—for a while. That wasn't always obvious. When I asked Barry Bingham and Wilson Wyatt whether there really was a separate place named Louisville, whether people considered themselves part of that place, both men, both over seventy, answered, "Oh, yes!" They figured that 95 percent of the people in Louisville were "from someplace around here." When I asked the same question of Dann Byck, in his early forties, and his wife, Marsha Norman, at thirty-one considered one of America's most promising dramatists, they said that more than half the people they knew in Louisville came from other parts of the country. Byck's seventeen-year-old daughter, Amy, said only a quarter of the people she knew came, originally, from Kentucky. When Byck, out of curiosity, tried to trace the family of John Brent McIlvaine, the "greatest merchant" who talked with Tocqueville, he found only one "McIlvaine" listed in the area telephone books. He called and asked the woman who answered, "Has your family been in Louisville a long time?"

"Yes," she said. "We came here six years ago from Pittsburgh."

"Instant roots" was a phrase used by Ruth Clark of Yankelovich, Skelley & White, who had supervised the readership surveys for the American Society of Newspaper Editors and had also done studies for the *Courier-Journal*. "We often find," she said, "that the people most interested in local news have just moved to a new area." When the McIlvaine family, the one Dann Byck called, came to Louisville from Pittsburgh, they may have been intensely interested in how the place worked, how it was different from Pittsburgh. It doesn't look different. Not much does in America.

"This may sound trivial," said Barry Bingham in one of our conversations, "but one of the greatest changes I've noticed in my lifetime is the erasing of distinctions between rural and city people. Country people used to look and talk differently, probably thought differently. Now you can't tell the difference—education, travel, television, I guess."

It did not sound trivial at all to me. I had found the differences in Americans, no matter how fervently celebrated locally, overwhelmed by the similarities. The sameness of tract homes, shopping centers, and hamburger stands—man's contributions to the countryside, rural and urban, northern and southern, eastern and western—seemed a deliberate, if unconscious, defense against the trauma of mobility. Most Americans moving away do not have to go to a strange place. There is relocation without dislocation—the highways built to the rigid specifications of the federal government, the homes built from efficient standard plans, the hamburgers prepared to a juiciness determined in Chicago by market research. It is not new, it is progressive—and inevitable. "The man you left behind in the streets of New York," Tocqueville wrote in an essay, "you will find him again in the midst of almost impenetrable solitudes: same dress, same spirit, same language, same habits and the same pleasures."

"The time must come," he wrote in *Democracy in America*, "when there will be in North America one hundred and fifty million people all equal one to the other, belonging to the same family, having the same point of departure, the same civilization, language, religion, habits, and mores, and among whom thought will circulate in similar forms and with like nuances. All else is doubtful, but that is sure."

The number was a little low and it has not happened yet—not quite yet. People will always strive to differentiate or define themselves by where they live, or what they read, or how they worship, and fortunes are still being made by people figuring out new ways in which Americans differ—usually to identify a group that will buy something if they know about it. Coming back from Louisville, I met a "management consultant," James Kelly, who worked out of Boston. He was, he said, helping to prepare a plan for the American Telephone and Telegraph Company, the national telephone monopoly, to reorganize along "market" rather than geographical lines. "Market" was a euphemism for "demographic"—to one of America's largest institutions it would not matter at all whether the McIlvaines were in Louisville or in Pittsburgh; Mrs. McIlvaine would be defined in terms of how much money she was capable of spending on personal and professional communications services.

The Yankelovich firm, according to Ruth Clark, categorized newspaper readers or consumers by age, race, income, education, and their "values," as determined by 39 questions related to attitudes about work, leisure, self. It was important, she said, for the researcher to know whether individuals believe in sacrificing for their children; where they lived was irrelevant. Another company, SRI International, was selling a service called VALS II—the acronym was for "Values" and "Life-Styles"—which divided Americans into three groups: Outer-Directed, Inner-Directed, and Need-Driven. They were then divided into nine subgroups: achievers, societally conscious, I-am-Me, belongers, sustainers, survivors, integrated, and two classes of emulators. I wasn't sure what all those words meant—company officials said they could be used to tell which magazine or stock someone would pay money for—but I did know they had nothing to do with whether someone lived in Louisville.

Barry Bingham had spoken of values at our lunch. I had asked him what he thought determined "right and wrong" in modern America. He said he couldn't be sure anymore. "The old values," he said, "are being destroyed. We see it in new employees and pilferage. People believe that if you want something you have the right to go ahead and take it. They begin by saying 'do your own thing,' but it really comes down to 'the end justifies the means.'"

What do you think changed those values?

"Freud," he said. Bingham, it seemed clear to me, was not so much talking about a man, Sigmund Freud, or his theories. "Freud," as he talked on, was an all-embracing word collecting

ideas and circumstances that redefined an individual's relationship to society and personal accountability for his or her own actions. I was beginning to get used to that answer.

Many things had changed in his lifetime, including his city.
The Louisville of history and memory will die a little more with
Barry Bingham, Wilson Wyatt, and their leadership generation.
The torch is flickering now—Dann Byck doesn't want it. Leadership is passing in the general direction of the absentee benefi-
ciaries of local commerce and industry, and to federal officials
who see the place as "Your Community," and to what Byck
called "the garbage," a class of professional politicians willing to
act as receptacles of citizen complaints in return for reasonable
creature comforts and the narcotic of seeing their names in the
papers and being validated regularly on television.*

The political leaders of Louisville were on television that
night. Meetings of the Board of Aldermen, the city's council,
were televised on the second and fourth Tuesdays of each month
on Channel 13. The meeting on January 9, 1979, was called to
order promptly at 7:00 P.M. by the board's president, Reverend
W. J. Hodge. He was black—as was 20 percent of the city's population—and so were the chairman of the local board of education and the chairman of the board of trustees of the University
of Louisville, a private institution for 123 years before it was
taken over by the state in 1970.

"There has been a great move here to put blacks in prominent, visible positions in recent years," said Wyatt, and we then
had this exchange:

Q. Isn't that a way for the white majority to say that there is

* "Estate taxes are what is destroying Louisville," said Joseph Ardery,
secretary of the Louisville Area Chamber of Commerce. "People
somewhere in Washington began applying meritocracy theories in
the 1970s to try to cut the influence of inherited wealth. One of the
things they are accomplishing is stripping medium-sized cities of
their natural leadership class, local businessmen. In Louisville, the
families that have traditionally supported the arts and other civic improvements are being forced to sell out—and probably to abandon
the city." Perhaps. But a new national administration elected in 1980,
the Reagan Administration, responded to complaints like that by
sharply reducing such taxes—and I, for one, doubted that the new
regulations would significantly check the decline of family businesses
and local civic leadership.

no racial problem? Is there a consensus among whites that the society has done enough for blacks? We can say: "Look at the important positions some of them have now."

A. Yes, I think that's what has happened here. The majority is not willing to do any more, even if the basic situation for most blacks has not changed very much. Black people are about as poor as they've always been. At the university, the white and black students are legally desegregated, but they resegregate themselves.

Q. I've heard blacks say that we're practicing a colonial policy. Do we just pick off the incipient black leadership—pick them off as soon as we find them and get them to Harvard Law School and into good, visible jobs—because we know they are the ones who could cause real trouble in the society?

A. Yes, they're probably right. We allow blacks to become members of this club, the Louisville Club, and I suppose a lot of people here feel we've done as much as can be expected. We've taken care of the problem. But, of course, the real problem is still out there.

Reverend Hodge proceeded to the main business of the aldermen's meeting, the "State of the City" message of Mayor William Stansbury. The mayor was something of a comic figure; his credibility had been destroyed during the past year by information, specifically a short series of stories in Bingham's newspapers. Stansbury had announced that he would be out of the city for a few days at a meeting of city officials in Atlanta, Georgia, but a reporter had discovered that he was actually in New Orleans, registered at a hotel with a woman, a former assistant. With the press reporting every word and facial expression, the mayor tried to explain. He couldn't, but he gave a reasonable demonstration of why New York's Governor Carey was bitter and why Dann Byck and many other Americans didn't want to get involved in a business, politics, in which the public's right to know, and the press's inclination to report, encompassed every moment, public and private.

The mayor talked on that night about a city that existed only in his own mind: "The major priority is the rebuilding of our downtown. In downtown Louisville, the prospects for the future are unlimited . . ."

It was what mayors were expected to say. But, in fact, the future of Louisville as the river port on the Falls of the Ohio was behind it. The downtown was usually deserted. A couple of new hotels to accommodate visiting management consultants check-ing out branch operations of national corporations were not going to change sad reality: Louisville was just a place where a few hundred thousand Americans happen to live at the moment.

In my notebook on one of those cold days along the Ohio River, I wrote and underlined: "There is no Louisville." It was too flat a statement, but I was not surprised when I learned, in May of 1981, that Dann Byck, the natural inheritor of local lead-ership, had moved to New York City.

9
NASHVILLE
AND MEMPHIS

"Andrew Jackson . . . and Elvis Presley . . ."

"Nothing is more rare than to encounter a house of brick in Kentucky; we didn't see ten in Tennessee, Nashville excepted," Tocqueville wrote in his notebooks during the ten-day, 260-mile journey from Louisville to Memphis that awful winter. "The [log] cabin of the Kentucky and Tennessee country . . . attests to the indolence of the master even more than his poverty. You find a clean enough bed, some chairs, a good gun, often books, and almost always a newspaper, but the walls are so full of chinks that the outside air enters from all sides . . . Nothing would be easier than to protect oneself from bad weather and stop the chinks, but the master of the place is incapable of taking such care."

Why? He asked one of the masters, a man named Harris living off the primitive road from Nashville to Memphis, and the American answered: "Slavery. We are habituated to do nothing for ourselves. There are no farmers in Tennessee so poor that they do not have one or two blacks."

"We made the acquaintance there of a kind of man and a way of life that we had no conception of," the traveler wrote to his father. "This part of the world is peopled by a single type of man only, the Virginians. They have retained the physical and moral character that belongs to them; they form a people apart, with national prejudices and a distinctive character."

Nashville became a city of 475,000 people; Memphis a city of 650,000. The "Virginians"—Tocqueville saw the frontier being pushed back by two distinct groups, Virginians and New Englanders—the Virginians are no more. "There is no 'South' anymore. That's all a game," said John Seigenthaler, publisher of the *Nashville Tennessean*. "There are no regions left in the country. Sixty-five percent of the new starts, subscriptions, we get at the newspaper are people coming from other parts of the United States. It's absolutely insane to talk about the values of the frontier or of an agrarian society. What we do here is try to bring in industry from the North."

And sell a little, too. Nashville sold country music to the rest of the nation; Memphis sold Holiday Inns, 1,760 almost identical inns along the roadsides of America, built after the first one, in 1953, was successful in that city.

The newspapers Tocqueville saw in almost every cabin did it. The newspapers and the roads.

"The roads, the canals and the mails play a prodigious part in the prosperity of the Union," he wrote in his notebook in Tennessee. "America, which is the country enjoying the greatest sum of prosperity ever yet accorded a nation, is also the country which, proportional to its age and means, has made the greatest efforts to procure the easy communications I was speaking of . . . There is not a cabin so isolated, not a valley so wild, that it does not receive letters and newspapers at least once a week; we saw it ourselves."

The distinctive character of the "Virginians," the men and women who settled a quarter of the country from southern coastal communities, could not survive in an environment of roads, information, and ideas running along lines that, almost invariably, went from North to South and from East to West. "As they mingle," Tocqueville wrote in *Democracy in America*, "the Americans become assimilated; the differences which climate, origin, and institutions had created among them become less great. They all get closer to one type."

That one American type was never destined to be the southerner. Fatally weakened by its dependence on slavery, the Virginian nation was inevitably sliced up by lines of communication and, one day, absorbed in the American mingling. Trying to break away from the United States thirty years after Tocqueville passed through was a logical but bloodily futile southern response. Now, more than a hundred years after that civil war, regional resistance was reduced to words, the romantic, bitter sermons of the evangelical preachers I heard everywhere along the road from Louisville to Memphis, and the complaints of a generation that knew they were being overwhelmed as other southerners had been overwhelmed in battle in the 1860s.

"Give us a chance," said Ann Rickey, a member of the board governing WKNO, the public television station in Memphis, during a long lunch in that city's Tennessee Club. "We have no chance to survive as a place with the pictures, the information all coming from someplace else. We can't compete without alternate channels of communication."

"The information—the news and the ideas—all comes from New York and Washington. And Los Angeles, too," said Michael Grehl, editor of the *Memphis Commercial Appeal.* "Their views are not congruent with ours, but what can we do against them? It's happening with everything. I look forward to the day when the whole country will be fed pap from an underground kitchen in Nebraska . . . We'll fight it to the bitter end."

The end is near. "It used to be enough for Memphis to be what it always was, the shopping center for everybody from Tupelo, Mississippi, north to here," Grehl said. "But that's not good enough for the new people. The people coming here from New York and Pennsylvania want something different. They want it to be more like what they're used to." Grehl, though, like most Americans, was new people himself; he came south from Chicago in 1957 to work for, and eventually become editor of the *Commercial Appeal,* one of 47 newspapers owned by the Scripps-Howard Corporation of Cincinnati.*

---

* "The new people here are from every place up North, but it seems you hear more about Chicago, New Jersey, and Pennsylvania," said Ken Shapero, the twenty-three-year old editor of the *Harpeth Herald,* a weekly newspaper serving Brentwood, Tennessee, near Nashville. He went on to describe the almost inevitable tension between new people and the older residents of areas that are rural or southern, or both. "The new residents are willing to support higher taxes because they want schools as good as the ones they're used to in Jersey. The local people who own farm land desperately want to keep taxes low so that they can keep the land until big development reaches them and then sell out at the highest possible price."

Grehl's complaint that Americans want what they're used to certainly helped explain the success of Memphis' most famous commercial enterprise, Holiday Inns. The company's success was based on providing identical boxy rooms with the light switches in the same spots so that travelers could turn them on without thinking about which city or state they were sleeping in that night; the inns were a multiplying tribute to the fact that Americans get what they want. America is a mass market—and Americans want it that way. "Who runs America?" said William Safire, a *New York Times* columnist, repeating my question. "The consumer. The consumer. The consumer. The consumer is king!" Nashville and Memphis were neither as isolated nor as manipulated as some of their more thoughtful citizens argued to me; both places played a part in creating and satisfying and profiting from that mass appetite. Nashville was the home of America's country music industry; Memphis was the home of the industry's most successful practitioner, Elvis Presley, a true hero of mass culture. Nashville was the home of Andrew Jackson, President when Tocqueville was here, and more than 300,-000 people each year visited the house where he lived, the Hermitage. More than ten times as many, more than three million visited the city's twin monuments of country music, Opryland U.S.A. and the Grand Ole Opry. And, in Memphis, another two million visited the house where Presley lived and died, Graceland.

"There is an irresistible force within democracy—movement toward the broadest possible base of selection," said Michael Jay Robinson, a professor of political science at George Washington University. "And it's not only in politics that you see that . . . In a real democracy, there would have to be an inevitable rise of a great popular culture. Any system of entertainment, for instance, that is directly tied to public response is going to have more and more universal appeal. A democratically based mass culture would tend to drive out other forms and ideas wherever it goes."

Tocqueville and Beaumont would have been appalled by that thought. They were appalled, again and again. "We spend our life enduring howling of which one has no conception in the old world . . ." wrote Tocqueville of American singing. "It resembled what one hears in the booths at a fair . . ." he said of one of

New York's finer orchestras. "Tocqueville and I laughed like the blessed . . ." Beaumont said after visiting the American Museum on Broadway and discovering its main exhibit was stuffed birds. "The fine arts are here in their infancy," Beamont wrote to his family. "The commerce and industry which are the source of riches do not at the same time produce good taste."

"So far," Tocqueville would write in *Democracy in America*, "America has had only a very small number of noteworthy writers, no great historians, and not a single poet. The inhabitants have a sort of prejudice against anything really worthy of the name of literature, and there are towns of the third rank in Europe which yearly publish more literary works than all the twenty-four states of the Union put together."

The Americans maintained their prejudices. "We get to them from underneath," said Ted Ashley, a former chairman of Warner Brothers, who had been responsible for the making of more than a hundred television series. "Once you establish that you will be able to sell entertainment to the public unencumbered by government, then what happens is inevitable. I'm free to sell anything I want to as many people as possible, so I stick to the fundamentals of common-denominator mass entertainment. The first two fundamentals, always, are: one, you identify with the hero; two, you know what's coming next."

"Cartoons, fantasy and action-adventure have the potential for reaching everyone or almost everyone," Ashley said. "Drama and other forms that are more complicated depend on compatibility of emotional experience. You may be eliminating part of the audience, which is exactly what you're trying to avoid in mass entertainment."

"The style will often be strange, incorrect, overburdened and loose, and almost always strong and bold," said Tocqueville of the literature he thought would develop with democracy. "Short works will be commoner than long books, wit than erudition, imagination than depth. There will be a rude and untutored vigor of thought with great variety and singular fecundity. Authors will strive to astonish more than to please, and to stir passions rather than charm taste."

That, in general, is probably true. Certainly it was within the context of the structured and mannered work of aristocracies with which the Frenchman was comparing American writing and howling. But Tocqueville may have underestimated the American skill, in both production and marketing, to make vigorous, strange, and incorrect styles into accepted forms. "Traditionally, not very much entertainment has crossed national borders," Ashley said. "But a hell of a lot more American stuff has, because when it comes to reaching masses of people, we're years and years ahead of anyone else . . . Technically, we can dazzle them from time to time. But it is probably more important that because we are almost always trying to reach *all* the people, we have found common denominator values that no other society can match."*

Ashley, who had succeeded in it, was describing a business dedicated to understanding, exploiting, and accelerating a tendency Tocqueville wrote about, prophetically, 150 years before:

"What I say about the Americans applies to almost all men nowadays. Variety is disappearing from the human race; the same ways of behaving, thinking, and feeling are found in every corner of the world. This is not only because nations are more in touch with each other and able to copy each other more closely, but because the men of each country, more and more completely discarding the ideas and feelings peculiar to one caste, profession, or family, are all the same getting closer to what is essential in man, and that is everywhere the same."

Those are really more graceful words for . . . for "lowest common denominator." Those same ways of behaving, thinking, and feeling are most likely to be transmitted through mass entertainment—in films, on television. "Television as entertainment or just for passing time seems to me infinitely more important than attempts to use it to shape opinions," said Stanley Hoffman, the Harvard government professor who is chairman of the univer-

---

* Ashley pointed to the American obsession with standings and "Top Ten" lists—of books sold, movie revenues, stock earnings, television ratings, attendance, and so on—to underscore the society's emphasis on finishing first. I thought that the effect of constant exposure to those lists—in daily newspapers, for instance—might be compared with the effect of the games Tocqueville saw American children playing. When he saw ten year olds choosing their own leader or voting on the rules of a game or of behavior, he concluded they were being trained in the habits of democracy. Modern American children are apparently being trained to understand the difference between Number One, Number Two, and—God forbid!—Number Eleven.

sity's Center for European Studies. "The medium's impact is in shaping mores." And it was Tocqueville's conviction, repeated throughout his work, that: "It is their mores, then, that make the Americans . . . capable of maintaining the rule of democracy." Then there came a day and technologies that made it possible and profitable for the Americans to begin broadcasting their mores—their habits, their customs, their everyday ideas—to every corner of the world. The films and television series of Hollywood and the Holiday Inns of Memphis—there were 271 Holiday Inns in other countries by the end of the 1970s—the Nashville sound, and the sounds of the English language, Coca-Cola, blue jeans, sweatshirts, shaking hands, majority rule, and freedom of the press seem to appeal to something essential in men and women. The ideas and things of America—many of them developed in that direct contact between seller and buyer—do sometimes seem irresistible.*

"I do not think the intervening ocean really separates America from Europe," Tocqueville wrote in the second volume of *Democracy in America*. "The people of the United States are that portion of the English people whose fate it is to explore the forest of the New World . . ." Their fate, too, was to explore the

---

* According to studies by the United Nations (UNESCO): 35 percent of the feature films shown in 24 countries were American made; 35 countries import more than 35 percent of their television programming, usually from the United States, which has huge backlogs of old programming for sale at prices as low as $30 per half-hour; Associated Press news reports are used in about 4,000 newspapers outside the United States; in ten of the world's most important nations, at least three of the five largest advertising agencies have Madison Avenue names; and in 20 more countries, the largest single ad agency is American. Statistics like that have triggered complaints and investigations around the globe about American "media imperialism." But there is nothing new about that. In the 1920s, the Canadians were griping about a brain drain caused by American publications' trumpeting of the States' "unlimited promise, higher wages, better living conditions and good times." In 1944, William Haley, director general of the British Broadcasting Corporation, warned that "in the entertainment field it is essential that the use of . . . Bob Hope, Jack Benny and other [radio] programs does not become a Frankenstein." One of Haley's associates at that time, in a government report, added, "If any hundred British troops are invited to choose their own records, ninety percent of the choice will be the American stuff." That's the way it is: Given a choice, most people will pick that American stuff.

wilderness of cultural democracy, to create a democratic culture. Americans made the direct link between what people want
and what they can get. The commerce, as Beaumont noted, may
not produce good taste, but it is powerful stuff. It may be irresistible stuff.

It bridges intervening oceans—some of the stuff does that literally and electronically from communications satellite to communications satellite. The people of the world could one day
become that portion of the American people whose fate it is to
live farther from the center of cultural democracy than Memphis or Nashville.

But no matter where they were geographically in relation to
the center of mass culture and what contribution they made to
its popular mix, Nashville and Memphis, like Louisville, were
not going to be very important as distinct and identifiable
places. John Siegenthaler, the Nashville publisher, worried that
the way his city would one day be identified within its own region would be racially.

We were talking about the *Tennessean*'s growing inability to
influence black readers in a city where blacks made up more
than 25 percent of the population. (In Memphis, the black proportion was more than 40 percent.) "The black population keeps
expanding," he said, citing higher black birth rates. "Black politicians are going to take over this city and a lot more, and I don't
think the establishment press, the white-owned press, has much
credibility with much of the black population. A black mayor of
Nashville could ignore criticism from this newspaper and, if that
happens, the press is going to lose its watchdog role. Local political systems are breaking down in a fundamental way."

Our conversation drifted from blacks as newspaper readers to
blacks as Americans, and soon we were echoing the conversation
I had had the day before in Louisville with Wilson Wyatt.

"I think white America has reached a consensus on black
America," said Siegenthaler, who as executive assistant to Attorney General Robert Kennedy had been a leading figure in the
federal government's efforts to force desegregation of the South
in the early 1960s.

What is the consensus?

"Look, we've done enough for the bastards. If they can make
it, fine. If they can't, that's their problem."

The next night, at a dinner attended by nine of Nashville's leading citizens—including the publisher, a federal judge, the city historian, the chaplain of Vanderbilt University, all white—Fate Thomas, a blunt-spoken professional politician who is sheriff of Davidson County, said of blacks: "They've had their day. The moment is past." There was a long discussion around the table; no one disagreed with Sheriff Thomas.

In Memphis, a place haunted by the fact that America's greatest modern black leader, Martin Luther King, Jr., was assassinated there in 1968, a similar meeting with local leaders at the Tennessee Club produced equally direct conversation.

"We have done a lot for them," said Albert C. Rickey, one of the city's leading attorneys. "Look"—he waved an arm—"I never thought I'd see the day when black people would be eating in this club."

A couple of black men were there, it's true. But Lamar Willis, the city's director of libraries, then told a story of darkness in the American spirit. The summer before, in 1978, the members of the Memphis Fire Department, which is almost totally white, had gone on strike against the city and actually began to burn down abandoned buildings to demonstrate their power over people's lives. One of the buildings they chose was on Vamce Street, next to the Vamce Street Branch Library, traditionally the city's "black" library. The flames from the abandoned building reached the library and it, too, began to burn. As it was destroyed, the white firemen stood in the street cheering.

There was sadness in Willis' voice as he told the story. But the emotion may have been for the burning books. Of black people he said, "It's really too bad, you know. We hire them here, but they won't work very hard. They're not really capable of developing loyalty to an institution."

"They don't know how to work," said Paul Cappock, a Memphis historian. "They're people who have been given everything and just don't know how to work for things. What does it matter? About half of them are going to get shot anyway."

"Everything isn't enough, is it?" said Ann Rickey, who has been active in civil rights work. "There are two black underclasses here. One is centered in public housing projects and they are dangerous people. The other is the Mississippi blacks and they are very tender people. But there's nothing we can do for either of them. That's the way it is."

Her husband, Albert Rickey, said he had been talking to someone about Andrew Jackson. "He was saying," Rickey continued, "that Jackson wasn't such a bad man, he just didn't believe Indians were human beings."

Our own conversation—about blacks this century—didn't seem that different to me.*

In Nashville, the dinner conversation about blacks ended abruptly when a black city councilman, Mansfield Douglas III, joined the table. The conversation drifted to other topics, drifted, in fact, into group melancholy.

For almost an hour, the eight men and one woman—Penny Edwards, an assistant to Tennessee's lieutenant governor—speculated on whether dishonesty was still looked down on in America. Political scandal was discussed—the state's governor was involved in a couple of investigations—and there was agreement that public reaction was mild and cynical, rather accepting of corruption as the political norm. "Sure he's stealing money, but . . ." and "He's lying, but after all . . ."—that was what Tennesseans were saying, according to the people at the table. Stealing was becoming a right, John Siegenthaler said, when I asked him about the guards, gates, and cameras in the lobby of his newspaper's building. He said the company used local racial violence as an excuse to install security systems to prevent pilferage. Employees were stealing so much, he said, that in effect they were being locked inside the building.

Penny Edwards complained that the politicians and public officials she worked with and knew were men and women with-

* The people talking about blacks that day at the Tennessee Club were not young. In Tennessee, and in other places, I heard many things like this remark from John Siegenthaler: "I think younger people, like my own children, are becoming essentially color-blind." But I was also told something that stuck with me by a white cab driver in Memphis, an aspiring film writer named Vernon Richards: "The people I know are becoming bigots, too. It's just not personal or passionate anymore. A stockbroker I know here is in his early thirties and he was pretty radical once. The other day he said: 'Hell, I don't mind being around blacks, but for the things that are important to me, my wife, my kids, my home, my job, they can only hurt me.' "

out conviction, that they were "creatures of polls," of the market researching of opinion that had become almost mandatory before public and private decision making in America. Beverly Asbury, the chaplain of Vanderbilt, said that the average income of the parents of students at the private university was over $50,-000, that a new elite was being created as only the sons and daughters of the wealthy could afford the rising tuitions at the country's best universities. Hugh Walker, Nashville's official historian and a college professor himself, said that people of means were being driven to private education because social experiments like busing were destroying the public system. Federal Judge Gilbert Merritt, of the Sixth Circuit in Cincinnati, worried that charity and private initiatives in general were being destroyed by government programs and services such as legal aid to poor people. Siegenthaler said corporations were running and ruining the country, that lawyers had created organisms beyond the control of government by taking advantage of laws designed to control the behavior not of organizations but of individuals.

It would not have been hard that night in Mario's restaurant in Nashville to come away with the impression that the country was falling apart. The people at the table lamented, several times, that they had "no control over what's happening." They would have kept at it all night, but most of them had to get up early the next morning to go about the business of running the country.

Granted, Americans have a tendency to gripe because, as Tocqueville wrote, things aren't perfect and Americans "all have a lively faith in human perfectibility," but there was something laughable about our protestations of decline and despair. And I did laugh the next morning with Henry Kantor, who ran a small furniture store on Nashville's faded Broadway. "Life is just so much better here than it was," said Kantor, who was seventy years old and had come south from New York City in 1931. "When I came here, the newspapers ran job ads that specified 'Christians Only.' Black people were treated as animals or children. People who think the past was better in Nashville don't remember it."

"Concepts of right and wrong haven't changed," he said. "Basically, I think, they come from the Bible. Everyone learns ethics the same way. By the time you learn, you're dead. People always had the same instincts, like cheating in school. But in my day there were proctors and you couldn't. Now the discipline is gone, so people cheat. In my store today"—he sells the cheapest kind of furniture to poor people, usually black poor people—"fully 10 percent of the people who come in don't intend to pay. I am not talking about slow payers. I mean people who fully intend to cheat me. That's an extraordinary increase from what it used to be.

"There is no discipline and I think it was destroyed by mobility. Because, now, there is no peer pressure. No one knows who you are anymore as people move around, so there is no shame attached. People cheat. The morality, the ethics—they're constant. Right and wrong, that's a middle-class thing. The upper classes never gave a damn about right and wrong for themselves anyway, neither did poor people."*

"My grandchildren will probably live better lives than we do. Maybe not materially, because things are running out. But spiritually better. Different, sure. They won't be Jewish the way I'm Jewish. You can see the Jews dying out in Nashville. Intermarriage. People having fewer children. We'll all be American Americans. I don't think they'll have to fight a war. America tried to fight a lower-class war in Vietnam. Nobody gave a damn about it because poor whites and poor blacks were the ones dying. Now, we can't try that again. I don't think America will fight a war for a hundred years unless we're attacked. That's better than it used to be. Most things are."

---

* In January of 1832, while traveling through South Carolina, Tocqueville met Joel Roberts Poinsett, a former congressman and ambassador, and asked him about the "extreme purity of morals" in the United States. Poinsett answered, "I don't believe either that we are more virtuous than other peoples; the purity of our morals is the result rather of special circumstances and particularly of the total absence of a class of men having the time and means to attack the virtue of women."

10
NEW ORLEANS

"The First Law of Democracy . . ."

"There is not a white but has the right to maltreat the unhappy person in his way and thrust him into the muck crying: 'Get out of the way, mulatto!' " Thus the French consul in New Orleans, Monsieur Guillemin, explained the law and custom of the American city to his countryman, Monsieur de Tocqueville, on the first day of 1832. When I arrived, a descendant of those mulattoes was the mayor of the city on the delta where the Mississippi River meets the Gulf of Mexico.

The mayor, Ernest Morial, the son of a cigar maker and a seamstress who traced their ancestry not to slaves but to Creoles, early settlers of mixed blood, was testifying before a traveling Congressional subcommittee on the day I arrived in his city. "You must provide a higher level of funding," Morial said to the members of the House Judiciary Committee's Subcommittee on Crime.*

Life, as Henry Kantor had said in Nashville, was certainly better. But it was also hard not to notice that as some black Americans—and despite his light skin, Morial said he was black in a city whose population was 56 percent black—completed the rise from gutter muck to political control of local govern-

* In strict definition, the Creoles of Louisiana are descendants of white conquerors from Spain and France. In usage, the word defines the descendants of those conquerors and, often, free blacks.

ments, the chemistry of national government and international commerce was reducing local governors to . . .

"Children . . . They treat us like children, like their slaves," said Brod Bagert, the white member of the New Orleans City Council who was so angry about the red-white-and-blue signs announcing, "Jobs for Your Community." "They treat us like dirt. We're the American people, but you'd never know that when you have to go to Washington to beg."

Washington, actually, was coming to New Orleans, in the flow of news, at least. The city still had two newspapers when I was there, and over that three-day period in February of 1979, the *Times-Picayune* and the *States-Item* were chronicling the daily interaction with national government, usually as reported by the Associated Press:

WASHINGTON (AP)—Any state raising the speed limit higher than 55 miles per hour will lose its Federal highway funds, Transportation Secretary Brock Adams said Wednesday . . .

WASHINGTON (AP)—The nation's largest single supplier of home mortgage funds said Tuesday it will more than triple its urban loan program to spur investment in inner cities.

The Federal National Mortgage Association decision to increase its participation in the loan program was made public by Vice President Walter F. Mondale. . . .

WASHINGTON (AP)—The Carter administration is considering forcing gasoline stations to close on Sunday as part of a program to reduce oil consumption and build public awareness of the energy crisis . . .

NEW ORLEANS—A series of studies designed to improve the city's transit system will be paid for with a $300,000 grant from the Urban Mass Transit Administration, Mayor Ernest N. Morial said today. . . .

The most interesting story about the governed and the governors, though, was not from Washington, but from a small town in the Delta just southeast of New Orleans, a place called Pointe La Hache, reported on the front page of that day's *Times-Picayune:*

A representative of the U. S. Food and Drug Administration Wednesday said Louisiana would be cited for non-compliance with the national shellfish standards if Plaquemines Parish [county] did not close the harvesting areas east of the Mississippi River.

Parish oyster growers were told that the bacteria count in waters from the Mississippi River which breached levees during high water times, such as now, are polluting the oysters and making them unfit for consumption.

Victor L. Casper, regional specialist for the federal agency, said he would notify the U. S. Department of Health and Human Resources of Louisiana's non-compliance . . .

Plaquemines Parish Commission Council President Chalin O. Perez said he would not ask the parish governing body "to be part of this nefarious federal scheme." He said no parish agency or parish industry-based group had approved of the national standard. "This was a standard arbitrarily developed by a bureaucratic federal agency and stuffed down the throats of the people in the industry," he said.

The U. S. Food and Drug Administration contends that the backwaters of the east bank of the parish are being polluted by fresh water from the Mississippi River. The waters are said to pour over the levees which Perez said were severely damaged during hurricanes.

He contends that the U. S. Fish and Wildlife Service has prohibited the Army Corps of Engineers and the parish from repairing or improving the levees in the area because of the area's determination as wetlands . . .

Perez asked Carter if his agency would recommend to the U. S. Fish and Wildlife Service that it remove its objections to the construction necessary on the levees to keep the river waters from entering the marsh back waters.

Carter said no federal agency could interfere with the jurisdiction of another federal agency and that his only recourse was to cite the state on its non-compliance posture . . .

Darrel Sercovich of Buras, owner and operator of D. D. Sercovich Oyster Growers, said if action taken by either the state or federal agency "causes me to go out of business or lose business I intend to file suit to see where we stand once and for all."

The federal government does things. Good things: the Army Corps of Engineers has traditionally been responsible for the maintenance of the country's coastlines, protecting them against erosion and protecting inland areas against flooding; the Fish and Wildlife Service was responsible for protecting the natural habitats of native species, including the birds and water life of the marshy wetlands of the Mississippi Delta; the Food and Drug Administration was responsible for protecting Americans against poisoned or tainted foodstuffs. None of those agencies existed in 1832, when it was assumed that state and local governments—or the people of an area—would do those good things in their own self-interest. It didn't always work that way. There was always the option of moving on if nature or man had spoiled the land or the water. And there were people who stayed behind in Canandaigua, N. Y., or other older places and just would not tax themselves to finance some public improvements. And there were black people, almost always getting as few good things as possible. Then, of course, there would be a public outcry, often organized, demanding that government take action to protect land, or water, or health, sometimes people. Democratic affairs of state seemed something like the affairs of matter and energy, and there was a First Law of Democracy analogous to a layman's definition of the First Law of Physics: for every action there is an equal and opposite reaction. The cries, the reaction, would almost inevitably rise toward the highest level of government, the level with the greatest taxing power. The people who planned, inspected, enforced, and recorded all the good works made up the spreading national government.

It was before that national government that more and more Americans offered their pleas and made their demands. On the day Morial pleaded for money to fight crime, other Louisianians drove huge tractors across the grassy mall behind the Capitol of the United States in Washington. They were part of a demonstration organized by the American Agricultural Movement, a national association of farmers demanding higher federal subsidies for the crops they grew back home.

The farmers of the land and the farmer of the sea, Darrel Sercovich, the oysterman, were at the same time tugging at the two levers of power that often seemed most useful to the citizens of the modern democracy: publicity and lawsuits. Modern communications technology, especially television, tended to make the governor and the governed the same size as they presented their messages to the public—antagonists, both sides, usually got 20 seconds on a 19-inch television screen and viewers were free to choose between them. In court, all men were theoretically equal—and, often, practically so. If the jurisdictional conflict involving the Army Engineers, the Fish and Wildlife Service, the Food and Drug Administration, and the livelihood of Darrel Sercovich were to be resolved it would probably be resolved by a judge, a federal judge appointed by the President of the United States with the advice and consent of the United States Senate.

Those angry citizens instinctively and institutionally decided to deal with the federal government. Chalin Perez and Ernest Morial had very little to do with all this. Indeed, local government appeared to be collapsing around me as I walked through Morial's charming city, still dominated, visually, by the history and architecture of French and Spanish colonial periods. The elements of the governments of the city and region were turning on themselves, concentrating on struggles among themselves.

"Strikes expected by Monday" was the lead headline in the *States-Item;* the paper reported that both the policemen and the sanitation workers of New Orleans planned to walk away from their public duties in five days in a dispute over wages. More than 200 Louisiana welfare workers, employees of the Office of Family Security, were off the job in the city that day, demanding that the federal Department of Health and Human Resources provide more financial aid to pay for their overtime work. In Jefferson Parish, the city's southern neighbor, bus service was shut down because drivers were striking for more money, and the parish's ambulance drivers had scheduled a strike for the next day.

The front pages were filled with stories about the employees of government, who seemed to constitute a class with interests quite separate from those of the general public, fighting among themselves over the division of public revenues. Inside the newspapers were stories of struggles between ethnic groups for private resources. "The influx of Vietnamese refugees" was cited during a hearing of the Mayor's Housing Committee at City Hall the night I arrived as a reason for the displacement of local blacks from scarce housing and low-income jobs. "Next Monday," the *States-Item* reported, "the sixth and final public hearing will be held on how to increase housing for low-income and minority persons."

"New Orleans is a patchwork of peoples," Etienne Mazureau, a lawyer who had been born in France, told Tocqueville. "Not a country in America or Europe but has sent us some representatives." That was still true a century and a half later: New Orleans was more than half black by the early 1970s, and at the end of that decade a new immigrant group came to the city—the Vietnamese, families displaced from their homes 10,000 miles away because they had sided with the Americans in a war in Southeast Asia. Four years after the last Americans had been driven out of Vietnam, three columns of the New Orleans telephone book listed people named "Nguyen," the Vietnamese equivalent of "Smith."

Many of the new immigrants, like millions before them, were finding opportunity in America. But the resources of the country did not seem as unlimited as they had in the early nineteenth century. "Everybody works," Tocqueville wrote home to his father, "and the mine is still so rich that those who work rapidly succeed in acquiring that which renders existence happy." The resources of New Orleans seemed rather clearly defined now, and the black majority within the city limits didn't have many of them beyond the subsistence level provided by government. They were put in their place by *New Orleans,* a glossy magazine selling for $1.50 a copy each month. The February issue had 100 pages; the only black faces in the entire publication were two waiters seen serving white patrons in an advertisement for a restaurant named Pat O'Brien's.

"There's a story around here that someone offered a job to a black man and the man said, 'That's too tough—give it to a Vietnamese,' " said Lawrence Eustis III, a local mortgage broker. "I don't know whether that's true, but I do know that the Vietnamese aren't used to getting something for nothing from the government and they really work. Within six months they've learned enough of the language and saved enough money that they're coming to my place looking to borrow the money to buy a house or start a business."

"The blacks will totally dominate local politics in a very short period of time," said James Glassman, founder of a local weekly newspaper named *Figaro.* "But they won't be involved in anything else. The business life of the city is closed to them. There is literally nothing much for them to do here—New Orleans has the highest percentage of people living below the poverty level of any American city—because the old families who dominate business life didn't want the city to grow. Now it's like a banana republic and there are only jobs like being waiters in the restaurants. There's no place for poor people to move up here. The political power will give black people nothing but impressive titles."*

"Nothing but impressive titles"—Glassman's phrase was meant to be an exaggeration. So, I suppose, was the talk I had heard from "brothers" and "sisters" on the radio as I had driven through Newport, Rhode Island, listening to black men and women angrily describing a colonial policy of elevating talented blacks into impressive positions to remove potential leadership from the dismal mainstreams of American black life. But how much exaggeration? How much truth? In New Orleans, a long time before, Tocqueville had heard another version of the same hard thinking in his conversations with Guillemin, the French consul, about the free blacks and their descendants then in the city—Mayor Morial's ancestors—the men required to state *homme de couleur* on legal documents whatever the actual shade of their skin. The shadings of talent were not covered in official forms.

"Free, they can hope for nothing," Guillemin told Tocqueville, according to the younger man's notes. "Yet among them, I know men of virtue and of means. It's in isolating itself thus obstinately from all the rest that the aristocracy of the whites exposes itself to danger on the American continent . . . If, without giving the negro rights, it had at least taken in those of the colored men whose birth and education most nearly approximated its own, the latter would infallibly have attached to its cause, for they are in reality much closer to the whites than to the blacks. Only brute force would have remained for the negroes. By repelling the mulattoes, however, the white aristocracy gives the slaves, on the contrary, the only weapon needed to become free: intelligence and leadership."

---

* Like other upwardly mobile Americans I met traveling, Glassman moved on. By 1981 he was in Washington, D.C., as publisher of a national magazine, the *New Republic*.

Majority America, white America, by the time I arrived, seemed to have heard Guillemin; it had taken in Ernest Morial, a man of virtue with the impressive title of Mayor. That had not been accomplished until late in the country's second century— and there had been black riots before the federal government adopted laws with names like "The Voting Rights Act of 1965," and court interpretations of phrases like "affirmative action" began elevating substantial numbers of black men and women into the world of political titles. It took centuries and the full force of the national government to overcome local law and custom in New Orleans and give Morial that title. Whatever the relationship between events and circumstance, Monsieur Guillemin was a prophet: the "only weapon" of real black revolt had been removed. What was left, in this city and others, was "brute force." "The projects out there," Lawrence Eustis said, pointing toward one of the city's poor black neighborhoods, "are filled with dangerous people. Savages—young guys with nothing to lose." But random crime and occasional riot only disturbed the peace; they did not disrupt the established order.*

And brute force was available to both sides. More than three-quarters of the city's police force were white—"Our trained rednecks," Councilman Bagert said, "they treat the blacks like animals"—and New Orleans regularly had the highest number of police brutality complaints of any city in the United States.†

* In 1960, before the passage and enforcement of the Voting Rights Act of 1965, approximately 29 percent of the adult black citizens of the Old South were registered to vote. By 1976 that statistic had increased to 63 percent.

† In 1980, the FBI investigated 105 police brutality complaints in New Orleans. The *Washington Post* of June 11, 1981, reporting on investigations of nine shootings of blacks by policemen—seven of them fatal—said this:

"Ernest N. (Dutch) Morial, New Orleans' first black mayor, has resisted outcries from the black community that he fire police who are accused of using excessive force. He says civil service regulations tie his hands.

"But privately, he anguishes over his 'Catch-22' dilemma. Firings that didn't stick would inflame police to brutalize more blacks to show that Morial is powerless to protect them. Firings also could cost him support among white police backers. Both would hurt his chances for reelection next year."

The brutality complaints—more than double the number filed in New York City, with twelve times the population of New Orleans—were made to the U. S. Justice Department. The complaint papers could be filled out on Camp Street, in the Federal Courthouse there. It looked like a dangerous place. Armed guards and television cameras scanned the huge, columned lobby; citizens who entered were forced to pass through what appeared to be a doorway separate from any wall, but was actually an electronic disarming device designed to detect the metal of knives and guns.

Perhaps the security was simply a tribute to the power in the building. One of the institutions that had changed American race relations was inside: the United States Court of Appeals for the Fifth District. "Powerful?" said Judge Robert Ainsworth, who had sat on the nation's second-highest court since 1962, the beneficiary of one of the lifetime appointments that, for better or worse, made judges different from other politicians in America. "I don't feel powerful. But no one seems to these days. I think that's because no one can get anything done by themselves."

That frustration was built into the American system. Democracy was supposed to give people power—or, perhaps, a sense of empowerment, the sense that, in some small degree, each individual had control over his or her own life. But, realistically, how much power could I have, or should you have? "The power of association," to use the phrase Tocqueville returned to repeatedly in his notebooks and in *Democracy in America,* was the result: "an appeal to individual powers working in concert." Americans weren't literally supposed to be able to do anything by themselves then. Now each American had greater empowerment—each individual modern American had more power, or potential power, over public affairs than each one had had 150 years ago. There were many reasons for that, but one of the principal ones was individual accessibility to Judge Ainsworth's court and the greater power and role of that court. The expansion of the judicial role, particularly on the federal level, sometimes seemed to give citizens more rights than the political system could process. Things could be done that individuals and institutions couldn't seem to get done. And that produced a frustrated people—as I had heard in Nashville the night I listened to some of its leading citizens despairing of their power-lessness. "Everyone feels powerless these days," Ainsworth despaired as we talked in his chambers. "Chief Justice Burger," he said, "told me a while ago that he feels powerless. He feels one man can't control the Supreme Court because each member can go his own way."*

How did the courts get the power they have today?

"The legislative and executive branches failed in their jobs."

Judge Ainsworth, who had been a Louisiana state senator for four terms, was stating the obvious. But it was that obvious fact—the failure of elected public officials to equally distribute the benefits, real or desired, of democracy to all the citizens of the democracy—that had, for most practical purposes, led to a relatively peaceful revolution in the United States in his professional lifetime. He had been there, part of the problem and part of the solution.

The problem was race. The problem was Americans of color thrust into the muck. Black Americans, formally and informally, by law and custom, were denied some of the rights of citizenship and many of the rewards of industry. In Louisiana, when Ainsworth was a legislator, complicated and deliberate tradition prevented *les hommes de couleur* from voting, from holding public office, and, as in Louisville and a thousand other places, from going to better public and private schools, almost exclusively white schools. It was almost impossible for a black man or woman to win—to win the political power or the education to compete for influence or money with white men and women. The restrictions were more formal in places like Louisiana, in the South, but they were no less real in other parts of the country.

In Philadelphia, Tocqueville had talked with the city librarian, John Jay Smith, and made some notes that were similar to the cases presented to the Fifth Circuit Court of Appeals:

---

* In May 1981, federal judges, not feeling powerful enough, decided to associate to advance their own cause within the government. A report of their activities in the *Washington Post* on June 10, 1981, began: "A group of Federal judges, much to the dismay of Chief Justice Warren E. Burger, has proposed organizing the federal judiciary into a Federal Judges Association to lobby for higher salaries and fringe benefits . . ."

"Mr. Smith, a very able and well-informed Quaker, said to us to-day that he was perfectly convinced that the negroes were of the same race as we, just as a black cow is of the same race as a white cow . . .

"We asked him if blacks had the rights of citizenship. He replied: Yes, in law. But they can't present themselves at the polls.

"Why so?

"They would be mistreated.

"And what becomes of the reign of law in this case?

"The law with us is nothing if it is not supported by public opinion. Slavery is abolished in Pennsylvania . . . [but] the people are imbued with the greatest prejudice against the negroes, and the magistrates don't feel strong enough to enforce the laws favorable to them."

The political system had failed for the descendants of America's slaves. For almost a century that system, responsive to what was undoubtedly the majority will, had ignored—when it did not implement—society's legal and social racism. And the magistrates, through lack of strength or will, did the same. In 1892, a man named Homer Plessy, whose skin was white but who had a black great-grandfather, tried to sit in the "Whites Only" section of a train in New Orleans and was arrested when he refused to move. Four years later, after several appeals, the United States Supreme Court ruled that the conductor who refused to seat Plessy was right and so was the Louisiana law directing railroads "to provide equal but separate accommodations for the white and colored races." It was not until the late 1930s that the high court began to suggest that there should be some questioning of whether, sometimes, "separate" facilities were actually "equal"—and legal separation itself was not then questioned. That didn't happen until 1951. It happened outside the South, in Topeka, Kansas.

A minister in Topeka, Oliver Brown, who was black, attempted to enroll his nine-year-old daughter in the fourth grade of one of the city's all-white elementary schools, legally segregated under Kansas law. She was turned away and he sued, with the backing of other local black parents and an American "association," the National Association for the Advancement of Colored People. The parents lost and lost again in court, finally appealing to the Supreme Court. On May 17, 1954, the Chief

Justice of the United States, Earl Warren, read the unanimous decision of the Court:

> Today, education is perhaps the most important function of state and local governments. Compulsory school attendance laws and the great expenditures for education both demonstrate our recognition of the importance of education to our democratic society. It is required in the performance of our most basic public responsibilities, even service in the armed forces. It is the very foundation of good citizenship . . . [It] is a right which must be made available to all on equal terms . . . Separate educational facilities are inherently unequal.

A year later, the Supreme Court ruled that local and state governments must implement the desegregation of schools "with all deliberate speed." With even more speed—"It all began with *Brown* v. *Topeka*," said Judge Ainsworth—the courts, particularly federal courts, began to be overwhelmed with class-action suits attempting to force government, usually local and state government, to do what it did not want to do or to prevent it from doing what it wanted. Trivial things and profound things—the Fifth Circuit had ruled on the case of a Florida man who sued to force the government to allow him to use food stamps to feed his cat (he lost) and on the cases that moved the Congress to guarantee full voting rights for black Americans. When the Supreme Court upheld the constitutionality of the Voting Rights Act of 1965, Chief Justice Warren said, speaking for the majority: "Hopefully millions of non-white Americans will now be able to participate for the first time on an equal basis in this government under which they live."

"Class actions became a critical part of the political process," Ainsworth said. "When I became a judge, someone couldn't just come in and enjoin the government to prevent the building of a highway, but you can now . . . You used to have to post a bond to pay for the damages if you lost the case. No more. In one of my cases, road construction was stopped through a park in San Antonio, Texas, and the state lost $10 million because of that. One of the problems of the courts' political, governmental role is that the courts can stop anything, but they can't start anything. We are making law, there's no doubt about it—and there is already too much law."

"Read this," he said, handing me a speech by the vice chancellor of the University of Alabama, Richard Thigpen.*

"We have seen a proliferation of lawsuits across this land which is unprecedented at any time in our history and indeed the history of any civilized nation," said Dr. Thigpen, a former professor of law.

> Between 1970 and 1977 alone, civil case filings in the federal district courts grew by 49 percent ... For example, suits seeking access to government files are increasing rapidly; federal and state environmental laws have brought a new wave of litigation unheard of a decade ago; individuals are filing more claims involving race, sex, and age discrimination.
>
> In our nation today, whether the matter concerns civil rights or town planning or the economics of the marketplace or labor-management relations, or whatever, the judiciary will generally play a key, and often determining, role in its outcome ... It may be the highest compliment a free people can pay an instrumentality of their government. For despite pressures of case-overload, deadlines, and delay, the fact is that our courts are the only instrument of government which regularly and consistently and visibly gets things done ... It is not so much that Americans have made extreme demands of the legal system, as it is that they have raised their expectations of society in general, and government in particular. As a result, governmental and legal remedies are now deemed appropriate for all varieties of social problems which were formerly dealt with privately, within the context of families, schools and churches. And policymakers, both in and out of government, have added new rights and expanded the range of available remedies faster than they have been able to develop the capacity to enforce or protect them.†

* Judge Ainsworth died in December of 1981.

† The statistics of litigation and the legal profession do show dramatic increases and tend to support some people's contention that the rise in court activity is proportional to the number of lawyers looking for work. "We may well be on our way to a society overrun by hordes of lawyers, hungry as locusts," Chief Justice Burger said in a 1977

"We should be proud of that overload," another judge told me later, in a statement that, for a moment, struck me as silly. "Americans are exercising rights they never had before. Americans are freer. America is more democratic," continued G. Mennen Williams, an associate justice of the Michigan Supreme Court and a former governor of that state.

He was absolutely right. The overuse of the courts was a management problem that followed the rights explosion after the 1954 desegregation decision. But if clogged courtroom calendars were the price of *Brown* v. *Board of Education of Topeka*, it was one of the greatest bargains in American history, the best buy since the country picked up New Orleans and what eventually became 13 states from France for $15 million in the Louisiana Purchase.

The political problem was the centralization of authority that inevitably flowed from the appeals process itself. When representative democracy, the Republic, was deliberately unresponsive, as it was to black Americans, self-interested individuals found a mechanism to begin constructing a new political system, judicial appeals became the politics of the day and the appellate process became the process of governing. There were national answers to local questions, then there were fewer and fewer local questions.

More and more the questions of the day were answered by individual interpretations of a document of fewer than 5,000 words written, by a committee, almost 200 years ago. "Americans love their Constitution," said Gilbert Bochet, the French consul in New Orleans when I was there. "What an illusion— that something written in the eighteenth century could thrive in the late twentieth century.

"What is called American democracy is a thing of the past. In Africa, for instance, American democracy is seen as a reaction to European aristocracy—a white man's affair. That's what Tocqueville saw here, the reaction to aristocracy."

---

speech. At the end of 1978, according to the American Bar Association, there were 464,851 practicing lawyers in the United States— compared with 12,000 in Japan, an industrial society with half the population—but an even more interesting figure was the number of students in accredited U.S. law schools at that time: 114,688.

I wondered. Perhaps it did begin that way. But Tocqueville, I suspect, saw more than either Bochet or I. He must have, because he wrote: ". . . the Constitution of the United States so contrived things (and this was its master stroke) that the federal courts, acting in the name of the laws, should never have to deal with any but individuals."

The document Bochet read was a compact between 13 sovereign governments, and it was an illusion now. The document Tocqueville saw became a contract between a national government and millions of individuals. It was the reason Darrel Sercovich believed he had to go to federal court to find out where he stood once and for all. It was the reason Ernest Morial, with his impressive title, was forced to plead for his city before the nation and government of the white American majority.

11
MONTGOMERY

"Those Words Are America . . ."

"I have just made a fascinating but very fatiguing journey," Tocqueville wrote to a friend from Norfolk, Virginia, after a twelve-day trip across the South from New Orleans, "accompanied each day by the thousand annoyances that have been pursuing us for the last two months: carriages broken and overturned, bridges carried away, rivers swollen, no room in the stage; these are the ordinary events of our life."*

It was easier 147 years later. I drove to the New Orleans airport . . . and I came upon a scene that seemed very much part of the ordinary events of modern American life. Three small boys were lined up against the wall at a Delta Airlines gate. They were frightened and confused, trying to reassure one another in French. Only the oldest one, about twelve years old, spoke any

* Tocqueville's exact route through the South is impossible to determine. In the definitive study of Tocqueville's American travels, *Tocqueville and Beaumont in America*, by George W. Pierson, published in 1938 by the Oxford University Press, a footnote in Chapter 48 reads: "The strong probability is that they followed a stage-coach route from Montgomery to Fort Mitchell, to Knoxville, to Macon, to Milledgeville, to Augusta, to Columbia, to Fayetteville, to Norfolk.... For this difficult journey, Tocqueville manufactured his fourth and fifth small pocket diaries (*Cahiers portatifs* IV & V), and kept his notes in pencil. These fugitive entries are very hard to decipher today."

English, and he finally understood that the uniformed security guards—placed there by orders of one of the federal government's aviation agencies—wanted his little brother to surrender his plastic flashlight. The thing was shaped like a toy pistol, a derringer.

"Aren't you overreacting?" asked the pilot of a Delta jet. One guard, a woman assigned to the doorway-shaped metal detector, looked up for a moment and said: "We've got rules here!" So we do. Everywhere. A foreigner traveling this route, seeing guards and gates at so many doors, might have guessed that he was in a police state. In a way he would be right. There was a private police state growing up around me—blank-eyed men and women in uniforms of many colors, plastic identification tags, television cameras in halls, barbed wire along fences, hand-held two-way radios and mysterious buzzers and beepers on walls and on hips. In *New Orleans* magazine, the glossy chronicle of the city's white life, amidst page after page of advertisements for expensive restaurants and perfumes there was an ad showing a woman posed beside a metal shutter. Its message began: "Available in many decorator colors, BURGLARY PROTECTION. No need for burglar bars because Reel Shutters give you excellent burglary protection. . . ."

In Louisville, while I was there, the city's Free Public Library announced the completion of a $50,000 system to summon guards electrically if patrons attempted to leave the building without going through the normal check-out procedure.

All this was the reaction to what Barry Bingham, the Louisville publisher, thought was the breakdown of "the old values"; and in his city the library's traditional honor system was abandoned only after the theft of 80,000 of the 400,000 volumes in the main branch—one out of five books was gone. There did not seem to be enough honor in Louisville. There was not enough peer pressure on Broadway in Nashville, Henry Kantor said. Old religions were losing their frightening, disciplining grip—and that was part of the reason for the panic in the voices of many of the radio preachers who accompanied me across the South. Whatever happened to "Thou shalt not steal"? Perhaps the same thing that was happening to "Honor thy father and mother"? And what was replacing those old things?

Laws. Rules. Detectors. Guards. "There is also the increasing tendency of American society to be governed by regulation," Richard Thigpen had said in his speech to the new lawyers of Alabama. "It has been estimated that each year the state legislatures and the Congress pass an estimated 150,000 bills. More importantly, however, it also has been estimated that, for each piece of legislation passed, there are promulgated by agencies of our growing bureaucracy ten regulations for each bill, or a total of one-and-a-half million regulations per year." Stephen Lemann, the attorney who wrote the charter of Total Community Action, New Orleans' antipoverty agency, had told me: "The book of regulations for employing low-level workers was about eight inches thick and almost all those regulations were designed to prevent anyone from stealing a penny."*

The matter of pennies unstolen made for a petty ethic—and that was a subject that kept coming up as I traveled. In New York City, Dr. Eugene Galanter, director of the Psychophysics Laboratory at Columbia University, linked the modern vigilance with the confusing after-effects of the democratic decision to transfer some of the honoring of fathers and mothers to the state. "The country changed profoundly when people accepted Social Security and the idea that they weren't responsible for their parents anymore," he said. "We dropped something that had been accepted over thousands of years. Our way of dealing with that decision as an ethical question was to make sure that people didn't steal money from nursing homes. We put in new accounting systems as a substitute for ethics."

I wasn't as sure about how it began, but it was obvious that the web of regulations, public and private, was a substitute for morality—nets intricately woven to catch people and to hold them within limits once defined by religion, by common morality, by tradition or just snoopy neighbors. By trust. And I was also pretty sure I knew how it ended. Three days after I saw that little scene in the New Orleans airport, an Air Force sergeant named Laurence Chamberlain, a black man, drove into the town of Raton, New Mexico, in a snowstorm. He was out of gas and out of cash because of car repairs he had paid for as he drove

---

* Months later, in New York, that city's corporation counsel, Alan Schwartz, took up the same subject: "We have built in so many checks to prevent corruption that we have mandated a government that can barely get anything done—it has to be incompetent."

from a military base in California to another in New Mexico. The three banks in Raton refused to cash a check from Chamberlain's California bank. Security regulations, they said politely. No out-of-town checks cashed. Chamberlain slept in his car that night; the temperature in Raton dropped to six degrees above zero Fahrenheit. His wet feet froze and ten days later, because of the frostbite, both his feet were amputated.

There were heavy steel gates across the lobby of the offices of the Montgomery, Alabama, newspapers, the *Advertiser* and the *Alabama Journal*. I had been told which buttons to push and the right words to say, so I was admitted. Tocqueville, at a comparable moment, made this note: "On arriving in Montgomery, we learned that a man had been killed in the street by a pistol shot."

"There was a time we needed those gates and a lot more to defend ourselves," said Ray Jenkins, editor of the *Advertiser*, one of the first papers in the South to advocate the desegregation of public facilities—schools, lunch counters, and buses—in the state. "We were bombed and mobs, white mobs, did try to break in here."

"There is no one here who is not carrying arms under his coat," a young lawyer had told Tocqueville in Montgomery, the capital of Alabama, on January 6, 1832. "In the smallest dispute, you pull out a knife or a pistol." The lawyer showed the shocked young Frenchman the scars of his own battles, duels to protect an offended sense of honor. Tocqueville asked whether he had pressed charges against his assailants and the lawyer replied, "God! No. I tried to give back as good!"

That confirmed for Tocqueville what he had heard about the violence underlying the courtliness and rural chivalry of the South. A century and a half later, many still bore the scars. One was John Seigenthaler of Nashville, who was beaten unconscious on the streets of Montgomery in 1961, when he went there to report to the Attorney General on the mob violence that greeted incoming busloads of civil rights workers.

Montgomery, which in 1861 had become the first capital of the Confederate States of America, once again became more than the capital of a state; it was the capital of the moral and legal struggle for black political and civil rights. On December 1, 1955, a black woman named Rosa Parks refused to move when a Montgomery bus driver shouted his usual order: "Niggers get back!" She was arrested, just as Homer Plessy had been more than 50 years before in New Orleans. "We are tired," a young black minister, the Reverend Martin Luther King, Jr., preached from the pulpit of the Holt Street Baptist Church six nights later, when he helped organize a boycott of the city buses by the more than 50,000 black people then living in Montgomery. "Tired of being segregated and humiliated. . . . If you will protest courageously, and yet with dignity and Christian love, future historians will say, 'There lived a great people—a black people!' "

By 1963, King was the most visible leader of the black movement surging back and forth across the South. In April of that year, not for the first time, he was in an Alabama jail, the Birmingham city jail. "A Letter from Birmingham Jail," written during the four days that King awaited trial for parading without a permit, was essentially a plea for justice from the white American majority, but it was also, like the most effective of the black leader's rhetoric, a challenge Americans could not readily repudiate because it was framed in the national rhetoric:

"We will reach the goal of freedom in Birmingham and all over the nation, because the goal of America is freedom. . . . We will win our freedom because the sacred heritage of our nation and the eternal will of God are embodied in our echoing demands . . . carrying our whole nation back to the great wells of democracy which were dug deep by the founding fathers in the formulation of the Constitution and the Declaration of Independence."

The appeal was to the declared public morality of Americans, to the words and ideas which evolved from Protestant Bibles and, more than geography, became the United States of America. But that morality could not then be enforced by or upon elected officials. The battles of Martin Luther King were fought in the streets and won in federal courtrooms, usually in the courtroom of a single judge, Frank M. Johnson, Jr., of the United States District Court for the Middle District of Alabama. He sat on the three-judge panel that issued the order desegregating Montgomery's buses on June 4, 1956. The order that was published that day—coauthored by Judge Richard Rivès—was based on the Fourteenth Amendment to the Constitution, which was to become the essential weapon of the battle for black equality, and, repeated in decision after decision over two decades, an essential sentence of American rhetoric: "No State shall ... deny to any person within its jurisdiction the equal protection of the laws." Johnson cited those words again and again during a 20-year period when he was routinely guarded by federal agents because of threats to his life, as the federal courts desegregated the city's museums and parks and forcibly integrated the school system.

By the end of the 1970s, when I was there, Frank Johnson was, for all practical purposes, governing the entire state of Alabama. He had assumed direct control over state functions and agencies that included prisons, schools, hospitals, parks, and voter-registration systems—taking control each time after considering a lawsuit in which there was overwhelming evidence of the denial of equal protection or the inability to deliver public services to black citizens by predominantly white administrators and elected officials. A judge acting out his role as arbiter between the individual and the state was routinely gaining power over both. The pattern developed everywhere in the United States, but Judge Johnson was the best example because, seeing more injustice in Alabama, he used more of that power.°

Using the Constitution's ban on "cruel and inhuman punishment" as legal justification, for example, the judge assumed, in

---

° Judge Johnson's actions were, for the most part, affirmed by the Fifth Circuit of the Court of Appeals and by the Supreme Court. But through the period of judicial activism triggered by civil rights suits there was a lively, often angry, debate over what was sometimes called "judicial imperialism." In some cases, lower courts were overruled, particularly as judicial actions peaked during the years I traveled the country. On April 20, 1981, for instance, the Supreme Court ruled by a 6-3 vote that federal judges in the Third Circuit had gone too far in ordering the State of Pennsylvania to correct "abominable" conditions at a state hospital and a school for the retarded (*Pennhurst State School* vs. *Halderman*). "If Congress intends to impose a condition on the grant of Federal monies, it must do so unambiguously," said the Supreme Court's majority decision, ruling that a district court judge who assumed control over the school in 1977 had overinterpreted the phrase "appropriate care" in a federal law. The debate, I was sure, would continue as long as the United States had three branches of government, but I was reasonably certain, with Tocqueville, that the power of the courts would expand as the rights of Americans expanded—and I expected those rights to keep growing.

1976, what amounted to personal control over the operations of a state prison system that, by most accounts, would have been a scandal even in Tocqueville's time—"the court concludes from the evidence that robbery, rape and assault remain everyday occurrences among the general prison population"—ruling from the bench that the state of Alabama and his agencies were "incapable of effective leadership."*

The judge's words, backed by the power of the federal government, were, in a sense, the conclusion of a conversation Tocqueville had while riding in a carriage from the Carolinas to Norfolk, Virginia. His traveling companion for five days was Joel Roberts Poinsett, the former South Carolina congressman, who was one day to become Secretary of War.†

"How are roads made and repaired in America?" the Frenchman asked.

"It's a great constitutional question whether Congress has the right to make anything but military roads," Poinsett answered. "Personally, I am convinced that the right exists; there being disagreement, however, practically no use, one might say, is made of it. It's the states that often undertake to open and keep up the roads traversing them. Most frequently these roads are at the expense of the counties. In general our roads are in very bad repair. We haven't the central authority to force the counties to do their duty. The inspection, being local, is biased and slack. Individuals, it is true, have the right to sue the communities which do not suitably repair their roads; but no one wants to have a suit with the local authority."

There came a day, of course, when Americans—Homer Plessy and Oliver Brown and Rosa Parks among them—were willing to sue the local authority. And there came a time when the na-

---

* While I was in Montgomery in February 1979, a new governor, Forrest H. James, Jr., negotiated an agreement with Judge Johnson in which the governor was named the court's "receiver" of the prison system. In effect, James was allowed to run the system—which meant that after three years it was again under state political control—as long as he continued to make improvements satisfactory to the federal court.

† Poinsett served as U. S. Ambassador to Mexico from 1825 to 1829 and brought back samples of a red flower he admired—it came to be known as the poinsettia.

tional government, the creation of both states and words—the words of the Declaration of Independence and the Constitution—had become powerful enough after the centralizing of authority resulting from economic collapse in the 1930s and war in the 1940s to delegate to itself old prerogatives of the states and to attempt legally to implement "these Truths" that the Declaration called self-evident. The law was used to enforce the rhetoric that said men were created equal and had certain inalienable rights. A rhetoric that was a bit grander than the American people as they expressed themselves through their politics.

The law enforced fairness. It might be reflected morality, as Justice Potter Stewart had suggested in Cincinnati. It might even be confused with morality itself—for a moment.

"This is the most immoral book I have ever read," said the newspaper editor, Ray Jenkins, walking to the bookshelves in his office and picking out *Corporations . . . Cases and Materials*, by Harry G. Henn. "This was a standard textbook when I went to law school."

Jenkins, a veteran of the civil rights revolution, had seen what the law and the legal profession could do, and at the age of forty-four, he had entered the local law school of the University of Alabama. He had lost any illusions about law as morality long before he was admitted to the state bar in 1978. "This book," he said, tapping it, "is simply one case after another of greedy people fighting greedy people. Occasionally some poor soul surfaces to question a corporation on the grounds of common decency and is immediately shot down."*

* *Corporations*, a standard text in many law schools, is part of the American Casebook Series, published by the West Publishing Co. of St. Paul, Minnesota.
Jenkins' example of the type of case that persuaded him not to practice his new profession was Pillsbury *v.* Honeywell, Inc., a 1971 case decided in United States District Court and upheld by the U. S. Court of Appeals. A petitioner named Pillsbury, a shareholder in Honeywell, Inc., had protested the corporation's refusal to allow him to see corporate records to determine the company's involvement in production of war matériel. He was refused access, by the courts, because his interest in persuading the company to discontinue such production was "not a proper purpose germane to his economic interest."

"The law can't stand the strain," he said sadly. "There are things the law cannot do. It cannot replace faith or trust, it cannot replace religion, it cannot change human nature."

Jenkins had learned what Justice Stewart knew—"society expects too much. . . . We have been given power beyond the ken of the courts"—and what Judge Johnson understood even as he enforced fairness in Alabama: while the law might sometimes be a tool of morality that did not make it a moral thing. "When you have a voting rights case," Johnson said, "and you find there's been a pattern in practice of discrimination against the blacks in registering to vote, you don't register the blacks to vote so that they can gain political power in Macon County or Lowndes or Sumter or Perry. You are faced with some legal issues and if they are entitled to relief you give them relief and you order that they be registered. Now the effect of their registering and voting and electing a sheriff and other county officials is something that the court's not concerned with, and has no interest in. . . ."

The effect of voting rights cases and of "One Man, One Vote" decisions, based on the Fourteenth Amendment, in Lowndes County—the county seat is Selma, where in 1965 King began his most famous demonstration, a 45-mile march to Montgomery to demand voting rights—was, one day in 1970, the election of a black sheriff, John Hulet. "The fear is gone," Hulet said. "But everything else is the same." The fear, Jenkins added, is gone on both sides—the blacks' fear of discriminatory law enforcement and the whites' fear for their property rights. "The whites know," he said, "that their property will be protected by the state of Alabama and its courts and the U. S. courts, too.

"They also know that they will eventually take control of Lowndes again. Whites are moving in with northern industry. Industrial relocation is the new Reconstruction. There is savage competition among the small towns around here for the 'rag factories,' the factories that make cheap clothes and anything else cheap. There is less and less difference between the North and the South every day. There is much less social interaction— and sexual, too—between blacks and whites than there was when I was growing up. I'm very pessimistic about the way things are going. Southern cities—Atlanta, Birmingham, Miami—are developing black ghetto subcultures like Harlem or

Newark or Detroit. The South is going—television is one of the things doing it; people become the same all over."

Jenkins' confusion and moral disillusionment and Johnson's legal certainty made me think of a paragraph Tocqueville wrote near the beginning of the first volume of *Democracy in America*. The first chapter of that volume was his sweeping geographic overview, "The Physical Configuration of North America." The title of the second chapter was "Concerning Their Point of Departure and Its Importance for the Future of the Anglo-Americans"—and there the writer was searching, he said, for "the first cause of their prejudices, habits, dominating passions, and all that comes to be called the national character." The first causes, he concluded, were the Puritanism that traveled from England to New England and the political freedom settlers found, as if by accident, because they were so distant from European authority. So, he said:

"Thus, in the moral world everything is classified, coordinated, foreseen, and decided in advance. In the world of politics everything is in turmoil, contested, and uncertain. In the one case obedience is passive, though voluntary; in the other there is independence, contempt of experience, and jealousy of all authority."

There was, I thought, traveling through the South that winter, an argument for saying now that in the legal world everything was classified, coordinated, foreseen, and decided in advance. In the world of morality everything was in turmoil, contested and uncertain. I found myself wondering often what was right and wrong in America today. Who decides?

Churches certainly no longer decided in advance for many, many people, although there was still a great public attachment to them, and not just on the radio and in Sunday attendance figures. Jenkins' newspaper, the *Advertiser*, ran a small box, outlined in red, on the front page each day with the headline: "Pause to Pray." That day the little message began, "Cast out our fears, O Lord. Remind us we need not panic. . . ." The law might not always do it in advance, but the courts were where more and more Americans gathered to hear answers to the ethical questions of the day . . . including the obligations of the state and foster parents to orphans. In Norfolk, Virginia, on the road north from Montgomery, the *Virginian-Pilot* reported a week later: "A discrimination suit filed in Circuit Court alleges that two foster children have been unfairly deprived of the right to take driver education courses . . . depriving them of equal protection of the law under the 14th Amendment."*

The law could do only so much; it wasn't enough for Ray Jenkins. It was, after all, only an attempt at systematizing knowledge and reason, a try at creating a science. In his desk, the Montgomery newspaperman kept a typed copy of a quotation by a Harvard Law School professor, Paul Freund: "Religion is a great body of untruths leading to an ultimate truth. Science is a great body of truths leading to an ultimate untruth."

"I keep thinking that something big—and not something good—is building up in the country," Jenkins said. "I was raised on a farm in South Georgia, and when the farm came to me a while ago, I decided to keep it. I want to have someplace to go if something happens. Maybe I'll go there anyway and just grow food and read."

He didn't do that. Five months after our conversation, Ray Jenkins went to Washington as a special assistant to the President of the United States.

* The issue in the suit against the Chesapeake Social Services Bureau, according to the *Virginian-Pilot* of February 16, 1979, was that the municipal agency was requiring the foster parents of the two children to pay for insurance before they could take driver education courses, but such insurance was not mandatory for students living with their natural parents.

12
BALTIMORE

"The Richest Man in America . . ."

They were dancing in the streets when I arrived in Baltimore. A hundred thousand people were cheering. The mayor, William Schaefer, was at City Hall, shouting into a microphone: "Baltimore is the number-one city in the nation. . . . There is pride. There is togetherness."

Actually, Baltimore on that day—October 18, 1979—was number two. In baseball. The night before, the Baltimore Orioles had lost the seventh and deciding game of the World Series by a score of 4-to-1 to the Pittsburgh Pirates. The people had turned out for a parade to honor their losing players.

"It's a city with an inferiority complex," said Jon Katz, editor of the *Baltimore News American.* Even more than other old American cities, Baltimore, with a population drop from 905,787 in 1970 to 786,775 in 1980, was condemned to live in the shadow of Washington, because that's where it is. The capital is only forty miles south of Maryland's largest city. Katz's newspaper, in fact, had just published a series of articles detailing large-scale purchases of Baltimore town houses at depressed prices by Washington investors speculating that local real estate values would rise as more and more people commuted to jobs in the Washington area. Besides that, the Orioles, like the real estate, had just been bought by a group of Washington investors.*

No wonder Mayor Schaefer had ordered that no fat policemen be assigned to the city's Memorial Stadium during the World Series games; he wanted national television audiences to believe Baltimore cops were all fashionably slim. After one of the games, hundreds of Oriole fans had attacked a television sportscaster named Howard Cosell outside the stadium because they believed he was making fun of their team and city.

The street attack seemed to be something of a Baltimore tradition. Peter Hoffman Cruse, editor of the *Baltimore American* in 1831, told Tocqueville of attacks on local journalists who were not considered anti-British enough during the War of 1812. Then, watching the horse races at the city's Central Course, Beaumont witnessed a scene that he recorded in his notebook on October 29, 1831: "A Negro having taken the liberty of entering the arena with some whites, one of them gave him a volley of blows with his cane without this deed appearing to surprise either the crowd or the Negro himself."†

A few days later, Tocqueville and Beaumont met one of America's most precious relics: Charles Carroll of Carrollton, the last surviving signer of the Declaration of Independence. He was ninety-five years old and said to be the richest man in America. "He possesses the most vast domain existing today in America," Tocqueville wrote in his notes. "The estate on which he lives contains 13,000 acres of land and 300 Negro slaves. He has married his granddaughter to the Duke of Welesley [sic]. He is a Catholic . . . he is very erect, has no infirmity, his memory is uncertain. Still, he converses very well . . .

"We spoke of the government of the United States," Tocqueville continued. "Charles Carroll seems to show regret for the

---

* In November of 1981, Katz left Baltimore to become managing editor of the *Dallas Times-Herald*.

† The incident surprised Tocqueville and Beaumont. The latter was shocked enough to recount the scene fictionally in the book he published after their journey to America: *Marie, ou l'Esclavage aux États-Unis, Tableau de Moeurs américaines*. The novel, popular in its time, examined the conflict between the races in America through a romantic story with a predictably tragic ending: a young Frenchman's love for an American girl who appeared to be white but was actually a mulatto.

old aristocratic institutions of Maryland. In general, everything in his conversation breathed the tone and ideas of the English aristocracy, combined sometimes in original fashion with the ways of the democratic government under which he lives, and the glorious memories of the American Revolution. He ended by saying to us: 'a mere Democracy is a mob. The government of England is the only one suitable for you,' said he; 'if we get along with ours, it's because each year we can push our innovators into the west.' "

The Carrolls, though they were Catholic and originally Irish, had served England, King, and aristocracy, and their rewards had been great. Charles Carroll's great-great-grandfather, Daniel Carroll, raised a small army for King James II at the end of the 1600s and was granted 60,000 acres in the colony of Maryland. His son, the signer's great-grandfather, who was the first Charles Carroll, was appointed attorney to the Calverts, the proprietary governors of the royal colony north of the Potomac River. That Charles Carroll, "the Settler," came to America in 1688, and in 1737 his great-grandson was born, Charles Carroll of Carrollton, who would, before his fortieth birthday, pledge his life and fortune to American independence from England.

The signer's oldest son was named, again, Charles Carroll, and became known as Charles Carroll of Homewood. Homewood, one of the family's vast estates, later became the campus of Johns Hopkins University, in Baltimore. In the sixth generation of American Carrolls, Charles Carroll of Doughoregan was born. He had seven children, one of whom, Robert Goodloe Harper Carroll, became a cavalry officer in the Confederate Army.

Robert Goodloe Harper Carroll's son, a gentleman farmer born in 1873, was named Charles Carroll. His son, Charles Carroll, Jr., born in 1903, became a lawyer and spent 20 years as a member of the Maryland legislature.

Charles Carroll III was born in 1933 and his son, Charles Carroll IV, was born in 1955. The three of us met for dinner in Baltimore to talk about their lives and the story of the family since Charles Carroll III's great-great-great-great-great-grandfather signed the Declaration on July 4, 1776.

Charles Carroll III was an assistant vice president of the Chesapeake and Potomac Telephone Company. Charles Carroll IV was a medical student at the University of Maryland. The elder Carroll also had three other children: one was a salesman for a parts division of General Motors and the other two were still in school. His wife, Anne Johnson Carroll, was a speech teacher at a private school.

The father graduated from Princeton University—while he was there he converted from Catholicism and became an Episcopalian—and served as a lieutenant in the Army during the Korean War. "I think we're fairly ordinary people," he said. "Obviously we are not poor, but I would not say that we were rich, either. We're, I think, middle upper class." I took that to mean that this branch of the Carrolls—there were three lines of direct Carroll descendants—were doing just fine, since even the richest Americans often try to identify themselves as middle class.

"Work," he said, "was a later development in the family. My father's generation was really the one that broke the mold and faced up to the fact that working was becoming necessary."

Where did the money go?

"Beats the hell out of me," Carroll said. "Maybe the fact that people weren't working had something to do with it—that and the tax laws. There were a number of children in a couple of generations. There was also a time that some of the family— especially women—went back to Europe when they realized that there really wasn't going to be an aristocracy in America. They married minor nobility; I have cousins who are Belgian diplomats.

"It's exciting for me to think once in a while about the Signer," he said. "But it doesn't impress anyone and it doesn't have any impact on my life."*

"I have to be very careful about mentioning it," said his son, Charles Carroll IV. "The response is very mixed and I don't need that 'Oh, you're a blue-blood . . .' "

That was the way America had worked for one family, the richest family in the country at its founding. In the seventh generation, a son became a telephone company executive and his sons were selling automobile parts and studying medicine at a public university, not even the best medical school in the state.

* One of the few friends to mention his lineage, Charles Carroll III said, was Parren Mitchell, a black congressman from Baltimore, whose wife said she was descended from slaves of Charles Carroll of Carrollton.

The best school, which had no room for a Carroll, was in Baltimore, the Johns Hopkins University School of Medicine—the university built on old Carroll estates. Johns Hopkins, in fact, was one of the best in the world, and had been almost since its founding with a grant from a local Quaker merchant who gave it $7 million and his name.

"We pick the best," said Dr. Richard S. Ross, dean of Johns Hopkins Medical School. "We have 3,500 applicants each year for 100 places. The Admissions Committee does not know anything about families or family finances . . . the requirement is proved hard sciences capability.

"It is more competitive than it used to be, but it is fairer. It was different in the old days, or at least I've been told stories about how they got in here. The dean interviewed everybody and he just said, 'Okay, you can come; you can't.' This was an elite institution in every way. Now we have a complex, automated, computerized review system. In an attempt to be totally fair, we put an awful lot of emphasis on numerical properties."

But as Dr. Ross talked it became obvious that he was not entirely happy about the processes and regulations of enforced fairness and honesty. "Yes," he finally said, "I am an angry man. This school has been here to train leaders—people capable of thinking creatively, people who will make the medical advances of the future. The government keeps putting on more and more regulations. There was a time the attitude was to trust a place like Hopkins. Now we have to fill out forms, we have to have the right piece of paper at the right time to prove we're not doing anything wrong. . . . The regulations are all based on the assumption that all medical schools are the same. The government can't differentiate between research medicine and general practice, between Johns Hopkins and Harvard and run-of-the-mill medical schools."

How much do you depend on the government?

"Too much," he said. "We're dependent on federal money, mostly research money. It makes up about half our budget.

"A couple of years ago," Dr. Ross said, "the government decided that we had to accept third-year students educated in foreign schools and that those students couldn't be denied admission on the basis of academic qualifications. That's what happens when you deal with the government. They were lobbied by the parents of all the Americans who went to foreign medical schools because they couldn't even get into the second-rate ones here."

The federal action he was referring to—he almost sputtered as he talked about it—was Public Law 94-484, an amendment to the Health Professions Educational Assistance Act of 1976. The wording empowered the Secretary of Health, Education and Welfare to "equitably apportion a number of positions adequate to fill the needs of students described in subparagraph (B) among the schools of medicine in the States. . . . A school of medicine shall not be required to enroll a student described in subparagraph (B) if the individual does not meet, as determined under guidelines established by the Secretary by regulation, the entrance requirements of the school (other than requirements related to academic qualifications or to place of residence)."

The law, as written, seemed to do pretty much what Dr. Ross said it did—force Johns Hopkins and other institutions into accepting students who did not meet its academic qualifications.

"But," he said, "we beat them on that one."

How?

"We hired a smart Washington lawyer and he got that out of the law."

The incident, not worth the attention of the overwhelming majority of Americans, was instructive of an ordinary American cycle 200 years after Charles Carroll pledged his sacred honor to independence. Democratic pressures had been building up for years over the "unfairness" of medical education. Physicians, after all, were the highest-paid Americans and only a few people—8,000 a year—could become doctors. Those fortunate few were selected by medical schools according to criteria and qualifications that the leaders of the profession itself deemed reasonable. Many, many more were excluded, and the most energetic of those left home—left the United States—in an attempt to win the same rewards and benefits outside the established channels of the American medical profession. Over a period of time, those who felt excluded—students of foreign medical schools and others who were rejected in the United States—were able, with single-issue and single-minded determination, to bring enough political pressure on elected officials to persuade the government to take action. Publicity was a major weapon—distributing information about medical profession income and physician shortages, arguing that the profession itself was limiting entrance to insure the wealth of its members. The campaign worked—laws, regulations, and financial incentives were created to expand the profession. The number of students in American medical schools increased from 8,000 to 19,000 between 1968 and 1980. But an elite institution, distinguished by a record of unquestioned excellence, was able to block at least one of the incursions on its privilege by retaining—what else?—a lawyer capable of operating within the gray world that Tocqueville had compared with "occult science."*

But the natural law of egalitarian gravity had not been changed by Johns Hopkins' small victory. "We have no formal quotas for admission," Dr. Ross said. "But we do try to build each class as representative of the entire society. We have enough diversity to satisfy the government's requirements. The next graduating class, for instance, will have 34 women in it."

Is there a price for meeting those requirements for diversity?

"Yes," he said. "A medical school that has to admit people by group or by region inevitably loses quality. If every medical school has to be the same, medicine and health care suffer in the name of fairness. A society is enriched by institutions that emphasize excellence."

It was an old dilemma of democracy. "Fairness," as seen by Dr. Ross or by Magistrate Aug in Cincinnati, or "equal access," as defined by Darlene Kamine in the Ohio city, were indeed not the best tools with which to carve excellence—at least not the excellence associated with a medical leader or, for that matter, a political leader. But the excellence of a society is in the eye of the beholder. And if systems like the Johns Hopkins Medical School, geared to produce leaders, could not also produce black

* In the late 1960s, Johns Hopkins and other medical schools began receiving "capitation" money, a direct federal subsidy for each student. That program was initiated in the 1960s to encourage more admissions. The number of medical students then increased to the point that government study groups, including the Graduate Medical Education National Advisory Committee, began predicting a surplus in physicians by the 1990s. The GMENAC estimated that the United States would have 536,000 physicians by 1990, about 70,000 more than the country needed. The surplus by the year 2000, the committee reported, would be 145,000.

physicians or women physicians of any color, those systems were inevitably going to be modified or dismantled in a surging democracy.

"There is indeed a manly and legitimate passion for equality which rouses in all men a desire to be strong and respected. This passion tends to elevate the little man to the rank of the great," Tocqueville wrote in *Democracy in America.* "But the human heart also nourishes a debased taste for equality, which leads the weak to want to drag the strong down to their level and which induces men to prefer equality and servitude to inequality and freedom. It is not that people with a democratic social state naturally scorn freedom; on the contrary they have an instinctive taste for it. But freedom is not the chief and continual object of their desire; it is equality for which they feel an eternal love; they rush on freedom with quick and sudden impulses, but if they miss their mark they resign themselves to their disappointment; but nothing will satisfy them without equality, they would rather die than lose it."

His notes after meeting Charles Carroll reflected his own struggle to understand the meaning of what was already obvious in the United States. "All the ways and habits of mind of Charles Carroll make him completely resemble a European gentleman," wrote Tocqueville, who was of course one himself. "Probably the great proprietors of the South, at the time of the Revolution, were much on this model. This race of men is disappearing today, after having furnished America her greatest men. With them is being lost the tradition of the better born; the people is growing more enlightened, knowledge is spreading, a middling capacity is becoming common. The outstanding talents, the great characters are more rare. Society is less brilliant but more prosperous."

"Do you not regret that it should be thus?" he asked John H. B. Latrobe, a young Baltimore lawyer and author.

"Yes, from certain points of view," Latrobe answered. "This class was, in general, a nursery for distinguished men for the legislature and the army. They formed our best statesmen, our finest characters. All the great men of the Revolution, from the South, came from this class. And yet I am brought to believe that, taken altogether, the new order of things is better. The upper classes with us are less remarkable now, but the people is more enlightened; there are fewer distinguished men, but a more general happiness."

"What do you expect from society and its government?" Tocqueville wrote three years after that conversation. "We must be clear about that.

"Do you wish to raise mankind to an elevated and generous view of the things of this world? Do you want to inspire men with a certain scorn of material goods?

"Are you concerned with refining mores, elevating manners, and causing the arts to blossom? Do you desire poetry, renown and glory?

"Do you set out to organize a nation so that it will have a powerful influence over all others? Do you expect it to attempt great enterprises and, whatever may be the result of its efforts, to leave a great mark on history?

"If in your view that should be the main object of men in society, do not support democratic government; it surely will not lead you to that goal.

"But if you think it profitable to turn man's intellectual and moral activity toward the necessities of physical life and use them to produce well-being, if you think that reason is more use to men than genius, if your object is not to create heroic virtues but rather tranquil habits, if you would rather contemplate vices than crimes and prefer fewer transgressions at the cost of fewer splendid deeds, if in place of a brilliant society you are content to live in one that is prosperous, and finally, if in your view the main object of government is not to achieve the greatest strength or glory for the nation as a whole but to provide for every individual therein the utmost well-being, protecting him as far as possible from all afflictions, then it is good to make conditions equal and to establish a democratic government."

After Tocqueville listened to Charles Carroll's somewhat dim view of the democracy he had helped create, the Frenchman was pulled aside by a younger man, a relative, James Carroll, who said: "You mustn't exaggerate the inconveniences that 'democracy' has for us. No doubt in a mass of details, in a great number of particular cases, the people doesn't show common sense. Yet on the whole the machine goes and the State prospers. Certainly universal suffrage has its dangers, but it has this advantage that with it there does not exist a single class hostile to the others. There is a general satisfaction spread through the nation. . . . It still produces more good than misery. It spreads throughout the whole social body an activity and a life that another government would not know how to create."

There was the answer: Whatever mark, great or small, they would leave on history, the Americans knew what they were doing.

I don't think I showed any emotion during my dinner with the Carrolls—I tried not to—but I was thrilled. What was democracy? What was America? Whatever else it was, it was a system that worked in such a way that the richest man in the country couldn't be sure that his sons and his son's sons could get into the best schools and get the best jobs. We knew what we were doing with the Carrolls; we were trying to make room for the Reeveses.

PART THREE

Saginaw
to Detroit

13
SAGINAW

"Use It and Move On . . ."

"We bought pillows, a compass, brandy, sugar and ammunition. We hired two horses," Tocqueville wrote in his pocket notebook on July 23, 1831. He and Beaumont were in Detroit, in the Territory of Michigan, after crossing Lake Erie from Buffalo in a steamboat. The town had 3,000 people and was growing, but the young Frenchmen, for the moment, weren't interested in that. Detroit was the frontier; it was on the edge of the wilderness.

They sought out the government land agent for the territory, Major John Biddle, and pretended to be interested in buying land, then asked him where the last houses were in Michigan. "Towards the northwest," the American answered. "As far as Pontiac and in the neighborhood of that village some fairly good settlements have been established. But you must not think of settling farther on; the ground is covered by almost impenetrable forest, which stretches endlessly to the northwest, where one only finds wild beasts and Indians. . . . I say again, that is a part you should not think about."

It was the only part they wanted to think about just then. "We could not contain ourselves for joy," Tocqueville wrote, "for having at last discovered a place to which the torrent of European civilization had not yet come.

"We left at 11 o'clock. . . . Perfectly flat ground. One league without trees and under cultivation around Detroit. After that

177

Beaumont (standing), Tocqueville, and an Indian guide

we enter a thick forest through which a fine road has been cut. From time to time a little cleared space. A circle of wonderful trees around, mixed with burnt trees; a field covered with trunks; in the middle a log-house, often without windows. No poverty. Peasants well-clothed. Cattle bells around. . . . Houses become more and more scattered. Immediately after them the forest starts again. We went through some delightful marches; like English gardens where nature has paid all the expenses. . . . We arrived in Pontiac at 8 o'clock in the evening."*

The "fine road" the young Frenchmen followed into the wilderness became Woodward Avenue, bisecting the city of Detroit

* Tocqueville used the word "peasant" here to indicate that the work being done was land-clearing and farming. But he later noted in *Democracy in America:* "The Americans never use the word 'peasant'; the word is unused because the idea is unknown; the ignorance of primitive times, rural simplicity, and rustic villages have not been preserved with them, and they have no idea of the virtues or the vices or the rude habits and the naïve graces of a newborn civilization."

at an angle just off to the west of the north-south axis. The avenue, which is Michigan Route 1, began on the west bank of the
Detroit River—Windsor, Canada, is on the other side—almost
at the spot where another Frenchman, Antoine de la Mothe Cadillac, founded the city, or at least a fort, in 1701. When I began
the same trip that Tocqueville and Beaumont had taken, that
spot along the river was a mélange of planes of marble and concrete, glass and grass. It was new—new federal and county and
city office buildings, a new convention center, the new Renaissance Center with round glass towers of offices and hotel rooms,
all built as a symbol of the city's faith in itself after the terrible
riots of 1967. Hidden behind those bright and reflecting walls
and plazas was the triangle of older skyscrapers that was the
downtown the people of Detroit built in the 1920s, and, beyond
that, the city's residential neighborhoods and suburbs. In 1920,
city employees counted 18,424 automobiles—most of them built
right in Detroit—going through the intersection of Woodward
and Michigan Avenue, four blocks from the river, and proclaimed it the busiest intersection in the world. The population
of the city was then 993,700 and it continued growing to 1,670,-
000 in 1960—it was then the country's fourth largest city—before beginning the decline that reduced the number of people
living within the city limits to 1.2 million in 1980. Probably the
greatest manufacturing center the world had seen, it once even
switched in a few months from building automobiles to making
the trucks, tanks, guns, and planes that won World War II. That
achievement is commemorated by a memorial of screaming
eagles two blocks further up Woodward. War work was what
had brought hundreds of thousands of men and women, white
and black, up from the south, and by 1980 the population of the
city was 63.1 percent black.*

Past the old skyscrapers, Woodward belonged to merchants.
There were 66 clothing stores, 31 banks, 43 drinking places, and

---

* Woodward Avenue was named after Augustus B. Woodward, who
was appointed chief justice of the Territory of Michigan in 1805 by
his friend the President, Thomas Jefferson. Shortly after he arrived,
Detroit was almost destroyed by fire and he supervised the rebuilding
of the city before he ran into some problems with wine, women, and
swindle. He was last seen in the Territory of Florida, where he died in
1827 and was buried in an unmarked pauper's grave.

117 eating places—someone once counted them—and a young man named Michael selling gold-plated spoons, which could be used to inhale cocaine, at the base of the statue of Hazen S. Pingree, four times mayor of Detroit and twice governor of Michigan, near the intersection of Woodward with Adams Street. Within a few more blocks, where once the trees were burned to create farm land, more than half the buildings along the avenue were boarded up. Around and behind them, homes were charred and vacant—men deliberately started fires again during the riots of 1967. Urban desolation—blank, lifeless buildings and empty lots that seemed to grow garbage as well as weeds—was interrupted for several pleasant blocks by the city's cultural center, an area of impressive monumental museums and libraries. Detroit, a city of boulevards, a long time ago called itself "the Paris of the West," but the boulevards crossing Woodward were wrecked, lined in places with great turreted hulks which had once been the small castles of the auto makers and bankers who lived north and south of the towering gray mass of the headquarters of the world's largest manufacturer, the General Motors Corporation. The building that was once the headquarters of a smaller company, Motown Records, was abandoned, empty since the people who marketed to the world the sounds of the black streets and churches of the motor town became rich enough to move the whole thing to Hollywood. Another Detroit institution, Vernor's, a company built around a formula concocted by the city's first licensed pharmacist, was still operating on Woodward, but Vernor's Ginger Ale—like Falls City Beer in Louisville—had become just another product of a national corporation, United Brands.

Six miles from the river, the street signs along Woodward changed color from green to blue. That was the boundary, otherwise unmarked, of Highland Park, a smaller city within Detroit's borders. The faces of the people along the street had long ago changed from black and white to all black, but on one corner in Highland Park there was a reminder of the patchwork ethnic heritage Detroit and its parts have always celebrated: a small restaurant advertised "Rumanian Home Cooking." Then came the old factory building where in 1913 Henry Ford opened the first automobile plant with a moving assembly line to mass-produce a car he called the "Model T." The roadway in front of the factory was the first concrete highway in the United States. The next big building along Woodward was built like a fort, with huge white concrete walls; this was Highland Park High School and it had no windows—not one.

Most of the doorways I tested along Woodward in Highland Park were locked. Customers could get into stores only by buzzing and being inspected through the glass. One of those businesses was the A-Day Badge Company, just north of the Davison Freeway. Inside, they manufactured buttons saying almost anything you could think of to sell to small stores and sidewalk entrepreneurs for 22 cents before they were finally sold for a dollar. One of the popular numbers in the spring of 1980, when American diplomats were being held hostage in Iran, bore the message: "Iran Sucks." Americans were never much for paying attention to the details of foreign policy.

Before the street signs turned from blue back to green again, I saw the building of the Metropolitan Detroit Youth Foundation, with eleven clocks across the front; it was once the factory of a clock manufacturer named Centrix, which showed passersby the time in the capitals of the world. The clocks stopped years ago.

Back in Detroit, Woodward widened from a main street to a short superhighway. It ran along lovely green parkland built up with homes ranging from comfortable to Italianate mansions at prices ranging from $75,000 to $250,000, a fraction of what the same houses would cost in many other parts of the country. Joggers in expensive sweatsuits and running shoes pounded along the streets. The prices were lower around Palmer Park—named for U.S. Senator Thomas Palmer, who donated these 600 grassy acres to the city in 1893—which looked like hundreds of other rich neighborhoods in America. Except that the joggers were all black. The local precinct house, just off Woodward, with the sign saying: "Commander: Inspector Willis," looked about the same as any other in the United States. Except that Billie Willis is a black woman.

Nine miles from the river, the buildings along Woodward were fewer and lower. There were more white faces along the street—fewer faces than parked cars, though—as I finally left the city and was in a suburb called Ferndale. I could have been anywhere in America; Woodward Avenue there began on the

Sunrise Highway on Long Island and ended on Little Santa Monica Boulevard in Los Angeles. My American mind relaxed in the familiarity of passing gas stations and liquor stores and donut shops and a Taco Bell. I know, actually, that they were not passing; I was passing them. But what did it matter? The endless suburb. Home. America.

"Detroit's newest and handsomest suburb!"—that was the come-on in the 1890s, when Ferndale was being promoted as a development called Urbanrest. Lots sold for $17 up then, with an additional 60-cent charge for each fruit tree. "I think urban sprawl might be the first thing Tocqueville would notice if he were traveling now," said David Riesman, the Harvard professor who had written about the Frenchman's travels as well as writing *The Lonely Crowd.* "This is the only country whose living patterns were determined by real estate speculation." People moved wherever houses were built, and houses were built wherever other people could buy up land, preferably land with a couple of fruit trees.*

In a way, Tocqueville had seen the beginnings of the way Americans would choose to cover the countryside. "Nothing even resembles our villages," he wrote on his way to Detroit, noting that every settlement he saw, rich or poor, seemed a similar product of American spirit and custom. "The plane of a uniform civilization has passed over it."

"Everybody wants pretty much the same things in a house," said David Jensen, manager of a Chamberlain Realty office in the northwest suburbs. "Some of the men moved in here by their companies don't even look at the houses; they're the same as the ones they left. I've dealt with men who are sixty years old and their companies have transferred them to 17 cities. They don't care about charm or anything like that. They want security, which means they want to be away from the blacks, and they want minimum inconvenience. You hear a lot about people not moving because both the husband and wife are working, but that's the exception. They keep moving in and out of here just

* That little history of Ferndale and some other details concerning Woodward Avenue came to my attention in an article called "Walking Woodward" by Don Kubit, which was published in *Monthly Detroit* magazine in August 1980.

like they used to—every three or five years—and some of them, I swear, don't even know what town they're living in."

Five miles farther, past the suburb of Royal Oak, there was a small stone marker alongside Woodward, overgrown with weeds. "During the early summer of 1818," it read, "the first white men to systematically explore this region camped near this spot on the first night they spent in what is now Oakland County."

The road, still called Woodward Avenue, became a parkway 15 miles from where I had begun the trip. There were clusters of housing, developments built by speculators among the small hills, growing together to become suburbs. But as I went along the houses stood farther apart, hidden among low hills and high trees. This was Bloomfield Hills, where, I was told, land prices began at $150,000 an acre. Soon enough the name Woodward had disappeared and the old trail began to have different names as I moved along. I had traveled 27 miles and was in Pontiac, a gritty city of 76,700 people, named for a chief of the Ottawa Indians who led a revolt against British troops in the 1760s, but better known as the name of a line of General Motors' cars.

"Twenty very neat and pretty houses, forming so many well furnished shops, a transparent stream, a clearing a quarter of a league square, and the eternal forest about: there is the faithful tableau of Pontiac which in twenty years, perhaps, will be a city.*

"We had ourselves taken to the finest inn in Pontiac (for there are two), and we were introduced, as usual, into what is called the barroom; it's a room where you are given to drink and where the simplest as well as the richest traders of the place come to smoke, drink and talk politics together, on the footing of the most perfect exterior equality.

"He"—the innkeeper, Amasa Bagley—"led us into another room, spread with appropriate deliberation a map of Michigan on the oak table in the middle of the room and, putting the can-

* At this point, the account of Tocqueville's journey is not from his notebooks but from *"Quinze Jours au Désert"*—Fifteen Days in the Wilderness—a narrative that he wrote in August of 1831. It was not published until 1860 and is included in Pierson's *Tocqueville and Beaumont in America* (see Notes, p. 377).

dle between us three, waited in impassive silence for what we had to communicate to him. . . .

" 'You want to go to Saginaw!' cried he, 'to Saginaw Bay! Two reasonable men, two well educated foreigners want to go to Saginaw Bay! . . . do you realize what you are undertaking? Do you know that Saginaw is the last inhabited place till the Pacific Ocean; that from here to Saginaw hardly anything but wilderness and pathless solitudes are to be found?' "

There were still two inns on the route through Pontiac as I came by on a Saturday evening. The transparent stream, though, was now underground, part of the small city's sewerage system. The old road was called Route 10, the Dixie Highway; it was, before the construction of the federal interstate highway system after World War II, one of the line of state and local roads that led to Florida. There were two men in the barroom of the Holiday Inn, both watching a televised motorcycle race from San Jose, California. In the Delta Queen Lounge of the Sheraton Inn down the road, there was only one patron, a man watching a science fiction show, "Star Trek." Not a word was spoken in either place.

A huge painting of Jesus Christ, more than 20 feet high, loomed over the highway north of Pontiac, placed there by the Dixie Baptist Church with the legend: "Are You on the Right Road?" I was. Michigan Route 10 eventually became U. S. Route 475, a six-lane, controlled-access interstate highway through rolling land with a few stands of trees and modest homes—developments made possible by the new roads that reduced travel time between many points in the United States by more than half in only a little more than ten years. I was the beneficiary of a stunning $80-billion achievement of government and engineering, which made it possible for Americans to live farther from their workplace than any people in the world, created new towns, even cities, and reduced the national traffic fatality rate to 1.55 per hundred million miles traveled from the 6.28 per hundred million miles recorded before the first seven miles of the 42,500-mile system were opened in Kansas in 1956.

The highways—free highways that in some places connected with existing state toll roads—had been authorized in 1944 as a defense measure to facilitate the movement of military vehicles in case of war. The federal government agreed to pay 50 percent of the cost, but once construction began that share was quickly raised to 90 percent. The money came from taxes on gasoline and automobiles and all the parts that went into the machine Henry Ford had first mass-produced. There was no war at home, of course. But there was a revolution: Americans had more freedom to live where they wanted and millions of them chose not to live where they had been, in cities like Detroit. The old cities were drained, first of people, the local taxpayers, then of commerce and manufacturing, as shops and factories relocated along the sprawling roads. Innovative Americans were on the move again. A man on roads like this—speeding along at 70 miles per hour even though the posted limit was 55—could get from Detroit to New York, or Atlanta, or St. Louis in the nine hours it had taken Tocqueville and Beaumont to travel the 22 miles from the edge of the city to Pontiac.

"We pursued our way in the woods," Tocqueville wrote. "From time to time a small lake (this district is full of them) appears like a sheet of silver under the forest foliage. It is difficult to imagine the charm which surrounds these pretty places. . . .

"This valley where I found myself seemed to form an immense amphitheater, surrounded by the foliage of the woods on all sides, as by black drapery, in whose center the rays of the moon, breaking, came to create a thousand fantastic beings which played with each other silently . . . three quarters of an hour from there we finally caught sight of a clearing, two or three cabins and, what pleased us even more, a light. . . .

"Soon, in fact, the baying of dogs made the woods ring and we found ourselves before a log house, separated from it by a single barrier. As we were preparing to cross it, the moon showed us on the other side a great black bear which, upright on its hind feet and drawing its chain in, showed as clearly as it could its intention to give us a fraternal accolade.

"What a devilish country is this, said I, where they have bears for watchdogs. . . .

"We shouted then, at the top of our lungs and so well that a man finally put his head out the window. After having examined us in the moonlight,—Enter gentlemen, said he. Trink, go lie down! To your kennel, I say, these are not thieves."

That was Flint, Michigan. The man with the bear was John Todd, Flint's first settler. The site of his cabin is in the center of the city—a declining city of 160,000 where 60 percent of the male population have traditionally worked for one employer, General Motors. The point at which Tocqueville crossed the Flint River became Saginaw Street. The river itself was contained in concrete banks. There was, as I crossed, a red-white-and-blue sign reading: "Flint River Flood Control and River Beautification Project. Cost: $22,073,872." A federal project, a concrete and wood park planned as part of downtown redevelopment, and the city's share of the project was listed as $6,375,400.

I saw a hard, dreary town, a working-man's town of white men and black men who traced their roots to the pre–World War II South and earned, on the average, the highest industrial wages in the United States. When they worked—for the fortunes of Flint went up and down with auto sales and they were going down as the 1980s began. In 1967, a hundred white men wearing the robes and sashes of the Ku Klux Klan marched down Saginaw Street as blacks rioted in the city. The riots were calmed by the mayor of Flint, Floyd McCree, a Buick foreman, a black man.

"A wilderness of fifteen leagues separates Flint River from Saginaw, and the road there is only a narrow path, scarcely recognizable to the eye. Our host approved of our plan, and soon after he brought us two Indians in whom he assured us we could place every confidence. . . . One had carefully painted on his face lines of black and red in the most symmetrical way; a ring passed through the membrane of his nose, a necklace and earrings completed his apparel. His accoutrements of war were no less remarkable. On one side the battle-axe, the celebrated tomahawk; on the other a long sharp knife, with whose aid the savages lift the scalps of the vanquished. . . .

"The American, hastening to speak, told us what the savage asked would be valued at two dollars. As these poor Indians, added our host charitably, do not know the value of money, you will give me the dollars and I shall willingly undertake to furnish him with the equivalent.

"I was curious to see what the worthy man called the equivalent of two dollars, and I followed him very softly to the place where the bargain was consummated. I saw him deliver our guide a pair of moccasins and a pocket handkerchief, objects whose total value certainly did not reach half the sum. . . .

"Furthermore, it's not only the Indians whom the American pioneers take for dupes. We were ourselves daily victims of their extreme avidity for gain. It's very true they do not steal, they are too enlightened to commit such an imprudence. . . ."

Then Saginaw—and wonder:

"Each of these trees rises by the shortest way to seek the air and the light. As straight as the mast of a vessel, it shoots up beyond all the surrounding forest, and it is only in the upper regions that it tranquilly spreads its branches and envelops itself in their shade. Others soon follow it into that elevated sphere and all, interlacing their branches, form, as it were, an immense dais, above the earth which bears them. . . . A majestic order reigns above your head. . . .

"In a few years these impenetrable forests will have fallen, the noise of civilization and of industry will break the silence of the Saginaw. Docks will imprison its banks: its waters which today flow unknown and tranquil through a nameless wilderness will be thrust back in their flow by the prows of vessels."

So it was. The virgin forest was raped. The woods were the greatest stand of white pine on the face of the earth—"Green Gold!" In thirty years, from the 1860s to the 1890s, the Americans leveled the wilderness, braving the marshes and malaria, taking out more than 23 billion board feet of lumber from the valley of the Saginaw to frame a civilization. Everything was leveled, old trees and young, big and small; no shoots, no seeds were left for renewal. It was gone, over. That was the American way: Use it and move on—like nomads.

The Michigan lumbering boom netted four billion dollars, one billion dollars more than the California gold rush. Saginaw thrived and then survived—sort of. The settlement of thirty men, women, and children—Americans, French Canadians, Indians, and half-breeds—which Tocqueville and Beaumont found on the Saginaw River became a boom town in the lumbering days, grew into a prosperous automotive manufacturing city, and declined into a place where, when I was there, the grandest downtown hotel, the Bancroft, required guests to leave their driver's licenses and three-dollar deposits to get room keys. The hotel was one of the sights from the bridge over the river where Tocqueville had launched a dugout canoe and lost himself in reveries of peaceful majesty. I saw one of the ugliest spots in America. The west bank was gray with tired buildings, their sides painted with advertisements for places and things that no longer exist: the Temple Theater, Showplace of Northeastern Michigan; Swan Ice Cream; Michigan National Bank; and Feigens Furniture. The east bank was newer, a bit more colorful with brighter signs for Garver Buick, Carpet Barn, Taco Bell, and Montgomery Ward. The city, with a population of 77,500 in 1980, showed its gratitude for Tocqueville's description of its primeval splendor by modeling its federal building, which became the Saginaw County Building, dedicated on July 4, 1898, after Château de Tocqueville, the family home in Normandy.

"I am going to describe them here once and for all . . ." Tocqueville wrote of the homes and the men who made America, "as these establishments bear a perfect resemblance to each other, whether they are to be found in the depths of Michigan or at the gate of New York.

"The bell the pioneer is careful to hang around the necks of his cattle in order to be able to find them in the thick woods announces from afar the approach to the clearing. Soon you hear the ringing of the axe. . . . You proceed and come into a wood all of whose trees seem to have been struck by sudden death; in midsummer their branches still present only the image of winter. On examining them more closely you perceive that they have been circled by a deep trench cut in the bark, which, arresting the flow of sap, has not been slow to make them die. It's really with all this that the planter usually begins. Being incapable the first year of cutting all the trees which garnish his new property he sows corn under their branches and, by killing them, prevents their shading his crop.

"After this field, the rough sketch, the first step in civilization in the wilderness, you suddenly perceive the cabin of the proprietor. It is generally placed in the center of a piece of land more carefully cultivated than the rest but where man still sustains an unequal struggle against nature. . . .

"Like the surrounding field this rustic dwelling betrays recent and hasty work. Its length rarely exceeds thirty feet. It is twenty wide, fifteen high. The walls, like the roof, are formed of un-squared tree trunks, between which moss and earth have been placed to prevent the cold and rain penetrating into the interior of the house. . . .

"Generally, this cabin has only one single window, on which is sometimes hung a muslin curtain. . . . On the hearth of trodden earth flames a resinous fire which better than daylight illumi-nates the interior of the building. Above this rustic hearth tro-phies of war or the hunt are to be seen: a long rifle, a deerskin, eagle feathers. On the right of the chimney is stretched a map of the United States which the wind, coming in through the cracks of the wall, ceaselessly lifts and agitates. Near it, on a solitary shelf of badly squared boards, are placed some ill-assorted books; there you find a Bible whose cover and edges are already worn by the piety of two generations, a book of prayers, and some-times a song of Milton or a tragedy of Shakespeare. Along the wall are ranged some rude benches, fruit of the proprietor's in-dustry: trunks instead of clothes cupboards, farming tools, and some samples of the harvest. In the center of the room stands a table whose uneven legs, still garnished with foliage, seem to have grown from the soil where it stands. It's there that the whole family comes together for meals. A teapot of English por-celain, spoons most often of wood, a few chipped cups, and some newspapers are there to be seen.

"The appearance of the master of the house is no less remark-able than the place that serves him as asylum. The angular mus-cles and long thin arms and legs make you recognize at first glance the native of New England. This man was not born in the solitude where he dwells: his constitution alone proclaims that. His first years were passed in the bosom of an intellectual and reasoning society. It's his own desire that has thrown him into the labors of the wilderness for which he does not seem made . . . to become well-to-do he has braved exile, the loneliness and the numberless miseries of the savage life, he has slept on the bare ground, he has exposed himself to the forest fevers and the toma-hawk of the Indian. . . .

"Intent on the one goal of making his fortune, the emigrant has finally created for himself an altogether individual existence.

Family sentiments have come to fuse themselves in a vast egoism, and it is doubtful if in his wife and children he sees anything
else than a detached portion of himself. . . .

"This unknown man is the representative of a race to which
belongs the future of the new world: a restless, reasoning, adventurous race which does coldly what only the ardour of passion
can explain; a race cold and passionate, which trafficks in everything, not excepting morality and religion; a nation of conquerors who submit themselves to the savage life without ever allowing themselves to be seduced by it, who in civilization and
enlightenment love only what is useful to well-being, and who
shut themselves in the American solitudes with an axe and some
newspapers.

"A people, which like all great peoples, has but one thought,
and which is advancing toward the acquisition of riches, sole
goal of its efforts, with a perseverance and a scorn for life that
one might call heroic, if that name fitted other than virtuous
things.

"It's this nomad people which the rivers and lakes do not stop,
before which the forests fall and the prairies are covered with
shade, and which, after having reached the Pacific ocean, will
reverse its steps to trouble and destroy the societies which it will
have formed behind it."

14

GREEN BAY

"Puritan Republic to Selfish Democracy ..."

Tocqueville had been wrong about Saginaw. It was not really the last American outpost of civilization. Americans had moved farther west by then, into what was to become the middle of the country. A newspaper was already being published more than a thousand miles to the west, in Santa Fe, and there were already more than a thousand people, fifty of them Americans, living at a place on the Pacific Ocean called *El Pueblo de Nuestra Señora la Reina de Los Angeles*. But that was Spanish, and, since 1822, Mexican territory; the Frenchman, as American history itself would, accepted the English version of the settlement of the new continent.

He was wrong, of course, or partly wrong about many things. He underestimated the potential power and reach of the executive branch of the new government, of the President and the millions of administrators who would one day act in the name of that office. Bureaus were relentlessly created and oaths taken again and again to protect the rights of individual Americans. And new rights were found to protect. When Tocqueville was in Saginaw in 1831, there were fewer than a thousand civilian employees of the federal government; when I was there, the number was approaching three million.*

* In 1980, the total number of government employees at all levels was 15,971,000, according to statistics compiled by *U. S. News & World*

In Saginaw, the very long, strong arm of Washington had reached the squash courts of a local club. Government had threatened to close down the courts there, as in other places, if the small doors leading onto them were not modified to accommodate people in wheelchairs.

My questions about courts—of squash, not law—led me back to the Department of Health, Education and Welfare in Washington and to its interpretation of a sentence in the Rehabilitation Act of 1973: "No otherwise qualified handicapped individual . . . shall, solely by reason of his handicap, be excluded from participation in . . . any program or activity receiving federal financial assistance." By then, three-quarters of the *state* agencies in the country were wholly or partly financed by federal funds; since then, in half the states, including Michigan, new law had been written extending that clause to include all buildings and facilities used by the public—including racquet clubs. The federal program—requiring ramps, elevators, lowered telephone booths, and other facilities needed by Americans in wheelchairs—was administered in Washington by the Architectural and Transportation Barriers Compliance Board of the Department of Health, Education and Welfare. Larry Allison, a spokesman for that board, informed me that its estimates indicated that 70 million Americans might qualify as "handicapped." That was one out of three people in the United States—including me, it turned out, because of an eye injury I had forgotten many years ago. "All have a lively faith in human perfectibility," Tocqueville had written of the Americans; he had expanded on that thought in a short chapter with a headline dry enough to imply satire: "How Equality Suggests to the Americans the Idea of the Indefinite Perfectibility of Man."

Certainly a great deal of American law and custom seemed to be based on that idea, both charming and powerful. If all men and women were created equal, obviously each had the right to play squash. And the right to a perfect body—on the roads along Saginaw Bay, in what is now Bay City, more than 1,500 citizens

---

Report magazine. There were only 13 million people in the United States when Tocqueville visited. The 1980 figures were 2,869,000 federal employees, 3,699,000 state employees, and 9,403,000 local, county, and regional governmental employees. The largest number of those civil servants were teachers.

were grimacing in apparent agony in a quest for self-improvement in the little city's first marathon. The idea, to Tocqueville, had continuing implications, as he mentioned in a letter to a friend as he was traveling in New York State: "The idea of perfection, of a continuous and endless amelioration of social conditions, this idea is presented to the American unceasingly, in all its aspects." Perfectibility, though, was an expensive idea to enforce when it was applied to things like the social conditions of the physically handicapped. But the federal government began trying to do just that in the 1970s, and a lively political debate inevitably began—the First Law of Democratic Physics was working—over the common sense of federal orders requiring cities to spend $400,000 each for buses that could kneel down in the front to accept wheelchairs.*

Bay City—50,000 people living near the point where the Saginaw River runs into Saginaw Bay on Lake Huron—was the place where the lumber of Michigan passed through on its way across the Great Lakes to become the houses of America from New York City to every settlement along the Mississippi River. "It's a beer-and-shot town," said David Rogers, who was born there, and grew up to become editorial-page editor of the *Bay City Times*, the local paper—which was owned by the Newhouse chain. "Beer. Bowling. And work. The city is very ethnic. More than 50 percent Catholic. People don't move in and out very much. . . . It's very conservative here. There is a little public housing, but the neighbors harass the people in projects— shouting 'Welfare Cheat!' or not talking to them at all. . . . There are only 1,500 black people in the whole county. No one likes to talk about it, but new industry has really been discouraged here because people think it would bring more black people.

* In the summer of 1981, the federal government began relaxing many of its regulations concerning the rights of the handicapped, after the U. S. Court of Appeals ruled—in a suit brought by David and Rhea Dopico, on behalf of a group of handicapped New Yorkers—that public transportation did not have to be "fully accessible" to all. But neither the courts nor the federal government fundamentally questioned the right of equal access. They debated only how far and expensively public and private agencies were required to go to make "appropriate efforts" for the handicapped—for instance, giving them the money to hire taxis for transportation as the moral equivalent of kneeling buses.

"It's funny, though," he said as we drove along Center Street, blocks of large Victorian houses built by owners of the lumber companies. "One of the biggest houses along here was just sold to James Weldon Baker, who's my paper's attorney. He's black." I wasn't surprised. I thought, perhaps too facilely: Baker can be rich, Baker can be perfect; what he can't be is white; he can be in the majority only by accepting its rules.

Tocqueville and Beaumont retraced their trail from Saginaw Bay back to Detroit. On the day they returned they learned that a steamboat, the *Superior*, was scheduled for a ten-day excursion around the Lower Peninsula of Michigan, up the St. Clair River and then north on Lake Huron, passing onto Lake Michigan and crossing it southward to Fort Howard at a place called Green Bay. Bad weather kept them two days at Fort Gratiot (which became the small city of Port Huron, Michigan), where the St. Clair meets Lake Huron.*

On the lake, the passengers amused themselves by watching the crew throw potatoes overboard and then seeing the things drop slowly 40 feet and more in the clear water. When I was at the same place, the waters were not that clear, but, I was told again and again, they were much better than they had been 15 years before, when silt and muck choked off the fish of the area. In that time the federal government had forced (and largely financed) projects that local and state governments had rejected, the construction of sewage treatment plants along the Great Lakes—and fishermen were catching Coho salmon and perch again in the lake and in the St. Clair and Saginaw Rivers.

On their trip around those lakes, the Frenchmen's most en-

---

* The *Superior* anchored for two days off the Fort Gratiot lighthouse, which was still in use when I came through in 1979. A little more than twenty years after Tocqueville's visit, the lighthouse got a new keeper, a man named Samuel Edison, who had a small son people called Alva. Thomas Alva Edison, who grew up in Port Huron, was to become the personification of this Tocquevillian insight into Americans: "For people in this frame of mind every new way of getting wealth more quickly, every machine which lessens work, every means of diminishing the costs of production, every invention which makes pleasures easier or greater, seems the most magnificent achievement of the human mind . . . more profit will be made out of discoveries immediately applicable to industry, bringing renown and even power to their inventors."

gaging companion was a zealous Catholic priest named James Ignatius Mullon, who planned to stop off at Michilimackinac Island, where Lake Huron meets Lake Superior, to debate Protestants, something he dearly loved to do. "These Presbyterians are wicked as vipers," Father Mullon said to Tocqueville and Beaumont, "you crush their heads and they rise on their tails."

Roman Catholicism, the priest said, was thriving under this democracy. "All religious beliefs are on the same footing here," he said. "The government neither sustains nor persecutes any one; and doubtless there is not a country in the world where the Catholic religion counts adherents more fervent and proselytes more numerous. I repeat, the less religion and its ministers are mixed with civil government, the less part will they take in political dissensions, and the more power religious ideas will gain."

"At bottom as intolerant as they have ever been, as intolerant in a word as people who believe," Tocqueville had written of his fellow Catholics after meeting a few of them in his first days in the United States. That impression hadn't been shaken in Detroit, where he had talked with Father Gabriel Richard, priest, publisher of the first newspaper in Michigan, and a territorial delegate to Congress. "Their sects are without number. There are now 450 of them, they don't believe anything at all, they're neither Episcopalians nor Methodists nor Presbyterians: they are *rienists!*" Father Richard said of the Protestant majority, expanding the French word meaning "nothing."

Yet the Protestants Tocqueville challenged about the growth of Catholicism reacted without passion. In Boston, Joseph Coolidge, a shipping merchant and husband of Thomas Jefferson's granddaughter, said: "We are not afraid of Catholicism in the United States because we are persuaded that here it will modify itself so that it will have no influence on our political *moeurs.*"

Tocqueville doubted that. So did I. I had not been raised a Catholic, but I had been raised in a Catholic city—Jersey City, New Jersey—and even though I had not been to mass in twenty years, I remembered, as I walked into St. Agnes Church in Green Bay, Wisconsin, the soaring darkness of the churches I knew and the fear and guilt of Catholic friends who had to know them better.

From the outside, St. Agnes Church was a pleasant building of brick and glass, set off by a big parking lot on a street of modern one-family homes. Inside, I was struck by the light: sunlight streamed through high windows onto more than a thousand worshipers. They were in polo shirts and slacks, some in shorts, the costumes of America in summer. A high-school gymnasium— that was what the yellow brick, the light, and the casual crowd reminded me of, a high school gymnasium. Someone was playing a xylophone. Three young people were strumming guitars. We stood and sang a song, a bouncy little number with words that went, "The Spirit is A'Moving All Over, All Over the World." There were only two statues in the church—if they could be called that, simple wooden representations of Christ on the cross and of his mother, Mary. Behind the altar, which was really just a raised platform, there was brightly colored tapestry with a dove and a cross in a jumbled pattern of almost childlike letters which spelled: "We Are One in the Spirit of the Father, the Son and the Holy Ghost."

The priest, who seemed very young and smiled as he spoke, had an enormous head of tightly curled blond hair, a blond Afro, the kind that is shaped in beauty parlors, and he wore a bright red robe decorated with a white dove. The church bulletin, complete with two pages of advertisements for restaurants, insurance, travel agencies, A&W Root Beer, and Budweiser, offered these thoughts: "Think you've been shortchanged in life? . . . Look at the bright side: you have the Spirit. The Spirit caused a public sensation one day two thousand years ago in Jerusalem. The same Spirit can cause a sensation in your life today. Don't hold yourself back for fear of being different. The world can use all the Spirit-filled people it can get." There was a modern drawing of Christ in the booklet; He was kneeling, but the parishioners never did. At the end of the mass—we were standing—the man next to me turned suddenly and thrust his hand at me with a smile. I had to force myself not to flinch. He said, "Have a nice day!" It was all part of the ritual: the greeting of peace.

I left St. Agnes humming—and stunned. I had been aware that Vatican Councils in the early 1960s had allowed a liberalization of the Church's liturgical rules and that the mass was being said in English and had become more colloquial. What I hadn't known was that colloquy would sound like the dialogue and conversation of a small college dramatic society. It was as if I were Rip Van Winkle, asleep for twenty years. I had dozed off, kneeling, to the smell of incense and the sound of murmuring Latin in a majestic gray light. I woke in the middle of this peppy fun. Let's hear it for the Spirit! Even Presbyterians—those *rienists!*—would have looked down on this. *Roman* Catholic? This was an American church—as American as Budweiser and A&W Root Beer.

I couldn't believe it. St. Agnes was the largest Catholic Church in a very Catholic city, but I had to find another one—a real one! I went downtown to the gray center of the old working city, through streets of warehouses and stores that seemed not to have changed at all in those twenty years, to St. Willebrord's, the old cathedral. It looked more like a church—dark, Gothic. The parishioners, many standing because the pews were all filled, were older and more formally dressed. The priest was young, a tall, handsome man in a beard and white robes. "Hey!" he was saying as I walked in. "Hey, I've accepted Christ . . . The Spirit shows itself through, through what? Through sharing! Through giving yourself to others, Through being open. . . ."

This was Roman Catholicism in Green Bay. The determined and dogmatic church with an awesome history of its own had done just what Joseph Coolidge had thought it would do 150 years before. The church, not America, modified itself. What I had seen was a reformed church, more American than Roman. It was . . . "nice"; the masses I saw were celebrations and they were, amazingly, celebrations of what researchers and sociologists had been telling me were the "new values." The guitar, rather than the organ, provided suitable backup for these pleasant young men urging parishioners to be different, to be themselves, to be open, to share. "The old values are being destroyed," Barry Bingham had said in Louisville. "They begin by saying, 'do your own thing' . . ."

Value systems, new and old, are of course in the eye of the beholder. Daniel Yankelovich, president of the firm doing research for newspapers around the country, tried to describe the old and new value structures in a 1978 essay which touched on some of the things and themes I had seen: " . . . We see the beginnings of an ethic built around the concept of duty to oneself, in glaring contrast to the traditional ethic of obligation to others. In reaching for 'something more than success,' (they) also press for greater freedom for the individual—freedom to express impulses and desires that people have been accustomed to suppress. Sexual desires are the most obvious, hence the greater openness of homosexuality, pornography, nakedness, and casual sexual encounters. But other forms of freedom 'to do what I want to do' are almost as prominent: freedom to enjoy life now rather than in some distant future; freedom to elevate one's own desires to the rank of entitlements; freedom to give one's own ego more room in which to maneuver; freedom to pull up stakes and move on without having to pick up the pieces."*

What changed those values?

"Freud" was the answer I had usually gotten when I asked that question.

" 'Let it all hang out' and other idiocies have been elevated to values by the popularizers of psychology," said David Riesman of Harvard, who had written perceptively about the impact of Freud and psychology in general on American behavior and ethics. "When Freud appeared we didn't have the intellectual ballast to deal with his ideas. We went overboard from the beginning. So it would be more correct to say that it was not Freud, but misinterpretations of Freud which have had profound impact in the United States."

Sigmund Freud, the Viennese founder of psychoanalysis, would not have sought credit for any American values. "America is gigantic," he said after his one visit, in 1909, "but a gigantic mistake." He was also appalled, according to his friend and biographer Fritz Wittels, by wild American enthusiasm for his ideas and believed, prophetically, that "this craze would preserve little more of his life's work than the name and the most elementary connections. . . ."

He was a smart man—something like that seemed to have happened. "Freud," as I heard it used repeatedly, was the name not of a man but of a body of confused ideas and pressures. "Freud," in those conversations, stood for almost anything that challenged or displaced the old values seen or imagined by the

* Yankelovich's essay, "Work, Values, and the New Breed," appeared in *Work in America: The Decade Ahead*, Clark Kerr and Jerome Rosow, eds. (Van Nostrand and Reinhold, New York, 1979), pp. 3-34.

speaker. This "Freud" was practically all things to all men—the word encompassed the swirling impact, interpretations, and random misinterpretations of the most prominent of the great thinkers whose views began reshaping much of the world as the nineteenth century turned into the twentieth. What seemed so threatening, and enticing, to Americans then was the suggestion that people somehow were not responsible for their own behavior, that they were somehow controlled by mysterious forces—unconscious or psychological (or sexual!) forces in the analyses of Sigmund Freud, and economic imperatives in the analyses of Karl Marx. During the same period, the biological research and theories of Charles Darwin, which have more than once been challenged in American courts, went so far as to challenge, in the eyes of many, the teachings of the Bible itself. By the time I traveled, those ideas, those new ways of looking at the world and each other, had essentially been absorbed into the experiences and characters of Americans—even if, in 1981, the state of Arkansas was in its own courts trying to prove that God created the earth in six days and rested on the seventh. Part of that process of dealing with new information—a very American part and a very American method—was, as far as I could tell, to personalize it. The American way, as often as not, was to reduce concepts and movements to personalities for mass consumption. The personality for this mélange of ideas, information and misinformation, "values," and "life styles" was the Viennese doctor with a goatee and pince-nez glasses, "Freud."

Psychology in all its manifestations, from the profound to the idiotic, seemed irresistible to Americans. In the 1970s there were more than 31,000 psychiatrists in the United States, compared with an estimated 1,000 in France. In a society founded and deeply influenced by Puritans, there was bound to be a response to an artful science that seemed capable of casting out the devils of mind and spirit, bringing a man or woman along the lively paths of American perfectibility. The whole idea of the thing could have been American: it was both democratic and individualistic; the answers did not come from a God or anyone else in high office, the answers were within each of us. What Freud did was to legitimize and, eventually, institutionalize an emphasis on the individual and self. American democracy did just about the same thing. "In the long run," Tocqueville wrote, "I am sure that democracy turns man's imagination away from externals to concentrate it on himself alone. . . . It is about themselves that [the Americans] are really excited."

The democracy and the psychoanalyst were made for each other. They were synergistic. The press and the entertainment business spotted that almost immediately. Psychology and psychiatry were aggressively processed through the marvelous machinery of American mass information and mass culture—in newspaper headlines, magazine articles, and popular films. Magazines from *Good Housekeeping* to the *New Republic* began inflating Freud and psychoanalysis as both a cure for most of man's illnesses and a poison for God's reign. In 1924, the largest newspapers in the country offered to pay Freud any price he would name to psychoanalyze famous murderers, while filling their columns with sensational information and misinformation about therapy, complexes, fantasies, neuroses, psychoses, inhibitions, and repressions. In that year, one of America's most successful film producers, Samuel Goldwyn, set sail for Europe announcing that he intended to offer a screenwriting contract to "the greatest love specialist in the world," Professor Sigmund Freud.

Making money from ideas—that was an American reaction that Tocqueville would have understood. The Frenchman might have thrown the whole "new values" system—or those many value systems—into what he saw as the vague American stew of pecuniary Protestantism. Some things here struck him as extraordinary, not because he was perceptive but because he was French. His views of multiplying sects—routine stuff to an American—have to be considered in the context of his country of one true faith. So he wrote to a friend: "It's incredible to see the infinite number of subdivisions into which the sects of America have split . . . each new sect separates a little further, while nearing pure Deism. . . . The reformed religion is a sort of compromise.

"The Catholic faith is the immovable point from which each sect separates a little further . . . like circles traced successively about the same point, each new one a little farther away from the next. . . ." he went on, foreseeing continuing tension between the hard center of Catholicism and the Deists, those who sort of believed in a Higher Authority, the Americans Father

Richard called *rienists*. From what I observed, the center had not held. Catholicism—at least much of American Catholicism—had been compromised; the church of Tocqueville's fathers had become part of the outer circle. That circle, in the America I traveled, included everyone from the happily singing Catholics of Green Bay to the tolerant folk of mainstream Protestantism to Freudian antireligionists. The word "antireligion" had been suggested to me in Rochester by Christopher Lasch, the pessimistic historian. "Economic man himself has given way to the psychological man of our times—the final product of bourgeois individualism," he wrote. "Therapy constitutes an antireligion . . . the hope of achieving the modern equivalent of salvation, 'mental health.' "

But what was the new center? I had been hearing the voices of it as I traveled across the country. Protestant Fundamentalism was the immovable point, and the radio preachers I had been hearing everywhere spoke for a hard, truly American center. Those ministers and many thousands of others—the "hawkers" of religion who had amused Tocqueville—spoke to and for many millions of Americans who took their religions seriously, their Bibles literally, and who publicly, often pugnaciously, proclaimed themselves Christians, sometimes announcing that fact to strangers at the beginning of conversations. They were the spiritual ancestors of Americans who astounded Tocqueville by voting, in many towns, to post the names of heavy drinkers in taverns so that any barkeeper serving them could be punished; they were called, and called themselves, by many names—Fundamentalists, evangelicals, charismatics, "Born Agains." The last phrase, denoting a new spiritual birth after a personal experience with Christ, indicated, at least to me, that the movement was another variation on American democratic individualism—each born-again Christian was claiming one-on-one communication with Higher Authority.

Ninety percent of the American people told pollsters that they believed in God and 85 percent considered the Bible His word—that's what I had heard on the radio back in Newport—so there was and had always been fertile ground in the New World for this kind of very basic Christianity. "Sunday is rigorously observed," Tocqueville wrote, ". . . public opinion, much stronger than the law, obliges everyone to show himself at church and abstain from all diversions. And yet, either I am much mistaken or there is a great depth of doubt and indifference hidden under these external forms." Except that I would have mentioned that shopping had become Sunday's most rigorous activity, I could have written that same last sentence. But I also saw that the external forms, the professions of religion, tended to increase as the value system of traditional Christianity was publicly questioned or threatened. And in the mid–twentieth century, those "old values" had been successfully challenged within churches themselves—first in the mainstream Protestant churches that had evolved from the Puritan congregations of New England, then in Catholic churches too.

"The old Protestantism of individualism and work was replaced by a social ethic and that was very disturbing to many people," said Kristor Stendahl, dean of Harvard Divinity School. "American religious thinkers, particularly Reinhold Niebuhr, defined that social ethic, which was basically that just making people guilty wasn't good enough for religion. That does nothing for hungry people. The new ethic redefined evil, as it were, to a corporate evil—the evil of having poor people in America. It was quite distinct from the old American Christianity. . . .

"So religion, particularly Protestantism, was no longer a common denominator in the society. Instead of a glue, it's become one of the wellsprings of sensitivity, of maturity, of vitality. . . . It can give its adherents an identity within the larger unit. They can become part of a community within the community, in this case a community of faith. . . . More and more, the young people we attract are searching for community rather than values."

But the Divinity School really doesn't attract that many people—about 300 people apply each year compared with 7,000 applicants at Harvard Law School—and faith based on "sensitizing" and a sense of societal evil has always been rejected by significant numbers of Americans. "I'm a bit of a Fundamentalist myself," said Richard Nixon, a former President who was raised as a Quaker. "When religion started talking about the masses rather than about what it could do for the individual, then religion went—" He thrust his thumbs down and made a noise something like "Phfffft!"

"The rise of Fundamentalism," he said as we talked in New York City, "is a reaction to the social gospel, which is really a decay of religion, of religious values. The social gospel and the introduction of psychological jargon into religion led to the whole attitude that you're not responsible for your own actions. . . ."

Again! The last part of that sentence must have been repeated in half the conversations I heard as I traveled. Talking about politics, religion, or psychology, work, welfare or justice, Americans, white and black, religious and antireligious, politically liberal and conservative, as often as not would end thoughts with words like . . . "people don't feel responsible for their own actions anymore."

"The worst thing that's happening in America is that abhorrent behavior can always be explained now," said Robert Schrank, a former laborer and labor union official who was writing studies of work for the Ford Foundation. "It's dangerous to somehow apply Freudian thinking to justify people acting out their hostilities by stealing. But now it's explained. 'I'm not responsible because my mother and father didn't like me and I was brought up in a terrible way' . . . In a democracy, if the individual isn't responsible then we're finished as a free people. If the individual isn't responsible, then the government becomes responsible for behavior. Freedom will be lost because the government is then going to regulate behavior and tell people what to do and what not to do. The perfect example of that is the welfare system—in return for payments, the government claims the right to regulate behavior and the people on welfare develop their own culture to try to beat the system."

The government's regulation of behavior—partly an attempt to transform the social gospel, a gospel of perfectibility, into official action—inevitably brought two great American forces of the twentieth century, religion and antireligion, into political conflict. That clash, which I have greatly simplified and somewhat distorted by representing the opposing forces as "Freud" and "Fundamentalism," was at the heart of the continuing struggles over the relationship between the national government and the individual. If students at Cornell University—and many other Americans I interviewed—guiltlessly believed that "the government" was responsible for the care of elderly parents, the roots of those beliefs may have gone back to the time their parents were born. "The Roosevelt years and the efforts to deal with the Depression changed the psychology of Americans," said Richard Wald, a vice president of ABC News. "My father was a small dress manufacturer and his business failed in 1934. He felt tremendously guilty because he couldn't get a job to support the family. He believed it was his own fault. Franklin Roosevelt convinced him and convinced millions of other people that it wasn't their fault. They weren't responsible because there were forces beyond their control. . . . It was part of the American embracing of Freud in everything from government to the movies; it was a changing of the concepts of right and wrong in America."*

The antireligious forces, although they may have been outnumbered, tended to win those struggles over the decades as government absorbed the functions once classified as Christian charity and—often through court action—almost surgically applied the same First Amendment that guaranteed freedom of speech and religion to complete the separation of church and state in one public place and activity after another. The most symbolic action in this chain was the Supreme Court decision of 1962 that banned prayer and regular Bible readings in public schools.

But the religionists fought on, labeling their opponents, quite accurately, as "secular humanists," and their successes and failures came in waves on a downward curve. As I traveled in the South, I came across the beginnings of direct political action by Fundamentalist ministers and their congregations, sometimes grouped in national organizations with grandly pretentious names like the Moral Majority. I was in Alachua County, Florida, on my winding route from New Orleans to Norfolk, when a Baptist minister and Moral Majority organizer named Gene

---

* Samuel Goldwyn's 1924 trip to Vienna in an unsuccessful attempt to recruit Dr. Freud as a screenwriter was not the end of American film's fascination with psychological therapists. Toward the end of my travels, one of the most popular movies in the country was *Ordinary People*, in which a therapist helps a family become more open in relationships with each other. They do—and the family splits up. The mother leaves as father and son embrace in what was accepted as a happy ending.

Keith organized the members of his congregation to win 42 of the 122 seats on the county's Democratic Executive Committee. Keith wanted to be a Florida state senator, his wife told me, because "God told Gene to run for this seat."

God, however, was willing to go only so far. The Reverend Mr. Keith lost the election. That seemed fitting to me, because the Fundamentalists were winning occasional battles in a war they had already lost.

"While the law allows the American people to do everything," Tocqueville wrote, after four years of consideration, in the first volume of *Democracy in America*, "there are things which religion prevents them from imagining and forbids them to dare. . . . I do not know if all Americans have faith in their religion—for who can read the secrets of the heart?—but I am sure that they think it necessary to the maintenance of Republican institutions. That is not the view of one class or party among the citizens, but of the whole nation."

Five years after that, in the second volume, Tocqueville added: "In ages of faith the final aim of life is placed beyond life. . . . Religions instill a general habit of behaving with the future in view. In this respect they work as much in favor of happiness in this world as of felicity in the next. That is one of their most salient political characteristics. But as the light of faith grows dim, man's range of vision grows more circumscribed, and it would seem as if the object of human endeavors came daily closer. . . . Governments must study means to give men back that interest in the future which neither religion nor social conditions any longer inspire, and without specifically saying so, give daily practical examples to the citizens proving that wealth, renown, and power are the rewards of work, that great success comes when it has been long desired, and that nothing of lasting value is achieved without trouble."

The nation I saw no longer shared the view that public religion was necessary for the survival of republican institutions. Or, it seemed possible to me, the nation instinctively realized that republican institutions—representative government—were not necessarily essential to the survival of democracy once the technology existed for direct and constant communication between governed and governors. The unofficial dismantling of the republic, which was being accomplished by the centralization of authority and the decentralization of information, would be, to use a word adopted by Freud, a traumatic experience for Americans. But the acceptance of the changes of the twentieth century, living with "new values," has also been traumatic—and somewhat similar to what seems to be coming. The absorption of "Freud"—and of Marx and Darwin and others—demonstrated some ability to look at the world in new ways. That same ability is what will become more and more necessary for each citizen of the democracy as a rush of technology replaces that rush of ideas, changing what people know and when they know it.

So I was somehow encouraged to see that Tocqueville's pessimism about the dimming of faith sounded so modern. "Governments must study means to give men back that interest in the future which neither religion nor social conditions any longer inspire. . . ." I would have written those words without changing a syllable. That meant to me that the United States and the Americans had already survived the transition from Puritan Republic to some new kind of selfish democracy.

15
DETROIT

"The Tyranny of the Majority . . ."

After their excursions to the wilds of Saginaw Bay and the American and Canadian settlements across the tops of Lake Michigan and Lake Huron, Tocqueville and Beaumont left Green Bay by steamboat on August 10, 1831, for their third stop at Detroit. They had come first, three weeks before, still shocked from their first good look at the natives of America, the Indians. Buffalo was a Lake Erie trading center of 10,000 people, and the Frenchmen had arrived there on a day when Indians were gathering at a government office to receive pay for the lands the white men were taking from them.*

"Walk in the town," Tocqueville wrote in his notebook. "A multitude of savages in the street (day of payment). . . . Their ugliness . . . Population brutalized by our wines and liquors. More horrible than equally brutalized peoples of Europe . . . Contrast with the moral and civilized population all about."

"I don't believe I've ever experienced a more complete disappointment than at the sight of those Indians," he was to write years later. He stayed in Buffalo for just a day, then boarded the first steamboat crossing the lake. "Soon after the shores of Can-

---

* Tocqueville and Beaumont spent two weeks in Canada, seeing Sault Ste. Marie, Montreal, and Quebec, talking mostly to French Canadians in those places. I did not retrace that part of their trip.

ada seemed to approach rapidly, and we saw the Detroit River opening before us and the walls of Fort Malden appearing in the distance. This place, founded by the French, still bears numerous traces of its origin. The houses there are shaped and placed like the houses of our peasants; in the center of the hamlet rises the Catholic steeple surmounted by a cock. One would say a village near Caen or Evreux. While, not without emotion, we were considering this image of France, our attention was distracted by a singular spectacle. At our right, on the bank (on the Canadian side), a Scotch soldier stood on guard in full uniform. . . . On our left, and as if to furnish a contrast, two Indians, entirely naked, their bodies streaked with paint, their noses pierced by rings, put off at the same moment from the opposite bank. They were in a bark canoe . . . they quietly went fishing near the English soldier who, still shining and motionless, seemed placed there as the representative of the brilliant and armed civilization of Europe. . . .

". . . a striking emblem of American society. Everything is in violent contrast, unforeseen. Everywhere extreme civilization and nature abandoned to herself find themselves together and as it were face to face."

In Detroit, I stayed in Grosse Point Park, a shining suburb of expensive homes, almost small estates, on the city's northern border. The main route from there into downtown Detroit ran along the shore of Lake St. Clair and, then, the Detroit River. The name of the street changed at the border, from Lakeshore Drive to Jefferson Avenue. A few hundred yards, a quarter of a mile or so, and the civilization of Grosse Pointe came face to face, as it were, with a city abandoned.

I drove a block on either side of Jefferson, along streets named Chalmers, Marlborough, Philip, Manistique, Ashland, and Alter. Devastated blocks. There were twenty-nine boarded-up houses and twenty vacant lots where houses had been not long ago on those six streets. They had once been tree-lined blocks of solid two-story brick homes. Now small, dirty children played among the ruins, picking up bits of stone among the glass on the street and flinging them at my car. Black children.

Those homes and 16,000 more like them had been destroyed by the United States government. It had cost taxpayers almost one billion dollars. And it all seemed like a good idea at the time.

The time was 1968 and, partly as a result of the racial rioting in Detroit the year before, Congress passed the Housing Act of 1968 under strong pressure from President Lyndon Johnson. It was one of the last laws of the social and welfare programs Johnson proudly labeled "the Great Society." "The Great Society rests on abundance and liberty for all," he said. "It demands an end to poverty and racial injustice."

Under that act, poor families, with mortgages guaranteed by the Department of Housing and Urban Development through the Federal Housing Administration, would be able to buy inner-city homes with down payments as low as $200. When Richard Nixon was elected President at the end of that year, he appointed a former governor of Michigan, George Romney, Secretary of HUD, and Romney decided to use the program to rebuild his home town, Detroit. HUD acquired thousands of homes in "changing neighborhoods"—inner-city neighborhoods with a great number of houses for sale because white residents were abandoning their streets to a growing poor, black population—then hired local contractors and agencies to fix them up and resell them to poor people eligible for the FHA-guaranteed mortgages.

The troubles began when greedy contractors faked the repairs and bribed FHA inspectors to certify that competent work had been done; there were more than two hundred convictions and indictments in the 1970s in what came to be known as "the HUD scandals." Then it turned out that many of the new residents, some of them with houses in far worse shape than official papers reported, were unable or unwilling to maintain the properties or pay the mortgages. Banks began foreclosing, with HUD paying the bills and getting back the houses. The process was usually repeated for a second time by a government both hopeful and incompetent—or, much of the time, corrupted. Finally, in embarrassment, HUD began destroying the evidence of what had really happened—it began razing the houses.

By the time I was on Jefferson Avenue, more than 11 percent of Detroit's housing stock had been destroyed, leveled to vacant lots, and more houses—including the twenty-nine I saw that morning, some of which had to be worth $75,000 in most cities—were boarded up hulks waiting for the wreckers. They were stripped by bands of vandals searching for anything that could be sold, particularly copper plumbing, and serving as homes—"flophouses" was the local term—for drug addicts and dangerous playpens for children, tinder for fires that plagued the city.

The intent was good and the theory seemed plausible. But . . . Early in his travels, on October 1, 1831, in Boston, Tocqueville had written himself a note that rambled on a bit about "great social principles" and made the point that "the happy mean in these theories is difficult to seize."

"Each individual being the most competent judge of his own interest," he wrote then, "society must not push too far in its solicitude for him, for fear that he will end by counting on society and will load it thus with a task which it is incapable of performing." That, he wrote, was "another principle of American society that one must never lose sight of . . ."

Americans, however, being Americans, were condemned to regularly lose sight of that principle—and of their limitations and the limitations of their government. The same bent toward perfectibility, the same optimism, the same openness to change—"Change is a way of life with these people," Tocqueville said—that has served the nation so well inevitably leads it into excess, overloading the government in tasks, great and small, which it proves incapable of performing. And the greatest American tasks—and failures—have been in expressing the solicitude, what solicitude there is, of the conquering white race toward people of color.

Five miles more toward the center of Detroit, the sign marking the intersection of Superior and Orleans streets stands in a weedy plain, almost in the shadow of the Renaissance Center, the gleaming cluster of office and hotel towers built as a symbol of the city's proclaimed rebirth after the 1967 riots. The streets around Superior and Orleans had been leveled at about the same time to make way for public housing that was never built. The empty fields were punctuated with fire hydrants marking what had been the curbs of the erased streets.

The fields of hydrants were bordered by railroad tracks. On the inhabited side of those tracks, the landscape was littered with rusting and rotting cars and refrigerators and smaller junk, with sagging wooden houses that were little more than shacks when they were built 50 or 100 years ago, with charred wood from the fires that seemed to have blackened parts of every standing structure. It was littered with people, too—black Americans lived there, beaten and strangely hopeful that some higher authority cared. Of the 410 households in a 36-square-block area along those tracks, from East Forest to Mack Street along Chene Street, 382 were receiving some form of government assistance, some kind of welfare. In the winter, I was told, these streets were sometimes closed for weeks by snow and ice. There were 109 vacant lots in the area, and 15 store-front churches. In three blocks along St. Aubin Street, I passed the Life Tabernacle of Detroit, the True Vine Temple of Christ, the Ephesian Church of God in Christ, the Life and Light Temple, and the Temple of New Life Thru Awakened Vision.*

Mrs. Dorothy Pruitt, a fifty-one-year-old widow, headed one of those 410 households. She had been on welfare for more than 20 years, since her husband was laid off at Chrysler. He was dead and she paid $100 a month to live in a decaying wooden house that was built when the neighborhood was called "Poletown." It had been, 100 years before, the first American home of poor Poles from Prussia who emigrated to Detroit. The porch of the building was collapsing when I was there. The home had no central heating and one electrical outlet. Mrs. Pruitt received $117 a month in welfare. Her daughter, Betty Ann Kendrick, thirty-one, lived in the house along with her fifteen-year-old daughter, Sherrie; Mrs. Kendrick received $395 per month in government assistance, plus $72 in food stamps.

Mrs. Pruitt is black. More than 63 percent of the 1,203,339 persons listed as living in Detroit in the 1980 Census were black. In the 1970 Census, 43.7 percent of Detroit's 1,511,482 people were black, but more than half the city's white residents left the city during that decade.

"How do people get by here?" I asked Jason Lovett, Jr., a

---

* The statistics on the neighborhood bordered by the Grand Trunk and Western Railroad tracks, Mack Street, Chene Street, and East Forest Street were contained in a study of the neighborhood published in the September 1980 issue of *Monthly Detroit* magazine.

In February 1981, according to Mayor Coleman Young, Detroit's unemployment rate was 20 percent and 60 percent of the city's residents were receiving some form of public assistance, usually welfare or unemployment benefits.

thirty-seven-year-old black photographer and writer, who showed me around Mrs. Pruitt's neighborhood. "There's an underground economy," he said. "Gambling, narcotics. Almost everything that goes on here is against the law. But nobody bothers." Paul Thomas, a black patrolman from the Seventh Precinct, which covered the area, confirmed that, after kidding for a few minutes with a prostitute working Mack Avenue: "On the streets she can make a couple of hundred a night. She doesn't hurt no one and we watch out for her ... I could be running them all in. But why? We're here to protect all the community, not terrorize it."

The prostitutes, the numbers runners, the guards in front of the "casino" on Chene Street, small-time drug dealers and users were usually left alone there, as long as they didn't kill each other or bother people on the outside. It seemed to be a separate country receiving aid from the United States—in the form of the welfare and assistance checks that reached almost every house—and spending and circulating that money by local custom. One "party store" on St. Joseph's Street with a "blind pig" (an illegal tavern) in the back—these things were not secret in the neighborhood—took in $45,000 in food stamps in 1980, almost all of that to pay for liquor.

Live and let live. Lovett and I were driving along Woodward Avenue, Detroit's main street, looking for a public telephone. They were few and far between, but we found one with two men standing nearby. Lovett got out of the car, walked up to the booth, exchanged a few words, and came back to the car. "They're going to be awhile," he said. "They're trying to rob the coin box."

Detroit had its first racial riot less than two years after Tocqueville and Beaumont saw the town in the summer of 1831. On June 14, 1833, a sheriff arrested Thornton Blackburn and his wife as fugitive slaves from Kentucky. For a day and a half, a crowd of armed blacks, free residents of the city, surrounded the jail, finally helping the Blackburns escape to Canada as the sheriff and several blacks were shot and wounded. Order was restored by a company of cavalry from Fort Gratiot up the river, the first of many army units called to Detroit over the decades to separate the races.

Thirty years later, on March 6, 1863, white gangs, trying to lynch a dark-skinned man named William Faulkner who had been accused (falsely) of sexual assault, ran shooting along Beaubien Street, yelling, "Kill all the damned niggers!" Troops were called in again, to guard the area around what is now the site of the Renaissance Center.

By 1943, the Negro population of Detroit had reached about 50,000. Black families had begun migrating to the city from the South to seek employment in the automobile industry in the 1920s. (One result was that a Ku Klux Klan candidate won the 1924 Republican mayoral primary with write-in votes that were later disqualified by the courts.) The migration had speeded up as an aggressively tolerant union, The United Auto Workers, gained power in the plants. Then, defense work during World War II—and threats of national demonstrations by black labor leaders if blacks were refused employment in defense plants—created more and more jobs, and more and more black men took the trains north from Mississippi and Alabama. On June 20, 1943, fist fights between black and white men on Belle Isle, an island park in the Detroit River, escalated into bloody rioting as rumors swept through the city of dead women and children of both races. By the time federal troops had restored order, 25 blacks and nine whites had been killed. It was, up to that time, the worst racial riot in American history.

At 3:45 on a Sunday morning, July 23, 1967, Detroit vice officers raided a "blind pig" and began arresting the 82 patrons. The club was on the corner of Twelfth and Clairmount streets and it was called, rather grandly, the United Community and Civic League. A crowd gathered there as a hot dawn began showing to the east. There were curses, then a few rocks were thrown. The police began moving in reinforcements. Someone set fire to a store. In the next four days, 43 people were killed—33 black and ten white—and there was more than $40 million in property damage as blacks wrecked their own neighborhoods, battling police and federal troops.

Twelfth Street is called a boulevard now—Rosa Parks Boulevard, named after the black woman who refused to go to the back of the bus in Montgomery—and it is lined with neat, two-story units of public housing. "You have to imagine a crowded street of bars and nightclubs, candy stores, barberships, wig stores," said Jason Lovett. "It was a cultural center. They always find a way to destroy the black centers—a new highway, urban renewal, they keep moving us out."

"What happened after the riots?" I asked.

"They did things like this, built some housing. There were programs and jobs for a while. And the scag came."

"Scag?"

"Pinkish-red capsules," Lovett said. "They were everywhere. I'd never seen them before, but suddenly everybody had scag for 25 cents a cap. Weed and everything else dried up, but you could get all the scag you wanted. It gave you this mellow high. You didn't want no trouble with nobody. . . .

"It was, I think, low grade Mexican heroin. Mixed with milk sugar or quinine or something. Whatever it was, it took you away from here. People needed to go somewhere, but you can't go anywhere if you don't have money. Scag took you away . . . and that was the beginning of heroin in Detroit.

"It was no accident," he said. "I don't know how it happened, but I think it was part of somebody's pacification program."

"You think drugs are a control agent here?"

"Yeah, I do."

"How many other black people think that?"

"Most of them. They don't talk about it that much and white people wouldn't believe them. . . . But we've seen it all. There was no outcry about heroin or any other kind of drugs until it hit white neighborhoods. When it was in Grosse Pointe messing up white kids, then someone cared."

Lovett was a sophisticated man. Among other things, he had earned a degree in political science from Michigan State University. And his calculating view of American race relations was one I heard again and again in Detroit and other places. "Handing out heroin on the streets is easier and cheaper than giving the police machine guns," said Kenneth Cockrell, a black Detroit city councilman, a successful lawyer and a self-proclaimed Marxist. "That's the way it is in this society."

"No one ever gave a damn about drugs in the black community," said Roy Levy Williams, executive director of the Detroit Urban League and former executive assistant to the governor of Michigan. "I'm one of those Americans who is convinced that America can do anything it wants to. If you can get to the moon, you can. . . . So, I'm not sure that America ever wanted to control drugs in the black community."

"Brandy," said another man in another time, "is the great cause of destruction for the aborigines of America." That was Sam Houston, the "Squaw Man," as recorded in Tocqueville's notebook after their conversation on the steamboat from Memphis to New Orleans.

"It's a racist society," Williams said. "What we're concerned about is the level of racism at any time. What will they do to us if something happens?"

"There is a lot of racism, personal and institutionalized, and nothing is ever going to change that," said William Beckham, director of administration of one of the country's largest companies, the Burroughs Corporation, and, among many other credentials, a former deputy mayor of Detroit. He was the first black in modern times to serve as a professional on the staff of a United States senator, Philip Hart of Michigan. "Phil Hart," he said, "told me one thing I have never forgotten: You can tell from 50 feet away that a person is black and your mind adjusts.

"On that level," Beckham continued, "there is no assimilation and there never will be. I can feel it each time I meet someone: 'My God, he's black. I don't want to discriminate. I wonder if he's smart? I wonder if he's militant? What do I do?' That's what most whites, as far as I can tell, see and that's what they think. . . . You never forget you're black. Never. They never let you. Maybe they can't. I tell my wife that if I were white, I'd be further along in life."

I said that most whites would attribute his obvious success—Beckham had also served as Assistant Secretary of the Treasury and Deputy Secretary of Transportation back in Washington—to the fact that he was black and a beneficiary of affirmative action laws and programs designed to compensate for past discrimination. "What people resent is this business of some colleges pushing blacks too far for their own good, making them doctors and everything else," said one white man, a former President, Richard Nixon.

"We don't see it that way," Beckham said. "A black has to be a little bit smarter than a white to get to the same place." I checked that perception later with Roy Levy Williams of the

Urban League. "I feel that I had to work harder than any white to get where I am," he said. "I am sure all successful blacks, middle-class blacks, feel that way. We saw the obstacles everywhere."

What then, I asked Beckham, made it possible for him—he was forty-two years old when we talked—to be appointed to and hired for a string of prestigious public and private positions?

"Focused violence," he said. "Violence, the riots of the 1960s, brought whatever movement there was in the society, the softening of the rigidity of American institutions. It was the whites' fear of urban violence that made it possible for blacks to become mayors of cities like Detroit. Whatever its troubles, Detroit is a significant American institution and the white people with financial interests here believed those interests would best be preserved by working with the political power of black numbers. When Coleman Young became the first black mayor of Detroit and I was a deputy mayor, some of us used to argue that he wasn't militant enough and he would say: 'We've got the political power because we've got the votes, but we don't have a dime. We have to cut a deal. . . .'

"Now," Beckham said, speaking in early 1981, "the violence, that kind anyway, has passed and the old rigidity is returning. The golden time is over for people like me. The white reaction to the riots was defensive. Next time it will be offensive."

Do you think the white majority is capable of turning violently on the black minority?

Robert Battle III, a regional director of the United Auto Workers and one of the union's most prominent black leaders for more than 40 years, paused for a long time before he answered.

"Yes," he said. "Twenty years ago in this city, if a black person called the police for help, there was a good chance he'd end up in more trouble than when he began. There was a war here and they were the enemy. . . . Racism comes through in waves and right now"—we were talking in May 1981—"there's one going through and no one is doing anything to stop it because they think we got too much after the riots in 1967. . . . I look in the papers every day—the *Detroit Free Press* and the *New York Times,* not fly-by-night papers—and for no reason they keep reporting census figures, so many whites and so many blacks. Why? The numbers of blacks are always much lower and I think the message is: You have nothing to fear from blacks if there's trouble—they're outnumbered. . . . I think it would take only one heavy incident right now for a war to begin, for it to be worse than it was when I started out in the 1930s. Some whites—Ku Klux Klan nuts—could shoot down black children and then blacks would riot and the whites would respond, heavily. The pattern is here."

"I can conceive of open warfare," said William Beckham. "White fear of crime or something else could lead to that.

"More likely, I think what we might see is the government taking total effective control over the lives of large numbers of people, most of them black. We have two things going on at the same time. We're raising the standards of education for every job in the society and we have a class of people, a class getting larger and larger, that has less and less education. It is a volatile situation and no government is going to let people like that roam around loose forever. It will take control of their lives in one way or another—in the military, or in some sort of work-training programs."

I interrupted Beckham to ask whether he had ever seen Highland Park High School, which was about six miles from where we were. That was the building without windows I had seen looming over Woodward Avenue as I followed Tocqueville's route to the wilderness.

"That's riot architecture," Jason Lovett had said as we drove up. "I'd call it neo-penal," I replied.

"Highland Park Pen, that's what we call it," said Antonio Green, a seventeen-year-old senior. "You go crazy looking at the walls. . . . But it's got the best industrial program in the state."

"Are there whites here?" I asked.

"Sure," he said, "a couple of the teachers are white."

Industrial arts—work training. There was a row of store-fronts alongside the school. One was a food stamps office—welfare. The next three were recruiting offices for the United States Navy, the United States Marines, and the United States Air Force—military. Beckham's people were being warehoused—and some of the warehouses had no windows.

That view from black America, that black view of America, was not new to me. After months of traveling the United States asking the questions Tocqueville had asked, I was not surprised anymore by the cold and fearful words of black Americans. Some of it, I thought, was exaggerated—a bit of posing to shake the white man and lobby the government for a little more. But the pattern of conversations was too consistent, too clear to be ignored. Black Americans were afraid; all Americans should be. In New York City, Lloyd Williams, a forty-year-old black businessman and a vice chairman of the Harlem Chamber of Commerce, had sat in a luncheonette with me, ticking off the names of his junior-high classmates—"a junkie" ... "dead, shot in a bar" ... "jail" ... "dead, overdosed." He thought half the boys might be dead or drugged or had disappeared—after a while, he said, you stopped thinking of it as accident or coincidence. That is what happens to young black male Americans.*

On the other side of the country, the Pacific Coast that Tocqueville never reached, a black member of the Los Angeles Board of Education, Diane Watson, said, "If we really wanted to crack down on drugs, we could make a real dent. But we're not trying. In my moments of paranoia—and they are many—I think there must be a master plan, a conspiracy to keep the poor spaced-out, oppressed, suppressed. I just see it flowing too freely in this city and in our schools."

Maxine Waters, who was thirty-nine when we talked, had been elected to the California State Assembly from South Central Los Angeles—from Watts, the black neighborhood where, in August of 1965, 34 people were killed in the worst racial rioting in the United States between the Detroit riot of 1943 and the

---

* Tocqueville, using Philadelphia's medical statistics, reported in a footnote: "There is a great difference between white and black mortality rates in the states in which slavery has been abolished: from 1820 to 1831 only 1 white in 42 died, whereas the figure for blacks was 1 in 20. The mortality rate is not nearly so high among Negro slaves."

In 1978, according to *Vital Statistics of the United States,* the average life expectancy of white males was 70.2 years. For "other" males, the expectancy was 65 years. That gap—five years—had become dramatically lower over the years. In 1930, the life expectancy of white males was 59.7 years, and of "others," 47.3 years. In 1900, the figures were, respectively, 46.6 years and 32.5 years.

According to the 1830 census there were 120,520 blacks in states in which slavery had been abolished, compared with 6,565,434 whites. In slave states, there were 2,208,102 blacks and 3,960,814 whites. In the 1980 census, 25.6 million of 218 million Americans were black.

Detroit riot of 1967. Mrs. Waters, like Bill Beckham in Detroit, was extraordinarily successful; she had made it. When we talked, she had just been elected majority leader of the Assembly, one of the most powerful political offices in the nation's largest state. It was a long way from St. Louis, where she had been one of 13 children of a widow on welfare and went to work at seventeen doing piecework in a dress factory. She was an energetic affirmation of the American dream, cheerfully interrupting four hours of conversation to coordinate some clothes shopping with friends and a tennis date with her husband. But her words were not cheerful:

"There are too many hungry black people out there. And white people don't want to live in fear that those black people are going to rob them, are going to break into their homes, are going to kill them. . . . The fear is low-level, it's just bodily harm that people are worried about. From an institutional viewpoint, the blacks are under control—the poor blacks are no threat to an oil company or to the Bank of America. But those blacks—the underclass—are too potentially dangerous to too many white people, and I'm not sure the majority will let that continue. The next big step in America will probably be the dispersal of blacks. . . .

"I don't think the rhetoric of America or of Christianity would allow the equivalent of concentration camps . . . but I could see plans to systematically relocate people. They wouldn't be presented as hostile plans, but as economic plans. You already hear talk of breaking up the ghettos, or of industrial and economic zones in cities. If the whites want the centers of the cities back because of energy shortages or something else, the blacks will be moved out. And where they are moved out to will not be happenstance. I don't think the relocation decision will be a benevolent decision, even if it will be made palatable with paid transportation and moving, and with technical and vocational instruction and slogans like 'Matching people with jobs.'"

She stopped.

"I'm surprised to hear myself talking this way," she said after a moment. "But look around you. The white institutions—Sears, Roebuck, Firestone Tire—are pulling out of South Central L.A. The institutions are abandoning the people here. What are they left with? What increases—with government permission? Liquor stores. . . . And dope. A lot of blacks would say dope is purposeful here. Maybe they're right. What are you supposed to think when you read that the Central Intelligence Agency has been secretly testing drugs on people around the country?

" 'The blacks just can't handle it. See, they're all shooting up'—when I hear that kind of talk, I hear other people getting ready to say that they'll make the decisions for the poor doped-up blacks."

I had not been prepared for the reasoned mistrust of white Americans that I heard everywhere from black Americans—especially from the talented black men and women who had been publicly accepted into and acclaimed by the majority white society. "The system works to find us, train us, and help us," said Maxine Waters, whose personal path from poverty in St. Louis to honor and power in Sacramento, the capital of the nation's largest state, passed through the telephone company, where she was rapidly promoted, into government antipoverty programs, where, as an aide and instructor, she learned the skills and made the contacts that helped her begin her political career. "Talented blacks are picked up very quickly and moved up."

"Are those the most dangerous blacks?" I asked. "The ones who might organize and lead others?"

"Yes," she said, "and I'm one of them. I could have been a very angry person out there if no one knew who I was." The two of us had completed the conversation that Tocqueville began 150 years ago with Monsieur Guillemin, the French consul in New Orleans, who wondered why white Americans did not welcome the most talented, and most dangerous, blacks and mulattoes into the majority society. One day, we did.

The alternatives to that, in Tocqueville's thinking, were much worse. At one point, assuming that black Americans would continue to be concentrated in southern states, he speculated about race war along the Gulf of Mexico. "If the whites of North America remain united," he wrote, "it is difficult to believe that the Negroes will escape the destruction threatening them; the sword of misery will bring them down."

The Frenchman linked Indians and blacks in that misery, and it was obvious to him that the Indians were being exterminated.

"Is it that the Indians do not realize that sooner or later their race will be annihilated by ours?" he asked Canadian trappers in the woods of Michigan.

"It is obvious," he wrote in *Democracy in America*, "that there are three naturally distinct, one might also say hostile races. Education, law, origin, and external features too have raised almost insurmountable barriers between them; chance has brought them together on the same soil, but they have mixed without combining, and each follows a separate destiny.

" . . . These two unlucky races [Indians and blacks]. . . . Both occupy an equally inferior position in the land where they dwell; both suffer the effects of tyranny, and, though their afflictions are different, they have the same people to blame for them."

And he was not gentle in defining that blame, writing in his final work:

"The Spaniards let their dogs loose on the Indians as if they were wild beasts; they pillaged the New World like a city taken by storm, without discrimination or mercy; but one cannot destroy everything, and frenzy has a limit; the remnant of the Indian population, which escaped the massacres, in the end mixed with the conquerors and adopted their religion and mores.

"On the other hand, the conduct of the United States Americans towards the natives was inspired by the most chaste affection for legal formalities. As long as the Indians remained in their savage state, the Americans did not interfere in their affairs at all and treated them as independent peoples; they did not allow their lands to be occupied unless they had been properly acquired by contract; and if by chance an Indian nation cannot live on its territory, they take them by the hand in brotherly fashion and lead them away to die far from the land of their fathers.

"The Spaniards, by unparalleled atrocities which brand them with indelible shame, did not succeed in exterminating the Indian race and could not even prevent them from sharing their rights; the United States Americans have attained both these results with wonderful ease, quietly, legally, and philanthropically, without spilling blood and without violating a single one of the great principles of morality in the eyes of the world. It is impossible to destroy men with more respect to the laws of humanity.

"The Indians," he continued, "die as they have lived, in isolation; but the fate of the Negroes is in a sense linked with that of the Europeans. The two races are bound one to the other without mingling; it is equally difficult for them to separate completely or to unite."

It was the American anguish and hypocrisy, and Tocqueville sensed it everywhere he went. In Louisville, John Brent McIlvaine, the merchant, had said, "In Kentucky the majority would be found to be for the abolition of slavery. But we don't know what to do with the slaves. Our fathers did us a horrible injury by bringing them among us." In Philadelphia, Peter Duponceau, an elderly and distinguished lawyer who had first come to America in 1777 to help drill George Washington's troops, said, "The great rankling sore of the United States is slavery. The evil only grows. The spirit of the century tends toward giving slaves their liberty. I don't doubt that the blacks will eventually all become free. But I believe that one day their race will disappear from our soil."

And in Boston, a former President, John Quincy Adams, had this exchange with Tocqueville:

"There are two facts which have had a great influence on our character. In the North, the political and religious doctrines of the founders of New England; in the South, slavery."

"Q. Do you look on slavery as a great plague for the United States?"

"A. Yes, certainly. That is the root of almost all the troubles of the present and the fears for the future."*

---

* Adams also offered this opinion: "I know nothing more insolent than a black, when he is not speaking to his master and is not afraid of a beating. It is not rare even to see Negroes treating their master very badly when they have to do with a weak man. The Negro women especially very often take advantage of their mistresses' kindness. They know that it is not the custom to inflict corporal punishment on them."

Adams' racial views may have been milder than those of one of his predecessors, Thomas Jefferson, who wrote of blacks and whites: " . . . the real distinctions that nature has made, and many other circum-

I asked former President Nixon whether he believed Americans were racist.

"They were. They were," he answered. "God knows they were in politics. The cynicism and hypocrisy that you saw—both parties had their 'house niggers.' The real revolution began in the 1950s—you have to give the courts credit. . . . A lot of people are just as racist now, but it's not fashionable anymore—and I think that's damned important. You can't talk about blacks like you once did. . . . The racism has receded, I think. But it's there and it always will be there."

After his conversations, Tocqueville concluded in the first volume of *Democracy in America*: "The most formidable evil threatening the future of the United States is the presence of the blacks on their soil. From whatever angle one sets out to inquire into the present embarrassment or future dangers facing the United States, one is almost always brought up against this fact."

It was a fact that was as basic in Detroit in 1981 as in 1831. Fifty years from now, or 150 years, what will people see when they look back at the United States of the 1980s? Will those men and women accept the version I had heard of the racial history of our times? Will they be persuaded by the words of William Beckham and Jason Lovett and Maxine Waters?

It is hard for me to conceive that people 150 years from now will not judge us harshly for life on Chene Street and the walls of Highland Park High School. The payments from the government and the drugs come into the neighborhood; people rarely get out. And for the ones who do come outside the walls, the first doors waiting for them are government doors—to more payments, to military service and discipline. If democracy moves forward by millions of individual decisions, then Americans, si-

---

stances, will divide us into parties and produce convulsions which will probably never end but in the extermination of the one or the other race. . . . They have less hair on the face and body. They secrete less by the kidneys and more by the glands of the skin, which gives them a very strong and disagreeable odour. . . . Comparing them by their faculties of memory, reason and imagination, it appears to me, that in memory they are equal to whites, in reason much inferior . . . and that in imagination they are dull, tasteless and anomalous. . . . In music they are generally more gifted than the whites. . . ."

lently, democratically, by unspoken consensus, made the decision that this is the way it would be in our time.

Writing in his time, Tocqueville was more direct about racism than is now considered acceptable—and Nixon was right, it was no small achievement to civilize the dialogue of civilization. "You can make the Negro free," the Frenchman said, "but you cannot prevent him from facing the European as a stranger.

"That is not all; this man born in degradation, this stranger brought by slavery into our midst, is hardly recognized as sharing the common features of humanity. His face appears to us hideous, his intelligence limited, and his tastes low; we almost take him for some intermediate between beast and man." After that paragraph Tocqueville put a footnote: "To induce the whites to abandon the opinion they have conceived of the intellectual and moral inferiority of their former slaves, the Negroes must change, but they cannot change as long as this opinion persists."

That opinion, judging by my own experience as a white American, persisted in my lifetime. Perhaps it always will. The blacks I talked with seemed more aware of that and more resigned to it. "You can't regulate thought," said Inspector Gilbert Hill of the Detroit Police Department, the black chief of the city's homicide squad. "But you can regulate behavior. I don't care if white people—some white people—don't like me, but don't let them hang me."

The word "some" is both civilized and accurate. The white American consensus I sensed—which encompassed many opinions more admirable than the ones I have discussed so far in this chapter—was not shared by every white American. Black Americans, as perceived by whites, were clearly divided into two huge groups—those who have "made it" by playing by the American rules and those who have been left behind on places like Chene Street. Or, reversing the order, whites are afraid of some blacks and not of others.*

---

*Ken Cockrell, the black city councilman, said that division of blacks was also immediately obvious to black children in school. "In high school," he said, "we instinctively broke up into two groups, the 'Thugs' and the 'Elites.' That's pronounced E-lights. Those are the people who read books and joined fraternities and became lawyers and doctors."

"The treatment of poor blacks is the test of our democracy," said Felix Rohatyn, a New York investment banker and expert on municipal finance who came to Detroit as an adviser to Mayor Young. "Democracy may be a great luxury that works only so long as there is growth to allocate. The system still hasn't been tested in allocating sacrifice. Will the middle class sacrifice to keep black mothers on welfare?

"I don't think so," he said. "We are coming toward a time of mutual terror."

The beginnings of the terror were in Detroit. "I do not let my wife leave the house at night," said Douglas Fraser, the president of the United Auto Workers, who lives in a town house inside the city. "It is just too dangerous here for that."

When Henry Ford II, the chairman of the Ford Motor Company and the moving force behind the construction of the Renaissance Center, announced that his company would move its headquarters into the new towers, a fraudulent but official-looking memorandum circulated through the Ford offices on the stationery of the Employee Communications Department:

"Subject: RELOCATION TO RENAISSANCE CENTER

". . . In the event that a move becomes necessary, all department personnel will be issued Smith and Wesson .38 caliber revolvers and bullet proof vests. . . .

"Each car pool will travel to the Renaissance Center by way of Grand Rapids in order to avoid possible trouble spots. . . .

"Department personnel are requested to make sure that all personal affairs are in order and that next of kin are listed alphabetically. . . ."

That phony memo, circulated in late 1976, was a reaction to the inheritors of Guillemin's "brute force," the blacks feared by white Americans—and by most other black Americans. The division of blacks between the upwardly mobile and the beaten down had widened since the riots of 1967 and the uplifting programs that, with the consent of the white majority, were the government's response in the 1970s. What happened was that upwardly mobile blacks, like any opportunistic Americans, and the most capable and aggressive of the truly poor—William Beckham, whose father was a UAW official, and Maxine Waters, who never met her father—took advantage of that boost. It wasn't quite the rich getting richer, but it was the best getting better off. The proportion of black households with incomes above $15,000 (in 1976 dollars, adjusted to account for inflation) increased from 19 to 30 percent in the ten years following the black riots in Detroit and other cities—but the proportion of blacks officially classified as jobless increased from 7.4 percent to 13.2 percent. In those ten good years for middle-class blacks, the number of unemployed blacks went from 638,000 to 1,492,000. By 1980, black Americans, who made up 11.7 percent of the nation's population, were receiving 43.9 percent of the Aid to Dependent Children, the largest federal welfare program.*

In one way or another, the blacks on the bottom—and, to a lesser extent, other poor Americans—will always pose a constant threat to the larger society. Constant trouble, but certainly manageable, either using the essentially benevolent responses of the late 1960s, or using repressive measures and, perhaps, creating zones, large or small, urban or isolated, with perimeters maintained by police power. Whatever such zones, official or unofficial, were called, they would be home to hundreds of thousands of Americans, most of them black, "pacified" in contained communities governed by laws and mores different from the political and social rules of the majority.

Modern equivalents of Indian reservations—that's what Maxine Waters had really been talking about. When Tocqueville, in 1831, saw his first Indians, saw them beaten under the blows of Western civilization, he wrote notes in his diary that have a sad but strong ring in neighborhoods of Detroit still scorched by the fires of 1967:

"One would say that the European is to other races of men what man in general is to all animated nature. When he cannot bend them to his use or make them indirectly serve his well-being, he destroys them and makes them little by little disappear before him ... Every ten years, about, the Indian tribes which have been pushed back into the wilderness of the west perceive

---

* More than half of those black recipients were women heading households without men, and more than half of the children involved were born out of wedlock. Comparable income figures for white Americans during the same period, 1967 to 1977, showed an increase in the proportion of households making more than $15,000 from 41 to 53 percent. Median black family income in 1967 was 58 percent of median white family income; in 1977, the figure was 59 percent.

that they have not gained by recoiling, and that the white race advances even faster than they withdraw. Irritated by the very feeling of powerlessness, or inflamed by some new injustice, they gather together and pour impetuously into the regions which they formerly inhabited and where now rise the dwellings of the Europeans, the rustic cabins of the pioneers and further back the first villages. They overrun the country, burn the houses, kill the cattle, lift a few scalps."

Then, after each raid or little war, the tide of white men and their ideas flowed on, around, past, and over incidents and obstacles. With the savages, it took soldiers. Now, ideas may be enough.

"It's a hell of a country—the best," Gilbert Hill, the police inspector, said after a long lunch in which he had recounted the prejudice he had seen as a young black officer coming into an overwhelmingly white department. He began talking about being called "nigger" . . . and ended, two hours later, complaining about two women he knew who quit working to accept welfare. "It's people like that," he said, "who are ruining America for everybody."

"Never forget," William Beckham said, "that black Americans are Americans. They buy the American idea."

I didn't argue with him. In Washington, Patrick Cadell, who supervised polling for President Carter, had told me: "Unless you put in a few racial questions to find out, when you look at surveys of political and social attitudes, black middle-class people are the same as white middle-class people."

What's the American idea? I asked Beckham.

"If you keep working at it, you'll get a decent job, a decent home in a decent neighborhood, and your kids will go to college."

"We do buy it, but with lowered expectations," Jason Lovett said. "This is the land of opportunity, but there are two kinds of opportunity—theirs and ours."

"Blacks here believe," said Roy Levy Williams of the Urban League. "They've seen democracy work for them. Blacks do run this city politically and that does make an enormous difference in terms of policing, of patronage, and just of self-image. . . . And I think blacks bought into the American Dream even more than whites. Blacks—at least blacks over thirty—probably have more

Puritan ethic than whites. They believe if you work for it in America you'll get it, or your kids will get it."

Why?

"They had to. There were no other options. They couldn't live off the stock market or off their kids. They had to believe in work because they had to have hope."*

Carefully, Williams, who was forty-four years old, said he was not certain whether what he had been saying would apply in the same degree to new generations of black Americans. "I believe that the only answer for American blacks is more and better education. We have to improve the schools and provide real quality education," he said, using words that Tocqueville would have considered characteristically American. "But it seems to be becoming more difficult to convince young blacks of that. They're not buying the bullshit of pull yourselves up by the bootstraps quite as enthusiastically as we did. When I was a street worker for the Urban League in the early 1970s, I traveled around here in old clothes, looking like a street dude, trying to convince kids to try it—try school and work. A lot of them, more and more, would say, 'I'm supposed to go back to high school and then go to four years of college and come out looking like you? Why?' They were seeing other options."

The other options were crime and drugs. The successful blacks they saw were not social workers but crooks seeming to thrive in the tolerant lawlessness of many neighborhoods in black Detroit. Their life experience was significantly different from that of other Americans, black and white—and if there was one lesson that Tocqueville wanted to hammer into the consciousness of his readers, it was that life and politics in the New World was the institutional translation of "the practical experience of the Americans."

And what many young black Americans gained experience in was another country, a country of welfare, violence, drug dealing, thieves' loot—and television. "It wasn't only that television showed poor young blacks what affluence looked like, how the other half lived," Williams said. "It also gave them the im-

* Tocqueville expressed a similar thought in writing about religion: "Religion . . . is only one particular form of hope, and it is as natural to the human heart as hope itself. . . . Incredulity is an accident; faith is the only permanent state of mankind."

pression with news stories about political corruption and movies about evil businessmen that the people at the top got there by ripping off other human beings. So why shouldn't they do it too?"*

Williams essentially believed in the system that Americans— from Eugene Genovese in Rochester to Henry Kantor in Nashville—had experienced and were convinced worked for most of the people most of the time. That is, the American system worked if you were in it. It seemed very questionable to me that many children on Chene Street and St. Joseph's Street were born inside that system—what real connection did those kids have to the nation or its institutions?—and they certainly were not living within it.

The young ones were dangerous individually; they were the guys in the projects whom Brod Bagert talked about in New Orleans, the guys with nothing to lose. That rootless and lawless underclass was inevitably expanding as, according to the 1980 census, America's black population was growing at about 1.6 percent each year while the white population grew at just under 0.7 percent. Because of the combination of higher fertility and mortality rates, the median age of America's 25 million blacks was twenty-four years, compared with a white median age above thirty.

"Once one admits," Tocqueville wrote near the end of the first volume of *Democracy in America*, "that whites and emancipated Negroes face each other like two foreign people on the same soil, it can easily be understood that there are only two possibilities for the future: the Negroes and the whites must either mingle completely or they must part.

"I have already expressed my conviction concerning the first possibility. I do not think that the white and black races will ever be brought anywhere to live on a footing of equality.

"But I think that the matter will be still harder in the United States than anywhere else. It can happen that a man will rise

*While Williams and I were talking in Detroit in May 1981, a U.S. District Court in Chicago was taking evidence in a class-action suit brought in behalf of thousands of Americans who had purchased Oldsmobiles and other higher-priced General Motors cars in 1977 and later discovered that the company was putting cheaper Chevrolet engines in its more expensive lines.

above prejudices of religion, country, and race, and if that man is a king, he can bring about astonishing transformations in society; but it is not possible for a whole people to rise, as it were, above itself."

I was not sure about that. The nature of the American experiment, I was beginning to think, was the attempt to rise, collectively, above one's self. If there had been democratic elevation, it had been difficult and fitful, but it seemed to me that even on the most difficult question—race—there had indeed been some. The lifting force, I thought, was the ideas, the theoretical ones about equality and the practical ones about hard work that Beckham and Williams and millions of other black Americans accepted. The ideas of America are indeed bigger and better than Americans—and as a people, organized as a government, we are often forced to confront our own evil to confirm the rhetoric to ourselves. The golden time for black Americans—as William Beckham had defined the 1970s—was not only the result of violence. It was also partly a result of the ability of black leaders—particularly Martin Luther King, Jr.—to force America's white majority to face up to and prove there was some truth in the American rhetoric. If the majority had not bent in those years, if white America had not allowed black America to dictate some of the national agenda, the ideas and words of American democracy would have been publicly cast down and stamped on in mockery. There were few Americans, white or black, who could let that happen. Without the rhetoric, there is no America—at least not the America which we so proudly hail.

"There is only so far that repression could go in America," said Maxine Waters in Los Angeles. "The rhetoric of the country, and Christianity, probably act as an effective brake to obvious repression."

In Detroit, Roy Levy Williams agreed that there were limits to America's capacity for repression, but he focused on enlightened self-interest as the primary reason. "We are not as capable of repression by the majority as we were 30 or 40 years ago. Part of that is Americans' view of themselves as a fair and decent people, but it's really because some intelligent whites realize that once you break the rules so openly, there's no predicting what could happen. They could be next once something

starts. . . . There is also one new factor: Because of the rising political importance of Third World countries—places with huge
brown and black populations—it is not in the economic interest
of the United States to have racial problems at home."

"Conscience," said William Beckham.

"The United States is a country of conscience. It, in the end,
believes in what it says about itself. Repression and violent reactions, at this point in our history, can go only so far. The danger
is always what course we walk before we become conscience-
stricken as a people."*

That will always be the danger as long as the races don't mingle—and there is not much evidence in America that they have
done that or ever will. In my little survey, black people and
white people weren't marrying each other in Cincinnati and
they weren't doing it anywhere else in the United States. The
relations and commitments between white Americans and black
Americans—often close and deep—were almost never complete. So the races are separate but not equal: one is the majority, one is the minority.†

"The absolute sovereignty of the will of the majority is the essence of democratic government, for in democracies there is
nothing outside the majority capable of resisting it." Thus
Tocqueville began the most famous chapter of *Democracy in
America*, the chapter that included his short essay, "Tyranny of
the Majority," in which he wrote:

"When a man or a party suffers an injustice in the United
States, to whom can he turn? To public opinion? That is what
forms the majority. To the legislative body? It represents the

* "How," I said, "could these people of conscience allow drugs to
move so openly in black communities?"
"I think the drug traffic would be stopped if the people visibly involved, the people making money, were white," Beckham answered.
"What salves white America's conscience is that so many of the people making money on drugs are black. So you look and say, 'They're
doing it to themselves!' The white man isn't responsible. His conscience is clear."

† There may be some significance in the fact that the number of in-
terracial marriages rose from 65,000 in 1970 to 166,000 in 1980. However, it must be remembered that those numbers are still extremely
low; and the 1980 figure does not take into account the vast number
of divorces and remarriages in the later decade.

majority and obeys it blindly. To the executive power? It is appointed by the majority and serves as its passive instrument. To the police? They are nothing but the majority under arms. A jury? The jury is the majority vested with the right to pronounce judgment; even the judges in certain states are elected by the majority. So, however iniquitous or unreasonable the measure which hurts you, you must submit. . . .

"I am not asserting that at the present time in America there are frequent acts of tyranny. I do say that one can find no guarantee against it there and the reasons for the government's gentleness must be sought in circumstances and mores rather than in the laws."

And later in the same chapter: "If ever freedom is lost in America, that will be due to the omnipotence of the majority driving the minorities to desperation and forcing them to appeal to physical force."

PART FOUR

Philadelphia
to Washington

16

PHILADELPHIA I

"Everyone Is the Same Size on Television . . ."

The noise of Philadelphia was black noise on the June morning I
arrived. The central streets of the city that William Penn and
the Society of Friends founded as a haven for religious dissenters
in 1682—they made up the name from the Greek words for
"City of Brotherly Love"—were crowded with people who
seemed to be doing things and going places. More than half of
the faces I saw were black—and, in 1980, more than a third of
the residents of America's fourth-largest city were the descendants of slaves. The exuberant patois called "Black English" was
in the air, blending with the Caribbean sound of steel drums
played on street corners, and with loud rock music pumped out
by store loudspeakers and suitcase radios carried like electronic
armor by young men. On Fifteenth Street, near City Hall,
twenty well-dressed black boys and girls happily sang spirituals
and held up signs transcribed with the verses from the third
chapter of the book of John. "Jesus answered and said unto
him," was printed on the card marked John 3:3, "Verily, verily, I
say unto thee, Except a man be born again, he cannot see the
kingdom of God."

"This place sure has worked for me," said George Childs, a
taxi driver, who was black. "My mother was a widow—my father was a cement finisher and he died when I was five years
old—and she brought up all of us, six children. It was hard, but

235

she did it. Now my daughter is a college professor, a professor in New Jersey, and her husband is a lawyer. I think that's pretty good."

So did I. And it wasn't the only good thing I heard that day.

"This city is very much more democratic than it was when I began here thirty years ago," said Frank C. P. McGlinn, a bank vice president, who was white. "The social stratification has broken down. It was used to keep out any outsiders. In those days, the city was run by the old families, the Pennsylvania Railroad, and the power company. The railroad or the power company could bring the banks in line just by threatening to withdraw their deposits. That's gone now. In fact, there's been a tendency in the last two years for the boards of the banks to replace presidents from old families with outsiders chosen for nothing but talent—a Bodine and an Ingersoll were replaced that way."

"If someone you didn't know walked into your bank today," I said, "and that person wanted a loan to buy a house or start a business, would his chances be better or worse than they were thirty years ago?"

"Oh, better. There's no comparison. The little guy has a much better chance today. He had almost no chance in the old days. Things are totally different now. If that's democracy, then banking is much, much more democratic."

"What if the little guy is black?"

"His chances may be even better. The government wants it that way."

That night, June 19, 1979, more than 1,500 black people crowded into Calvary Evangelical Lutheran Church in Southwest Philadelphia to discuss the shooting, two nights before, of three young boys, black boys. One of the boys, a thirteen-year-old named Tracey Chambers, was dead and the assumption was that his killer was a white sniper. "We're going to fight back," said Representative Milton Street, a black member of the Pennsylvania State Assembly. "We're going to pick up guns and fight back. We're going to make the situation so nasty that somebody does something about it. We're going to avenge that little boy's death." During the day, Representative Street had appeared on a local radio station and called for "5,000 to 10,000 black men" to purchase guns as a visible warning to "white men."

So this was Philadelphia, the City of Brotherly Love, the place where the contracts of American democracy—the Declaration of Independence and the Constitution—had been signed 200 years before. People were publicly calling for armed insurrection. The rebels had a cause, historic oppression and continuing degradation. They even had a martyr. Was civil war at hand?

The next morning, the city's leading newspaper, the *Inquirer*, reported, faithfully and accurately, Street's call—"encouraging blacks to arm themselves" was the paper's phrase—as the eighteenth paragraph of a long story on the investigation of Chambers' murder and the shooting of the other two boys.

I went to see the executive editor of the *Inquirer*, Eugene Roberts, an old friend, and together we tried to find out why the politician's call to arms was reported with such apparent casualness.

Was there a management decision not to emphasize Street's words, to minimize their impact on a city that was regularly described in its own newspapers as "racially troubled"? "No," Roberts said. "I'm 'management' and I didn't even know he said anything."

We found the subeditor who had made the decision about the use of the quotation.

Did you consider not using Street's words because they were so inflammatory?

"Of course not. We don't suppress the news."

Why was it played so far down in the story?

"I didn't think it was that important. Street always talks that way. A lot of people talk that way around here."

Big talk is the genius of American democracy. Loud talk. Crazy talk. Free talk. Freedom of speech. Freedom of assembly. Freedom of the press. It bothered and confused Tocqueville, as it has others before and since. He used the term "association"—associating together—to describe the use of freedom of assembly. Two days before arriving in Philadelphia in 1831, he wrote in his notebook: "They associate in the interests of commerce, for objects political, literary and religious." He was amazed, for instance, by temperance societies, "one of the most remarkable things in this country . . . an association of men who engage mutually to abstain from a vice." Then he learned that just before he came to the city, there had been a "Free Trade" convention in Philadelphia at the same time that a "Friends of Domestic Industry" convention was going on in New York—pro- and antitariff groups had organized the meetings. "Of all that I have seen in America," he wrote two days after his arrival, "it is this convention which has most struck me as being . . . a dangerous and impracticable consequence of the sovereignty of the people."*

The Frenchman shared his fears with a prominent lawyer and former legislator, Charles Jared Ingersoll, the son of a delegate to the Constitutional Convention and an ancestor of the bank president who lost his job to an outsider in 1978. Ingersoll argued that Tocqueville misunderstood both the process and the real function of political assemblies. "The dangers of which you are afraid are in my opinion less to be feared," the American said. "The object of the convention is not to act but to persuade. It represents an opinion, an interest . . . [it] starts from the fact that it does not represent the majority, but wishes to act on public opinion and change the majority by persuasion."

"But," Tocqueville said, "the opinion and interest you speak of is able to put its arguments forward daily by means of the press."

That's the whole idea, answered this Philadelphia lawyer of 150 years ago. The assembly, the convention, was a way to attract the attention of the press and to project arguments with greater weight and credibility than any single speaker, journalist, or journal might have. "There are some opinions," the American said, "which, by the very fact they are shared by the minority, would be forever repressed by the majority, if by the side of the public assemblies"—Congress, for example— "which express the all-powerful wishes of the majority there were not to be found gatherings (likewise supplied with the moral power that numbers give) which may plead the interests of the minority and make, not laws, but speeches calculated to win over the majority itself. . . .

"When men can speak in liberty, you can bet they won't act," said Charles Ingersoll. He was a wise man. The United

* Out of curiosity, I checked the membership of two modern "temperance" societies, one designed to serve a public purpose and the other purely commercial. There were, I learned, more than 900,000 members of Alcoholics Anonymous and more than 500,000 of Weight-Watchers, Inc.

States has bet that line for 200 years, and it has usually paid off.

Milton Street wasn't going to *act*—he was not going to pick up a gun, he was not even going to march, and nothing ever happened because of his words. He was going to go home and watch himself on television and wait for the next morning's *Inquirer* to see how much play and space he would get. He must have been disappointed to see his words so deep in the story, back on the "jump" page, the page on which front page stories are "continued." Street would have been the most surprised man in Philadelphia if anyone else had acted on his call. If a citizen had actually taken up a gun and gone to shoot down whites, Street would have been back on television and in the papers cluckingly denouncing the poor soul as a lunatic who understood neither the words he heard nor the American system. Representative Street was the system: he held precisely the same official legislative position once held by Charles Ingersoll, the son of a drafter of the Constitution.*

That's how it worked. The United States, in modern times, had been a remarkably stable country politically; more than that, the nation was a remarkably stable society. The political arguments I heard during my journey were about means, not ends—"There is only one party in America," Beaumont wrote in a letter, "the quarrels which are carried on in the newspapers or in society concern persons rather than things"—and not a single person I met talked about leaving the United States. Indeed, it was the rare man or woman who even suggested that Americans might learn anything from the experience and ideas of other societies. The United States, simply, had kept most, or at least enough, of its promises, economic and political—allowing, providing for, and sometimes fostering movement within the society. And that movement often included upwardly mobile dissent.

George Childs, the cab driver who grew up in hard poverty but whose grandchildren were the children of a college professor and a lawyer, was part of that. He believed that America had kept its promise to him, that if he worked Puritan hard, he would be "better off" than his parents, and his children could be

---

* Street was elected to Pennsylvania's upper house, the State Senate, five months after the killing of Tracy Chambers.

better off than he was. Milton Street and the evolution of his radicalism into pseudoradicalism, media-radicalism, was part of that stability, too. America had delivered on two promises to him: financial comfort and a measure of recognition. The recognition, though, was not really power, or it wasn't very much of it. Street just had fame: minutes, hours, days, or years of being heard, if not listened to. His rewards were the trade-off for preventing the secret plots of real insurrection. Tocqueville, despite his fear that American democracy was living on the edge of anarchy, came to understand that and he later wrote: "This form of freedom, howsoever dangerous, does provide guarantees in one direction: in countries where associations are free, secret societies are unknown. There are factions in America, but no conspirators."

Milton Street in Philadelphia and Maxine Waters in Los Angeles might have been conspirators; instead they were made into celebrities, recruited and protected by a grateful majority. They were on television, speaking to state or nation, part of the thunder and static that had impressed me back in Newport, and so were other dissenters who were still further from the center of the established order of the moment.

While I was traveling in New England, I had talked with Edmund G. Brown, Jr., the governor of California, whose father had also been governor. He was running, unsuccessfully, for President. What was the difference, I asked, between the times each of you—your father and you—were in office? "Television," he said. "Demonstrators and protesters of any kind have the same access to television as the governor of California. The person picketing my office is going to have the same chance, the same 30 seconds, to get his message across to all the people watching the news on television as I will have. He has the same power I have." That was probably an exaggeration. The same access is not necessarily the same power. But that equal access to public opinion is democratic and democratizing—I was struck again by the thought that everyone is the same size on television.

The debate itself, then, was the end of all this, not the means; America celebrated the dialogue, reasoned and angry. The dissenters were absorbed; monuments were built to them. It was not only Rosa Parks who had a boulevard named for her in Detroit; there were freeways there named for Martin Luther King and for Walter Reuther, the United Auto Workers leader who had been threatened, beaten, and jailed during the 1930s when he attempted to unionize the city's auto plants. "That's the way it's supposed to be," said Judith Shklar, a professor of government at Harvard University. "Everybody gets sucked into the culture of multiplicity. By protesting you become part of what you're protesting against. It goes all the way back: after the Revolution, the Federalists really wanted aristocracy, so they went out on the hustings and campaigned for it."

Times have changed to the extent that while the Federalists had to pay their own expenses on the campaign trail, modern dissenters often don't. Dissent began paying quite well after television created the demand for an almost endless supply of American celebrities—there were fees available from television shows and movie makers, publishers and lecture bureaus. In some countries late in the twentieth century, terrorists were seizing people and buildings, then demanding, as ransom, the privilege of appearing on television to articulate their cries of injustice and revolution; in the United States, networks and publishers were competing for the privilege of having star dissenters gently interviewed by star reporters. There were careers to be made here. The "revolutionaries" of one decade—Tom Hayden, a radical leader of the 1960s, was an example—built on the fame of the moment, the star interviews, to become the state assembly and U. S. Senate candidates of the next decade. Could their messages and threats, their calls to insurrection, have been more effectively suppressed by force? by imprisonment? by expulsion? by censorship?

"We've glorified tolerance in the twentieth century, haven't we?" said Edwin Bronner, a historian and the librarian of Haverford College, near Philadelphia. I had sought him out because he was a Quaker leader, chairman of the Friends World Committee for Consultation. He was speaking of both Americans and Quakers when he said "we." Both have raised tolerance to a fundamental value, but the religious group, the Society of Friends, probably learned too late the political power and benefits of celebrating tolerance and smothering dissent with attention and understanding. "In the old days," Bronner said, "Quakers disowned dissenters. Thousands and thousands of people were thrown out for marrying outside of meeting. During the

Civil War, young men were disowned for performing any military service. By Vietnam, the same offense was met with what we call 'loving disagreement.' "

But by then there were few Quakers left to either love or disagree with each other. When Tocqueville visited Philadelphia, then a city of about 80,000, there were more than 30,000 Quakers in the area. When I was there, the city's population was more than 1.5 million and the number of Quakers was down to 15,000, part of a worldwide community of some 200,000 men and women. There were many reasons for the decline of the Quakers—among them the fact that it was difficult in prospering, enterprising America to be both wealthy and a good Quaker—but the Society of Friends had contributed to its own decline by excluding rather than including dissenters at critical times in Quaker history. Americans in general, it seemed, discovered the effect and the value of loving disagreement before the Quakers. The Friends had been too rigid to absorb and suppress dissent with smiling, knowing skill.

Tocqueville seemed in awe of the Americans' encouragement of big political talk. In *Democracy in America,* he used the free trade convention in Philadelphia as an example of freedom of association and "just how far it is tolerated."

"In America," he wrote, "there is no limit to freedom of association for political ends. . . . The assembly, which in American fashion styled itself a convention, was constituted at Philadelphia; it counted more than two hundred members. The discussions were public . . . After ten days the assembly broke up, having issued an address to the American people. In that address it declared first that Congress had not the right to impose a tariff and that the existing tariff was unconstitutional . . ."

So? Pretty tame stuff to an American.

"It must be admitted," the visitor went on, with what may have been limited conviction, "that unlimited freedom of association in the political sphere has not yet produced in America the fatal results that one might anticipate from it elsewhere."

"The power of association has reached its uttermost development in America . . ." he had written in his notebook. "It is never by an appeal to a superior authority that success is sought, but by an appeal to individual resources, organized to act in harmony."

Those images of people doing for themselves, of improvised assemblies of citizens removing obstacles from roads and appealing to their fellow man rather than to government, may have been a bit exaggerated even in 1831. Certainly, in a functioning democracy, it is hard to differentiate between an appeal to the people and pleas or pressure directed at government. But whatever happened when a tree blocked the road in 1831, I already had the testimony of what happened 150 years later: people telephoned City Hall, and if a truck didn't come out, they called their councilman or assemblyman or congressman.

On a June day in Philadelphia in 1979, assemblies of citizens had been improvised in many places, not so much to do something themselves, but to attract enough public attention to persuade, or force, superior authority to take some action favorable to those concerned. The parents of some of the 46 students of the Fourth Street Academy for Emotionally Disturbed Children, a public school in North Philadelphia, were occupying the school to protest government plans to close it and relocate the children in other facilities. The parents' goal was, first, to direct public attention to their problem, and then to embarrass officials of the city and the Philadelphia School District into meeting their demands rather than being forced to go on television night after night to defend themselves against parents charging them with persecuting disabled children. After four days, school officials agreed to keep the school open while they negotiated with the angry parents.

At the same time, all around the city, "independent truckers"—drivers who owned and operated their own tractor-trailer trucks—were using their huge vehicles as obstacles in the road, blocking traffic to attract public attention and force government action. The owner-drivers were protesting the high prices of their fuel, diesel oil, and the national highway speed limit of 55 miles per hour, which reduced their income by requiring more time for each trip. Their demonstrations were aimed at the President of the United States; they wanted Federal orders and regulation giving them preferential treatment in fuel purchases. Millions of other drivers were inconvenienced, and the threats and anger on both sides were recorded nightly on television and daily in the newspapers until the President himself did say that he would try to work out something.

Freedom of assembly was alive and well in Philadelphia, but the demonstration had replaced the convention. The press, too, was still free—freer than it had ever been anywhere. But the press, technologically, had been revolutionized. The truckers' angry words on the Pennsylvania Turnpike that day were transmitted electronically, changing what people knew and when they knew it in homes in the California deserts, in Alaska, in the small islands reaching south from Florida. At the same hour, across the continent, millions of Americans saw these truckers threatening to make daily life miserable for most of the people most of the time unless government met certain demands. "We're just waiting for a confrontation," said one of them, Tom Haedrich, leaning against his rig, which was barricading a service station in Philadelphia.

This was not what used to be called debate; this technologically driven speedup of democracy was different from the slow building of public opinion that Tocqueville had seen and studied. Instantaneous electronic debate was, by its nature, confrontation. Haedrich's words could be shown, followed instantly by the words and anger of a motorist stranded hundreds of miles away, then by the President or another official forced to comment because of the public disruption of precious commerce. And by commenting he was being forced to accept responsibility, or appear to accept responsibility, for ending that disruption of the public order. All this had to be transmitted—and absorbed—in about one minute; that bit of information lightning was in competition for time and attention with hundreds of other stories sparking electronically around the world, ringing the globe itself, like weather.

The technologies, the miracles that were invented after Tocqueville—in communications there was the telegraph, the rotary press, radio and then television—inevitably changed the techniques of the political process he observed. Information is power; control over the flow of information in a democracy is essential to the exercise of political power. What we know, and when we know it inevitably determines our actions as individuals, citizens, officials—as a nation. The speed of the process, I supposed, would be blinding to a nineteenth-century Frenchman. It was confusing enough to a twentieth-century American. But it was only a tool, the product of marvelous machinery to

deliver messages, to make certain ideas the context for the decision making of a government of the people.

"These are tools of my trade," said John Morris, a union official, pointing to typewriters, small printing machines, a stack of
portable sound systems (bullhorns), and a shelf of law books at
his headquarters in North Philadelphia. "Organization is important," he said. "But first we want public opinion on our side, and
then these are the weapons." He nodded toward the lawbooks.
"The lifeline of this union, of all unions, is what we can do politically. Who gets elected and what laws are passed. That is life
and death for us."

Morris was the business agent of Local 115 of the International Brotherhood of Teamsters. His local represented 2,600 of
the 2.3 million members of the brotherhood, which was originally a truck drivers' union but had grown to include almost
every kind of American worker.

"Truck drivers," Morris growled as he watched the evening's
news on NBC television, "are not the same as 'truckers.' " The
network was reporting the chaos caused by the independent
truckers, the owner-drivers, on highways around the country. "If
we did what they're doing," Morris said, "I'd be in jail right
now. . . . It's not a strike and they're not labor. They're employers, businessmen. But they're going to stop union truck drivers
and everybody else until they get what they want. And they will
get what they want—because the laws are on their side."

Morris, watching the independent truckers making their demands on government, was a study in bitter frustration. He was
probably correct in guessing that he would be in jail if his members, Teamsters, were doing the same thing—that is, shutting
down companies other than the ones that employed them. If
union members had done that, it would have been a secondary
boycott, against the law. The owner-drivers did it and it was just
another demonstration—not because that was logical but because that bit of law favored owners over employees.

Morris had been a union organizer for 31 years, beginning in a
Philadelphia department store, where he was a checker in the
lingerie department. For at least the last twenty of those years,
he said, he had realized that organized labor was in decline. "I
think," he said, "that if the corporations wanted to finish us off
they could do it. But why should they? Things are going fine for

them and they've always got the unions to blame for their own screw-ups."

Many Americans would have been astounded by that statement; many saw unions as all-powerful, massive organizations using strikes, the threat of strikes, and political activism and contributions to get whatever they wanted. The Teamsters sometimes seemed to be the best example of that power: members earned a minimum of $10.30 an hour and periodically thundered threats of a national transportation strike and hinted at violence directed at opposing workers and managements.

Morris' eye was clearer. His view was from inside a movement that had peaked long ago, losing a long struggle for public opinion and the day-to-day political contest for control over the laws and their interpretation. He had seen the rise and the fall of American labor—which was quite different from the pattern in other countries, where once the rise began it tended to become irresistible—a rise and fall that provided some insight into the character of Americans, the workings of their government, and the dynamics of democracy.

Labor unionism—the association of employees in an industry or company—had risen as a democratic reaction to the "manufacturing aristocracy" that Tocqueville saw as "one of the hardest that have appeared on earth." By 1945, with substantial help from federal laws designed to enforce fair protection of individual employees after employers had shown a general disinclination to do that, more than 35 percent of America's nonagricultural workforce was unionized. By the end of the 1970s, less than 25 percent of the same workforce belonged to unions.

The movement, even at its peak, was never at peace with American individualism. Certainly nothing in the nation's history ever indicated that Americans were really comfortable with one of the tenets of unionism: economic equality. The egalitarianism of Americans has tended toward the political and social over the years. Americans have generally seemed determined to protect themselves economically in case they should become rich. Americans did not want to overthrow the rich, they wanted to join them. Beyond that, the Constitution—specifically the make-up of the United States Senate—was designed to prevent regional domination, and organized labor was never more than a regional phenomenon. Even when labor probably had the real support of a majority of Americans, its strength was concentrated in only a dozen states. Eighty percent of union members were in the cities of the Northeast and Middle West, where the man-crushing inequities of the Industrial Revolution had been most apparent, and in California, Oregon, and Washington along the West Coast, where a frontier populism, a Tocquevillian association, had taken hold in lumber camps and then paper mills and canneries. In the end, you couldn't win in the United States Senate with 38 states, no matter how small, voting against you. Labor was beaten down by small towns and by the South and Southwest, and the decline accelerated as new transportations and technologies made it easier for managers to move their companies to those places.

The Senate, in fact, was a major focus of Morris' anger. "I don't think we ever really recovered from the Senate Rackets Committee hearings in the 1950s," he said. "The McClellan Committee hearings. People think we're all gangsters. That, helped along by public resentment over strikes by policemen and teachers, public employees, created a climate that made it easy for our enemies, for the corporations, the chambers of commerce, conservatives from the South. We have not been able to do anything about the laws. Corporations can sue for damages in a strike, but unions can only sue for back pay for members. Union officers are restricted to three-year terms, so you're constantly going into negotiations with inexperienced leadership. But, mainly, it's the Taft-Hartley Act, the injunction against secondary boycotts, the fines and contempt citations that keep hitting us. It's just crippled the American labor movement."

But it was democracy, not a cabal of industrial aristocrats, that produced the laws that hobbled organized labor. The movement served a larger purpose and then its limits were redefined by an American consensus. Democracy worked. For every action there is an equal and opposite reaction; for every movement there will eventually be an equal and opposite movement.

What happened always—and what should have encouraged John Morris about the future of the balance of power between labor and management—was a push toward the middle. The republic itself, Tocqueville was told in Philadelphia, was "the victory and the rule of the middle classes." Those were the words of the mayor of the city, Benjamin W. Richards, a popular execu-

tive who was then in the process of being reelected by the Select
and Common Councils.

The city was once again choosing a mayor when I arrived in
1979. The choice this time, of course, would be made by popular
election—the country, again, was institutionally much more
democratic than it was in 1831—and the man who would win
the 1979 election was William J. Green III. When I asked him
which classes, which elements of Philadelphia, would rule when
he was mayor, Green answered softly, "All of them."

His slogan, in fact, was: "Green—If you want a mayor who'll
stop the fighting between us by fighting for all of us." *

Mayor Richards was described by contemporaries as "imposing" and "handsome." So was Green. He was almost flawlessly
handsome—and tall and dark—like the simple paintings of
heroes on the covers of romantic paperback novels. His name,
too, was imposing, at least in Philadelphia. His father was William J. Green, Jr., a Democratic congressman for 12 years and
the city's undisputed political leader for most of that time.
When the elder Green died, his son, then a twenty-five-year-old
law student, was elected in his place. That was in 1964, and
Green had run for political office eight times in the ensuing 15
years. Obviously that was his business, running for office.

Why did he want to be mayor? Because, as far as I could tell,
it's there. This is a verbatim account of the heart of our conversation:

Q. What groups or interests do you have to appeal to and to
represent to be mayor of Philadelphia?

A. I represent everybody. I want a constituency that includes
everybody.

Q. How do you put a constituency like that together?

A. By visiting everyone.

(I waited.)

A. By meeting with them.

(I waited again.)

A. By telling them what I want to do.

---

* Green's slogan and much of his campaign was planned to contrast
him with the incumbent Democratic mayor, Frank Rizzo, who was
seen, by many, as a divisive figure deliberately favoring whites over
blacks.

Q. What do you tell them you want to do?

A. Bring the city together.

(I waited. I was probably staring.)

A. End the confrontation.

(I waited.)

A. End the corruption.

(I waited.)

A. End waste. Government wastes a lot of money.

(I waited again. But by then he was on to the game. He said nothing and I, concluding that I had heard the entire Green program, was forced to fill the silence with another question.)

Q. Are the decisions concerning government help for the poor people of Philadelphia made in Philadelphia itself, or are they made in Washington?

A. They're made in many places.

Q. Where should those decisions be made?

A. In many places.

Q. How would you define political power?

A. As the ability to relate to others.

There were other questions. And other answers. Among them:

"I don't want to be quoted on that subject."

"I don't want to guess at that."

"I don't want to criticize anybody."

"It was good talking with you," Green said as we finished. "It's exciting to talk about ideas instead of just being out there campaigning. . . ." He went on, but I didn't catch it all. I was talking to myself, which was what I thought I had been doing for the past hour or so.

I was still talking to myself as I walked through the energetic hustle of Philadelphia's center city to Frank McGlinn's office. McGlinn was not only vice president of the Western Savings Bank but former treasurer of the national Republican party and now an adviser to Green's Republican opponent for mayor, David Marston, who had been United States Attorney for the Southern District of Pennsylvania.

"I just met one of your candidates for mayor," I said, naming no names but describing the conversation.

"I have been around politics for a long time," McGlinn said. "Most of the people who go into it are mediocrities who need it as a means of existence—financial and psychological existence. First-rate people can make their livings and their names in other fields." I laughed at how close the banker's words were to those of his counterparts who had talked with Tocqueville 150 years before. I laughed again a few weeks later when, after a local newspaper reported that I had talked with Green, McGlinn sent me a note saying: "It's amusing, but when you were speaking of interviewing a noncommitting candidate for Mayor, I assumed it was Marston."*

"They're insecure men," said Richard Doran, a Democrat, former executive secretary to the governor of Pennsylvania and a friend and adviser to Bill Green. "Bill is afraid of losing this election, afraid that if he says anything it'll be used against him. He means well and he wants people to like him. . . . No, he wasn't hiding anything from you. He has no real program beyond being elected."

Doran had left politics, officially, at least. Unofficially he was Green's speechwriter. When we spoke he was executive director of the Greater Philadelphia Partnership, an association of local corporate and business leaders organized, according to the founding committee's statement, as "a unique blend of business, academic, and community leaders pooling their resources and talents to help improve Philadelphia economically and socially."

The people and institutions with a stake in Philadelphia thought it needed that kind of help. The city's population had declined almost 15 percent—to about 1.7 million people—between 1970 and 1980. It shared the problems of all the country's older cities, particularly older northern cities—loss of people and commerce, of tax revenues as corporations and individuals moved away to escape high taxes or high wages, black people or cold weather; or to find . . . to find whatever it is that Americans are energetically chasing in what Tocqueville, a bit sarcastically, called the American's "futile pursuit of that complete felicity which always escapes him."

"Philadelphia is being shaken down to what it will be in the future," Doran said. "The corporations that are still here—the ones that haven't moved out—either can't move or have strong

---

* Green, the Democrat, defeated Marston, the Republican, 297,205 votes to 164,978.

family commitments to Philadelphia. The banks can't move because they are really state institutions and the laws hold them here, and companies like Smith, Kline, the drug firm, stay even though consultants have told them they would be better off moving. Fantus, the people who move companies, recommended that Smith, Kline move to South Carolina for tax reasons, but they bucked the tide and decided to stay."*

"The elements and the forces that will change the national character, that will shape our future are already here," said Eugene Roberts of the *Inquirer*. "They are in place in Philadelphia."

He was optimistic about that national future. "Sometimes you think the country has run out of energy and you want to cry," he said. "Or laugh. I was in Bangor, Maine, the other day and I was taken to what they said was the best restaurant in town. Naturally I asked for lobster, Maine lobster. They didn't have any. They served Alaska king crab, flown in frozen. America *is* homogenized, but it is not static. Look at the Cubans in Miami. They've transformed the city, turned it into a boom town; they brought the same energy here that our great-grandparents, or whoever, did in their time. And they will spread from Miami. It starts in one place and spreads into the country, like the Jews spread out from New York seventy, eighty years ago. The same thing is happening now in other places, with other people driving for the middle class, driving to be Americans. People want to be Americans. They want what we have. They are already here and they will keep coming—Chicanos, Iranians, Koreans, Puerto Ricans . . ."

And what about blacks? Black Americans.

A few blocks beyond the lively, noisy, black and white center city where Roberts and I were spending $70 for dinner—a few blocks in almost every direction—were miles of the meanest urban slums I had ever seen. The decay and the degradation

---

* The banks did stay in the city, but they continually made efforts to expand their operations into the suburbs, other parts of Pennsylvania, and other parts of the country. Among other things, they tended to remove "Philadelphia" from the names, so that Philadelphia Fidelity Bank became Fidelity Trust. The city's newspapers did the same thing: the *Philadelphia Inquirer* and the *Philadelphia Bulletin* became the *Inquirer* and the *Bulletin*.

were worse than in many other places because the housing was older; it had been built in the late eighteenth and early nineteenth century. Some of the worst buildings were the houses of which Beaumont wrote in a letter home: "This city of 200,000 souls . . . is of a regularity that one is tempted to find too perfect. Not a street but traverses the whole city in one direction or another; and all of them are laid out with geometric precision. All the edifices are neat, kept up with extreme care . . . its sole defect I repeat is to be monotonous in its beauty."*

Roberts, who had grown up in a town named Pikeville in South Georgia, had made his reputation, a distinguished one, writing about black people—about the civil rights movement in the South and riots in the North. His answer surprised me.

"The blacks are making it. They will always be there. Moving slow—but steady."

My surprise must have shown because Roberts said, "You have to have seen what I've seen. I remember being in a place called Pugh City, Mississippi, in the Delta above New Orleans, in late 1967. One of the Pughs, sitting in a room full of black men, began talking about 'how many head of nigger' he had working for him. In Pikeville, I remember a boy I knew who followed his parents down the street as they pulled along a child's wagon selling fish they had just caught. He, my friend, is now the biggest contractor around there. And the sons and daughters of the 'lintheads,' the white folks who worked in the cotton mills, are doctors. It may not seem like much to you, but what I see is blacks where whites were in the 1940s and 1950s.

"No society can quickly absorb a peasantry. Some European countries have not been able to do it all—and at least in Europe, peasant families were preserved. We broke up the black family during slavery, then left blacks in 75 years of peasantry, then when they moved to the cities, we only let the women work—as maids. There was nothing for the men to do.

"But they keep moving up the ladder. They shall overcome."

---

* Beaumont overestimated the population. Tocqueville, writing home, said: "Philadelphia is, I believe, the only city in the world where it has occurred to people to distinguish the streets by numbers and not by names. . . . Europeans never fail to join an idea to each external object, be it a saint, a famous man, an event. But these people here know only arithmetic."

17

PHILADELPHIA II

"The Reign of Terror . . ."

A scene stuck with me after my visit to Philadelphia. I took the train west from the city to the village of Haverford to meet the Quaker leader Edwin Bronner. Less than a mile from the railroad station, I turned into the stone gateway of the college and walked down a long road through a perfect landscape of small hills. There was a duck pond just on the other side of the split-rail fence along the roadway, and a child's bicycle leaned against the fence near the pond.

As I got closer, I saw that the bike was chained and locked to the fence.

Crime, or, more precisely, crime and punishment, had brought Alexis de Tocqueville and Gustave de Beaumont to the United States. The principal reason, in fact, for the young Frenchmen's visit to Philadelphia was to see one of the wonders of Pennsylvania and of the Quakers, the Eastern State Penitentiary. The two-year-old prison, built under the supervision of a Quaker group called the Society for Alleviating the Miseries of the Public Prisons, was, if nothing else, the most expensive in the world, costing $432,000, or more than $2,000 for each of 200 cells. "The prison is truly a palace," Beaumont observed, "each prisoner enjoys all the comforts of life."

Not quite. It only looked like a palace, or seemed like one, in comparison to most of the other prisons of the day in both Europe and America. Along with the prisons at Ossining and Au-

Eastern State Penitentiary near Philadelphia

burn, Eastern State was the first of what might be called modern penitentiaries—walled structures with individual cells, rather than common rooms and yards for men, women, and children. The new penitentiaries, an American innovation, were the first to institutionalize on a large scale the use of detention itself as punishment for crime. Almost all other prisons of the day—and of previous history—tended to use detention as just that, the detaining of prisoners until they could be judged and condemned to death, beating, branding, or exile.

In fifteen of the twenty-four American states of 1831 there was no attempt and little thought given to improving prison systems that architecturally and spiritually went back to the invention of the wall. That was one conclusion of Beaumont and Tocqueville's official report to the French government, "On the Penitentiary System in the United States and Its Application to France."* In New Orleans, they reported, prison-

* The study was published in Paris in June 1833—two years before publication of the first volume of *Democracy in America*—under the title: *"Du Système Pénitentiaire aux États-Unis et de son application*

ers were housed with hogs. In Cincinnati, half the prisoners were in chains.

Eastern State, then, seemed to be humanitarian, even luxurious. It was neither. It was a thoughtless and arrogant experiment, the kind of thing that gives good intentions, and reformers, a bad name. Each prisoner was kept in solitary confinement, the theory being that reflection and Bible reading would lead to self-reform, self-rehabilitation. Often they led to insanity. Eleven years after Tocqueville was there, another visitor to the famous prison, Charles Dickens, wrote: "In its intention I am well convinced that it is kind, humane and meant for reformation; but I am persuaded that those who devised the system and those benevolent gentlemen who carry it into execution do not know what it is they are doing. . . . I hold this slow and daily tampering with the mysteries of the brain to be immeasurably worse than any torture of the body. . . ."

Tocqueville, after listening to the best citizens of Philadelphia extoll the virtues of their expensive new prison, stunned them by asking to talk with prisoners. And so he did, with one after another in their clean and airy cubicles, each including an attached, walled exercise yard. Each isolated from all others. He took extensive notes:

"No. 41—This inmate is a young man; he admits that he is a criminal; he weeps during the whole course of our conversation. . . ."

"No. 61—Horse-stealing . . . No one, he says, can conceive what horror there is in continued solitude. On being asked how he manages to pass the time, answers that he has but two pleasures: working and reading his Bible . . . he can't speak for very long without being moved and having tears in his eyes. (We have made the same observation with all those seen up to the present.) . . ."

And with Number 28, the first prisoner he saw:

"Q. Do you see the keepers often?"

"A. About six times a day."

"Q. Is it a consolation to you to see them?"

---

en France, suivi d'un appendice sur les colonies pénales et de notes statisques." Par MM. G. de Beaumont et A. de Tocqueville, avocats à la Cour royale de Paris, membres de la société historique de Pennsylvanie.

"A. Yes, Sir: it's sort of a joy to glimpse their faces. This summer a cricket came into my yard. *It looked like company for me.* When a butterfly or any other animal enters my cell, I never do it any harm."

Eastern State Penitentiary was in use for more than a hundred years before the last prisoners were moved out in the early 1930s. The buildings still stood, in crumbling disrepair, on Fairmount Avenue in North Philadelphia; they were used for the storage of state trucks, snowplows, other heavy equipment. The function of the famous prison was taken over by the Graterford Correctional Institute, which was built between 1928 and 1932 in the farm country 30 miles northwest of the city.

Graterford was one of the largest prisons in the world, a huge structure standing, low and stark, against the sky like a Saharan fort. The undecorated walls, thirty feet high above the ground and thirty feet below the ground to prevent tunneling escapes, seven feet thick at ground level and 22 inches thick at the top, enclosed 62 acres containing 2,000 cells in five parallel blocks, four stories high and 692 feet long. Each cell was 12 feet long by 6 feet wide, with a 9½ foot ceiling. There were a toilet and sink in the corner of each concrete-and-steel room. There were 1,600 acres of state-owned farms outside the walls. The total staff of the institution was 530, including 316 guards; only those stationed in nine towers around the walls carried rifles and pistols. The number of prisoners in Graterford on the day I was there was 1,750. Of those men, 1,444 were black.*

---

* A study of the criminal justice system in Philadelphia, published in 1976 by Professor Franklin Zimring of the University of Chicago Law School, reported that blacks convicted of homicide generally receive longer prison sentences than whites, especially if the victim was white.

Two robbery cases handled by criminal courts in the city during 1980 were reported this way in the *New York Times* of March 8, 1981: "Thomas Szumski, 21, and Jerry Ivy, 19 . . . stood for sentencing before two different judges in Philadelphia. Szumski's judge, sitting without a jury, found him guilty of robbery, conspiracy and aggravated assault; a jury returned the same verdict in a case against Ivy. Szumski and another white man had held up a drugstore. After the unresisting pharmacist turned over his cash and narcotics, Szumski fired a shot, wounding the druggist in the side. Jerry Ivy, a black, had pointed a gun at the head of a white bus driver and demanded cash.

"Stories of how bad prison life is are exaggerated," said Vebley Wells, Jr. "Being locked up is punishment enough—being away from your family and your friends and being helpless." Wells, inmate Number M0353, a forty-one-year-old black man, was serving a life sentence. In 1969, in his back yard in Bethlehem, Pennsylvania, he killed a policeman with a shotgun. "It can be dangerous here, but the violence is not as bad as they say. If you watch yourself, it's okay. . . . They don't really rehabilitate anyone here. Maybe they can rehabilitate some younger man, but you can't really rehabilitate most people. But you can break them."

"Only one in a thousand prisoners refuses to break," said Thomas Stachelek, assistant to the prison's superintendent. Like other prison administrators I had met during my travels, he used one word over and over again in describing the institution's operations. The word was "control." As Warden Robert Henderson had said at Auburn Prison, Stachelek and other Graterford officials told me that maintaining control was easier because a single group, blacks, constituted a working majority of the inmate population. Both he and Henderson cited California prisons as "problem" prisons because administrators had to deal with the power struggle between two groups of prisoners with rough numerical equality, blacks and Mexican-Americans, Chicanos. At Graterford, as at Auburn, prison officials actively sought out and attempted to develop an inmate leadership class. The idea, as Henderson had told me and Stachelek and others confirmed, was to make prisoners "accept responsibility for control themselves in return for the rewards that are almost always totally psychological."

The whip, which Elam Lynds, founder of the Auburn system,

Ivy's juvenile accomplice, also a black, collected money from the four white passengers. No one was hurt. Szumski had a prior drug conviction. Ivy had been found guilty of robbery as a juvenile. Law enforcement personnel regarded the two men's crimes and records as roughly equal." Szumski was put on probation for five years by Judge Alfred Di Bona on January 18, 1980. Ivy was sentenced to serve 15 to 30 years in the state penitentiary by Judge Levy Anderson on July 1, 1980. (On August 18, 1980, Szumski was arrested in Philadelphia and charged with burglary, theft by unlawful taking, criminal trespass, and criminal conspiracy.)

had considered essential 150 years before, was gone, but psychology, laid on prisoners with the same intent and purpose, seemed as effective. My conversations with keepers and inmates led to the same conclusions that Tocqueville recorded in his notebook in 1831: "During the whole course of this conversation which, often resumed, lasted several hours, Mr. Elam Lynds returned constantly to this idea that it was above all necessary to bend the prisoner to a *passive obedience.* That point obtained, everything became easy, whatever was the situation of the prison, the kind or place of work. . . ."

"What do they teach you here?" I asked Rexcell Cook, inmate F3925, a twenty-eight-year-old black man who had served six years of a six-to-eighteen-year term for armed robbery. "They teach us to respect the institution," he said. "They teach us to get along."

Cook, a big man, gregarious, said he was caught robbing a jewelry store in Philadelphia. It was his fifth armed robbery, his first arrest. "I wasn't treated fairly," he said. Like other inmates, he did not deny committing the crime for which he was convicted but did complain that police or the court system had dealt too harshly with him and his case. "There's guys in here for two-and-a-half-to-five for homicide and I never killed nobody. Nobody didn't get hurt from me. Sure, they were frightened. Anybody'd be frightened if you stick a pistol in their face.

"A guy was stabbed here five times last night. You can get killed here for a pack of cigarettes . . . You have to be part of something to protect yourself"—he was one of 500 Black Muslims in Graterford—"most guys go with people from where they come from. They may not have known each other on the outside, but here you get together because you're from South Philadelphia or North, or Germantown. That's how it breaks down here."

Miguel Rivera, inmate F4976, repeated one of Cook's phrases: "They'll kill ya in here for a pack of cigarettes." A thirty-one-year-old native of Puerto Rico, he was one of 56 Hispanics in Graterford, most of them Chicanos from California. He was serving a life sentence after being convicted of third-degree murder in a 1974 gang rape and murder in a Philadelphia park. He was also the only inmate I talked with in any prison who denied his guilt. If he was lying, it was necessary—child molesters and rapists are judged the lowest of the low in prison society. "I hate the thought of being in the same place with people like that," Rexcell Cook had said. Rivera, who said he was often afraid in Graterford, told me: "There is not as much violence as they say, but you never know who it's going to come from or when. That is the fear."

James Charlton, inmate F5265, was a twenty-six-year-old white man from a town named Ambler, 18 miles from Philadelphia. He was serving five to ten years for forgery and burglary. After two years at Graterford, he had been allowed to work on the farms outside the walls, and he had escaped. Recaptured, he had decided, he said, to become a "model prisoner," and he hoped to be paroled soon to attend Villanova University. He had completed two years of Villanova courses as part of a program offered at the prison.

Q. Why were you stealing?

A. I needed the money. I was a heroin addict—since I was sixteen.

Q. How were you caught?

A. They caught me in the act. A cop just happened to be driving by when I broke into a place I used to work. There are only two ways you can get caught—in the act or if someone squeals on you. It's not hard to get away with crime. The police have no way of figuring out who did something unless they see it or someone who knows tells them. But the thing is, once you're arrested, they'll convict you if they want to—you'll be convicted of something. The police will lie, they'll fabricate evidence, they'll do whatever they have to. They did it to me. They do it to everybody. . . . If I had it to do over again, I would be more careful and work absolutely alone.

Q. Will you do it again?

A. I'll tell you what would keep me from doing it again—fear of coming back here. This is not pleasant. Not being around women is the worst part of it and I'm worried about what I'll be like with women when I get out. Believe me, no moral fiber has been developed in me here. What you learn here is how to get around things. The good jobs and the favors here depend on who you know. It's all connections and money. And money is very important. Most of the violence here is over debts that aren't paid. You can buy any kind of swag in here [the term, as at Auburn, meant any contraband from weapons and drugs to fruit and pornography] so you have to have cash and credit. . . . It's just a little America in here. The difference is that there are more wild people here.

"I doubt whether in any other country crime so seldom escapes punishment," Tocqueville wrote in *Democracy in America*. "The reason is that everyone thinks he has an interest in furnishing proofs of an offense and in arresting the guilty man. . . . In Europe the criminal is a luckless man fighting to save his head from the authorities; in a sense the population are mere spectators of the struggle. In America he is an enemy of the human race and every human being is against him."

They would laugh at that now in Philadelphia, and almost every other place in America. But there would be no humor in the laughter. The perception on the outside was the same as James Charlton's inside Graterford Prison: criminals were rarely caught and even more rarely punished in the United States. No arrests were made for most crimes in the United States—in cities like Philadelphia, police often did not even bother to investigate routine crimes such as automobile theft or burglary—and when arrests were actually made, the odds were that nothing more would happen than a seemingly endless string of court appearances leading almost inevitably to freedom for the accused. A review of 1976 felony arrests in six jurisdictions—Baltimore, Detroit, Washington, D. C., Chicago, Los Angeles, and San Diego—indicated that 60 percent of those arrested were not convicted and 80 percent were not imprisoned. In San Jose, California, a newer city than Philadelphia, with criminal justice systems that might be expected to be more efficient, one judge was expected to handle 294 felony cases in a single sitting on a day in February 1981. He did—California Superior Court Judge Peter Stone used an average of 20 seconds to deal with the matters and motions concerning 9 killings, 31 robberies, 84 burglaries, 2 kidnapings, one indecent exposure, and a case of alleged salmon poaching. "It's like watching a conveyor belt going by," he said at the end of the day. "A lot of the items you see week after week, with a lot of new stuff . . . at the end of the belt, only a few trickle off."

The system did become overloaded. There was more crime in America. Perhaps the best indicator of that increase was homicide rates. Statistics, particularly crime statistics, are usually debatable, but murder victims are hard to hide, and the murder rate in the country increased from 4.5 per 100,000 Americans in 1965 to 10.0 per 100,000 at the end of the 1970s. In Pennsylvania, the number of arrests almost doubled during the 1970s and the population of the state's prisons rose from about 5,000 persons to 9,000. Across the country, the prison population, state and federal, increased from 196,000 to 314,000 between 1973 and 1980.

Part of the increase, certainly, represented little more than an inevitable demographic trend. That is, there were more young male Americans, and if confusing and contradictory studies of crime showed anything over the years, they showed that arrests and other indicators of criminal activity were somewhat proportional to the number of young males in a society. Young men, statistically, are the people who commit crimes—and the number of males in the country between the ages of fifteen and twenty-nine in 1980 was more than 30 million, compared with an average of less than 18 million between 1940 and 1960, and averages between 18 million and 25 million during the 1960s. They were the young men of the "baby boom," the American fertility explosion in the prosperous 15 years after the men of the nation came home from World War II.*

The increase in crime, though, no matter how inevitable or how great, did not explain the concern—almost panic—that a traveler heard, even felt, in America in the late 1970s and early 1980s. "It is not simply the increase in crimes of violence that has promoted public fear and the increased expenditure of public funds to combat crime," said Marvin Wolfgang, director of the Center for Studies in Criminology and Criminal Law at the University of Pennsylvania. "It is the expansion of crimes of violence to groups that have the power to enforce their beliefs, namely, the large middle class and the upper middle class in

---

* By the late 1970s the U. S. fertility rate—babies born each year per 100 persons—had dropped to approximately 1.8, compared with 3.77 in 1957. Those numbers meant that there would almost certainly be a significant decrease in violent crime in the late 1980s and the 1990s, I was told by Professor Richard Easterlin, a demographer at the University of Pennsylvania who was president of the Population Association of America.

American society, who have increasingly become victims of crimes of violence."

"The traditional residential segregation crime control system has been altered," Professor Wolfgang had written, arguing that

> the increasing importance attributed to equality of opportunity [and] the value placed upon political equality [had breached] the major crime control system in Western civilization. . . .
>
> From the time of the ancient Greeks in Athens through classical Rome, the Middle Ages on the continent of Europe, and in the United States, the slaves, the 'criminal classes,' the beggars of society . . . have always been residentially kept within their own densely populated, propinquitous areas. . . .
>
> In the United States, the under class, which has always included a high proportion of blacks since the days of slavery, has conveniently been residentially segregated from the middle class. . . . So long as the poor and the blacks were raping, robbing and killing one another, the general majority public concern with crimes of violence was minimal.

It was not minimal as I traveled. In almost every city, ordinary people talked of fear, and extraordinary language came from extraordinary places. "A reign of terror," said the Chief Justice of the United States, Warren Burger. "A crisis of violence," said the governor of New York, Hugh Carey. By March of 1981, a national poll sponsored by the *Los Angeles Times* indicated that 37 percent of the respondents considered crime the "most critical problem" in their communities.

The fear was pervasive, even taking into account the fact that polling, the very act of asking certain questions, probably tends to elicit responses that confirm the questioner's thesis. In Los Angeles, where there had been extensive publicity of recent crimes against middle- and upper-class residents, 82 percent of the respondents said they felt "unsafe" using public transportation at night. Nationally, that figure was 66 percent. And who did people blame for the state of affairs? The courts.

Americans, as the 1970s became the 1980s, obviously believed the courts were foolishly lenient with marauding criminals. Again taking into account the obvious slanting and limitations of opinion polling, 77 percent of another *Los Angeles Times* national survey, this one done in January 1981, said that the courts did not "deal harshly enough with criminals." When those respondents, 2,063 Americans, were asked the purposes of imprisonment, only one in five mentioned "rehabilitation." "Isolation" was mentioned by 52 percent; "deterrence" by 38 percent. Thirty percent—just about one out of three people—used the word "vengeance."

Perhaps it was ever thus. "Throughout history," Wolfgang said, "an eye for an eye, the payment of one's debt to society through expiation, general deterrence of crime by exemplary punishment and specific or special deterrence of an individual offender, reformation of the individual so that he will not commit further crime, and protection of society against criminality by detaining or imprisoning offenders have been the principal rationales for disposition of criminal offenders."

Then, in the nineteenth century, in his analysis, there came "a different and new rationale for disposing of criminal offenders: rehabilitation." The Quakers of Philadelphia—"elite leaders," Wolfgang called them—and their prison, Eastern State, were part of it.

"Coercive reformation thus began and later changed its language but not its style," Wolfgang wrote in an academic journal. "The invasion of medicine, especially psychiatry . . . changed sin and evil to sickness and disease . . . offenders were to be treated rather than punished. . . .

"The voices of punishment and retribution from the folk culture remained hushed for over a century," he wrote. But then— in a section he called "Triumph of the Public Mind"—he argued that the technology of mass media, which would include public opinion surveys and the dissemination of their results, enabled the ideas of "the general public mind" to be diffused upward in the society and be accepted by "elite leaders." Opinions and ideas moving quickly upward from masses to elites was obviously a reversal of much of human history—an extraordinary testament to the democratizing effect of technology, in this case public opinion polling. The America he saw in the late 1970s, a more democratic country, was ready to abandon reformation and rehabilitation for what most people really always wanted: "Deterrence, retribution and punishment."

That kind of thinking was often controversial in the United

States, not because of the conclusions but because of the inclusion of race as a factor in crime—or, more precisely in the majority's perceptions and fear of crime. In the polite writings of the society, professors used at their own risk such phrases as: "So long as the poor and the blacks were raping, robbing, and killing one another, the general majority public concern with crimes of violence was minimal."

Public dialogue and public opinion polls were not designed—perhaps deliberately not designed—to get at the roots of much of the modern fear of crime. Those roots were racial: the majority was white and middle class; the most visibly dangerous of the poor in most parts of the country were black. Discussions of those facts were usually private or, when they were public—with a traveling reporter, for instance—people asked that their names not be used.

Thus the deputy mayor of one of the largest cities in the country told me, "We know who is committing crime and we know what people are afraid of. We could cut crime in the good neighborhoods of this city by half in one day—and we would cut the fear of crime by even more. All we have to do is what we used to do years ago: let the police start hassling any young black men they see in neighborhoods where they don't belong. Stop them, search them once in a while, chase them out. We might bruise the feelings of a few medical students on their way home from school, but we'd stop the muggings and the burglaries. But we can't do that anymore. The courts now protect everyone's rights. Black organizations would raise hell and they would be backed up by the newspapers and most of this town's important people—at least in public."

When I was in Washington, in one of the city's better neighborhoods, a young couple, who considered themselves liberal on race and every other political question, argued one morning about whether to contribute money to a new "Neighborhood Watch" program, an association organized by their neighbors to watch streets and alleys as burglaries in the area doubled and tripled with the escalations of gold and silver prices. (The burglars who had hit three houses on one street in a week were obviously sophisticated and professional enough to follow precious-metal prices, and to know that the most respectable jewelers in town were competing for the greedy privilege of, in effect, fencing stolen goods, advertising day after day: "We Buy Old Gold and Silver.")

"We can't get involved in this," the wife said. "All they want to do is keep blacks out of the neighborhood. All they'll do is scream for the cops every time a young black man walks around or drives through."

"So?" her husband said. "Who do you think is breaking into these houses? Middle-aged white women?"

In Washington, a city whose population was almost 70 percent black, 96 percent of the persons arrested for robbery in 1974 were black, 94 percent of those arrested for burglary and 95 percent of those arrested for homicide were black. Ninety-four percent of those arrested for the three crimes were males, with a median age of twenty-three. Juveniles, those under eighteen, were not included in these statistics.*

In Pennsylvania, a state whose population was approximately 10 percent black, the prison population was more than 50 percent black—and that percentage was growing steadily, partly because blacks had a higher birth rate than whites (about 35 percent higher). In 1831, when blacks made up about 2 percent of the population of the northern states, the percentage of blacks in Eastern State Penitentiary was more than 20 percent, according to Tocqueville and Beaumont's report to the French government.

Guilty or innocent, 1831 or 1981, a black man in similar circumstances was more likely to be suspected, arrested, convicted, and incarcerated. No doubt young black males did commit much more than their share of violent crime—the majority public fear was justified—but it was also their bad luck to be caught in a racist society. As it was in 1831. When Tocqueville visited the Walnut Street prison, the old Philadelphia city prison, he saw that black prisoners were totally segregated from white. (Eastern State could not be compared, since all prisoners were in solitary confinement.) At the House of Refuge, a charity home for children, he asked why there were no black children and was told by the director, "It would be degrading to the white children to associate them with beings held up to public scorn."

* The statistics, the most comprehensive I could find for any city, were compiled by the Prosecutor's Management Information System of the Washington, D. C., Superior Court.

Two weeks after his visit to the House of Refuge, Tocqueville, on October 25, 1831, made the first note that would lead him to his discussion of the possibility of tyranny by an American majority. " 'The people is always right,' that is the dogma of the republic just as 'the king can do no wrong' is the religion of the monarchic states," he wrote after his conversation with John Jay Smith, the Quaker leader, who told him about white intimidation to prevent free blacks from voting in Philadelphia. "It is a great question to decide whether the one is more false than the other: but what is very sure is that neither the one nor the other is true."

In *Democracy in America*, he rephrased those thoughts, and that was when he said: ". . . in democracies there is nothing outside the majority capable of resisting it."

And then: "The majority in the United States has immense actual power and a power of opinion which is almost as great. When once its mind is made up on any question, there are, so to say, no obstacles which can retard, much less halt its progress and give it time to hear the wails of those it crushes as it passes.

"The consequences of this state of affairs are fate-laden and dangerous for the future."

No less now than then. It did not take a leap of imagination—it only required being white and listening—to travel the United States 150 years later and conclude that the white majority is quite capable, perhaps always will be, of tyrannizing the black minority. Marvin Wolfgang's "Triumph of the Public Mind"— "the voices of punishment and retribution from the folk culture"—would be a triumph of public opinion. It would be an easy triumph, a democratic triumph, over the brute force of the minority, a popular reaction to what the highest judge in the land called a reign of terror. The Chief Justice and many Americans were attacking what they saw as the tyranny of the criminal minority. But, in the democracy, the ultimate power was with the majority. If there were to be tyranny in America, I was convinced it would be a tyranny of the majority—and it would begin by making the streets safe for that majority.

18
BOSTON I

"Everyone Should Make Harvard Law Review . . ."

On September 12, 1831, at a rally of more than 2,000 people at Faneuil Hall in Boston to express support for revolutionaries fighting for independence in Poland, Tocqueville met Josiah Quincy, Jr., a former mayor of Boston whom he identified in his notes as "the President of the University of Cambridge." It was Harvard University. Quincy gave the young Frenchman a catalogue of the school and a book describing local government in New England. The title was: *Town Officer.*

In September 1979, the twenty-fifth president of Harvard, Derek Bok, also gave me a catalogue and a book. This one, called *Adaptation to Life,* was by Dr. George E. Vaillant, a professor of psychiatry at Harvard Medical School, and it was a study of the lives of 268 Harvard graduates over a period of 35 years. The book's purpose and the principal questions it deals with are summarized on the cover as: ". . . to chart the ways in which a group of promising individuals coped with their lives over a period of time. . . . Why do some of us cope so well with the portion life offers us? . . . Why do some of us achieve happiness in our personal and professional lives, while others are doomed to be miserable themselves and to make others miserable as well?"*

"Coping," it seemed, was a word I could not escape. It had

*The book was published in 1977 by Little, Brown and Company, Boston.

been the favored word of the American Society of Newspaper Editors study, "Changing Needs of Changing Readers." Gannett newspapers, the country's largest chain, published sections with that title, "Coping." The verb—"to cope"—is derived from Old French, from *couper*—to slash, to strike. An aggressive word. In Dr. Vaillant's book, it had a Freudian meaning, according to the author's introduction: " . . . the so-called *defense* mechanisms of psychoanalytic theory will often be referred to as coping or adaptive mechanisms." I was laughing to myself as I looked at the book; I hoped that President Bok didn't notice. America turned upside down—from aggression to defense, from books on public solutions to books on private problems, from republicanism to psychiatry.*

"Public policy is of almost no interest to the people here today, the students," said Philip Morrison, University Professor of Physics at Cambridge's other great educational institution, Massachusetts Institute of Technology, which was founded thirty years after Tocqueville met with Quincy. I had come, that September morning, to talk about science and government's role in it—among other things, Dr. Morrison was the author of a book on the country's defense budget—about creativity and innovation. But the conversation turned to the students he had seen in 41 years of teaching.

"They are looking for private solutions," he said. "They are not interested in government, in community questions, public questions. They take no career risks and no intellectual risks. If they have a code, this is it: You pretend you're square so that General Motors will hire you and pay you, then you think whatever you want to—pretending all the time. There is a duality and they are much more cynical—much less ingenuous than the students of, say, twenty years ago, in the 1960s. They have separate cultures which are not shared by other people. Drugs, sex, taste—tastes in music, for instance."

"Will these people change the country when they take over?" I asked.

"They're not going to try.

"Let me give you an example," he continued. "They smoke a

* There is another derivation of "cope," as a noun, again from Old French, meaning "cape" or "cloak."

lot of marijuana, but they don't care whether it's legal or not. It's easier to buy pot and go off by yourself than to try and persuade state legislatures to legalize the stuff. The private solution."

Drugs—altering one's own mind—was a very private solution, the most individualistic way to cope. "There seem to be about 20 million marijuana users in the country today, most of them comparatively young," said Dr. Norman Zinberg, another Harvard Medical School psychiatrist and a member of the National Advisory Council on Drug Abuse. "The number of alcohol users is 105 million, and the amount of alcohol use has been constant for the past seven years. There are more people, so we're drinking less—really what is happening is that they are favoring lighter drinks, wine and beer rather than whiskey. People today drink much less than they did in Tocqueville's day. The per capita use of alcohol is a third or a quarter what it was in Colonial times."*

"Americans, in general, are controlled, disciplined people," said Dr. Zinberg. "The language of American drinking, I think, is very significant. 'Let's have *a* drink,'—that phrase condones drinking but limits it. 'The sun is over the yardarm, it's time for a drink,'—that restricts the hours of usage. People, many people, do the same things with drugs—limiting their own use by budgeting time or money, or by using drugs only with select people in select places. Americans are people who know what they're doing most of the time."†

* The oldest consumption figures I could find, from the Distilled Spirits Association, were from 1840, when the per capita consumption of whiskey and brandy was recorded as 3.04 gallons per year. The 1978 figure was 2.04 gallons. Consumption in 1831 was probably higher—that was the reason for the formation of the temperance societies and by 1840 they were having some effect. Americans have been altering their minds for a long time, and drugs serve the same numbing purpose that more alcohol once did.

† Dr. Zinberg's views on controlled drug use were somewhat controversial. He did, however, work directly with drug users in his capacity as psychiatrist in chief at the Washingtonian Center for Addictions in Jamaica Plain, Massachusetts. He told me that he knew large numbers of controlled users of marijuana, cocaine, and heroin. "Heroin?" I said. "Do I know or would I know—would someone like me know controlled heroin users?" He answered, "Yes, you would—it would be very unlikely not to come in contact with controlled users in the world you live in."

There was nothing new, I supposed, about double lives—especially in Puritan societies—and Tocqueville touched on that in a diary note he seemed to enjoy putting down: "Mr. Clay, who appears to have occupied himself with statistical researches on this point, told Beaumont that at Boston the prostitutes numbered about 2,000 (I have great difficulty believing this). They are recruited among country girls who, after having been seduced, are obliged to flee their district and family, and find themselves without resources. It seems that the young blood of the city frequents them, but the fact is concealed with extreme care, and the evil stops there, without ever crossing the domestic threshold or troubling the families. A man who should not be convicted but only suspected of having an intrigue would immediately be excluded from society. All doors would be shut to him."*

A group of 25 young men and women, students I met with after talking with Professor Morrison, certainly thought they knew what they were doing. "Playing the game" was the phrase they used to describe their attitudes and actions. I was their guest lecturer at a joint political science class for students from M.I.T. and from nearby Wellesley College. They were attractive people, well dressed and articulate—men and women who, by the very fact of being juniors and seniors at two elite universities, would also certainly be, one day, among the people running the United States. At least they had that option, or the option to try.

I did not lecture. I told them what Professor Morrison had said about them. "What does he expect?" said one young woman. "We were brought up playing games. Your parents and your teachers make it clear what they want and you give it to them. They make it clear what they don't want to know—and you go along with that, to get what you want. And to be left alone."

"Your professor's too simplistic," said a young man. "It's not duality. We play many roles. I'm different for every class. I'm whoever the professor wants me to be—for that hour."

It went on. A Wellesley student said she had watched the

* Mr. Clay was a Georgia planter visiting Boston. He obviously did have his numbers a little wrong—the city's population was only 60,000 in 1831.

President on television the other night with four other people, two of them, like her, in their early twenties and two in their late forties. The President, she said, used the word "patriotism," and the three young people looked at each other behind their elders' backs and—her word—"snickered."

"The whole thing here is personal betterment," said one of the young women, an M.I.T. student. "You play the game and get out of here and there's a good job waiting for you. Then you can do what you want." Like others, she made it clear that the betterment she was talking about was very personal: it had much, much more to do with the pursuit of happiness than the pursuit of excellence. "What is the point of being the best, or making more money than you need or 'doing things for the community'—what community?" a young man said with a cynicism that seemed both too certain and too self-conscious for me. But a few of the others around the long semicircular table nodded as he spoke.

"They're a cool bunch, aren't they?" Edwin Diamond, the political science seminar's regular lecturer, said to me. That was another word I kept hearing—"cool," in the sense of being without passion or commitment, of being detached. In New York, Richard Wald, the vice president of ABC News, had used it as we talked about ethnic prejudice when each of us was growing up around New York City. "People used to really hate other people then," he said. "Being Jewish then was a fact of life. You didn't need Italo-American Day to know people called you a 'Guinea.' Now the entire society seems to have cooled down. It's not so much that there are fewer opinions and prejudices, it's just that there's less steam behind them. . . . You see this cool, passionless country." The same day, in an office four blocks across Manhattan, the word was used—with passion—by Felix Rohatyn, the investment banker. A partner in the investment banking firm Lazard Frères, he had won a national reputation for working out plans for the government of New York City to avoid bankruptcy. New York had kept expanding municipal services despite a decline in tax revenues caused by the loss of some of its population and some of its traditional economic functions. "Cool," he said. "America has become cool—there is a lack of commitment at all levels of society. Businessmen are working for their own stock options and to get their pictures on the cover of *Business Week*; they're not producing for the society. 'Cool' is a philosophy of decline. The Roman Empire was probably cool." Then, across the Charles River from where I was meeting with students, David Riesman, the Harvard sociologist, said, when I asked him about American values: "To be 'cool'—to be surprised by nothing—has become a value. It's a dangerous one."

Among the passions declining in this cooler society, according to my students, was the most American one: ambition—ambition for wealth. These young men and women, proudly announcing their youthful cynicism, were, for better or worse, the inheritors of the labors of the Americans Tocqueville was describing when he wrote: "To clear, cultivate, and transform the huge uninhabited continent which is their domain, the Americans need the everyday support of an energetic passion; that passion can only be the love of wealth. . . . The American will describe as noble and estimable ambition that which our medieval ancestors would have called base cupidity." I thought of Henry Kantor in Nashville, not young, not cynical, saying that "things" were running out in America—the woods of Saginaw had been ravaged—but that he thought the lives of his grandchildren, the two sons and daughter of an attorney in Los Angeles, would be "better." Ambition depended, among other things, on how you defined "better." It certainly seemed possible that if, in a democratic society, progress was the sum of individual decisions and wills—and I was more convinced than ever of the truth of that—then expectations, aspirations, and behavior would change naturally with circumstance and perception. Perhaps that was another law of democratic nature. I had never quite known what to make of something told me by a lawyer in Buffalo. Robert Milonzi, who had been an assistant to a President, Harry Truman, and was a commissioner of the New York State Public Utility Commission, said, "Americans will be fine when they learn to live in a second-rate country—when everything doesn't go their way."

"Perhaps there is some sort of invisible hand at work," Professor Morrison said, quite seriously. "In a growing nation that needed more and more work, ambition was necessary. Now, if we are in a basically no-growth situation, and I believe we are, ambition is not needed and it does seem to be declining.... A lot of this is well within the American tradition—the individual takes care of himself. Whether the individual is battling with the frontier, as it were, or dealing with a corporate structure."

If ambition as Americans traditionally knew and exploited it were no longer essential to the society, would it decline or be redirected?

"There is great tension in the society about that question," said David Riesman. "The word 'workaholic'—the idea that work and ambition can be carried too far, to the point of being called a disease—is a symbol of that tension.... I see the balance tipping toward leisure. There will be exceptions, of course—you can see that in medical schools, islands of work like that."

"The most modern Americans I know," said Professor Morrison, "are a small new class of what might be called itinerant workers. They are computer technicians, highly educated and highly skilled—highly paid, too. They work for several months for the electronic companies around here, or in California, and then they drop out of the system for as long as the money lasts. They're very good workers, I'm told." Some of the creative and driven technicians of yesterday and tomorrow, it seemed, were spending today in the sun and drugs of places like Taos, New Mexico, Big Sur, California, and other farther, mellower reaches of the Pacific Coast. Thus the double lives of some of the descendants of the hard nomad people who felled the forests of Saginaw Bay and reached the Pacific Ocean—searching for gold—less than twenty years after Tocqueville left America.[*]

Duality, cynicism, detachment—none of the students I met with at M.I.T. seemed to disagree with Professor Morrison's dour analysis until the session's final minute. A young woman stood up. "This is nonsense," she said.

"I'm British"—her accent made the statement unnecessary—

---

[*] "Computer jocks" was the description someone used for the itinerant programmers. One of them, Howard Pearlmutter, who was twenty-four years old and had studied at Princeton University, said he "was capable" of earning $15,000 in two months. In fact, when we spoke in Northern California, he had just spent five days teaching software programming in El Paso, Texas. He said he had worked in eight countries and five states in three years.

"I've been here for a year listening to this kind of talk. It's not true and you know it. To me it sounds like play-cynicism. There is no cynicism in America—no cynicism that a European would recognize. You're the luckiest people in the world. There's opportunity here. People can move up. They can do what they want to do. That's not true where I come from—people are locked in by where they were born, by who their parents are. That's why I . . . people like me . . . my friends, all my friends, want to come to America. And you all know that's true. You believe in this."

End of class. As the students left, I stopped one who had been most vocal.

"What did you think of that?" I asked.

"She's right."

"It's a hell of a country—the best," Gilbert Hill, the black police inspector had said in Detroit after spending two hours talking about discrimination. And he wasn't the only one. At the end of a hundred conversations, more, the person I was with would stop and, after beginning the exchange of parting pleasantries, would use the word "best" . . . or "wonderful" . . . or "love." I wasn't sure that *always* happened, but my memory was that it did.

"The people has the Republic to the marrow of the bones," Tocqueville was told in Boston on September 22, 1831, by a brilliant young German immigrant, Francis Lieber, founder of the Encyclopedia Americana. "One of the problems we still have with European governments," Michael Mandelbaum, a young professor of government at Harvard, told me in Boston on a September day 148 years later, "is that they always have trouble understanding that we believe what we say. We don't talk about 'human rights' as a cynical ploy to embarrass other governments. There may be some cynicism among the leaders doing the talking, but the American people believe in human rights. We believe in our own rhetoric." His colleague Judith Shklar, who was born in Germany and whose specialty is European political thought, added: "Americans alone do not believe that the moral problems of the world have been solved."*

* Lieber later translated Tocqueville and Beaumont's *Du Système Pénitentiaire* into English in 1833 and in the process apparently invented several new words. One of them was "bureaucracy."

Americans, in their marrow, seem to think that moral problems *can* be solved—and that the last best hope for solving those dilemmas is this nation itself, America. "For fifty years," Tocqueville wrote, "the inhabitants of the United States have been repeatedly and constantly told that they are the only religious, enlightened, and free people. They see that democratic institutions flourish among them, whereas they come to grief in the rest of the world; consequently they have an immensely high opinion of themselves and are not far from believing that they form a species apart from the rest of the human race."

That went on for a lot more than fifty years. Tocqueville was not the first and not the last foreigner to wonder at Americans' capacity for telling each other how moral and decent and better they all were; he damned it at regular intervals in his notes and his final work—"this irritable patriotism . . . this boasting . . . this conceit." He would have been amused to know that someday students at a great university would snicker among themselves at the same things. But like the young woman from England, the Frenchman might not have been totally convinced by the cool detachment of the young Americans.

I wasn't. The same old feelings were there, as far as I could tell traveling Tocqueville's route—they were just held back a little longer in the name of sophistication. The cool young cynicism of M.I.T. and Wellesley in 1979 was a veneer over faith as the boastful patriotism of 1831 covered the doubts and insecurity of a new people building a new system. The doubts—like almost everything else in America—were now bandied about in the name of "openness," another new value. There was what seemed to be a double life of patriotism, too. I came home after more than a year with at least one clear impression: the American was still, instinctively, the loud flag-waving patriot. Below that red-white-and-blue surface there was often confusion and frustration, especially about the fairness of the economic system and the effectiveness of the political system, and it was fashionable for many people to function rhetorically at that cool level of disdain. But late at night, at the end of class or conversation, Americans believed in it! They bought the ideas of their fathers, of their fathers' fathers. There was a faith, a set of beliefs shared by almost all of the people almost all of the time.

After my M.I.T. class, while I was still thinking about shared beliefs, I talked with Gary Orren, a professor of political science at Brandeis University, outside Boston, who had also been the director of public opinion surveys—the pollster—for two of the country's most influential newspapers, the *New York Times* and the *Washington Post*.

What do Americans believe?

"A lot of things, some of them true," Orren said with a smile. "But I think a good place to start is to remember that we are pro-democracy and anti-government."

"Most of what we believe," he continued, "comes down to ideas that are essentially anti-authority and tend toward personal self-regulation. If there were an American creed, I think it might begin:

"One. Government is best that governs least.

"Two. Majority rule.

"Three. Equality of opportunity."

That seemed about right, but my first thought was that even those three tenets had proved contradictory—like so much in American life and, to use a phrase that no one will ever satisfactorily define, the American character. Personal self-regulation had not always worked in the United States, and, often, the enforcement of one belief—equality of opportunity, for one—required the violation of another—less government. More government was necessary, and central government at that, to enforce equality of many opportunities, including the opportunity to vote in Philadelphia and sit near the front of a bus in Montgomery.

The contradictions, however, only shook and did not shatter the faith. Many of the things I heard and thought on the road—about race, about dissent, about faith—came together for a moment one rainy afternoon in May of 1981 at a bar called Grimel's in Detroit. I was talking with Rick Martin, a black laborer around the blast furnaces in a Ford plant who had hustled his way to the presidency of his United Auto Workers local three years before, at the age of twenty-six. Here was Rick Martin speaking at a union meeting:

"I want to reveal the strategy of the multinational corporations and what they're trying to do to the working class of this country . . . the multinationals saw that with union progress the working-class people were moving up. We were able to put a roof over our heads without having rats . . . When the multinationals saw this and they saw that working-class people were moving into luxury and otherwise, they knew then that they had to destroy it and wipe it out; and this is what they started doing . . . they got the United States government as an accomplice to this crime . . ."

He went on, ending with a call: "We are going to have to go back to the old days. We are going to have to march!"

Afterward, we were sitting talking about conspiracies. What are you going to do next?

"I'd like to get me some education. Pre-law. I hope to get into politics. What I'd really like some day is to get elected to Congress. I believe in the system and I really want to make it work.

"Education is what counts," he said. "When I was in the ninth grade at MacKenzie High I was getting bad grades and messing around. My father came home in the kitchen one night with a pair of Ford work pants and he threw them in my face. 'Put these on,' he said. 'Because you're going to be wearing them the rest of your life if you don't get an education.' "

"Education—the national blessing" was how it was toasted when Tocqueville and Beaumont were in New York. Tocqueville wondered then at the universal American acceptance of the benefits of mass education. In Boston, after a long conversation with Francis Lieber, he elaborated in his notebook: "Reflection: What disturbs us the most in Europe are the men who, born in an inferior rank, have received an education which gives them the desire to leave it, without furnishing the means. In America, this inconvenience of education is hardly felt; instruction always furnishes the natural means to enrich oneself, and creates no social unrest."

"The effort made in this country to spread instruction is truly prodigious," he wrote home to a friend, a professor in Paris. "The universal and sincere faith that they profess here in the efficaciousness of education seems to be one of the most remarkable features of America, the more so as I confess that for me the question is not yet entirely decided." But for the Americans it was decided: Education was even more than the process that furnished the means to enrich oneself; education was the means. At least that was one of the many things Americans believed.

Rick Martin and his father believed that. The leader of Martin's union, Douglas Fraser, president of the United Auto Workers, believed it too. He was even willing to lie for it. We were sitting in his office in Detroit—in Solidarity House, UAW headquarters, built on land that was once the estate of Henry Ford's son—and I asked him about his boyhood. He told me of coming to the United States from Glasgow, Scotland, with his family at the age of eight, and then talked about growing up American and his pride at graduating from high school.

"I want to go back to something," he said a while later. "I wasn't telling the truth about high school. I never finished. I quit in the twelfth grade to take a job at De Soto. It's funny—after all these years I still lie about it. Because the fact is I still think it was a stupid thing to do. I should have finished my education."

"Education is the gateway. Even in an egalitarian society, and I think ours is getting close to that, there have to be gateways, funnels to positions of power and influence," said Derek Bok, the president of Harvard. "Universities control the gateway to jobs . . . and Harvard . . ." He let the sentence trail off, modestly, as we lunched in a small, airy restaurant near the campus, a place called Ferdinand's, where professors, Cambridge business people, and students chatted and ordered little salads and small white wines—an egalitarian setting chosen, not accidentally I was sure, by the president.

". . . and Harvard . . ." Fair Harvard. Founded in 1636, the first college in the New World, one of a hundred universities (all church-affiliated) in the United States when Tocqueville met Josiah Quincy. Of the 72 Americans quoted extensively in Tocqueville's journals, 18 were Harvard graduates.*

Fair Harvard was some funnel. The university was the alma mater of eight signers of the Declaration of Independence; five Presidents of the United States (Harvard Law School graduated a sixth); one out of four of the country's Secretaries of State. With Massachusetts Institute of Technology, its neighbor, the

---

* This is part of a footnote from George W. Pierson's *Tocqueville and Beaumont in America:* "Their manuscripts contain the names of more than 250 individuals, of both sexes, whom they met in America. Of these about 32 were foreigners, or Canadians, and a like number are not sufficiently identified to make any judgment possible. Of the remaining 177, however, a surprisingly large number had been college-trained. Harvard contributed 18 (possibly 21) to the list, Yale 9 (counting two non-graduates), Columbia 8, Princeton (College of New Jersey) 11, and Pennsylvania 5. . . ."

University and its graduate schools formed the core of the most formidable academic complex in the United States. *Science* magazine, cataloguing a list of the 41 major advances in social science in the United States between the years 1930 and 1965, concluded that nine originated in Cambridge, compared with five each in New York City and Washington.

There are a lot of ways to make it economically, politically, intellectually and socially in America, but if there is a better place to start, a better gateway than a Harvard education and Harvard connections, I have never noticed it. As I had in Philadelphia when I asked Frank McGlinn whether it was easier to get a business loan than it had been when he first became a banker, I thought the question of equality of opportunity to get into Harvard was a pretty good test of how democratic America actually was.

"There is much, much more competition than there used to be, so in that sense it is more difficult to get into Harvard," Bok answered. "But for any individual, a student in any high school anywhere in the United States, the system is much more open than it was in the past. If a young man or a young woman wants to go to Harvard, he or she begins with just about the same chance as any other student. Isn't that egalitarianism?"*

"There has been a startling change in who gets into Harvard over the past 25 years—startling," said William Fitzsimmons, the director of admissions—and the changes he talked about constituted an explosion of opportunity in those years. Almost 14,000 students applied for admission to Harvard's class of 1984, and more than 12,000 of them were judged academically qualified—2,148, about 15 percent, were admitted.† Twenty-five

---

* On one level at least, Harvard could claim something close to literal egalitarianism. By the middle of the 1970s, about 87 percent of the university's graduates were graduating with honors. In 1974, only 246 students graduated with no honors of any kind; 779 graduated *cum laude,* 373 graduated *magna cum laude,* and 53 graduated *summa cum laude.*

† The ratios were also high between applications and acceptances in the major graduate schools of Harvard. In 1980, Harvard Law School selected 545 students from more than 7,000 applicants. The numbers for schools of medicine and business were, respectively, 4,593 applications and 166 acceptances, and 7,712 applications and 700 acceptances.

years before, in 1956, 63 percent of the applicants were admitted. Before World War II, about 90 percent of all applicants were admitted; those applicants, some two-thirds of them graduates of private preparatory schools, knew their place and their place was Harvard.

By the late 1960s, a lot of other students began thinking that Harvard could be their place. More than three-quarters of those accepted in 1980 for the class of 1984 were public-school graduates. They may not have been as well educated as the old private-school graduate, but they were probably smarter: scores on standard aptitude tests taken by Harvard applicants increased by more than 15 percent during the democratization of admissions procedures. More than 20 percent of the class of 1984 were members of minority groups—blacks, Hispanics and Asians.

Test scores were not the only thing that increased with the democratization of Harvard. The number that increased most dramatically was the number of students who were Jewish.

"What is the percentage of Jewish students at Harvard now?" I asked Bok.

"I don't know. We don't keep records like that," he said after we had spent twenty minutes going over detailed head counts of black and Hispanic students. The next five minutes were uncomfortable as I persisted in asking for a number and he insisted that no one had any way of knowing.

"Some professors have told me 40 percent of their students are Jewish," I said.

"That's too high," Bok said.

"Twenty-eight percent is the best number I've heard," said Leonard Fein, a professor of sociology at Brandeis University and editor of the Jewish magazine *Moment.* "Not bad, huh? Twenty-eight percent of the students at Harvard are Jewish. Seven of the hundred United States Senators are Jewish. . . . We don't worry about the lies about the power of Jews in America. What we worry about is the truth—it's both embarrassing and comforting for someone like me to know that there are people in positions of influence who are looking out for Jewish interests. Our general inclination is to keep quiet about it and hope that nobody notices. . . . This country has been so extraordinarily generous to us. We are fewer than six million people, 2.5 percent of the population. But we are treated as if we were a third: the nation is always referred to as Protestant, Catholic, and Jewish. Nowhere else is there a phrase like 'the Judeo-Christian ethic.' "

Tocqueville never mentioned Jews or Jewishness in his notes—which is hardly surprising since there were probably fewer than 10,000 Jews in the entire country when he was here. Large-scale Jewish immigration from Germany began in 1836; the massive immigrations from violent anti-Semitism in eastern Europe and Russia began in 1881. In 1922, A. Lawrence Lowell, the twenty-second president of Harvard, recommended that the school impose a quota of 15 percent on the number of Jewish students admitted with each class because of "excessive" concentrations.

"I came from Russia at the age of three," said Will Maslow, a historian and the general counsel of the American Jewish Congress in New York. "My father was a tailor. We believed in one thing: education. I won a scholarship to Cornell and in 1927 I told one of my professors that I, too, wanted to be an economics professor. He told me to forget it, there were only three Jewish economics professors in the entire United States—and there was not a single Jewish professor of English or the classics. Now there are 60,000 Jews teaching in American universities. . . . We are, apparently, the richest ethnic group in America. We are the most affluent and best educated people in 5,000 years of Jewish history."*

"Judaism enthroned study as an ideal," said Rabbi Alexander Schindler, president of the Union of American Hebrew Congregations, and thus the head of the Reformed Jewish religion in

---

* Seventy percent of American Jews hold positions classified as "professional," "technical," "manager" or "administrator," compared to 29.4 percent of the general population holding such positions, according to the National Jewish Population Study (1974). That is only one of many indices of Jewish professional and educational position in the society. Seventy-eight percent of Jewish males between the ages of twenty-five and twenty-nine have had some college training; 48 percent of that group has earned a professional degree or had some postgraduate education. Politically, according to Cambridge Opinion Research, Inc., Jews, less than 3 percent of the population, cast 6 percent of America's votes because their average age, registration, and turnout are all high. Black Americans, by comparison, compose almost 12 percent of the population but cast only 7 percent of the vote.

America. "It is the cornerstone of our belief structure—which made us at one with American beliefs. Study, study, study, is what Jewish children hear at home, and they will always go further in school than anyone else. The reason Jews are so successful and so prominent in America is that Jewish families were making sure their children went to college before anyone else was."*

"It's a miracle that Jews have survived anywhere in the world," Fein said, worrying, as Henry Kantor had in Nashville, that low birth rates and intermarriage were steadily reducing the American Jewish population. "But in America, we have thrived. There will always be some anti-Semitism everywhere, but it lags behind here because of the consensus of decency and fairness in America. There is not much, not much at all. The *Federalist Papers* are the most morally impressive documents in the history of the world. The United States offered Jews the greatest space we have ever had. But of course we had to pay a price."

What was the price?

"We had to be like everybody else."

That was indeed the American price: to be an American like everybody else. Jews paid and paid a little more—some became more Yankee than the Yankees—and part of the reward was education. At best, a Harvard education.

All members of one group of Americans were denied admission to Harvard. They were not a minority like blacks or Jews. They were half the nation. They were women. Perhaps the most radical thing about Harvard's class of 1984 is that 846 of the 2,148 members are women. In 1879—nine years after the first black man, Richard Greener, was admitted to Harvard—the Society for the Collegiate Instruction of Women was formed to make private arrangements with individual members of the

---

* A similar pattern of individual success stories in education seemed also to be developing among Asian students as I traveled. In California, students of Asian origin were being admitted to the best schools in the state's university system in ratios much higher than their proportion of the population. In Texas, when I was there in 1981, the valedictorians of two of the state's best high schools—Highland Park in Dallas and Lanier in Austin—were both recent immigrants from Vietnam.

Harvard faculty to instruct women students at an institution which later became known as Radcliffe College. In 1943, with a shortage of instructors because of World War II, Radcliffe women began attending some classes with Harvard men. The two schools effectively merged in 1975, when their admissions departments and procedures were combined.

Blacks, male and female, made up almost 10 percent of the student body when I visited Harvard. In the class of 1961, blacks had constituted less than 1 percent—eight of more than 1,200 graduates. In March of that year, the President of the United States, John F. Kennedy, a member of the class of 1940, issued Executive Order Number 10925, which concerned the employment policies of private companies eligible to receive contracts for government work: "The contractor will take affirmative action to ensure that applicants are employed, and that employees are treated, during employment, without regard to their race, creed, color or national origin. . . ."

More government. More equal opportunity. That one phrase, "affirmative action," took on legislative meaning and the power of law when it was used in the Civil Rights Act of 1964. At first the words had seemed to mean that employers had an obligation to take some action to inform members of minority groups—blacks, really—that they did not discriminate. But it soon took on expanded meanings, and by 1972 the Equal Employment Opportunity Commission, a creation of the Civil Rights Act, was issuing annual reports with statements like this: "As the Commission stated in Decision No. 72-0265, Title VII imposes an affirmative duty on employers and unions to end the chilling effects of past discrimination and that a continuing lack of Negro applicants for once all-white jobs only indicated that the effectiveness, thoroughness, and frequency of whatever efforts the respondent was making to inform Negroes that it no longer discriminates against them fall short of what is necessary."

Similar interpretations by federal courts and federal agencies were soon being applied to college admissions. You did not have to be a Harvard graduate to figure out that the government, in effect, was saying that the only acceptable proof of nondiscrimination was the percentage of Negroes on the job or in the class. Americans, after all, are a practical people—"American know-how"—a people who demand not only results but proof of results. Harvard, which had admitted young men because of their privileged background, began accepting some because of their underprivileged background, and because the federal government had the power to threaten the 25 percent of the university's budget that came from public funds.*

"The gap between the minority students and the rest of the student body is very small now," Bok told me. "There has been a significant improvement in them. Overall, they're better than our football players. We are, of course, getting the best minority students in the country."

But even the best blacks sometimes did not seem good enough within the self-conscious meritocracy of the Harvard community. With almost seasonal regularity Harvard, which had always held itself up to the society as a national symbol for excellence, was forced to deal with criticism and, sometimes, demonstrations that flared up along the tension lines between merit and fairness, between inflexible standards and "affirmative action," between quality and equality.†

In the fall of 1980, preliminary drafts of a report to Bok on admissions were obtained and—freedom of the press being in young American marrow—published by the student newspaper, the *Crimson*. "The astonishingly small numbers of blacks at the right tail," the draft said, referring to the high-score "tail" of standardized test result curves, "imply, I believe, significant

* After Kennedy's 1961 order, the language of fairness expanded from groups defined by race or physical capabilities to include those who defined themselves by sexual practice, particularly homosexuality. The 1980–81 Harvard catalogue contained this statement: "As a matter of policy Harvard and Radcliffe do not discriminate on the basis of race, religion, sex, age, sexual orientation, national and ethnic origin or physical handicap in the administration of educational policies, scholarship and loan programs, and athletic or other college-administered programs."

† "Affirmative action may be, by its very nature, a one-generation phenomenon," Bok said. "We find tremendous pressure from black faculty members who do not want their own credentials demeaned by the awarding of the same credentials to a new generation of blacks seen as less deserving." For that reason and others—particularly white resentment over visible black professional advances—it seems likely to me that "affirmative action," or something like it, will be a cyclical "solution"—perhaps skipping generations—to continuing black middle-class frustrations.

changes in one's thinking about affirmative action ... If elite universities did not compete so heavily for blacks, these students might attend slightly lesser institutions where they might compete as intellectual equals."

In the winter of 1980–81, the *Harvard Law Review*, which had picked 86 editors from the law school each year by grade rankings and writing competitions, announced that some female and minority students would henceforth be named to the *Review* without regard to scholastic achievement. There were, at the time, only 11 women and not a single black among the editors—who were all virtually guaranteed success in their careers, since *Review* editors traditionally moved on to clerkships for important judges. The *New York Times*, another elite institution regularly in dispute or negotiation with female and black employees, editorialized a bit plaintively:

> When an institution that has always defined and upheld merit for an entire profession shrinks from the burden, it sends an unwelcome message through the entire society. It says that not even in the academic stratosphere can the dreams, and delusions, of absolute merit survive the claims of fair play and opportunity. The cause of affirmative action is thus made the adversary of merit. It should not have to bear such a burden from such a place.

At one point, the controversy was such that Bok felt compelled to publish "An Open Letter on Issues of Race at Harvard":

> The opportunities for minority students to contribute to the understanding of their fellow students and to the welfare of society as a whole seem sufficiently important to us to justify an effort to enroll a significant number of applicants from these racial groups. This policy leads us to admit some minority students with prior grades and test scores somewhat below those of other applicants whom we must turn aside. Like any admissions policy, the rationale just described is based on informed judgment rather than established fact. It does seem reasonable to suppose that special efforts to assemble a diverse student body will add to racial understanding and that well-prepared blacks, Hispanics and other minority graduates will have important contribu-

tions to make, especially during the next generation. Indeed the nation faces a bleak and dispiriting future if our assumptions turn out to be incorrect. It is true that these assumptions . . . have neither been demonstrated empirically nor been free of criticism. Nevertheless, I believe them to be sound and will uphold them at Harvard and defend them . . . against any effort . . . to overrule our policies and limit our authority to use our own judgment in admitting students to this institution.

The reasoning was tortured, climaxing with a concluding statement that was exactly the opposite of reality. Harvard was neither defending nor upholding "our own judgment." The judgment was the federal government's. That judgment, enforced after the middle 1960s, was, in its simplest terms, that because of the injustices of past discrimination and the possibility of continuing civil disorder—Bok's "bleak and dispiriting future" presumably referred to riots and, perhaps, organized terrorism—claims of fair play would have to take precedence over delusions of a society based on absolute merit. Black Americans had their dreams, too; white America had nightmares of a race war. The president of Harvard became, in many ways, not the leader of a great private institution but an agent of the central government enforcing a consensus national policy. Harvard was not that private anymore, receiving more than $80 million each year from the federal government, mainly in the form of tuition aid and research grants.

"I spend from 10 to 15 percent of my time dealing with the federal government," Bok said. "Mostly on compliance with regulations—on affirmative action, safety in laboratories, restrictions on research, things like the use of human subjects, and, now, privacy amendments, what we must do with student records. When I began eight years ago, there was almost none of that. Then, there was one person here who dealt with federal matters and that took only one-eighth of his time, an hour a day. Now we have four people full time."*

* Harvard University maintains a full-time office in Washington. The job of the university's representative there may be made easier by the fact that, as Bok and I talked in 1979, 17 of the 100 members of the United States Senate held degrees from Harvard or one of its graduate schools.

"Government had to take over higher education," said the dean of Harvard's own Divinity School, Kristor Stendahl, "because there was no other way to give that education to the poor."

Indeed there was "no other way . . ." Stendahl's perception complemented what George Ewing, the newspaper publisher, had told me in Canandaigua, N. Y. The people of his town—and individuals and small groups of Americans everywhere—just weren't going to do certain things. Not if they thought those damned things—building sewer plants and giving poor people a better shot—were going to take money out of their own pockets. The government was making people do it, but the people, sovereign after all, and professing that they didn't believe in it, still accepted more government.

It was an American contradiction and a proud American cycle. The black students at Harvard, whether or not they would have been able to compete in a true and structured meritocracy, were part of it.

Americans believed their own rhetoric, as Michael Mandelbaum had said, and although they might resent criticism of the gap between rhetoric and reality, they would respond to it. They, the majority, consensus America, would act under the prodding of moral or moralistic leaders and arguments—of Martin Luther King, Jr., or millions of his fellow blacks shouting that this was not fair, this violated the sacred heritage of our nation. "We are a nation with a conscience," said James Reston, a columnist for the *New York Times*. "Usually it's a troubled conscience, because we are not living up to what we were taught we were . . . So we are always vulnerable to appeals to the best in ourselves."

The modern governing of America was based on fairness and appeals to fairness—"enforced fairness," as Vincent Aug had described the function of the courts in Cincinnati—and the enforcer had to be the government itself, government at the highest levels, the levels which deal with fundamental questions. No American question could be more fundamental than equality of opportunity. The national government, the enforcer of fairness, guaranteed equality, and education, in the American mind, guaranteed opportunity. The match was made—the government would police the "gateway." Then came the question of proof, of finding some way to prove that there was equality of opportunity, that things were fair. The answer was obvious, even if a bit foolish: the results had to prove equality. In a truly egalitarian society, everyone should make the *Harvard Law Review*.

The government, trusted and feared, obeyed and avoided, revered and disdained, had become very much like a religion. Its role was to confront evil for the rest of us. Somehow, it had to make us better than we knew we were because the ideas that were being enforced, the ideas of America, were bigger and better than Americans.

Most Americans, consensus America, supported that reinforcement of the national rhetoric, even while protesting the growth of the secular church to meet evils old or new, growing or being redefined. The support, the basic trust of the public solution, existed even as the American congregation sought out private solutions—and new ways to evade the multiplying laws and bureaus, rules and enforcers. Which was, of course, the way people have always believed in and dealt with religions. No one can play by all those rules, all those commandments. But they can say they do and they can try. Americans try—and it makes them, often, hypocrites and fools. And decent. And democrats. Americans.

19

BOSTON II

"The Problem Is Across the Charles River . . ."

It was in Boston that Tocqueville gave in to the same temptation
that pushed Garry Orren and me into making our short list of
American beliefs: "Government is best that governs least . . .
Majority rule . . . Equality of opportunity." Tocqueville's list, in
his notes, was longer, and was headed "Causes of the social condition and the present political organization of America."

"1. *Their origin*, fine starting point, intimate mixture of religion and spirit of liberty. Cold and reasoning race.

"2. *Their geographical position.* No neighbors.

"3. *Their Activity*, commercial and industry. Even their vices
are now helpful to them.

"4. *The Material Happiness* which they enjoy.

"5. *The religious spirit which reigns.* A Republican and egalitarian religion.

"6. The diffusion of *useful* education.

"7. Very pure morals.

"8. Their division into small states. They are incapable of a
great state.

"9. The lack of a large capital where everything is central.
Care in avoiding such a large place.

"10. Communal and provincial activity, which enables every
one to find employment at home."

That list, written five months after Tocqueville's landing at

Newport, outlined many of the themes which would later be expanded in *Democracy in America*. It also showed the importance to his thinking of the ideas and opinions of the Reverend Jared Sparks of Boston, the leader of the Unitarian Church, the principal institution of *rienism*, and a distinguished historian and editor who collected and published the papers of George Washington. The first item, in fact, was almost directly from Sparks, who told Tocqueville, "I believe that our origin is the fact which best explains our government and our ways. We came here republicans and religious enthusiasts. We found ourselves abandoned to our own devices, forgotten in this corner of the world."

"The idea that the majority has a right based on enlightenment to govern society was brought to the United States by its first inhabitants," Tocqueville would later write, "and this idea, which would of itself be enough to create a free nation, has by now passed into mores. . . ."

"Mores"—in French, *moeurs*—would be used over and over again in *Democracy in America*. "I here mean the term 'mores' . . ." Tocqueville wrote, "to have its original Latin meaning; I mean it to apply not only to *'moeurs'* in the strict sense, which might be called the habits of the heart, but also to the different notions possessed by men, the various opinions current among them, and the sum of ideas that shape mental habits. . . . The importance of mores is a universal truth . . . If in the course of this book I have not succeeded in making the reader feel the importance I attach to the practical experience of the Americans, to their habits, opinions, and, in a word, their mores, in maintaining their laws, I have failed in the main object of my work. . . .

"It is their mores, then, that make the Americans of the United States, alone among Americans, capable of maintaining the rule of democracy . . ." he said. "Mexico, as happily situated as the Anglo-American Union, has adopted these same laws but cannot get used to democratic government."

The word "Anglo" is not much used in the United States except by Hispanics, especially, ironically, by Mexicans and Mexican-Americans living in the country. They use the term to differentiate between themselves and the majority white population. There were, as I traveled, millions of men and women of Mexican descent living and working in the United States, and many of them were having a difficult time adjusting to "Anglo" ways because their native culture was continually reinforced across the 1,946-mile border shared by the two American countries. The Mexican-American Culture Center of San Antonio, Texas—a growing city of 785,000 people, 53.7 percent of them of Hispanic origin—prepared a booklet for the use of Mexican-Americans explaining the strange ways of the Anglos. Another list—like Tocqueville's, an outside perception of the American majority. One chart was titled "Comparative Overview of Anglo-Saxon and Mexican Historical Cultural Patterns":

FUNDAMENTAL INSTITUTIONS (STATE)

Anglo	*Mexican*
The people are the government.	The people versus the government.

FUNDAMENTAL VALUES

Anglo	*Mexican*
Control of oneself, of others, of nature.	Harmony. Within oneself, among others, within nature.

SYSTEM OF SOCIAL ORGANIZATION;
RESPONSE TO STRESS

Anglo	*Mexican*
Immediate and constant action. . . . modify the environment to meet our needs.	Passive endurance and Resistance . . . modify ourselves to meet the environment.

That little summary was another reminder to me that the constant grumbling about government had to be kept in perspective. Americans did have a fundamental faith in their own government. A touching faith, really. And if I needed any more evidence of Americans' belief that they were capable of organizing themselves and nature, I found it walking around Massachusetts Institute of Technology. There, in offices and laboratories along Memorial Drive in Cambridge, the government of the people was taking action that would have humbled deities: it was trying to create creativity at a place called the Innovation Center.

Innovation—or lack of it—was becoming a national issue. The annual report of the U.S. Patent and Trademark Office, which was issued while I was in Cambridge, showed that in the preceding year, 70,292 patents had been issued in the United States, more than 4,000 patents below the average for the preceding ten years. Thirty-seven percent of those patents, 25,833, were issued to foreigners, compared with only a 17-percent share for foreigners in 1960. In Washington, the Senate was then considering a $60-million-a-year "National Technology Innovation Act." According to the bill, S-1250, "Technology and industrial innovation are central to the economic, environmental, and social well-being of the citizens of the United States. . . . Industrial innovation in the United States may be lagging when compared to historical patterns and other industrialized nations. . . . No national policy exists to enhance technological innovation for commercial and public purposes."

Actually, the Innovation Centers, first established in 1973 on an experimental basis by the National Science Foundation at a cost of about $5 million—80 percent of that from the federal government—might be considered the beginnings of a national policy. "The idea was to see if it was possible to teach entrepreneurship and invention," said David G. Jansson, director of the center. "What we teach is 'invention methodology' and we think we can increase the probability of something creative coming out . . . It is like the methods a swimming coach would use to teach the proper motions. It's designed to bring people up to the actual point of creativity."*

A decline in American creativity—or "innovation," the word more commonly used—was a subject of concerned and regular debate as the 1970s turned into the 1980s. The decline in American patents was one indicator cited in newspapers, magazines, and speeches by professors and politicians; another was the decline of the proportion of the Gross National Product going to research and development, a drop from 3 percent to 2.25 percent from 1963 to 1976. One long story, in the *Los Angeles Times* of April 16, 1978, began:

> WASHINGTON—For decades, every new technology or its product seemed to have made-in-America stamped on it,

---

* The M.I.T. Innovation Center was one of four in the country. The others were at the University of Oregon, the Carnegie-Mellon Institute, and the University of Utah.

from instant copying and instant photography to advanced computers, nuclear reactors, oral contraceptives, synthetic fibers and jet airliners.

Things have changed. . . . There is the alarming prospect of the "loss of our scientific and technological empire," as one historian of science put it. . . .

The story began on page one and was continued, under the headline "Decline in U.S. Technology Lead," on page 23. The other story on page 23, a United Press International dispatch from Philadelphia, reported that Professor Thomas Naff of the University of Pennsylvania was planning to teach surgery to students in Calcutta, India, with videotapes and live satellite transmission from his operating room at the university hospital.

The problem was real, but relative. After enjoying the material happiness and other rewards of technological imperialism for more than a quarter of a century, when much of Europe and Asia was in ruins after World War II, many Americans were startled to realize that their new television set was made in Japan and the better automobile they wanted had been designed in Germany. The loss of monopoly—and the challenge to arrogance—were more shocking than a real or perceived loss of something as hard to quantify as innovation. The problem, it seemed to me, had more to do with American decision making than with national talent.

It wasn't hard to visualize the problem; I saw it in front of me, right across the Charles River. I walked across the Lars Anderson Bridge from Harvard University to the Harvard University Graduate School of Business Administration. "The mission of the school," according to its dean, Lawrence Fouraker, "is to prepare competent and responsible general managers . . ." And it does just that. Harvard Business School had graduated 47,000 men and women—the first women were admitted in 1963—and, in 1978, an estimated 12,000 of them currently held "top" management positions. Of the top three officers of the 500 largest American manufacturing companies (as compiled by *Fortune* magazine) one out of each five was a Harvard Business School graduate. The median income (in 1978) of graduates who had been out of school for five years was $48,400; for graduates out 25 years, it was $100,300 and their median net worth exceeded $750,000. One out of ten applicants to the school was accepted each year. The place could not have defined itself better than to quote Tocqueville, who wrote: "I cannot express my thoughts better than by saying that the Americans put something heroic into their way of trading.

"It will always be very difficult," he continued, "for a European merchant to imitate his American competitor in this." But, 150 years later, competitors in both Europe and Asia were trying and imitating. "You must not underrate the energy of the Americans," Gilbert Bochet, the French consul, told me in New Orleans. "The competitiveness is of heroic proportions. Business, for example. The world has to follow American procedures in marketing and accounting. American business standards are becoming the world's business standards."

Harvard's Masters of Business Administration were the new heroes of American trading, inheritors of the roles and rewards of the hard manufacturing aristocracy that Tocqueville had seen arising on America's fertile commercial soil. The "competent and responsible general managers" were running the organizations created by the hard, innovative captains of the Industrial Revolution.

The officers commissioned by Harvard Business School were trained in and by "case study." Students were bombarded, week after week, with business situations, usually taken from real life, and asked: What would you do? The theory was that the students, most of whom already had some business experience, would evolve into managers with a practiced set of conditioned responses. The right responses were "number" responses—the manager was being trained to maximize profits. It was not what Tocqueville would have called "education." This was merely "useful education"—instruction.

"Although its curriculum is strong in quantitative courses, its teaching is designed to meet the information needs of general managers, not technical specialists," to quote a December 1979 assessment of the school's strategies by a committee of distinguished alumni. That sentence, designed to deflect criticism that H.B.S. was turning out bottom-line automatons without feeling or conscience, was followed by: "The School has been considering the study of ethics for more than 50 years and is actively addressing it now."

Usually, H.B.S. managers could make decisions a bit more

quickly than that. They were taught to use tools like "the decision tree." In courses with names like "Managerial Economics, Reporting, and Control," the students were given complicated case studies and asked what they would do.

"A decision tree," wrote a 1970 H.B.S. graduate, Peter Cohen, "is really a way to order complicated decisions on a piece of paper. It is a diagram based on three simple but useful observations:

"The first observation holds that even the most complex decision must end in a simple choice: to do or not to do a certain thing.

"The second observation notes that all decisions have at least one consequence. And that even no consequence is a consequence.

"The third observation states that all, even the most uncertain consequences, have one certainty about them: They either occur or they do not occur."

So, starting from the original question of what to do—whether to finance more research on a better mousetrap, say—the manager begins by forming a "decision fork" with "Do" or "Don't" tines. Then, branching off from each of the two lines of the fork, he forms an "event fork" based on the predictable consequences of the "Do" decision or the "Don't" decision. A dollar amount—zero, plus, or minus—is then placed at each fork and line, along with a percentage figure on the likelihood of a consequence occurring.

"Half an hour of diagramming," Cohen wrote, "and what seemed an impenetrable mess of a problem is presenting itself as a sequence of logical, easily graspable steps, and all that is left for you to do is to pick the sequence where the numbers show the greatest likelihood of making the most money (or suffering the least loss)."

Simple. It may be wrong or stupid, but it is logical and defensible. With decision trees and the other tools producing a number or two at the end—plus X or minus Y dollars—the student, the American manager, is relieved of thinking, of taking responsibility for the nonfinancial consequences of decision making. Nonfinancial consequences don't grow on trees.

A simple-minded plan, but all the more frightening for that—

and for the fact that a creative young Frenchman was able to visualize it before it existed. In *Democracy in America*, arguing that Americans would be most likely to apply science to the development of comfort and productivity, Tocqueville wrote:

"Nowadays the need is to keep men interested in theory. They will look after the practical side of things for themselves. So, instead of perpetually concentrating attention on the minute examination of secondary effects, it is good to distract it therefrom sometimes and lift it to the contemplation of first causes. . . . If the lights that guide us ever go out, they will fade little by little, as if of their own accord. Confining ourselves to practice, we may lose sight of basic principles, and when these have been entirely forgotten we may apply the methods derived from them badly; we might be left without the capacity to invent new methods and only able to make a clumsy and an unintelligent use of wise procedures no longer understood."

That sounded like Harvard's competent and responsible general managers to me, competent at making decisions simple and largely responsible for the debated decline in innovation. "Instead of meeting the challenge of the changing world, American business today is making small, short-term adjustments by cutting costs and by turning to the government for temporary relief," wrote Ryohei Suzuki, a visiting Japanese economist, in an article that spring for the *Sloan Management Review*, the journal of M.I.T.'s business school on the other side of the Charles. "Success in trade is the result of patient and meticulous preparations, with a long period of market preparation before the rewards are available. . . . To undertake such commitments is hardly in the interest of a manager who is only concerned with his or her next quarterly earnings reports."

Suzuki's analysis was later incorporated in H.B.S's own journal, the *Harvard Business Review*. A "controversial diagnosis," the magazine said in introducing the article, "Managing Our Way to Economic Decline," by two business school professors, Robert H. Hayes and William J. Abernathy.

Those authors quoted a corporate executive, who sounded as if he had just climbed out of a decision tree: "It's much more difficult to come up with a synthetic meat product than a lemon-lime cake mix. But you work on the lemon-lime cake mix because you know exactly what the return is going to be. A synthetic steak is going to take a lot longer, require a much bigger investment, and the risk of failure will be greater."

"These managers are not alone," said Hayes and Abernathy, "they speak for many. Why, they ask, should they invest dollars that are hard to earn back when it is so easy—and so much less risky—to make money in other ways? Why ignore a ready-made situation in cake mixes for the deferred and far less certain prospects in synthetic steaks? Why shoulder the competitive risks of making better, more innovative products?"

With a few exceptions—successful exceptions, particularly in agriculture and computers and other electronic technology—American managers were taking American business out of applied research, to say nothing of "first causes." Much of what was being budgeted as industrial research, I was told again and again, was actually "development," development of products even less useful than lemon-lime cake mixes and of new labels, bottles, and boxes.

Business, even at its best, had always been a secondary factor in first causes. Basic research—the expansion of knowledge for knowledge's sake without regard for immediate or predictable need, usefulness, consequence, or profitability—and much of the complicated or esoteric applied research being done at any time was largely funded by the federal government. The government was left, again, to do the good things people probably wouldn't do themselves—and not-so-nice things, too, in the endless quest for more effective ways to destroy people in war. The roots of the government's involvement in research went back at least to the 1860s and the establishment of A&M (agricultural and mechanical) colleges to help develop the economies of new western territories. "It could be argued," said James Reston of the *New York Times*, "that the greatest thing America has ever produced is the agriculture that came out of those A&M colleges." That involvement continued through public health studies and aeronautical and other mechanical research funded during the administration of Theodore Roosevelt at the beginning of the twentieth century. Then the federal involvement began growing as that research became increasingly expensive—equipment became more sophisticated and began being built on the massive scale of nuclear accelerators.

"Science and technology have traditionally been the core of

the power of this nation," said Philip Morrison, the M.I.T. physicist. "There are probably enough of the nation's resources allocated toward science right now, but they are misallocated. There is a distortion favoring the military as there was a distortion toward the space program. Going to the moon is not science. It's an engineering accomplishment fueled by nationalism . . . But that's what the government wanted and government influence is now determining here. The money comes from the Department of Defense, the Department of Energy, which has picked up the old Atomic Energy Commission contracts, and the National Institutes of Health. The government determines and it is becoming much stricter in regulating the use of the money."

"Research today has to be publicly financed because the scale is so big," said Daniel Martire, head of the Department of Inorganic Chemistry at Georgetown University in Washington, D. C. He had spent 15 years doing basic research on the chemistry of liquid crystals. "There is money available for research. The question is: Who decides how it will be used?"*

Who does decide what research is done?

"Lawyers," Martire said. "The people who write the government's regulations."

* Martire began his research in 1963, at the age of twenty-five. Thirteen years later, some of the experimental techniques he developed because he thought liquid crystals were "intriguing" were adopted for use in separating and classifying carcinogens—probably as good an example as any of the way basic research evolves into applied research.

The fact that Martire began so young was also typical, and pointed up a potential problem for the immediate future of all American scholarship. Because of the large numbers of American children born between the late 1940s and 1960—the "baby boom" years—universities expanded their faculties as those children came of college age beginning in the late 1960s. The new instructors, inevitably, became tenured professors and, like Martire, were in their early forties when the number of young men and women applying to universities began to decline in the late 1970s. "It's going to cause some sort of slowdown in research," said Philip Smith, when he was assistant director of the federal Office of Science and Technology Policy. "There is no doubt that young professors are critical to research because of their energy, their fresh insights. They bring the new ideas. But there is going to be no room for them when faculty cutbacks inevitably begin. There will be no place for the young and the enthusiastic among tired tenured faculties."

"You're kidding!"

"No," he said. "The government decided a few years ago that a lot of money was being wasted in research. Which, of course, was true—a scientist wants to stumble around and follow his nose, that's what basic research is all about. They passed the Mansfield amendment in 1969—which said that research had to be 'relevant.' The research I do has to be relevant to society's needs.*

"The question then becomes who decides what's relevant? And the answer seems to be a ladder of bureaucrats leading up to a cabinet member, usually the Secretary of Defense. But those people are just working from lists of regulations drawn up by the lawyers, and the lawyers, of course, are the only ones who can interpret what they wrote down in the first place. You spend a lot of time filling out forms to show how relevant you are—that you're going to get us into space, or cure cancer or conserve energy, whatever they want you to say at the moment."

You mean . . .

"You lie," he said, describing an underground commerce of ideas. "You make it up. It wastes a lot of time and energy and it probably prevents a lot of quality research from being done. By quality, I mean research that will be 'relevant' thirty years from now, but no one knows how or why yet."

Business, increasingly, wanted to know neither how nor why. Even given the possibility of a certain democratic lack of interest in first causes—many of America's most distinguished scientists have been European, born and trained abroad—the interest in anything but the most profitable knowledge was declining. That was, Hayes and Abernathy wrote, "evidence of a broad managerial failure—a failure of both vision and leadership— that over time has eroded both the inclination and the capacity of U. S. companies to innovate."

The managers were failing America, but they were failing in ways that were both democratic and American. The managers of

---

* The amendment, named after Senator Mike Mansfield of Oklahoma, was passed on November 19, 1969, as part of the Military Construction Act. It stated, "None of the funds authorized to be appropriated by this Act may be used to carry out any research project or study unless such project or study has a direct and apparent relationship to a special military function or operation."

industrial combines were no different from the managers of Gannett newspapers—Harvard helps produce that sameness—in giving Americans products they say they want. "Americans are naturally inclined to require nothing of science but its limited application to the useful arts and ways of making life comfortable . . ." Tocqueville wrote. "In America the purely practical side of science is cultivated admirably, and trouble is taken about the theoretical side immediately necessary to application. On this side the Americans always display a clear, free, original, and creative turn of mind. But hardly anyone in the United States devotes himself to the essentially theoretical and abstract side of human knowledge."

"Investment in both new equipment and research and development, as a percentage of Gross National Product, was significantly higher 20 years ago than today," Hayes and Abernathy wrote in the spring of 1980. They related that decline to the dramatic increase in the number of presidents of large corporations with financial or legal backgrounds—as opposed to production or marketing backgrounds—during the same period:

> When executive suites are dominated by people with financial or legal skills, it is not surprising that top management should increasingly allocate time and energy to such concerns as cash management and the whole process of corporate acquisitions and mergers . . .
>
> During the past two decades American managers have increasingly relied on principles which prize analytical detachment and methodological elegance over insight, based on experience, into the subtleties and complexities of strategic decisions. As a result, maximum short-term financial returns have become the overriding criteria for many companies . . . By their preference for servicing existing markets rather than creating new ones and by their devotion to short-term returns and "management by the numbers," many of them have effectively forsworn long-term technological superiority as a competitive weapon.

The masters of the short-term adjustment—with degrees from Harvard and other prestigious institutions to prove their mastery—became to me the metaphorical counterparts of the clouds of mosquitoes that plagued Tocqueville and Beaumont's journey through the wilderness of Saginaw. They were everywhere.

"When we were making *Fantasia* there were fourteen hundred artists and animators on staff," said Frank Thomas, who was retiring at the age of sixty-five after more than 40 years as an animator on the staff of Walt Disney Studios, once an innovative hub of American popular culture. "Today we've got fourteen hundred accountants and lawyers." That was in Hollywood, California. In Detroit, where they sell cars instead of cartoons, Edward Reingold, a former *Time* magazine bureau chief there, said: "To understand the decline in the quality and salability of American automobiles, you have to know the people who run General Motors and Ford. The car companies went into the money management business. Their idea was that every American would give them $300 a month to invest and they would supply a new car every three years. The investments became the company's business, not the cars." In New York, Richard Wald, vice president of ABC News and former president of NBC News, said: "This company is one of the few still in the entrepreneurial phase. It's still run by the people who founded it. NBC was in the managerial phase. The lawyers and the accountants, who began as advisers, began taking over. What the managerial phase is about, after all, is preserving and milking the property under complicated rules, rules written by and for lawyers."

Those were not pleasant conversations. Each of these men sounded bitter. The young men and women I met at M.I.T. were only cynical. What they were already doing was protecting themselves against the possibility of the same bitterness; one of the reasons for their duality, their determination to use corporations rather than be used themselves, was family experiences some of them had shared when their fathers' energy or work had been discarded for one managerial imperative or another. Despite Professor Morrison's prediction of their passivity, those young Americans might be forced to associate as a movement opposing the managers and their phases. Unionism had declined during the prosperity that followed World War II—that was also a time of a certain enlightened and self-interested paternalism that made many employees feel secure within the association of a corporation itself. But with the insecurity of being a variable in a management case that was real instead of a study, the sons and daughters of employees whose dreams or illusions were shattered in mergers, acquisitions, and productivity and efficiency programs seemed destined to recreate the power of a movement something like organized labor—to use their organized power to make government become the unfailing protector of their security.

Democracy worked, Tocqueville wrote to his friend Ernest de Chabrol, and one reason was that: "Not a man but may reasonably hope to gain the comforts of life; not one who does not know that with love of work his future is certain." Democracy will continue to work. It will not always do everything each of its American adherents would have it do, but it will by its very nature—the sovereignty of the people—follow natural tendencies to insure the comforts of life and a future as secure as any prophecy to those people. As students they might cling to private solutions—and most would always have somewhere to hide from the society—but they would join together one day when the cynicism of youth was no longer enough. Their solution would be public; they would, if American history was a guide, associate to make the government provide the security and certainty that love of work did a long time ago.

20

BOSTON
TO NEW YORK

"The World Turned Upside Down ... "

While I was spending time at Harvard Business School, a new class entered—the class of 1982. There were 190 women among the 785 members of that class. That was more than all the women who graduated from all the country's business schools in 1960—that number was 167. It was more than all the women who had applied to H.B.S. in 1971—155. The number of female applicants for H.B.S.'s class of '82 was 1707. In 1980, 6,281 women earned master's in business degrees from universities around the country.*

I was walking back from a meeting at the business school, along Boylston Street in Cambridge, when I heard a roar of cheers and applause coming from the main building of Harvard's Kennedy Institute of Politics. I looked inside and saw a crowd of several hundred students milling around a speaker. All the students, or almost all, were women. "When I got out of Smith College," the speaker said, "I might have gone to Harvard Law School, but Harvard Law School did not take women." The speaker, Betty Friedan, had graduated from Smith, in Northampton, Massachusetts, in 1943. During World War II she worked as a newspaper reporter, voluntarily giving up her job after the war to a man, a returning veteran. Three years later,

---

* That same year, 23,905 men received master's in business degrees.

married, she was working as a reporter again when she became pregnant. She was fired.

"It seemed so unfair to me," she said. "But no one else thought it was. I talked to my boss. I talked to the union. I wanted to come back to my job after the baby was born."

She never got the job back, and she decided that one day she would write a book about that unfairness. *The Feminine Mystique*, published in 1963, was one of the sparks of what became known as Women's Liberation or the Women's Movement.

"The Fair Sex—Always entitled to our protection!"—that was the toast Tocqueville heard. There were, though, few public toasts and not much protection in the wilderness of Michigan, and it was from there that Tocqueville wrote of the pioneer man—"Family sentiments have come to fuse themselves in a vast egoism, and it is doubtful if in his wife and children he sees anything else than a detached portion of himself"—and woman: "Time has weighed heavily on her: in her prematurely pale face and her shrunken limbs it is easy to see that existence has been a heavy burden for her. . . . It is against the solitude of the forests that she has exchanged the charms of society and the joys of the home. It's on the bare ground of the forest that her nuptial couch was placed. To devote herself to austere duties, submit herself to privations which were unknown to her, embrace an existence for which she was not made, such was the occupation of the finest years of her life, such have been for her the delights of marriage. Want, suffering and loneliness have affected her constitution but not bowed her courage. 'Mid the profound sadness painted on her delicate features, you easily remark a religious resignation and profound peace and I know not what natural and tranquil firmness, confronting all the miseries of life without fearing or scorning them."

"In America, a woman loses her independence forever in the bonds of matrimony," Tocqueville wrote in the second volume of *Democracy in America*, published in 1840. In the first volume, published five years earlier, he had virtually ignored women, saying only that he believed they were more religious than men, and thus shaped the moral habits of the home and promoted "love of order" in affairs of state. Inexorable public opinion carefully keeps woman within the little sphere of domestic interests and duties and will not let her go beyond them," he continued in the second volume. "She knows beforehand what will be expected of her, and she herself has freely accepted the yoke. She suffers her new state bravely, for she has chosen it."*

But there was the obvious question.

"I have shown how democracy destroys or modifies those various inequalities which are in origin social. But is that the end of the matter?" Tocqueville wrote finally. "May it not ultimately come to change the great inequality between man and woman which has up till now seemed based on the eternal foundations of nature?"

Did it?

"Yes, absolutely," said Betty Friedan. "It's not accidental that the modern women's movement began in this country. The real ideology that shaped the movement was the ideas of America—equality, democracy, participation in the shaping of the decisions that affect your own life. There are things ingrained in Americans. Taking the responsibility and the opportunity to mold your own destiny—that's what I learned growing up in Peoria, Illinois. You can do something about things that are unfair. You can organize; you can associate yourself with other people. . . . Those were the ideas behind what women did. It couldn't happen in an authoritarian country, in a lot of other countries, because letting out those ideas would be too danger-

---

* American feminists sometimes quote the concluding section of one of the final chapters of the second volume of *Democracy in America:* "And now that I come near the end of this book in which I have recorded so many considerable achievements of the Americans, if anyone asks me what I think the chief cause of the extraordinary prosperity and growing power of this nation, I should answer that it is due to the superiority of their women." That thought, however, seems to have been in praise of the domestic tranquillity facilitated by women who—in modern terminology—knew their place. It was preceded by lines such as this: "To sum up, the Americans do not think that a man and woman have the duty or right to do the same things, but they show an equal regard for the parts played by both. . . ." In Volume I of the same book, the same man ignored women in sentences like this: "In the United States, except for slaves, servants, and paupers, no one is without a vote. . . ." It may have been coincidence, but the man who forgot women in Volume I, published in January of 1835, and attributed national prosperity to their superiority in 1840, was married later in 1835. His wife, Mary Mottley, was noted, contemporaries reported, for her intellect and serenity.

ous. But here? Here it's all in the Constitution. It's all in the Declaration of Independence."

Why did it take so long?

"Women's lives were dictated by childbearing for so long; they were tied to the home. The Industrial Revolution sent men off to work, to do the big work, make the big decisions. Women stayed behind, and their role was diminished from what it had been in an agricultural society. Then Freud, the current of popularized Freud that ran through the country for so long—that put down women. Freud had no sense of women as people— they were vessels who fulfilled themselves with passive service to men . . . But, really, childbirth. You walk through old cemeteries and you can see what was happening—a lusty man might have three wives and three families because the women were dying young in childbirth."

Why did it happen when it did?

"Technology. Birth control. Earlier women's movements finally won the vote, but we found out that political power didn't mean much without an economic base. Birth control liberated women—it allowed them to use their brains and their education. Then it was a question of when you reached a critical mass of women who were educated but were being underutilized by the society. That began happening after World War II and I was part of it."

So, in Betty Friedan's analysis, one of Tocqueville's fears had been realized: universal education in the United States did indeed lead to social unrest. What the Frenchman—what most men—couldn't quite imagine was that it would be women who would become restless. Women demanded fairness.

That was a revolution! "The most important development of my lifetime," said David Riesman, the Harvard professor who had helped Americans define themselves for 50 years. There were figures and facts to demonstrate the extent of change— more than half of American women were part of the workforce by the late 1970s; the first women were admitted in 1976 as cadets at the United States Military Academy—but statistics and "firsts" were inadequate to describe the cracking of the eternal foundations of nature. The "mores"—what Tocqueville called the sum of ideas and habits of the heart—had changed and were changing. That was best described for me by a poet and novelist, Elizabeth Hardwick:

> The women's movement has crystallized in domestic life changes that have been going on for decades. Historically, the political and social expression of the themes of women's liberation coincides with the needs of a world in which there are almost as many divorces as marriages, with smaller families, longer lives, the economic expansion desired by the average household for which two incomes are required, education of women, diminishment of the need for heavy muscular work, which means that the lives of men and women—talking on the phone, sitting at the desk, managing—became more and more alike.
>
> The inner changes within women can scarcely be exaggerated. Ambition is natural to new groups freed, or demanding to be free and equal. No group demands equality for nothing, as a simple adornment of status. The arrival of women's ambition, transforming as it does private life, inner feeling, and public life, is not at all simple but instead resembles the subtle shiftings of human thought and life brought about by enormously challenging ideas such as evolution and Freudianism. Many hang back, just as many would stand on the literal truth of Genesis; but no matter what the ideological reluctance may be, every life is an inchoate but genuine reflection of the change. We begin to act upon new assumptions without even being aware of the singular changes.
>
> Society does not want women to lead a long life in the home. It is not prepared to support them and cannot give the old style true sanction. Children do not want their parents' lives to be given to them forever. Husbands cannot take the responsibilities for wives as an immutable duty, ordained by nature. Women's liberation suits society much more than society itself is prepared to admit. The wife economy is as obsolete as the slave economy.
>
> . . . It is a psychic and social migration, leaving behind a violently altered landscape.

The world was turned upside down. Like their grandmothers and mothers, women students at Harvard wanted security, according to one of them, Karen Rochlin of the class of 1982. But, looking at the broken marriages and unstable families of their own experiences, they believed careers offered more security than marriage. She summarized the attitudes of many of her classmates as: "You can't plan for a marriage, but you can plan for a career; it makes sense to pursue the career."

And the changes were just beginning. "This is the second wave of feminism in America," said Gloria Steinem, the editor of a feminist magazine, *Ms.*, who argued that the modern movement began as an outgrowth of black civil rights activity in the 1960s. "This has really only been going on for about ten years. The first wave—the drive to establish legal and political identities for women who weren't even allowed to sign contracts— lasted for about 150 years and ended when they won the right to vote in 1920. This wave, so far, has only been consciousness-raising on issues like equal pay for comparable work and the right of a woman to control her own body, to have an abortion. I think a majority consensus—of both women and men—has been reached on those issues and now will come the push to put those changes into effect.*

"There is going to be tremendous opposition to these things," she continued. "Fundamentalist groups, publicly, will lead the attack. We understand each other very well. . . . They understand revolution. Look at the things Howard Phillips is saying."

She knew her enemy. Howard Phillips, a former federal official, was the national director of a lobbying group called the Conservative Caucus. In a speech to a "Pro-Family" conference of California Citizens for a Biblical Majority in June of 1980, he said: "The family is increasingly being eliminated as the basic unit of self-government in America and being replaced by state control over the individual. . . . In the eighteen-hundreds, legislation was enacted which freed the wife of economic dependence on the husband. [Women] were given property rights. . . . We saw how women were liberated from the leadership of their husbands politically . . . we had one family, one vote. And we have seen the trend toward one person, one vote. And the ultimate extension of this philosophy has been the sexual liberation

* Steinem described Friedan as part of a "reformist" movement that represents the interests of educated middle-class housewives. Women were on the move; that did not mean they were always united. Like other democratic movements, feminism was a concourse of individual wills.

of the woman from the husband as our government and as our established elites in America have condoned adultery, promiscuity and other forms of immoral behavior which undermine the family. . . ."

Phillips, a serious man who was once director of the U. S. Office of Economic Opportunity, went on and was applauded again and again. So there were people out there who agreed with him. I wondered whether any of them thought he would succeed in his crusade—and I wondered whether he could have been politically successful even in 1831. That was the year Tocqueville wrote: "I repeat what I have said before, that the present tendency of American society seems to me to be toward ever increasing democracy."

If the Citizens for a Biblical Majority were the opposition, then the outcome of the struggle for women's equality was clear. While Phillips was arguing that things would be better if wives would do what their husbands told them, wives were leaving both their husbands and children, and one out of every ten students at the government institution training military leaders was a woman. The arguing was over. The question was: How would the landscape be altered?

Well, for one small thing, America was no longer going to be, as Tocqueville described it in a satirical letter to his sister-in-law, "the eldorado of husbands." He wondered at—and amused himself by writing letters home about—the placid subservience of American wives. "When a woman marries, it's as if she entered a convent, except however it is not taken ill that she have children, and even many of them. Otherwise, it's the life of a nun; no more balls; hardly any more society; a husband as estimable as cold for all company; and that to the life eternal. I ventured the other day to ask one of those charming recluses just how, exactly, a wife could pass her time in America. She answered me, with great *sang-froid:* in admiring her husband. I'm very sorry: but that's the literal translation of the English. I tell you this so that, should you happen to be bored at home, you may know what you have to do."

The liberation of women—for nothing less was happening—changed American lives at home and at work. The new assertiveness of women was changing the way Americans faced each other. Inevitably, it would change the way the nation faced the world. I became sure of that as I traveled the country during the 1980 election campaign between the President, Jimmy Carter, a Democrat, and his challenger, Ronald Reagan, the nominee of the Republican Party. Women, it seemed to me then, were much more favorable to the incumbent—and that perception was confirmed after the election, when surveys indicated that women split their votes about evenly between the two candidates while men strongly favored the Republican.*

One of the television networks, NBC, reported that its surveys, taken by questioners waiting outside polling booths—a device that with the aid of computerized past results gave networks the capability of announcing the winners of elections before many people had even voted—indicated that Reagan, the Republican, owed his winning margin of 10 percent entirely to male voters. Which meant there was a 20-point difference between the voting of men and women. (Another network, CBS, which surveyed in conjunction with the *New York Times,* reported a 14-point spread; their numbers showed Reagan winning 54-to-47 percent among men but only 48-to-45 among women.)

For the first time, women were voting in the same numbers as men, and for the first time, apparently, they were voting for dif-

---

* The two-party system is ingrained in both custom and law. Tocqueville argued that in a democracy custom would always take precedence over law, but the survival of the custom of choosing between two candidates nominated by the same two parties may be a triumph of law over customs prevented from changing. Election laws, still primarily established by the states, are essentially a contract between the two parties to insure the survival of both and to make challenges by other groups exceedingly difficult if not impossible. In the 1970s political reformers began proposing, with success at both national and state levels, plans for financing elections from tax revenues. The idea was to diminish the influence of individuals and private associations contributing money to candidates to pay for the rising costs of television and direct-mail advertising. One effect, however, was to institutionalize the two-party system. The aid formulas were based on the results of the preceding election—which, of course, was a contest between the same two parties. If the same public financing laws had been in effect during the 1856 election, the election in which the Republican Party was formed as a third party, the 1980 election would have been between the Democrats and the Whigs.

ferent candidates and different issues. "A tremendous change
has occurred in American politics almost without notice:
Women now hold the balance of voting power," Sandra Baxter
and Marjorie Lansing concluded in *Women and Politics*, a book
published just before the election. "Whatever happens to the . . .
feminist movement, plain statistics clearly show that the political opinions of women will count for more than those of men in
the 1980s and the decades beyond."

What Baxter and Lansing documented in their book was that
by the middle 1970s, after a history of relatively low interest,
women began participating in politics—talking and voting—at
the same levels as men. And since there were more women—
they live longer—their political ideas were inevitably going to
become more important than men's. They had become the majority in a country where the majority rules. Of course there
could only be a majority if it was made up of people who disagreed about something with a minority. What American women
and men disagreed about was militarism: they disagreed about
going to war.

Polls, surveys, and political scientists—and years of plain conversation—showed that, whatever the situation, women were
more opposed to military action than men. A small test of those
attitudes came up only four months after the 1980 elections. In
March of 1981, when the Reagan administration appeared to be
enormously popular and newspapers were competing with each
other to analyze how the new President had won the hearts and
minds of the people, the regular Gallup poll on public approval
of the President showed that Reagan's popularity had dropped
more than 20 percentage points in 60 days and that he had much
lower public approval than his predecessor, President Carter,
had had at the same point in his presidency. Polling is a more
inexact "science" than its practitioners pretend—the answers
depend on the questions and the only thing scientific about the
business is the number of respondents selected at random—but
it is most certain as a comparative device. And, comparatively,
this President was in trouble because of women, even though
they have traditionally been more supportive of presidents than
men. But this time his support among women had dropped
sharply—and it seemed clear, at least to me, that the reason was

a couple of belligerent White House statements raising the possibility that the United States might send military advisers to back the government of a small country, El Salvador, in a civil war.

"Women are closer to life, I think," Betty Friedan said. "If women were 50 percent of the United States Senate, we would not have continued the Vietnam War year after year. . . . Those kinds of changes will take time—we're still electing women officials who are really imitation men—but you will get a change in political behavior. Men will change, too, because they will have to share more and more of women's work, including the rearing of children. In the last analysis, women are going to be the ones answering the question: What is it worth to die?"

"Women are more inclined to mistrust violence," said Gloria Steinem. "We're not trained for it. And it's usually been used against us. . . . In high school, I remember the guys going off to the Korean War. Some of the girls cried, but there was a feeling it had to be done. Moreover, there was a feeling it was the right thing to do. I don't think that's true anymore, for women or for men. Communications are better, so you don't necessarily see the enemy as a monster. And you have women: we don't see violence as the inevitable solution."

I had seen Betty Friedan in Cambridge, but Gloria Steinem's office was only ten blocks from mine in Manhattan; I was on West Fiftieth Street and she was on West Fortieth. I walked. It was quite a trip.

I started from the thirty-seventh floor of the Time-Life Building. There were five people on the elevator down, one of them a dark-skinned young man—Puerto Rican, I guessed—wearing a T-shirt celebrating a rock group called "The Kinks" and khaki pants tucked into Army boots. He was carrying a suitcase-sized radio, the kind that enlivened Philadelphia—the things were called "Ghetto Blasters," and this one was blasting out a song, if that was the word, whose shouted lyrics were the days of the week chanted over and over again, "Sunday, Monday, Tuesday . . ." The elevator seemed to throb; the sound was physically painful. No one said a word. No one looked at the young man. I got off at the basement level of the building to pick up a newspaper, and other young men, black this time, were leaping over and diving under the subway turnstiles to avoid paying the

75-cent fare. People moved away to give them more running room for the leap.

Outside, the Avenue of the Americas—Sixth Avenue to New Yorkers—was wired with energy. More young men, black and white, were playing strings and horns for the enjoyment and coins of passers-by. Sticks of meat, sausages, sodas, nuts and dried fruits, hot dogs, cappuccino and espresso, ice cream, cups of fruit were being sold from under brightly colored umbrellas. A man was saying to a street-light pole, "You never come to see me anymore. . . ." Another and another were drinking cheap wine from bottles held inside paper bags—one man walking along, the other slumped against a building wall. Another was sprawled across the sidewalk and people stepped around and over him. A man wearing a large Mexican hat walked backward holding out a handful of shiny wallets, calling, "Four dollars! Four dollars! . . ." "Look at the way she's dressed," said one well-dressed middle-aged man to another, attentively following the progress of a young woman whose pubic hair scraggled out from under a pair of tight pink shorts. "It's no wonder they get raped all the time." A man handed me a green card with a drawing of a lounging woman: "$17. The Place for Single Swingers. Open 'Til 5 A.M. SILVER SLIPPER 121 West 45th Street." An old woman, white, with only a couple of teeth, shuffled past me, calling softly, "Sheee-yak . . . Sheeee-yak."

Outside the building I was looking for, on West Fortieth Street, four workmen were unloading desks and filing cabinets from a truck, passing back and forth a marijuana cigarette as they piled the things on the sidewalk, smiling at people who could not pass without walking into the street. Inside, in the elevator, two men were talking. "I started to yell, but then I thought he might have a shiv. They came running and he went down the stairs like lightning. . . ."

"Did you chase him?" the other said.

"No. He probably would've killed me."

"Yeah. Smart."

"We're going to take everything out of the showroom and we're keeping a crowbar under the counter. We'll get a gun. . . ."

The elevator arrived at the offices of *Ms.* magazine.

"Many people are threatened by the changes they see happening all around them," Gloria Steinem said. "The women's movement is part of the changes. It confuses people because they don't know what will change next. . . .

"They don't want women involved in the military. They want to maintain an obedient and violent presence in many places here and abroad. They think women will fuck that all up—and we probably will."

21
NEW YORK

"The American Dream Self-Destructs . . ."

"We understand that two magistrates, Messrs. de Beaumont and de Tonqueville [sic], have arrived in the ship *Havre*, sent here by order of the Minister of the Interior, to examine the various prisons in our country," the report in the New York *Mercantile Advertiser* had said on May 12, 1831, the second day Tocqueville and Beaumont were in the United States. ". . . we have no doubt that every facility will be extended to the gentlemen who have arrived."

The young Frenchmen stayed in New York for more than two weeks before leaving on a steamboat going up the Hudson River on May 29. They were to return three times, to spend a total of two months in the city before leaving for home. "To a Frenchman the aspect of the city is bizarre and not very agreeable," Tocqueville wrote to his mother on May 15. "One sees neither dome, nor bell tower, nor great edifice, with the result that one has the constant impression of being in a suburb. In its centre the city is built of brick, which gives it a most monotonous appearance. The houses have neither cornices, nor balustrades, nor *portes-cochères*. The streets are very badly paved, but sidewalks for pedestrians are to be found in all of them. We had all the trouble in the world getting lodgings because at this time of year strangers abound. . . . At length we succeeded in establishing

The Battery, New York City

ourselves admirably in the most fashionable street, called Broadway."*

"Saturday evening," Beaumont wrote to his family, "Tocqueville and I, while out walking, perceived a church that was open. Within were only a few pious souls wrapped in prayer. We found the door of the stairway leading to the steeple open. There we were climbing from attic to attic, by little staircases dark and steep. At last, after many tribulations, we got all the way to the top and enjoyed an admirable spectacle: that of a city of 240,000 inhabitants built on an island, surrounded on one side by the ocean and on the other by immense rivers, on which are to be seen an unending multitude of vessels and small boats. Its harbor is immensely wide. Its public buildings are few and as a rule of undistinguished construction."

But the visitors were considered distinguished indeed. No

* Their boarding house was at 66 Broadway, an address that no longer exists. The main part of New York City was concentrated between the Battery and Canal Street, with dirt roads—Third and Eighth avenues—leading north to the villages of Manhattanville and Harlem.

matter how young they were, France was very old and their official mission flattered the new United States. "Everyone here overwhelms us with courtesy and services," Beaumont told his family two days after the *Mercantile Advertiser* announced their arrival. "We shall soon be obliged to forbid our door. Our arrival in America has *created a sensation. . . .*"

One of the first to their door, figuratively, was the mayor of the fast-growing city, Walter Bowne, who was in the hardware business when he became Grand Sachem of the Tammany Society and then, in 1827, was appointed mayor by the Common Council. With 25 aldermen and various assistants, the cream of the Tammany Society, Mayor Bowne gathered up the two commissioners on May 25 for a carriage tour of New York's prisons and asylums. The climax was a formal dinner inside the Bellevue Almshouse and Penitentiary overlooking the East River from First Avenue between Twenty-seventh and Twenty-eighth streets.

"I should like to describe it to you, but the thing is difficult," Tocqueville wrote to a friend. "Picture to yourself, however, a long table like a refectory table at the high end of which the mayor flanked by your two servants was seated. Next came all the *convives, tous grands personnages à faire pleurer,* for they laugh mighty little on this side of the Atlantic.

"As for dinner itself, it represented the infancy of the art: the vegetables and fish before the meat, the oysters for dessert. In a word, complete barbarism. . . .

"The Mayor drank to our health in the English manner, which consists in filling a small glass, in raising it while looking at you, and in drinking it, the whole performed with great solemnity. The person to whom this civility is addressed has to respond to it by doing exactly the same thing. We each, then, drank our glass, always with befitting dignity. Up to that point everything was going well.

"But we began to tremble on perceiving that each of our table companions was getting ready to do us the same honour. We had the appearance of hares with a pack of dogs on their trail, and the fact is they would soon have had us in distress if we had allowed them to. But at the third glass I took the step of only swallowing a mouthful. . . .

"They bring lighted candles and serve you very neatly a certain number of cigars on a plate. Each one takes possession of one and, the society enveloping itself in a cloud of smoke, the toasts begin, muscles relax the least little bit, and they give themselves to the heaviest gaiety in the world."

"The toasts," the extravagantly patriotic thirteen, with music and cheers after each one, were hardly to the visitors' elegant taste. "These people seem to me stinking with national conceit," Tocqueville wrote to his mother, "it pierces through all their courtesy."*

Three miles north of the old Bellevue Almshouse and almost 150 years later, in a gracious eighteenth-century house called Gracie Mansion, I had dinner with the mayor of New York City. Our evening began, rather than ending, with a lustily patriotic burst of American conceit, still alive and well after all these years of thinking (and talking) of ourselves as a breed apart.

"Who the hell do these people think they are criticizing the United States every day?" said the mayor, Edward Koch. He was upset about the day's debate in the United Nations, forty blocks south of his official residence. "These two-bit dictators, killing and torturing their own people back where they come from— and they come here and talk about 'Freedom'! This is freedom. America is freedom."

"This is a classless society," said one of the guests, Richard Ravitch, a wealthy builder who was chairman of the Metropolitan Transportation Authority, the governmental agency that operated the city's buses and subways. "That's right!" others at the table said, and it immediately became apparent that the Americans in this old house equated freedom with opportunity—the opportunity, no matter who you were or where you came from, to make money or have power, or both. We began talking, enthusiastically, about what our parents and grandpar-

---

* Tocqueville and Beaumont had another reason for disliking the toasts. Almost invariably the Americans would toast the Marquis de Lafayette—"The Friend of Washington, the Champion of the Rights of Man—General Lafayette. Nine Cheers," was the toast at a Tammany dinner on May 12, 1831—and the touring Frenchmen were politically opposed to the old man and his dreams of an American-style republic in France.

ents did for a living, where they came from. The mayor's father and mother were Polish immigrants; he had worked as a tailor, she as a cloakroom attendant. "My grandfather came from Russia when he was fourteen," Ravitch said, and the conversation took off with others joining in, "My grandfather was a janitor in the Bronx and my father was a yarn salesman." "My father was a janitor too." "My grandfather sold from a pushcart in Boston, a peddler." "My mother was a salesgirl at Bloomingdale's . . ."

The mayor's official residence, on a small bluff overlooking the East River, was called a mansion, but it was not. It was once the home of a merchant named Archibald Gracie. It has to have been one of the houses Tocqueville saw when he came down from Newport in a Long Island Sound steamboat, the *President,* and wrote home: "Picture to yourself an attractively varied shoreline, the slopes covered by lawns and trees in bloom right down to the water, and more than all that, an unbelievable multitude of country houses, big as boxes of candy. . . ."

"Who would you like me to invite?" Koch had asked several times in the weeks preceding the dinner.

"Whoever you think are the most interesting people in New York," I had said.

He invited five men and a woman. Each of them worked for him, had worked for him, or held a public appointment he had proposed or approved. Not surprisingly, he dominated the conversation. And after the extravagant patriotism of the beginning, it was an angry conversation, rambling expressions of the frustrations of people who had sought the power of local self-government, then found that, at best, they were sharing the power with the central government. It was also self-serving, since by rhetorically shifting responsibility for local problems to the federal government, which he and other mayors and governors did regularly in public, Koch was also absolving himself, or trying to, of public blame for the troubles of the day.

"Washington just sits there and tells us to do this, do that, do it this way, do it that way," Koch said, beginning to be warmed by his own rhetoric. "Keep the hospitals open even if they don't have patients, or we'll cut off your aid. They'll cut off the money, they'll take us to court. It never ends. It's insane. Help the handicapped, help the children. Put white teachers in black schools. No, we changed our mind, put black teachers in black schools. Teach in Spanish. A judge says put one prisoner in a cell. Where the hell is the money, judge? We don't . . ."

"It's not just the courts," said Ronay Menschel, who had been on Koch's staff when he was a congressman and was now the city's executive administrator. "It's federal regulations. . . ."

"We keep getting these mandates from Washington without providing the money," Koch continued.

"We're a captive of federal revenue," said Alan Schwartz, the city's corporation counsel. "Washington offered all those bright new programs and the cities jumped into them because people wanted them, but they had to match part of the federal aid with local money and there was this tremendous dependence."

"It's insane," Koch said again. "I want to exercise the powers I have under the Charter of the City of New York. I can't do that. Washington is running everything. We have to take money from the cops and give it to the hospitals because they'll take us to court, they'll cut off our funding. They're giving us funding, making us take it to do things that don't need to be done. People being allowed to speak both Spanish and English in the schools is crazy."

"Ed," Schwartz said, "you voted for that." He had indeed. Koch was a member of Congress for nine years before being elected mayor.

"I know that," the mayor snapped back. "I was dumb. We all were. I voted for so much crap. Who knew? We got carried away with what the sociologists were telling us. We wanted to help people."

"Congress became more responsive," Menschel said. "The winds of change once would have come and gone, but now they are institutionalized through regulations and the courts."

"Times change but old plans have a life of their own," said David Brown, who was lecturing at Yale University after having served as Koch's deputy mayor. "They live on through the courts and through bureaucracies created to enforce regulations. One of the central problems you see from this perspective is administrative law. Washington sees a new constituency and creates a new right or corrects an old wrong; then a mechanism—rules and people—has to be created to enforce the new value. The value becomes institutionalized even though tomorrow there may be a new one. . . . The Constitution never contemplated the creation of those new constituencies and their governmental arms. We can't get this thing back in the bottle."

"How did it begin?" I asked.

"When money was tied to policy," Brown said.*

"The people out there had nothing to do with any of this," said Koch, waving his hand vaguely in the direction of what he saw as his devoted constituents in Queens and Brooklyn. Like many politicians of the day, he was maintaining a high level of popularity by echoing or leading the complaints of "ordinary" people, even when those complaints were aimed at his own areas of responsibility. "We permitted a small number of people, usually gifted people, to dominate the society. This was their view. It was never the majority view."

"I take it," I said, "you are not as concerned as Tocqueville was about a tyranny of the majority?"

"If there's a tyranny right now," he said, "it's a tyranny of a minority. The elitists."

The powerful minority that the mayor of the country's largest city was railing against had little riches and no troops. The feared few had only one thing: information.

"The bills I voted for in Washington came to the floor of the Congress in a form that compelled approval," Koch said in a later interview. "After all, who can vote against clean air and water, or better access and education for the handicapped? But as I look back it is hard to believe I could have been taken in by

---

* The proportion of federal and state aid in American municipal budgets increased from approximately 25 to 45 percent from the late 1940s to the middle 1970s, according to reports of the Advisory Committee on Intergovernmental Relations. In New York City, that percentage increased from 25.3 percent in 1950 to 46.8 percent in 1976, when it began to level off and then decline slightly. But, more significantly, the proportion of state aid during those years actually declined by a percentage point or two, while the federal share increased more than fivefold. Those figures are from the City Comptroller's annual reports.

"The City of New York," Mayor Koch said in a later interview, in May 1981, "is driven by 47 federal and state mandates. The total cost to the city of meeting these requirements over the next four years will be $711 million in capital expenditures, $6.25 billion in expense budget dollars, and $1.66 billion in lost revenue."

the simplicity of what the Congress was doing and by the flimsy empirical support—often no more than a carefully orchestrated hearing record or a single consultant's report."

The information of a few witnesses or a single professor, Koch argued, in effect, controlled democratic government. Information was power in the America I was traveling through—and that was becoming more true as the amount of information expanded. How could I select among the electrons of energy that I heard and saw spinning through Newport on the May day when I began traveling? My selections, my decisions about that determined what I wrote here. My decisions, my choice of information as a citizen, would determine what I would do as an American. Multiply that 200 million times, and you had the engine of American democracy. "What strikes every traveler in this country the most . . ." Tocqueville wrote in an exuberant letter, "is the spectacle of a society proceeding all alone, without guide or support, by the single fact of the concourse of individual wills." A tyrant, or a minority of tyrants, would, first, have to control that spinning, overwhelming flow of atmospheric dialogue and images.

A month later, the elected executive of the largest state in the country, Governor Jerry Brown of California, talked about control of information during a long conversation we had as he traveled across New Hampshire in an unsuccessful presidential campaign. Once he used the same phrase that Koch had used, "tyranny of the minority."

"I see very deep questions about the future of individual freedom," said Brown, an inconsistent man, both unpredictable and thoughtful. "As free citizens, we are increasingly dependent on distant bureaucracies that give us permission to think. . . .

"Life becomes like health, or like medicine, the medical profession. You go to a doctor to find out about your own body, even though there is a great deal about your body you could learn yourself if the educational system were structured differently. So doctors, in effect, constitute an elite, controlling information. . . ." Brown was developing Tocqueville's thought about American lawyers—"somewhat like the Egyptian priests, being, as they were, the only interpreter of an occult science." The governor continued: "And more and more in the society, we are specializing and creating boxes of expertise, each controlled by its own elite. You turn people into children, into dependent beings who look to the elites for their central thoughts—whether it's in the university, or the medical establishment, or the television establishment or the political establishment.

"What you have is very different from the autonomous yeoman citizen that Thomas Jefferson had in mind. You develop a mass consciousness, in which a relatively small number of people can determine the thoughts and ideas that all people possess."

Koch and Brown, the mayor and the governor, from the perspective of the modern city and state, were each frustrated and concerned by the concurrent fractionalization and centralization of power in the society. The centralization—the draining of traditional political and informational centers—had seemed striking and sad to me in Louisville. I was thinking there was no Louisville. Koch, throwing his arms wide with the palms up, shrugging his shoulders and saying, "What can I do? Washington makes all the decisions now," was exaggerating more than a bit to serve his own political purposes, but he was trying to say that there was no New York City. Brown, with his fear of distant fractionated bureaucracies, could have been worrying that there would be no Californians, no California.

"We . . ." said Barney Frank, the Massachusetts legislator who became a congressman, "we work in the margins." I repeated that line from an elected representative of the people to L. Clinton Hoch. "That's right," Hoch said, smiling. "Political boundaries are almost completely insignificant to us." He pulled down a wall-sized map of the United States. But it was united states without the states: the familiar middle swath of the North American continent was divided into grids of 500 miles by 500 miles and then subdivided into grids of 100 miles by 100 miles. Hoch tapped one of the smaller grids. "This," he said, "is the real United States."

Hoch was executive vice president of the Fantus Company. "Location Consultants" was printed below the company's name. Fantus—named after a Chicago furniture manufacturer, Felix Fantus, who moved his factory to Rushville, Indiana, in 1919, to "get a full day's work for a full day's pay"—handled 70 percent of the consulting work paid for in 1980 by American corporations considering the location or relocation of plants and offices.

Fantus did not work in the margins. The frustrations of Mayor

Koch—more accurately, the problems of his city—were rooted in economic decline, in the decentralization of the day-to-day operations of the nation's business rather than in the centralization of governing that he was attacking. Industrial and commercial functions—companies, jobs and taxpayers—had been leaving New York City for more than 20 years. The mayor's complaints about federal domination were essentially cries that the central government was not doing enough to maintain and preserve the facilities and services—from subway trains under the great rivers to free dental care for poor people—that could once be supported by local taxation of essential and growing industrial and commercial systems. In 1960, 150 of the 500 largest industrial corporations in the United States maintained their headquarters, their main offices, in New York. By 1980, only 83 of those headquarters remained in the city. Of the 67 that relocated, most had retained Fantus—the location consultants often knew of economic dislocations that would have material effects on the governing of the city months and years before any municipal or state officials.*

Fantus, in those years, was the guide (working for very large tips) showing corporations the way across frontiers—financial and life-style frontiers—from the North to the South, from the East to the West, and from large cities to smaller ones, even to towns. It was as if instead of seeing eastern families on the roads and rivers in search of fortune, Tocqueville had seen entire communities moving on. The companies were that and they were going—Anaconda, Akzona, Cities Service, Shell Oil, and Johns-Manville from New York to Denver, Asheville, Tulsa, Houston, and Denver. That was a beginning, predicted Keith Wheelock, the president of Fantus, speaking, in this case, of office relocation: "I anticipate that critical assessments of corporate activities and requirements will lead to further . . . positioning of operating headquarters and technical facilities that is determined by future opportunities rather than past historical circumstances."

It seemed such an American statement. We are, indeed, a na-

* Fantus, a subsidiary of Dun & Bradstreet Corp., maintained its own offices in the New York suburb of South Orange, New Jersey.

tion of leavers. "This nomad people," in Tocqueville's words, ". . . which after having reached the Pacific Ocean, will reverse its steps to trouble and destroy the societies it will have formed behind it." Those societies called Louisville, Memphis, Saginaw, Detroit, New York. All for the American reasons, old and new: money and an easier way of life.

"The reasons that companies give in public for moving are almost never the real reasons," said Hoch. "It's easier to blame government and people believe it. They can understand when someone says taxes are too high and all the rest. But the truth is that taxes are almost never a factor in relocations. There are tax breaks everywhere, in all the states. Real estate taxes vary more with community size than they vary with states.

"There are two different types of relocation. Plant moves, whatever is announced, are almost always simple bottom-line moves. Manufacturers are interested in dollar cost per unit manufactured. That means one thing: cheap labor. . . .

"Office relocations do not involve money. The figures are often fudged to make a move look like an economic decision. They are basically about quality of life—the ability to attract middle-management people or the simple fact that the chief executive officer can't tolerate the conditions where he is, whether it's crime or untrained, unpleasant secretaries or just that commuting is terrible and he wants his office where he wants to live. I'm working now in a city unnamed, corporation unnamed"—he tapped a stack of documents on his desk—"it's very big and very important. Several top executives or their families have been personally affected by crime, violent crime. The chief executive officer told me: 'I'm getting out. I can't stand it!' There's no way we can justify this move economically, but they're going to move and they're going to say it's for economic reasons. Offices, in fact, can relocate anyplace—the Cayman Islands, wherever—because the people they need, the banking people, advertising people, will come to them. And the support workforce is not all that important anymore. Dictating machines and 'automatic word systems' are replacing secretaries and clerks. The big cost is moving people—it costs $25,000 and up to move a family—and you want to keep everyone from the president down to the head bookkeeper. You want to keep your key people and, generally, they're family people making between $25,000 and $50,000 a year and they care about good schools, medical service, culture, recreation, climate. They care about quality of life and the company cares about them because their skills are hard to replace.*

"Manufacturing moves," Hoch continued, "are different. Workers are not hard to replace—the idea is to find cheaper workers to do the same thing. You only need to relocate two or three key people. After that, it's all numbers. Labor costs, transportation of supplies and product. Transportation costs effectively eliminate whole areas of the country from consideration in many relocations"—he pointed to the grids covering the state of Maine. "If you move a manufacturing operation from Boston to rural Missouri, you immediately save 15 percent in transportation costs. But the principal factor is still labor." Then he opened a map which color coded the country to indicate the percentage of the labor force that was unionized within each of the grids—ranging from less than 7 percent in the area of the Carolinas to almost 40 percent in large sections of the Northeast. That was a significant part of the reason why, in the middle 1970s, the difference between the prevailing industrial wage in the textile industry was lower in the South than in the Northeast—the average was $5.55 an hour in the Northeast compared with $3.49 in North and South Carolina.†

---

* Despite the fact that office moves, like manufacturing moves, tend to be from the North to the South, "climate" is apparently not a controlling factor in many Americans' personal definitions of "quality of life." In Fantus surveys, 90 percent of relocated executives listed "schools" as critical to their decisions on whether to move with their jobs, compared with 56 percent who cited "climate." The quality of "schools," I suspected, was considered a reliable indicator, by most relocating families, of the overall socioeconomic level of the neighborhood in which they would be living—and thus could be a category that effectively hid motivations that were essentially racial.

† The standard Fantus manufacturing report offered the client corporation three choices: a new facility in a plant's present location, a nearby facility (within the same small grid), and a distant facility selected to maximize annual savings. The final report to the client was as good an example as any of a type of modern American decision making. The communities in this example, supplied by Fantus, were unnamed because where they were was irrelevant to decision making.

	Present location versus recommended communities			
	Present Location	Community A	Community B	Community C
TRANSPORTATION				
Inbound	$ 385,900	$ 498,400	$ 418,400	$ 412,200
Outbound	941,200	874,600	1,019,200	865,000
LABOR				
Direct hourly	3,758,400	2,897,800	2,831,200	3,298,000
Indirect hourly	2,245,000	1,313,200	1,274,200	1,570,600
Salaried personnel	671,500	525,500	519,600	580,900
Fringe benefits	2,536,200	1,515,200	1,470,400	1,798,300
PLANT OVERHEAD				
Annualized occupancy cost based on construction costs or rental	336,300	387,300	395,600	422,400
Real estate taxes	77,600	56,600	54,200	78,200
Personal property taxes				
Machinery and equipment	55,300	0	58,800	51,700
Inventory	75,700	12,700	0	62,300
Fuel for heating	34,800	28,400	26,800	32,600
UTILITIES				
Power	169,800	122,600	154,700	171,600
Fuel	55,500	44,100	54,000	52,200
Water	37,000	16,400	16,200	18,400
Waste treatment	6,300	14,300	24,800	22,100
STATE AND PAYROLL TAXES				
State income and franchise taxes	73,400	64,200	62,600	60,700
Sales and related taxes	30,200	26,800	24,600	0
Workmen's compensation insurance	62,100	44,100	42,600	46,700
Total	$11,522,100	$8,342,200	$8,447,900	$9,543,900
Potential annual savings over present location		$3,209,900	$3,104,200	$2,008,200
Percentage saving		27.8%	26.9%	17.4%

But there is life beyond the Carolinas; the industrial frontier keeps moving—across oceans. "A recent consultant study revealed the extraordinary fact that semi-skilled labor in the U.S. is paid 14 times as much per hour as equivalent labor in the Far East," reported a Fantus booklet of which Hoch was coauthor. "The study compared hourly wages, fringe benefits, work week, labor practices, training and productivity. No planning approach can realistically ignore the global aspects of corporate survival."

"The Ford Motor company will survive," a vice president of the automobile company, Philip E. Benton, Jr., had told me in Detroit. "It may be much different than it is now. We have to face the fact that it costs an American automobile manufacturer more than $17 per man hour to produce a car and it costs a Japanese manufacturer only $9 per man hour. . . . We will do what we have to do. It may be international, but the company will survive. We can go offshore—we could manufacture cars and trucks for the American market anywhere. Say, South Korea."

In fact, Ford, the symbol of American innovation, the man and company of the pioneer assembly line in Highland Park, was already an international company. Benton, the new manager of the company's largest division, the one that actually manufactured cars in the United States, had made his reputation managing Ford's truck manufacture and marketing in Europe. He had seen the future. Many, many Americans saw the same things—more in private business than in government. One of democratic government's problems and charms was that it still operated with a time lag, essentially reacting to that "concourse of individual wills."

American industrial workers, men and women who build or make things, were almost certainly not going to be a critical part of the future Benton saw. "There is nothing wrong with the American worker," he said. By that he meant only that there was nothing inherently inferior about the end products of the hand-eye coordination of American humans. What was wrong, as far as Ford was concerned, was the price the company had to pay for the use of American bodies—which was why, as Benton and I talked, Ford was beginning construction of a $400-million plant in Mexico to manufacture engines for the American market after 1983. The "trainability of labor" factor, a Fantus category, had become high enough in parts of Latin America to accommodate the simplified skills of modern auto making.

"Americans don't serve most of the purposes of American industry anymore," said Robert Schrank, a foundation official who had both done and thought about work, having been a laborer, plumber, and machinist before moving on to lesser physical exertion as a union official and sociologist. "The dirty little secret is that people don't like to work. There is no intrinsic desire or drive to work. Americans want jobs—jobs provide status and social connection and interaction for many people—but they don't want to work. That's what I learned in factories, in mines, in fields. Without the Calvinist belief that work leads to salvation—and that ethic is fading—and the real financial necessity—and the welfare state is taking care of some of that—it will become harder and harder to motivate people to do the dirty work and the make-work that the society is generating to keep itself busy. It only takes 40 or 50 million people to keep the United States running."

Money aside for a moment, why do people do the dirty work?

"I've asked that question all over the world, and the answer is always the same," said Schrank, a project officer with the Ford Foundation, which was originally supported by some of Henry Ford's fortune. "In Detroit or in Moscow, people say they are willing to do what they are doing so that their children won't have to. 'My kids are never going to do this—never, never.' That's the answer I get."

That, in Detroit, was called the American Dream. If it worked, it self-destructed. At least it would if population were relatively stable. If no children had to do what their parents did, soon there would be no one left to do the dirty work. That was not a problem for a long time as waves of immigration washed over the United States. It inevitably became one when immigration was curtailed in 1924 and when growing numbers of black Americans were being sustained (by government welfare programs) outside work-reward systems.

It had, when it happened, traditionally, taken perhaps three generations for a family or the nation to go from the affirmation and living of that dream to questioning—and sometimes hostile—rejection. But time speeded up after World War II: events and information, actions and reactions, were telescoped by the new communications technology. Many men and women were going through both the affirmation and the questioning within their own lifetimes. Schrank thought the labor movement he had served was dying, because as work became less physically brutal there would be less possibility of confrontation between labor and management. "We're going," he said, "from *High Noon* to high expectations."

"We have no trouble getting good workers in most parts of the country, what we have trouble doing is meeting their expectations of what the work will do for them," said Jeremy Jacobs, the president of Sportssystems, in Buffalo. The company, owned by his family, had ten thousand full-time employees, most of them working at racetracks and ballparks at concessions selling anything spectators would buy. "They have to be enjoying what they do or they won't do it. They simply leave . . . As far as I can tell, there are many people who don't have to work. We've removed the necessity for working. There are government programs to take care of people, but I'm also talking about people who have removed the burden of other people from their lives. Young people, both counter clerks and executives. They're single. They have no families. They move on, looking for something—I don't know what."

They are the children of the "new values"—the Post-American Dream Americans—who distressed Barry Bingham. They could be the students Philip Morrison and David Riesman were watching in Cambridge; they were the people Yankelovich, Skelly & White were trying to define. "If you had to isolate one value of these people," said Ruth Clark, vice president of the New York research company, "it might be: 'I'm as important as my children are—if I choose to have children.'"

Daniel Yankelovich, the firm's president, had analyzed 25 years of opinion research and concluded that a majority of adult Americans—52 percent, he said, with the enviable certainty of the statistician—were rejecting the old value system based on self-sacrifice for children and visible symbols of success. The ultimate moment in that old life, it seemed, would have been leaving church and getting into a Cadillac to take the kids for college interviews.

The new majority, according to Yankelovich, did want jobs—

most still defined themselves by saying things like "I'm the assistant manager of . . ."—but that did not necessarily mean they wanted to work. "In principle, a person might be richly satisfied merely by holding a job without working at it seriously. And in practice, this is what a great many do. People will often start a job willing to work hard and be productive. But," he wrote, "if the job fails to meet their expectations—if it doesn't give them the incentives they are looking for—then they lose interest. They may use the job to satisfy their own needs but give little in return.

"The [new] values are, in essence, an extension of individualism to the workplace . . ." according to Yankelovich; "today's individualism can be defined as the quest for lifestyles that suit each individual's unique needs, potentials and values."

The only thing surprising about that, I thought, was that it took so long for it to happen. The curse of any materially advanced society had to be that one day people would want to enjoy the fruits of their labor. "People didn't go into factories all that willingly," Schrank said. "The year Henry Ford opened his first assembly line, 1913, there was a 370-percent turnover of his labor force." But you had to feed the kids before you sent them off to college, and the pulpits of the land, secular and nonsecular, thundered the glories of work and heaven, the shame of sloth and the everlasting fires of hell. The happy result, for management, was that the plant and office location decisions framed by Fantus were still made on the basis of the *cost* of a worker and the *quality of life* of an executive. It might be revolutionary, as Yankelovich argued, to realize that workers had a regard for the quality of their lives, too—but it was inevitable. "Some people care mainly about money," he said, in concluding that future corporate incentive systems will have to be more flexible and less directly linked to economic reward and suspect future security. "Some would rather be compensated by more leisure. Others seek status opportunities. Still others derive their satisfaction from the inherent challenge of the work itself. There are even some who still place the well-being of the organization or the society ahead of purely personal goals, and future rewards ahead of present ones."

"Leisure," here, is a somewhat misleading word. Freedom— or, less elegantly, free time—might be better. True, millions of

Americans would use whatever additional freedom they won to do nothing, or to watch television, which, according to surveys, many do for hours on end, or to indulge in the society's traditional escape, alcohol. But Americans are still the people Tocqueville met and wrote this about: "Choose any American at random, and he should be a man of burning desires, enterprising, adventurous, and, above all, an innovator. The same bent affects all he does . . . his domestic occupations."*

"Americans are people who think 'dropping out' is going to Denver to practice law," said Judith Shklar, the German-born professor at Harvard. She was laughing. "I've yet to meet an American who was out of work and had self-respect, including men of great and luxurious wealth. What does an American do when he has time off? He works on his house—refinishes the basement or something. He takes another job—moonlights."

National laziness will probably never be an American disease. But the United States was no longer the nation of enterprising farmers and merchants that Tocqueville saw. "The workers are totally defeated by a system that tries to turn them into robots and, if it can, will replace them with robots," said Enid Eckstein, who had spent seven years as an assembler, inspector, and shop steward in Plymouth's Lynch Road automobile plant in Detroit. "No matter how much they need the money, the conditions are so bad and the work so unsatisfying—Production! Production! Let the car go no matter how bad it is!—that the biggest demand in the shops is still the right to refuse to work overtime."

There are, of course, private solutions to that disillusionment and resentment. "The underground economy, entrepreneurs hustling for themselves, is probably the closest thing you'll find to the economy Tocqueville saw," Schrank said. "I would guess that 90 percent or more of Americans were self-employed when he was here, in the 1830s. Now we love to talk about entrepreneurship, but it's declining. Except on the streets."

The Ford Foundation's offices are on Forty-second Street, near the United Nations buildings, and when I left Schrank I walked north along Lexington Avenue on an eccentric little er-

---

* Television, whatever its failings, may be something of an alcohol substitute. It seems to serve the same relaxing and time-filling function for many older Americans that drugs do for many younger ones.

rand. I had left my pipe at home and wanted to buy an eighty-nine-cent corncob. Stopping in a dozen little stores along ten blocks of the avenue, I could not find anyone who spoke English well enough to deal with the words "corncob pipe"—Greek, French, Chinese, and Arabic, but not English. The streets of the city where I was born were alive again with accents—as they must have been eighty years before, when immigration to the United States was at a peak—and alive with enterprise. The underground economy was not only visible on the East Side of Manhattan, it was clamoring for attention with the calls of southern Europe and northern Africa, of Latin America. Outside the doors of the most fashionable stores in the city, young men pressed you to buy handbags, gloves, belts, perfume for a third of the prices advertised inside.

More than a year after that, in May of 1981, I was talking again with Mayor Koch. He was not complaining this time. He was more popular than ever and was preparing for an election campaign in which he would be the nominee of both major parties, the Democrats and the Republicans. Even his soaring frustration with federal regulations and mandates had been eased somewhat by a change of administrations in Washington. Between our conversations, in the 1980 elections, Republicans—conservative Republicans at that—had won the presidency and one house of Congress, the Senate. To Koch's delight, the new custodians of federal power were trying to dismantle parts of the centralized machinery that distributed aid and orders to states and cities. "They're giving us more time to meet the standards on dumping sludge in the ocean. Where else are we supposed to dump it?" he said. "They're removing the retro-fitting requirements of Section 504 of the Rehabilitation Act—so we'll get some sanity back into the business of making public transportation accessible to handicapped people. . . . For better or worse, they've moved the country a bit as far as federal involvement in local government. I also think I might be able to get some more money from them on a few things."

Everyone wanted just a few things. Including the new "rulers": The Republicans proclaimed their intentions of returning power to states and cities and villages and yeomen, but they seemed really to favor a slight shift in the path of the central glacier. Where they disagreed with the ends of federal power—forced racial integration of schools, for instance—they attempted to eliminate the means—in this case, legal action by the Justice Department. The lawyers of the federal government would no longer initiate or join lawsuits using transportation of students as a means to reduce school segregation. (That, however, would not and did not prevent other groups, or individuals, from taking such legal actions. As democracy expanded, the lawsuit could be mightier than the pen of the President.) But when they wanted something—the elimination of abortion and of some other things considered sinful by segments of their electoral majority, for example—the same people, like all their predecessors, attempted to legislate, regulate, mandate, and enforce—to use federal power as the means to their favored moral and economic ends.

Like Andrew Jackson, the President Tocqueville met, Ronald Reagan, the President I had traveled with just before his election, was from the Far West—Nashville in 1830, Los Angeles in 1980. The President from Tennessee presided over the end of the political domination of the East, of the original 13 states; the President from California was presiding over the end of the economic domination of the East and the Middle West. The old cities of the East and Midwest were being troubled and destroyed.*

The destruction was so obvious that it could have been deliberate. The growth toward a complete national government proceeded in fits and starts—checked, at times, by the American feeling that there *should* be less government—and local taxation and function was often preserved and encouraged in sentimental atrophy. When the decentralization of production began after World War II, the displacement of commerce and population that was, among other things, the core of Fantus' business, was inevitably reflected in a decline in local tax revenues. Without some systematic distribution of federal revenues—distribution not tied democratically to population and population trends—

---

* Beaumont's description of President Jackson, in a letter to his mother on January 20, 1832, was quite similar to the descriptions of Ronald Reagan, then campaigning for President, which could be read in almost any newspaper during 1980: "He is an old man, well preserved and seems to have retained all the vigor of his body and spirit. He is not a man of genius."

ruin had to result. And it did. The subways in Mayor Koch's
city—the largest mass transit system in the world, with 6.5 million riders daily—were a perfect example. The city could not
generate enough money through taxation or fares to maintain
the system. Fare increases led to decreased ridership and made
the city less attractive as a commercial base—so both fare and
tax revenues declined.

This is what had happened statistically during the four years
I worked on this book: the number of the 6,409 subway cars
out of service on a single day increased from 600 to 2,141; the
number of canceled trips each day increased from 86 to 300;
the number of fires per year increased from 2,243 to 4,908; and
the number of miles traveled between breakdowns decreased
from 13,900 to 6,000. A subway ride that took ten minutes in
1910 often took forty minutes in 1980.

The subways and buses, turned over to the city by private
owners when profitability began declining, were still the economic lifeline of the country's most populous and productive region. Those lines on maps and below and above the ground were
part of complex life-support systems spreading over three states.
"Developed ecology" was the phrase that came to my mind as I
followed Tocqueville's trail through the avenues, streets, and
highways of northern New Jersey, Manhattan, the Hudson River
Valley, and Connecticut—miles and miles of housing for millions and millions of people, roads and reservoirs, bridges and
tunnels, pipelines and tracks, factories, schools, stores, hospitals,
firehouses swirling out like the building blocks of life itself from
a central nucleus in dazzlingly intricate, interdependent patterns. And the same systems were there, somewhat smaller, in
the other cities—in Philadelphia, in Detroit, in Baltimore, in all
of them—because the new places Tocqueville went to are now
the older parts of America.

"Cities are not permanent," a presidential commission reported in January of 1981. "Many of the cities of the old industrial heartland—for example in the states of New York, Pennsylvania, Ohio, Michigan and Illinois—are losing their status as
thriving industrial capitals, a position they have held through
the first half of the century.

"These cities are not dying," said the report. "Rather they are
transforming—and in the future they will likely perform a nar-

rower range of vital and specialized tasks for the larger urban society. . . . Thus, as the major long-term goal of Federal urban policy, the Commission urges government to place greater emphasis on retraining and relocation assistance efforts designed to link people with economic opportunity, wherever that opportunity might be."

The commission, 45 private citizens appointed by the President, had no permanent official status and no power to enforce its recommendations, but that one on urban affairs prompted a brief public debate. For the first time, really, a national body was heard speaking the unspeakable: the government should stop trying to do so much for the losers and join the winners. Forget the places where people are from—Detroit, for example, where population had declined by 300,000 in ten years and where Texas newspapers were sold on the streets to men and women looking for new jobs and homes—and begin thinking about the places where they are going—to San Antonio, Texas, whose population had grown from 654,153 to 785,410 during the same period, and to San Diego, California, where the increase had been from 697,471 to 875,504.

New York City, with cracked and broken streets and trains, with miles of abandoned houses between towers of wealth at its center and older suburbs now falling into disrepair, was the greatest of those societies. Its vital and specialized tasks narrowing, the city's population had declined from 7,895,563 to 7,071,-030 between 1970 and 1980.

The old cities were becoming the places Americans were from—they were the societies these nomad people had formed behind themselves.

Still, Mayor Koch prattled on about how wonderful things were and what a great job he was doing. "Being perfectly objective," he said, "I've tried to figure out what I should be proudest of, besides balancing the city's budget and putting it, honestly, on a firm financial footing for the first time in many, many years. I've decided that I'm proudest of increasing the number of jobs in the city and improving the schools—the reading scores of our students are up for the first time in a long time."

There was a bit of the buffoon in Ed Koch. Having no family and no real interests other than politics, he happily grew, if that is the word, into a successful parody of the American politician.

But there was some truth in what he was saying. New York, the most arrogant and boastful place in a country stinking with conceit, seemed to be coping with its own decline—sporadically thriving on it. After a ten-year reduction of the number of jobs in the city of more than 500,000, an increase was recorded between 1977 and 1980 of more than 100,000 nongovernmental jobs by the U.S. Department of Labor. And the scores of the city's public-school students on standard national reading tests did exceed the national average for the first time in decades.

Why? How? The answer—part of the answer, anyhow—was on the streets as I left Robert Schrank's office on the East Side of Manhattan. The entrepreneurs, the storekeepers, the peddlers, the taxi drivers, the janitors—people making their own work and doing the dirty work—were immigrants. They were the kind of people that Ed Koch and his cronies had bragged that their parents and grandparents were when we all told our American stories that night at Gracie Mansion.

The languages, the accents, and the numbers were astounding; the impact on New York was impressive. "They're tremendous. They're wonderful," Koch said. "I love them. They're great family people, dedicated to hard work. . . . They're almost all working and from what we hear they are keeping what's left of the garment industry here. These are people who make their kids do homework—they're probably responsible for the better test scores. This is what New York must have been like at the turn of the century."

Where are they from?

"You name it," he said. "Lots of Latins and Central Americans. Santo Domingo. Colombia. Ecuador. Peru. Cuba. Haiti. West Indians. Asians."

Are they in the United States legally?

"Who knows?" he said with a shrug. He might have added: Who cares?

At the beginning of that year, 675,000 citizens of other countries—resident aliens—had registered at post offices in the city's five boroughs. Those were the legal aliens who bothered to fill out annual government forms. Obviously there were others who didn't. Then there were the illegal aliens, foreigners who in one way or another had slipped into the United States—not hard to do in an open society. The mayor's office estimated that there were 750,000 of them, although that unverifiable figure was probably exaggerated in an attempt to qualify for more federal aid under formulas based on population.°

There may be two million of them in New York City—chasing the American Dream. If history repeats itself, some will stay and some will move on to other parts of the country, following the dream, and a few will go back. Between 1901 and 1910, the peak years of the European immigration to the United States, seven million people came to the country through New York—including Ed Koch's parents, from Poland. They stayed.†

° Some of those registered aliens—elderly citizens of Italy and the Republic of Ireland, for example—had lived in New York for decades. But the overwhelming majority had immigrated to the United States since the country liberalized its immigration laws in 1965 after more than 50 years of extremely restrictive legislation. The largest number of aliens who registered in New York City in 1980—75,000—were from Santo Domingo. Other common countries of origin were: Italy, 45,000; Taiwan and Hong Kong, 42,000; Jamaica, 38,000; Ecuador, 26,000; Colombia, 25,000; Cuba, 23,000; Russia (almost all Jews), 19,-000; Greece, 15,000; India, 14,000; Korea, 12,000; Haiti, 11,000.

There were also approximately 900,000 Puerto Ricans in New York—they were American citizens, not aliens—giving miles of the city a decidedly Latin rhythm. The growing importance of the city's Hispanic community was institutionalized for me when Allen Neuharth of Gannett announced that the company was purchasing New York's Spanish-language daily newspaper, *El Diario–La Prensa*.

† There were, at the beginning of 1980, more than 5,381,107 registered aliens in the United States, according to the Immigration and Naturalization Service. The number of illegal aliens in the country may be more than that. The New York metropolitan area had the second-largest concentration of aliens, second to the enormous community of documented and undocumented Mexican aliens living among the Mexican-American community in the states from California to Texas. The number of American citizens of Mexican descent in the United States was more than 7,000,000 in 1980. The number of legal aliens from Mexico was 1,058,596, according to the Immigration and Naturalization Service. The number of illegal Mexican aliens—families temporarily or permanently fleeing unemployment rates as high as 50 percent in their native country—was probably between two and four million. My own experience living in Southern California for two years indicated that the illegals are probably creating jobs and maintaining some small industries that would have to close down or move overseas without cheap, un-American labor. Government studies have indicated that the United States made money on the illegals. One study, in San Diego county, California, reported that illegals ac-

That's the way America is supposed to work. For many years and many people, it has; for many, it still does. But the Dream needs dreamers. It cannot sustain itself with auto workers who demand more money as revenge for the mechanized indignities of their work lives, or with M.I.T. students hoping to redefine ambition to suit personal dreams of life without sacrifice. The American Dream always needs new Americans—and they can be made very quickly, from Englishmen, from Poles, from Mexicans. The ideas of America are just that powerful. So far, for most of the people most of the time, there seems to be nothing better than life, liberty, and the pursuit of happiness.

---

counted for up to $39 million in employment and sales and Social Security taxes, and spent up to $104 million locally, but received only $29 million in government services, mostly for the education of their children.

22
WASHINGTON

"The Democratization of War . . . and Peace . . . "

The American journey of Tocqueville and Beaumont was nearing an end on January 16, 1832, when, after their twelve-day
carriage ride across the South from New Orleans, they boarded a
steamboat in Norfolk for the trip up Chesapeake Bay to Washington. They shared the boat ride and the last five days of their
southern travels with Joel Roberts Poinsett, the former ambassador and South Carolina congressman who was to become Secretary of War in 1837.

"Conversations with Mr. Poinsett (from the 12th to the 17th
January 1832)" were the last extensive interviews recorded in
the fourteen pocket notebooks Tocqueville carried in the United
States. The Frenchman wrote out pages of questions and answers on subjects that ranged from the financing of the public
roads they were bouncing over to the cost and speed of American ships. "The American, on sea as on land, has a quality which
makes him singularly adapted to succeed and make his fortune,"
Poinsett said during a conversation that Tocqueville was to repeat often. "He is a highly civilized man thrown into a society
in formation, where trades have not had time to become absolutely classified. As a result each man of us knows a little of
everything, and is accustomed from childhood to do a little of
everything . . . There is a phrase which is always in our mouths

in face of any difficulty, and it gives our character perfectly: 'I will try.' "°

Summarizing the ideas that came out of these long talks, Tocqueville wrote in his notebook: "Only an ambitious or a foolish man could, after seeing America, maintain that in the actual state of the world, American political institutions could be applied elsewhere than there . . ."—American democracy, it seemed, often told more about Americans and America than about democracy itself—". . . Political liberty is a difficult food to digest. It is only extremely robust constitutions that can take it. But when it has been digested, albeit with pain, it gives the whole body social a nerve and an energy which surprises even those who expected the most from it."

Then, cryptically, he wrote: "Fatal influence of the military spirit and military obedience on liberty." It was his first mention of militarism in America—the United States had only a few thousand men under arms—and, in his notebooks, the last. But the enthusiasm for notes was fading. There were only ten short entries after the Poinsett conversations, even though Tocqueville and Beaumont were presented socially to President Andrew Jackson. "We find it hard to hold ourselves in America," Tocqueville wrote to his father, "our feet are burning."

° Poinsett also explained an American innovation that would one day have a name—planned obsolescence. This was the exchange, with Tocqueville asking the question:

"Q. One hears that generally your ships do not last long?"

"A. . . . One reason why our ships do not last long is that our merchants often have little capital at their disposal to begin with. It is a matter of calculation on their part. Provided that the ship lasts long enough to bring them a certain sum beyond their expenses, their aim is attained. Besides, there is a general feeling among us about everything which prevents us aiming at permanence; there reigns in America a popular and universal belief in the progress of the human spirit. We are always expecting an improvement to be found in everything. And in fact that is often correct. For instance, I asked our steamboat builders on the North Bank a few years ago why they made their vessels so weak. They answered that perhaps they might even last too long, because the art of steam navigation was making daily progress. In fact, these boats which made 8 or 9 knots, could not, a little time afterwards, compete with others whose construction allowed them to make 12 to 15 knots."

He was homesick and a bit disoriented by the fact that the capital "city" of the United States of America was more map than city. Forests had been replaced by great boulevards with no one to walk them. The population of the District of Columbia was less than 20,000. "Washington," he told his father, "offers the sight of an arid plain, burned by the sun, on which are scattered two or three sumptuous edifices and the five or six villages composing the town."

One hundred and fifty years later, the villages had grown together into a city of more than 700,000 people and there were hundreds of sumptuous edifices to house the departments and bureaus of the federal government. Washington, D.C., was two cities really: black Washington, a struggling and sprawling place that was home to more than 500,000 black Americans, the descendants of servants and southern slaves who had fled to the North during and after the Civil War; and white Washington, a smaller, prettier place for the representatives and staffs of the central government and the people who lived off the organism, the lawyers, the journalists, the experts, the people who sometimes had trouble explaining exactly what it was they did for a living. That second Washington—the one transmitted in laws, statements, and interpretations to the nation each day by television and newspapers—had codes of its own which were described quite well to me by Ray Jenkins, the Alabama newspaper publisher who had left Montgomery to work in the White House: "I'm a stranger here. Most Americans would be . . . People here see government as a game staged on a national scale for their own amusement. They've even created a separate language: gossip."

Jenkins was not impressed, thinking that Washington operated in its own vacuum. Tocqueville had not been impressed either. In a city of politicians, American congressmen were hardly up to the standards of an aristocratic French public servant whose last post had been Versailles. "When one enters the House of Representatives at Washington," he wrote, "one is struck by the vulgar demeanor of that great assembly. One can often look in vain for a single famous man. Almost all the members are obscure people whose names form no picture in one's mind. They are mostly village lawyers, tradesmen, or even men of the lowest classes. In a country where education is spread almost universally, it is said that the people's representatives do not always know how to write correctly."

That was written at least a year after Tocqueville had returned to France. It was then, and only briefly, that he considered military and foreign affairs in the democracy created by the Americans; there were only four discussions of war and peace in the first volume of *Democracy in America*, the volume published in 1835. Tocqueville dismissed contemporary European speculation that General Jackson had wished to establish a military dictatorship—"He would certainly have lost his political position and put his life in hazard, so he was not so rash as to attempt it"—and he praised the wisdom of the outspoken determination of Presidents Washington and Jefferson to avoid any entanglement in the battles and diplomacy of Europe. Then, in a one-page section entitled "Accidental Causes That May Increase the Influence of the Executive Power," he wrote:

"If the Union's existence were constantly menaced, and its great interests were continually interwoven with those of other powerful nations, one would see the prestige of the executive growing, because of what was expected from it and of what it did.

"It is true that the President of the United States is commander-in-chief of the army, but the army consists of six thousand soldiers; he commands the navy, but the navy has only a few ships; he conducts the Union's relations with foreign nations, but the Union has no neighbors. Separated by the ocean from the rest of the world, still too weak to want to rule the sea, it has no enemies and its interests are seldom in contact with those of the other nations of the globe. . . ."

So, he judged then, the United States did not particularly need either diplomats or soldiers. When the time came that the democracy needed to formulate foreign policy and raise armies? . . . Tocqueville did not know.

"In the half century since the Union took shape, its existence has only once been threatened, during the War of Independence," he wrote in that 1835 volume. "At the beginning of that long war there were extraordinary signs of enthusiasm for the country's service. But as the struggle was prolonged, habitual selfishness reappeared: money no longer reached the public treasury, men no longer volunteered for the army . . .

"To judge what sacrifices democracies are capable of imposing on themselves, we must await a time when the American nation will be forced to put half its income into the hands of the government, as England has done, or is bound to throw a twentieth of its population onto the battlefield as has been done by France.

"In America conscription is unknown; men are induced to enlist for pay. Compulsory recruitment is so contrary to the conceptions and alien to the habits of the people of the United States that I doubt whether anyone would ever dare to bring in such a law."

They did dare—within thirty years. During the Civil War, there was some conscription—and there were riots against that compulsory recruitment. The drafting of soldiers was instituted again during World War I and World War II—when 16 million Americans, more than a tenth of the nation, were in uniform—and during smaller conflicts for thirty years after the second of the twentieth century's multinational wars. (By the 1970s the American nation was putting close to a third of its income into the hands of local, state, and national government.*)

Five years later, in 1840, more than eight years after the January day in Norfolk when he had written himself that one-sentence note about the influence of the military spirit, Tocqueville seemed to come back to that point in the second volume of *Democracy in America*. There he wrote five short chapters—twenty pages in all—on militarism in democratic societies. The first one was titled: "Why Democratic Peoples Naturally Want Peace but Democratic Armies War."†

* The actual proportion of the national income going to all levels of government in 1980 was 28 percent, according to government statistics compiled by *U.S. News & World Report* magazine, published on May 11, 1981.

† The four other chapters were titled: "Which Is the Most Warlike and Revolutionary Class in Democratic Armies"; "What Makes Democratic Armies Weaker than Others at the Beginning of a Campaign but More Formidable in Prolonged Warfare"; "Of Discipline in Democratic Armies"; and "Some Considerations Concerning War in Democratic Societies." In those chapters, emphasizing what he believed would be the pacific temper of democratic citizens, he focused

The young Frenchman, who really wasn't all that young by then, constructed that title—particularly the words "Why Democratic Peoples Naturally Want Peace"—on two observations about Americans and their democracy. First, he believed that as social conditions became more equal, each person obviously had more knowledge of how other people lived and thought and, consequently, "as people become more like another, they show themselves reciprocally more compassionate, and the law of nations becomes more gentle." And he believed that the more widely personal property was distributed, the less inclined any people would be to support property-threatening mass political violence, and "in no other country in the world is the love of property keener or more alert than in the United States."

What he said, then, in those chapters on war was that it would be harder to trigger and generate national hatreds in what he called the "democratic ages ahead," and that it would rarely be in the "self-interest properly understood" of Americans to fight wars.

"The ever increasing number of men of property devoted to peace, the growth of personal property which war so rapidly devours, mildness of mores, gentleness of heart, that inclination to pity which equality inspires, that cold and calculating spirit which leaves little room for sensitivity to the poetic and violent emotions of wartime—all these causes act together to damp down warlike fervor," he said. "I think one can accept it as a general and constant rule that among civilized nations warlike passions become rarer and less active as social conditions get nearer to equality."

The history of civilized nations during the next 140 years did not always support that conclusion. Or perhaps Tocqueville, the student of democracy and equality, was just too far ahead of his time. Certainly that thought occurred to me, or perhaps hope

---

on "the restless ambition of the army." "Military revolutions," he wrote, "which are hardly ever a serious threat in aristocracies, are always to be feared in democracies." That danger, however, never developed in the United States. The American system worked well enough so that there was always infinitely more opportunity for influence, respect, and wealth for civilians than for soldiers. The overwhelming majority of America's military men seem to have been, at heart, civilians temporarily in uniform.

was springing in my breast, when, during my first interview in Washington, Senator Gary Hart of Colorado said: "In thinking about national defense today, you have to take into account the fact that Americans are becoming less warlike. It may be impossible to convince many people that anything is worth fighting for—or dying for."

There was no conscription in the United States when Senator Hart and I talked in March of 1979. The drafting of young men had ended six years before in the closing days of an unpopular American military involvement in Vietnam in Southeast Asia. But within a year, as national leaders from the President down issued statements about the inadequacies and expense of the country's volunteer army, draft registration was reinstated—not conscription, which would have required new laws, just the official listing of the names of the nation's young men.

But the boys wouldn't give their names—at least a lot of them wouldn't. The government, over two years and under two presidents, began issuing a confusing and contradictory barrage of statements and statistics, sometimes calling the registration of eighteen- to twenty-year olds "satisfactory" and announcing compliance as high as 93 percent, and at other times saying officials were "perturbed" because as many as 33 percent of the young men were not registering. Traveling the country in those years, I suspected that the registration percentages might be even lower than the official numbers. I kept coming across young people who said they would not register and many of their friends would not. That began in Louisville, when Dann Byck's seventeen-year-old daughter, Amy, seemed amazed when her father and I said we believed there were things worth fighting and dying for, and continued across the country to Roosevelt High School in East Los Angeles, where Mexican American seniors asked about registration routinely told me, "No way, José!"

"What if 'they' "—meaning some foreign enemy—"were in South Carolina? Coming this way," Byck said to his daughter. "Should we fight?"

"That would make no difference to me," Amy Byck said, defining her military responsibility, or denying it, as earlier her father had rejected civic leadership in the city where his father had been president of the City Council. The young woman's an-

swer may have been hasty, may have been exaggerated, but it
was sincere at the time. And it was important because it was
American; she was an American who was about to come of military age in a consciously egalitarian society that was just then
debating how to reconcile equality between the sexes and traditional male military responsibility. That political and legal dialogue would continue for a time, there would be decisions, com-
promises, and reversals, but the eventual direction of the
decision-making would not change without a reversal in the ho-
mogenizing trends of American history.

Any American military strategy based on conscription, dependent on mass participation of people who properly understood self-interest was, I thought, doomed. The present and future tendency of national militarism was framed by the
extraordinary fact that there were women in the cadet corps of
the United States Military Academy. Were women, with views
toward war and violence which seemed traditionally and unal-
terably different from those of men, going to change or be
changed? Or was it the U. S. Army and the military posture of
the society that would change?

And would women be drafted in this nation still tending toward millions of people all equal? In one way or another, I
thought: Yes, women will be drafted. If men are drafted. If anyone were drafted—if there could be such a thing as fair conscription, an egalitarian draft. In the twentieth century, American draft policy was based on the national tragedies of England
and France in the early days of World War I—both nations, in
nationalistic and patriotic frenzies, lost much of their future
leadership in Flanders' fields—and the United States then was
determined not to expend its educated, trained elite in the same
way. So youthful American elites were generally exempted from
service, and that educated and exempted elite also tended to be
a richer elite. That kind of draft and that kind of unfairness—no
matter how well-intentioned—would be extremely difficult, if
not impossible, to sustain and defend in a modern America
where the public's business is conducted in public. People, male
and female, who had that information before them—that they or
their children might die so that others or others' children might
live—might not be universally willing to chance the sacrifice of

themselves in what their leaders defined as the national interest.*

"National interest" was a phrase I heard often in Washington. I rarely—if ever—heard it outside Washington and New York— and Cambridge.

"There is a foreign policy/security community which lives in a not particularly magic circle of its own," said Stanley Hoffman of Harvard. "The great majority of people in almost every democratic country I know of want to be left alone . . . The average citizen in Omaha does not go to bed each night worrying about the vulnerability of Minuteman missiles.

"People, I think, deeply resent the risks of involvement in foreign troubles, but they realize that once the United States is as involved as it is, has as widespread economic interests in the world—well, one has to accept certain things even if there is no enthusiasm . . . Democracy has really affected foreign policy very little. One comes to the conclusion that foreign policy and the needs of it overwhelm democracy and its necessities . . . so these things are left to this small, slightly ominous community."

How many people are in that community? How many people actually control American foreign policy? "A few thousand," Hoffman said. "I think the group has expanded over the years. But it could be two thousand, three thousand . . ."

I asked the same question, months later, of former President Nixon.

* Depending on the consent of the governed, democratic conscription is a delicate instrument of governance. Relatively low levels of opposition can quickly and visibly disrupt a draft system in an open society. During the Vietnam period, according to figures compiled by the Federal Clemency Board created in 1975, 26,800,000 men were eligible for military service. Of those, 8,720,000 enlisted in the armed forces and 2,215,000 were drafted and served. A total of 15,980,000 never served; they were deferred, exempted, or disqualified for a variety of reasons. Only 570,000 apparently evaded the draft to the point of being classified as "draft offenders." Of those, 209,517 were actually charged with breaking the law and 11,750 were either convicted or became fugitives. At most, 2 percent of the eligible draft pool were willing to defy the government at risk to their own futures. But the disruptive effect on the society was such that it had some effect on both the conditions of the settlement of the military conflict and the end of Selective Service, the agency created to administer conscription.

"Very few," he said. "Two thousand? Three thousand. I'd put the number somewhere around there. That's how many people a President would find it worth talking to. They're very close—most of them in New York and Washington . . . And some of them you talk to because you have to. They're soft in the head—the ones who believe in nothing but peace, who cannot understand the reality of the world and of America's national interest."

The "national interest" elite—or the elite which believes that it is its duty and right to define the national interest in regard to foreign policy—is the closest thing to a governing aristocracy that has survived in American democracy. It is essentially a self-selected aristocracy made possible because the United States once did not need a foreign policy, and when it did need one, the information needed to formulate policy was remote and inaccessible to the general public. Americans lived and governed themselves on the basis of their own life experiences—the difference in the life experiences of black Americans generation after generation was a major factor isolating them from the white majority—and almost all Americans almost all the time had no experience in anything foreign. The foreign policy aristocracy came to be made up of the Americans who did have such experience—the Americans who studied, spoke, sold, bought, or went to anything or anywhere foreign. Those ventures beyond the usual American experience inevitably set them apart from the rest of the nation. They cared about foreign policy, so they made foreign policy.

That well-informed elite, while its members often disagreed among themselves over specifics of policy, consistently had an internationalist consensus—some would occasionally say "militaristic"—that had never, or rarely, been shared by the entire nation. That point was made for me again when, as I was traveling, the Chicago Council on Foreign Relations released one of its periodic studies on the foreign affairs attitudes held by two groups of Americans: "opinion leaders" and "average Americans." The same questions were asked, during late 1978 and early 1979, of 400 or so "leaders"—White House officials, members of Congress, important academics, corporate leaders and bankers, and the editors of important journals—and of the standard polling sample of 1,500 Americans selected at random, the "average" folk. There was, as there probably always has been, a striking difference between the willingness of leaders to use force internationally and the willingness of average people to be used as force. When, for example, the two groups were asked what the United States government should do if the Soviet Union invaded Western Europe, 97 percent of the "opinion leaders" said "send troops," but only 59 percent of the general public chose that answer.

"It is very difficult, it is becoming more difficult to convince our people that they must play this world role—that it is in their self-interest," Nixon said. "Americans are still, deep down, very idealistic. They believe that if we're good, the other side will be good ... It takes great leadership to convince our people that you're building for peace by taking certain measures."

But that kind of "great leadership"—by individuals and small groups—was becoming a thing of the past in American democracy. What the former President, and many thoughtful, concerned Americans, worried over, seemed to me to be the inevitable breaking down of one of the aristocracies. The key to that kind of leadership as the United States became more and more democratic and more and more open was control of information. Presidents and allied elites had controlled foreign policy by controlling the flow of information from abroad—until technology began distributing facts, opinions, and pictures indiscriminately. Radio, television, cables, satellites, jets, and telephones—the technology changed what we knew and when we knew it about other nations and the mysteries of diplomacy. The President, by the end of the twentieth century, was seeing the same battlefield on television news—or a premier's statement, or riots in Poland—at the same time his constituents saw it. He had no power in selecting the image, the timing, the words—and not enough influence in creating "average" opinions. Polls, those maddening instruments of democracy, were gathering opinions in baskets and throwing them at the doorsteps of leadership. The numbers, the images, the sensations, the ideas accelerated and collided, ricocheting to ... to Newport. That was the storm I had stepped into on the day I stood where Tocqueville had first stepped onto the land of America.

"To see what is happening to leadership in this town, you

must go into the basement of the Capitol," said James Reston, the columnist who had managed the Washington affairs of the *New York Times* for decades. "The television studios and video-taping facilities there are part of a revolution. The Congress today is the most intelligent I've seen, but members have no party loyalties and no institutional loyalties and they are using those facilities to broadcast back home, to make proclamations on issues on which they have only been very quickly briefed. Now, each one of them can—and does—act like a little President."

But the people watching those broadcasts each night were doing the same thing. We were all quickly briefed. We were all little Presidents. That was democracy! They say that Benjamin Franklin was once asked what we had here—a monarchy? a republic? a democracy? "A republic, if you can keep it," he said. We couldn't. The United States was becoming a real democracy writhing within the framework and traditions of a republic. The Americans I met called for leadership, but were not willing to delegate that much to representatives or "leaders" anymore.

Nixon lamented that as he talked about the future he saw: a world, by the middle of the twenty-first century, dominated by the East, by Asians. "Mao told me," he said, referring to Mao Tse-tung, the leader of the People's Republic of China when Nixon was President, "that his people will make any sacrifice, that 300 million Chinese would be willing to die."

"Do you think Americans are willing to die?" I asked.

"No. No, I don't think so. Do you?"

I didn't think so, either. I thought the democratizing of foreign affairs, a process that seemed certain to continue over a period of many years, would strain and test public and private life in the United States. Periodically there were and would be struggles over levels of public expenditures for the ceaseless refinement and expansion of almost incredibly complex and literally incredibly destructive weaponry. Those struggles seemed, to me at least, the understandable efforts of the threatened "national interest" aristocracy to mechanize the military capability and capacity they deemed necessary so that it would be available and usable with or without democratic consensus. The "Egyptian Priests of National Security," as Tocqueville might

have been tempted to call the keepers of the codes of thermonu-
clear destruction, were systematically attempting to find the ir-
reducible minimum number of men (and women) needed to
threaten, start, fight, and win wars, large and small. Democracy
in action was always more clumsy: the larger the number of
people who had control over weaponry, the less chance there
should be that it would be used. Benjamin Franklin, whose Republic might be lost, might also approve of that effect of the triumph of democracy. "There never was a good war or a bad
peace," that American wrote in 1773, in a letter to Josiah
Quincy, the father of the Harvard President Tocqueville met.

Becoming and creating a system of governance more likely to
lead—and be led by—its people to peace than to war would
leave that "great mark on history" that Tocqueville thought democracy might never be capable of writing. "What do you expect from society and its government?" he had written in the
first volume of *Democracy in America*. ". . . If in your view the
main object of government is not to achieve the greatest
strength or glory for the nation as a whole but to provide for
every individual therein the utmost well-being, protecting him
as far as possible from all afflictions, then it is good to make conditions equal and to establish a democratic government."

Then perhaps democracy itself was the great mark on history.
The survival of the form and ceaseless spreading of the ideas of
democracy and equality—an expansion I thought would be accomplished more by invention than by force, more by communication satellites than weapon satellites—that was history itself.
It was not that American democracy could be recreated in other
languages and societies. But the ideas and the inevitable push toward equality: those traveled, they could be understood in any
language. Democracy was the last, best form of governing hu-
mankind.

American democracy was not efficient—Tocqueville had certainly been right about that—but it was effective. It did, govern-
mentally, with fits and starts, waste and corruption, injustice and
national self-delusion, what it was supposed to do: translate,
peacefully, the will of the people—"the concourse of individual
wills" of millions of men and women—into public policies and
systems protecting life, liberty, and the pursuit of happiness.

And the government was only part of the democracy, the visible hand among others, invisible and often a bit shaky, that allowed people a chance to do and get what they want. "Bad laws, revolutions, and anarchy cannot destroy their taste for well-being or that spirit of enterprise which seems the characteristic feature of their race," Tocqueville wrote in the closing pages of his first volume on *les Américains.* So we are what we have always been and we want what we have always wanted—not glory and strength, but some comfort, some security, and the chance to try a few things that seem like good ideas at the time.

"In America," the French visitor wrote, "the taste for physical well-being is not always exclusive, but it is general; and although all do not feel it in the same manner, yet it is felt by all. Everyone is preoccupied caring for the slightest needs of the body and the trivial conveniences of life . . . When distinctions of rank are blurred and privileges abolished, when patrimonies are divided up and education and freedom spread, the poor conceive an eager desire to acquire comfort, and the rich think of the danger of losing it. A lot of middling fortunes are established. Their owners have enough physical enjoyment to get a taste for them, but not enough to content them. They never win them without effort or indulge in them without anxiety."

One hundred and forty years later, trying to satisfy such tastes was being described, as always, as giving in to a new and almost universal selfishness—joining the "Me" generation—but it also could have just been described as "American." American ambition might not be declining quite as much as it seemed to be to the analyzers of public opinion polls and to professors at M.I.T.; it could have been the same ambition that built the country, adapted, now, to an easier environment. Well-being was simply closer, in distance and in time, in 1981 than in 1831.

Democracy had done that—brought well-being closer—because that was what most of the people wanted most of the time. Democratic politicians might be mediocre, might even be more mediocre than the ones Tocqueville met, but politicians did not make or drive the larger system. The United States, the democracy, was a contract between each individual American and all Americans associated as a government.

The Republic and the federalism—the deliberate, "orderly" compact of sovereign states—that Tocqueville saw and wrote about no longer existed when I traveled along the same American roads. The structures were there, and so were multitudes of attitudes, misunderstandings, laws, departments, officials, lists, and forms in the style of the Republic. But much of what had been reality in 1831 was only living legend in 1981. Democratic governing and American rhetoric had created more durable myths than "The Republic" and "The Union"—Americans responded to "Democracy" and "Equality."

It was democracy that became the American value when the nation united to fight in the wars of the world—Americans in the twentieth century were persuaded to fight and die to make that world safe for democracy, not for republicanism. The new mythology was democracy and equality, expressed in many ways, from "All men are created equal . . ." to "One man, one vote."

There has always been pride and fear in that kind of equality, in being an American, in being one among many. "In times of equality no man is obliged to put his powers at the disposal of another, and no one has any claim of right to substantial support from his fellow man, each is both independent and weak," Tocqueville wrote in his second volume. ". . . He is full of confidence and pride in his independence among his equals, but from time to time his weakness makes him feel the need for some outside help which he cannot expect from any of his fellows, for they are both impotent and cold. In this extremity he naturally turns his eyes toward that huge entity . . . the central government." There was the footnote to that, a fair description of the America I saw: ". . . Democratic ages are times of experiment, innovation, and adventure. There are always a lot of men engaged in some difficult or new undertaking which they pursue apart, unencumbered by assistants. Such men will freely admit the general principle that the power of the state should not interfere in private affairs, but as an exception, each one of them wants the state to help in the special matter with which he is preoccupied, and he wants to lead the government on to take action in his domain, though he would like to restrict it in every other direction. . . . "

But who could control the directions of adventure? Democracy, trusting other people, was a risk. "Aristocratic nations are by their nature too much inclined to restrict the scope of human perfectibility; democratic nations sometimes stretch it beyond reason," Tocqueville wrote as he began his second volume. " . . . when castes disappear and classes are brought together, when men are jumbled together and habits, customs, and laws are changing, when new facts impinge and new truths are discovered, when old conceptions vanish and new ones take their place, then the human mind imagines the possibility of an ideal but always fugitive perfection. . . . Thus, searching always, falling, picking himself up again, often disappointed, never discouraged, he is ever striving toward that immense grandeur glimpsed indistinctly at the end of the long track humanity must follow."

It is "beyond reason," of course, that wars should end or castes disappear. But stumbling democracy—that's the track.

In January of 1832, on their trip north to Washington, Tocqueville and Beaumont rested by a stream near the cabin of a pioneer in the forests of Alabama. Tocqueville described what happened next:

" . . . an Indian woman came up (we were in the neighborhood of the Creek territory); she was holding by the hand a little girl of five or six who was of the white race and who, I supposed, must be the pioneer's daughter. A Negro woman followed her. There was a sort of barbarous luxury in the Indian woman's dress; metal rings hung from her nostrils and ears . . . the Negro was dressed in European clothes almost in shreds.

" . . . the young savage, taking the child in her arms, lavished upon her such fond caresses as mothers give; the Negro, too, sought, by a thousand innocent wiles, to attract the little Creole's attention. The latter showed by her slightest movements a sense of superiority which contrasted strangely with her weakness and her age, as if she received the attentions of her companions with a sort of condescension. . . . "

"I had often seen people of the three races inhabiting North America brought together in the same place; I had already noted very many different signs of white predominance, but there was something particularly touching in the scene I have just described; here a bond of affection united oppressors and oppressed, and nature bringing them closer together made the immense gap formed by prejudices and laws yet more striking."

Americans took out the laws, slowly, finally, after 150 years. There were new laws, programs, regulations, rules—most of which, really, could be traced back to the fact that in the land of equality a six-year-old white could look down in enforced scorn upon a black woman in tattered clothes.

On the first night of my journey to Newport, Rhode Island, I stayed at the Airport Hilton Hotel at Logan Airport, in Boston. It was May 8, 1979. While I waited to check in, a black man, tall and well dressed, said to the young woman, a white woman, behind the hotel desk, "I would like to cash a check for $25, please."

"We don't cash personal checks," she said.

"I'm a guest at the hotel," he said.

"I told you," she said, slowly and quite coldly, "we don't cash personal checks here."

"I'm a pilot for TWA and I . . ."

"Do you want to talk to the manager?" she said, cutting him off.

The half-dozen people around the desk were backing away, slowly stepping back into the lobby. There was a very real tension in the room as the woman disappeared.

"I understand you want to cash . . ." the manager said briskly, appearing from somewhere behind the desk.

The manager was black, too. The grim pilot suddenly smiled. We all smiled.

Tocqueville and Beaumont had been in the United States for almost nine months when they left Washington by stage for Philadelphia and New York on February 3. The time for taking notes was past, although the two Frenchmen gathered up trunks of books and documents their American acquaintances had shipped to New York City before their departure on the *Havre*, the same steamship on which they had arrived at Newport nine months earlier. They boarded the ship for home on February 20, 1832, and Tocqueville wrote a final letter to his brother, Edouard, worrying that he had not spent enough time in the United States to really understand democracy in America. "I hope," he said, "I have not wasted my time . . ."

He spent nine years writing the two books of *De la Démocratie en Amérique.* He began the conclusion of his work by saying:

"It is natural to suppose that not the particular prosperity of the few, but the greater well-being of all, is most pleasing in the sight of the Creator and Preserver of men. What seems to me decay is thus in His eyes progress; what pains me is acceptable to Him. Equality may be less elevated, but it is more just, and in its justice lies its greatness and beauty. . . .

"For myself, looking back now from the extreme end of my task and seeing at a distance, but collected together, all the various things which had attracted my close attention upon my way, I am full of fears and of hopes. I see great dangers which may be warded off and mighty evils which may be avoided or kept in check; and I am ever increasingly confirmed in my belief that for democratic nations to be virtuous and prosperous, it is enough if they will to be so. . . ."

"What do you expect from society and government?" he had asked. What do you expect from American democracy?

That it "work"?

That it be "great"?

It does work, but in the democracy each of us has the right and the power to disagree about what it should do. The glory and the frustration of American democracy is that greatness is defined by each American—and that's the way we meant it to be.

Tocqueville
and Beaumont

ALEXIS DE TOCQUEVILLE was born on July 29, 1805, into a family of Norman aristocrats. His father, Comte Hervé de Tocqueville, was made a peer of France by the last Bourbon king, Charles X. His great-grandfather, Chrétien de Malesherbes, considered one of the country's great statesmen, was beheaded during the French Revolution. Tocqueville studied law and was a junior magistrate at Versailles when he traveled to the United States in 1831 on a government-sponsored mission to study American penitentiaries. His analysis of American democracy, *De la Démocratie en Amérique,* published in two parts in 1835 and 1840, was a spectacular success at home, and he was honored for a time as one of France's great political thinkers. In 1837, he ran for the Chamber of Deputies and was defeated. He was elected in 1839 and served without great distinction for more than ten years, becoming foreign minister for six months in 1849. Two years later, he was arrested and jailed briefly after Louis Napoleon seized power. Retiring to private life after his release, he devoted himself to his second great work, *L'Ancien Régime et la Révolution* (*The Old Regime and the Revolution*), an analysis of the events and ideas leading up to the French Revolution, which was published in 1856. He was married in 1835 to Mary Mottley, an Englishwoman. Never in robust health, he died in 1859 at the age of 53.

GUSTAVE DE BEAUMONT was born February 6, 1802, into an aristocratic family in the Sarthe district. His life in many ways mirrored that of his friend Tocqueville. They met in 1825 as young magistrates in Versailles and traveled together to the United States. After that trip he published a novel, *Marie, ou l'Esclavage aux États-Unis* (*Marie, or Slavery in the United States*), which was a success. He also traveled extensively in Ireland and wrote *L'Irlande Sociale, Politique, et Religieuse*. He served in the Chamber of Deputies during the period Tocqueville was there and served briefly as France's ambassador to England and Austria. He married his cousin, Clémentine de Lafayette, the granddaughter of the French and American hero, the Marquis de Lafayette. He spent the last six years of his life editing a nine-volume collection of Tocqueville's writings. He died in 1866 at the age of 64.

Acknowledgments

In October of 1978, George Wilson Pierson of Yale University wrote me a note explaining how to find a copy of his 1938 book, *Tocqueville and Beaumont in America,* and wishing me well in my plans to retrace the travels of the young Frenchmen. Every day since then, Pierson has been with me. This book would not have been possible without the scholarship of his study.

This book also would not have been possible without the talent and skills of four people: Alice Mayhew, my friend and my editor at Simon and Schuster; Suzanne Gluck, my assistant during the writing of the book; Amy Peck, my assistant during the travels; and Lynn Nesbit, my friend and my agent, who encouraged me to do the book I wanted to do.

I am also grateful to a number of friends who were more than just helpful during the planning and traveling for the book: Richard Snyder, Margery Schwartz, Ken Auletta, Amanda Urban, Laura and Barrett Seaman, Felicity Barringer and Phil Taubman, Tom Drape, Clay Felker, Jonathan Moore, Nick Mitropoulos, Ned Whelan, Karin Dorsett, Jason Lovett, Jr., John Siegenthaler, Barry Bingham, Sr., Albert Rickey, Kathy Lang Guastaferro, Ed Koch, Byron Dobell, Larry Eustis, Cokic Roberts, Ann Godoff, Shep Morgan, Bruce Parker, James Schleifer.

My wife, Cathy O'Neill, and our children, Cindy and Jeff Reeves and Colin and Conor O'Neill, were there through the good and the bad of all this, and I hope I can show my gratitude with more than these few words.

Most of all, I am in debt to the hundreds of people who gave me parts of their lives and wisdom in conversations through the days and the nights around the country. Americans.

RICHARD REEVES
New York, November 1981

People Interviewed

This is a partial list of the men and women I interviewed for this book.

NEWPORT:
Albert Sherman, Jr.   General manager, *Newport Daily News*

ALBANY:
Hugh Carey   Governor of New York
Stanley Fink   Speaker, New York State Assembly

ITHACA AND AUBURN:
Thomas Buerkle   Editor, *Cornell Daily Sun*
Robert Henderson   Warden, Auburn Correctional Facility
Mario Izzo   Educational supervisor, Auburn Correctional Facility
Andrew Knobel   Editor in chief, *Cornell Daily Sun*
Walter Mills   Guard, Auburn Correctional Facility
Robert Murray   Editor, *Cornell Daily Sun*
Cushing Strout   Professor of history, Cornell University
L. Pearce Williams   Professor of history, Cornell University

CANANDAIGUA:
George Ewing   Publisher and editor, *Daily Messenger*

ROCHESTER:

Eugene Genovese	Professor of history, University of Rochester
Laurence Kirwan	Chairman, Monroe County Democratic Committee
Christopher Lasch	Professor of history, University of Rochester
Allen Neuharth	President and chairman of the board, Gannett Corporation
Alan Underberg	Attorney
Barbara Wilson	Social worker
Richard Wilson	Chairman, Monroe County Legislature
Andrew Wolfe	Newspaper publisher

BUFFALO:

William Gaiter	Chairman, People Enterprises, Inc.
William Hoyt	State Assembly member
Jeremy Jacobs	Chairman, Sportsystems
Robert Milonzi	Attorney, member New York State Public Utilities Commission

CINCINNATI:

J. Vincent Aug	Magistrate, U.S. Court of Appeals, Sixth Circuit
John Burlew	Attorney
David Flick	Reporter, *Cincinnati Post*
Dennis Guastaferro	Newspaper executive
Kathy Lang Guastaferro	Associate director, Cincinnati Bar Association
Charles Kamine	Attorney
Darlene Kamine	Attorney
Potter Stewart	Justice, Supreme Court of the United States
Theodore Weinkam	Attorney

LOUISVILLE:

Joseph Ardery	Secretary, Louisville Area Chamber of Commerce
Barry Bingham	Chairman, Louisville-Courier Journal Corporation
Amy Byck	Student
Dann Byck, Jr.	President, Byck's
Charles Farnsley	Former mayor
Elmer Hall	City editor, *Courier-Journal*
Marsha Norman	Playwright
Wilson Wyatt	Former mayor

NASHVILLE:

Beverly Asbury	Chaplain, Vanderbilt University
Mansfield Douglas III	City councilman
Penny Edwards	Assistant to the Lieutenant Governor of Tennessee
Henry Kantor	Furniture store owner
Gilbert Merritt	Judge, U. S. District Court
Ken Shapero	Editor, *Harpeth Herald*
John Siegenthaler	Publisher, *Tennessean*
Fate Thomas	Sheriff, Davidson County, Tennessee
Hugh Walker	Historian

MEMPHIS:

Paul Cappock	Historian
Charles Crawford	Historian
Michael Grehl	Editor, Memphis *Commercial Appeal*
Vernon Richards	Taxi driver
Albert C. Rickey	Attorney
Ann Rickey	Board member, WKNO-TV
Lamar Willis	City director of libraries

NEW ORLEANS:

Robert Ainsworth	Judge, U.S. Court of Appeals, Fifth District
Broderick Bagert	City Councilman
Gilbert Bochet	French consul
Jack Davis	City editor, New Orleans *States-Item*
Lawrence Eustis III	Mortgage broker
Hubert de Germiny	Press attaché, French Consulate
Karen Giger	Public television producer
James Glassman	Founder, *Figaro* newspaper
Susan Hess	Investor
William Hess	Investor
Stephan Lemann	Attorney

MONTGOMERY:

Ray Jenkins	Editor, *Montgomery Advertiser*

BALTIMORE:

Louis Azreal	Columnist, Baltimore *News American*
Charles Carroll III	Assistant vice-president, Chesapeake and Potomac Telephone Company

Charles Carroll IV	Medical student
Jon Katz	Editor, *The News-American*
Dr. Richard S. Ross	Dean, Johns Hopkins Medical School
Garry Wills	Writer

SAGINAW AND GREEN BAY:

David Rogers	Editorial page editor, *Bay City Times*

DETROIT:

Robert Battle III	Regional director, United Auto Workers
William Beckham	Director of administration, Burroughs Corporation
Philip E. Benton, Jr.	Vice president, Ford Motor Company
Kenneth Cockrell	City Councilman
Enid Eckstein	Auto worker
Douglas Fraser	President, United Auto Workers
Antonio Green	Student, Highland Park High School
Gilbert Hill	Chief, Homicide Squad, Detroit Police Department
David Jensen	Realtor
Jason Lovett, Jr.	Photographer and writer
Jon Lowell	Reporter, *Newsweek*
Rick Martin	President, Local 600, United Auto Workers
Dorothy Pruitt	Welfare recipient
Edward Reingold	Bureau chief, *Time*
Barrett Seaman	Bureau chief, *Time*
Laura Seaman	Housewife
Paul Thomas	Policeman
Remer Tyson	Reporter, *Detroit Free Press*
G. Mennen Williams	Justice, Michigan Supreme Court
Roy Levy Williams	Executive director, Detroit Urban League
Paul Witteman	Correspondent, *Time*

PHILADELPHIA:

Edwin Bronner	Librarian, Haverford College
James Charlton	Inmate, Graterford Correctional Institute
George Child	Taxi driver
Joseph Clark	Former U.S. Senator
Rexcell Cook	Inmate, Graterford Correctional Institute

Richard Doran	Executive director, Greater Philadelphia Partnership
Richard Easterlin	Professor of economics, University of Pennsylvania
William J. Green III	Mayoral candidate
Edwin Guthman	Editor, *Inquirer*
James Karyn	President, WHYY-TV
Frank C. P. McGlinn	Vice president, Western Savings Bank
Vebley Mills, Jr.	Inmate, Graterford Correctional Institute
John Morris	Business agent, Local 115, International Brotherhood of Teamsters
Miguel Rivera	Inmate, Graterford Correctional Institute
Eugene Roberts	Executive editor, *Inquirer*
Thomas Stachelek	Assistant to the superintendent, Graterford Correctional Institute

BOSTON:

Derek Bok	President, Harvard University
Edmund G. Brown, Jr.	Governor of California
Edwin Diamond	Lecturer in political science, Massachusetts Institute of Technology
Leonard Fein	Editor, *Moment* magazine
William Fitzsimmons	Director of admissions, Harvard College
Barney Frank	State Representative
Betty Friedan	Writer
Ellen Goodman	Columnist, *Boston Globe*
Stanley Hoffman	Professor of government, Harvard University
David G. Jannson	Director, Innovation Center, Massachusetts Institute of Technology
James Kelly	Management analyst
Anne Mandelbaum	Law student
Michael Mandelbaum	Associate professor of government, Harvard University
Jonathan Moore	Director, Kennedy Institute of Politics
Philip Morison	University Professor of Physics, Massachusetts Institute of Technology
Richard Neustadt	Professor of government, Harvard University
Gary Orren	Professor of political science, Brandeis University
Howard Pearlmutter	Computer Programmer

David Riesman	Professor of sociology, Harvard University
Judith Shklar	Professor of government, Harvard University
Kristor Stendahl	Dean, Harvard School of Divinity
Laurence Tribe	Professor, Harvard Law School
Daniel Yergin	Research fellow, Harvard Business School
Dr. Dorothy Zinberg	Psychiatrist
Dr. Norman Zinberg	Psychiatrist, Harvard Medical School

NEW YORK:

Ted Ashley	Former chairman, Warner Brothers
Ken Auletta	Writer
David Brown	Deputy mayor
Ruth Clark	Vice president, Yankelovich, Skelly & White
Judith Daniels	Editor, *Savvy* magazine
Clay Felker	Editor, *Daily News Tonight*
Dr. Eugene Galanter	Director, Psychophysics Laboratory, Columbia University
Simon Gourdine	Deputy Commissioner, National Basketball Assoc.
L. Clinton Hoch	Executive vice president, Fantus Corporation
Donald Katz	Writer
Edward Koch	Mayor
Jerzy Kozinski	Writer
Abraham Lass	Retired high-school principal
Will Maslow	General counsel, American Jewish Congress
Ronay Menschel	Executive administrator, New York City
Roger Mulvihill	Attorney
Richard Nixon	Former President of the United States
Andres Oppenheimer	Reporter, Associated Press
Tully Plesser	Pollster
Richard Ravitch	Chairman, Metropolitan Transportation Authority
Felix Rohatyn	Investment banker
Rabbi Alexander Schindler	President, Union of American Hebrew Congregations
Robert Schrank	Project officer, Ford Foundation
Allen Schwartz	Corporation counsel, City of New York

Peter Solomon	Commissioner of Economic Development
Gloria Steinem	Editor, *Ms.* magazine
Richard Wald	Vice president, ABC News
Lloyd Williams	Vice chairman, Harlem Chamber of Commerce

LOS ANGELES:

Steve Stockwell	Artist
Maxine Waters	California Assembly member
Diane Watson	Member, Los Angeles Board of Education

WASHINGTON:

Arthur Angel	Attorney
Patrick Caddell	Pollster
Joseph Early	Professor of chemistry, Georgetown University
Gary Hart	U.S. Senator from Colorado
Walter Isaacson	Correspondent, *Time*
Ray Jenkins	Deputy Press Secretary to the President
Nicholas Lemann	Editor, *Washington Monthly*
Daniel Martire	Chairman, Department of Inorganic Chemistry, Georgetown University
James Reston	Vice president and columnist, *New York Times*
Michael Jay Robinson	Political scientist, George Washington University
William Safire	Columnist, *New York Times*
Philip Smith	Assistant director, Office of Science and Technology Policy
Strobe Talbot	Diplomatic correspondent, *Time*
Steven Weisman	Correspondent, *New York Times*

Notes

PREFACE

13 "I shall go see there . . ." Tocqueville, letter to Charles Stoffels, from Versailles, August 26, 1830. From George Pierson, *Tocqueville and Beaumont in America* (Oxford University Press, New York, 1938), pp. 31–32. Hereafter Tocqueville's letters in that volume are cited *TocqL*.

Chapter 1: NEWPORT

22 Spending $13.25, I suddenly found printed reason to believe . . . The issues in which the quotations used in this chapter appear are, in the same order, *U.S. News and World Report*, Vol. 86, No. 19, May 14, 1979, p. 59; *Mother Jones*, Vol. 4, No. 6, July 1979, p. 27; *New Age*, Vol. 5, No. 1, July 1979, p. 15; *Harvard Business Review*, Vol. 57, No. 3, p. 22.
24 "Saturate your senses with a Sarah's Family acrylic bong . . ." The issue of *High Times* which I did not buy but quote is No. 50, October 1979. The advertisement appears on p. 11.
25 Twenty-two of its 36 pages . . . The issue of the *Newport Daily News* that I am discussing is Thursday, May 10, 1979.

Chapter 2: VERSAILLES TO NEWPORT

29 "the first philosophical book ever written on democracy . . ." John Stuart Mill's comments appeared in the *Edinburgh Review*, No. CXLV, October 1840, p. 3.

30 "We went to visit the town . . ." This portion of Tocqueville's letter to his mother was written on May 14, 1831. Pierson, p. 54.

30 "This race is entirely commercial . . ." Beaumont's letter to his family was written on May 14, 1831. Hereafter *BeauL*, Pierson, p. 55.

30 *"Caractère national des américains . . ."* The note on Mr. Schermerhorn commences Tocqueville's diary proper, hereafter *TocqD*. He had already begun writing letters home, portions of which would eventually make their way into his final work. Pierson, p. 49.

32 "I have long had the greatest desire . . ." *TocqL*, to Charles Stoffels, Versailles, August 26, 1830; Pierson, p. 31.

32 "You know just exactly . . ." *TocqL*, to Charles Stoffels, Paris, November 4, 1830; Pierson, p. 32.

33 He began *Democracy in America* . . . The English translation of *Democracy in America* cited here and throughout this volume is the 1966 translation by George Lawrence (J. P. Mayer, ed., Harper and Row, New York, 1966). Mr. Pierson's book uses the earlier translation by Henry Reeve (John Allyn Publishers, Boston, 1876, 6th ed.) Lawrence, pp. 17, 19, 24. (The Mayer-Lawrence edition has been reprinted by Doubleday Anchor Books, New York, 1969.)

34 "No novelty in the United States . . ." Lawrence, p. 3.

34 "The nations of our day . . ." Lawrence, p. 680.

35 "We understand that two magistrates . . ." Pierson, p. 58.

35 "Everyone here overwhelms us . . ." *BeauL*, Pierson, p. 59.

35 "American Usages . . ." *TocqD*, Pierson, p. 65.

Chapter 3: ALBANY

36 "a man of very simple manners . . ." *BeauL*, Pierson, p. 215.

36 "He took us for a walk in the woods . . ." *BeauL*, to his sister, July 14, 1831; Pierson, p. 215.

36 "I. What kind of men . . ." Tocqueville did not indicate which Livingston he talked with. *TocqD*, Pierson, p. 118.

37 "In the United States it is men . . ." Lawrence, p. 189.

37 "I was again assured today . . ." *TocqD*, Fifth Notebook; Pierson, p. 608.

38 "his person indicates physical . . ." *TocqD*, Fifth Notebook, December 31, 1831; Pierson, p. 611.

38 "Daniel Webster," . . . "like thousands of other . . ." Francis Lieber recalls Tocqueville's words in his letter to G. S. Hillard, December 1852, from T. S. Perry, *The Life and Letters of Francis Lieber*, p. 256.

38 "When the right of suffrage is *universal* . . ." *TocqD*, Fifth Notebook; Pierson, p. 608.

39 "In the United States . . ." Lawrence, p. 222.

41 "National prosperity is the prosperity . . ." From the Record of the New York State Legislature, Fifty-fifth Session.

41 "All fine corps . . ." Pierson, p. 180.

41 "It's the national guard . . ." *TocqL*, Pierson, p. 180.

42 "In a carriage . . ." *BeauL*, Pierson, p. 181.

42 "Nothing is more annoying . . ." Lawrence, p. 219.

42 "Once more, however . . ." *BeauL*, Pierson, p. 183.

42 "That was really a fine . . ." *TocqD*, Pierson, p. 183.

43 "We had wanted to stay . . ." *TocqL*, to Chabrol, Auburn, July 16, 1831; from the Yale Tocqueville Collection; Pierson, p. 185.

44 "All the details of social life . . ." Lawrence, p. 667.

44 "In a word" . . . "there are . . ." Lawrence, pp. 54, 103.

45 "In America" . . . "the Union's subjects . . ." Lawrence. p. 142.

45 "Here the central power acts . . ." Lawrence, p. 143.

47 "I think that, generally speaking . . ." Lawrence, pp. 530–531.

Chapter 4: ITHACA AND AUBURN

51 "I was saying that . . ." *BeauL*, to his sister Eugénie, July 14, 1831; Pierson, p. 193.

51 "breathless cupidity." Lawrence, p. 421.

52 "Men's main opinions . . ." Lawrence, pp. 616, 644.

53 "They prefer trade . . ." *BeauL*, to his sister Eugénie, July 14, 1831; Pierson, p. 215.

56 "a small town . . ." *TocqL*, to his mother, July 17, 1831; Pierson, p. 214.

57 "by the aid of an instrument . . ." *TocqL*, to Chabrol, Auburn, July 16, 1831; Pierson, p. 212.

57 "the most effective . . ." *TocqD*, Non-Alph. Notebook I; Pierson, p. 208.

57 "How much do you pay . . ." *TocqD*, Non-Alph. Notebook I; Pierson, p. 211.

58 "We must understand . . ." *TocqD*, Non-Alph. Notebook I; Pierson, p. 209.

Chapter 5: CANANDAIGUA

62 "Canandagua is on the road . . ." *BeauL*, July 22, 1831; Pierson, p. 216.

64 "I know Canadaigua lives by . . ." "Travels Through America," *Esquire*, February 1976, pp. 33–34.

66 The *Messenger* duly reported . . . The issue referred to is May 13, 1979.

66 "it was by promising . . ." Lawrence, p. 354.

66 "Better use has been made . . ." Lawrence, p. 174.

67 "How is your public education . . ." *TocqD*, July 17–18, 1831; Pierson, p. 221.

67 "All of the people I've seen . . ." *TocqD*, June 1, 1831; Pierson, p. 114.

68 Part of the entertainment . . . Pierson, p. 89.

69 "The Americans" . . . ". . . enjoy explaining . . ." Lawrence, pp. 498–499.

70 "A National Agenda for the Eighties." *Report of the President's Commission for a National Agenda for the Eighties* (Government Printing Office, Washington, D.C., 1980).

72 "The most distinguished man . . ." *BeauL*, to his mother, July 22, 1831; Pierson, p. 216.

72 "Q. What is the influence . . ." *TocqD*, July 17–18, 1831; Pierson, p. 219.

73 ". . . the number of periodical . . ." Lawrence, pp. 170–171.

73 "The first newspaper I saw . . ." Lawrence, pp. 168–169.

74 "The Press—The channel of public opinion . . ." *TocqD*, Pierson, p. 89.

74 "I admit" . . . "that I do not feel . . ." Lawrence, pp. 169–170.

Chapter 6: ROCHESTER

76 "Competition prevents any newspaper . . ." Lawrence, pp. 170–171.

78 "So the Americans have not yet . . ." Lawrence, p. 439.

78 "The nation's premier newspaper growth company . . ." The quotation is from the Gannett Annual Report for 1980.

79 "The hallmark of the American journalist . . ." Lawrence, p. 171.

79 "In times of equality . . ." Lawrence, p. 672.

83 "Authors are quick to see . . ." Lawrence, p. 458.

87 "The same historical development . . ." Christopher Lasch, *The Culture of Narcissism* (Norton, New York, 1978), p. 235.

88 ". . . public opinion is the dominant power." Lawrence, p. 399.

88 "The Union" . . . "principally exists . . ." Lawrence, p. 362.

90 "The contagion of unintelligibility . . ." Lasch, *The Culture of Narcissism*, p. 78.

Chapter 7: CINCINNATI

95 "There is one thing that America . . ." *TocqD*, Fifth Notebook, Nov. 30, 1831; Pierson, p. 548.

95 "Concerning Equality in America." *TocqD*, Fifth Notebook, November 30, 1831; Pierson, pp. 549–551.

96 "A singular spectacle . . ." *TocqD*, Fifth Notebook; Pierson, p. 552.

98 "Is it true," he asked . . . *TocqD*, Non-Alph. Notebook III; Pierson, p. 556.

99 "It is of the essence of judicial power . . ." Lawrence, pp. 672–673.

101 "I went today to view . . ." *TocqD*, Pierson, p. 560.

102 "We have yielded too much . . ." *TocqD*, Non-Alph. Notebook III; Pierson, p. 555.

102 "We have carried 'Democracy' . . ." *TocqD*, Non-Alph. Notebook III; Pierson, pp. 557–558, 561.

103 "Yet the state enjoys . . ." *TocqD*, Non-Alph. Notebook III; Pierson, p. 565.

106 ". . . nothing could be more obscure . . ." Lawrence, p. 246.

106 "There is hardly a political question . . ." Lawrence, pp. 248, 247.

106 "Naturally strongly opposed to . . ." Lawrence, p. 243.

Chapter 8: LOUISVILLE

108 "Just now the vessel . . ." *TocqD*, Pierson, p. 576.

108 "The thaw doesn't come . . ." *BeauD*, Pierson, p. 576.

110 "There are preachers hawking . . ." Lawrence, p. 506.

110 "business men of religion." *TocqD*, Pierson, p. 156.

110 "Sunday is rigorously observed . . ." *TocqL*, to L. de Kergolay, Yonkers, June 29, 1831; Pierson, p. 154.

111 "The South, whose men are ardent . . ." Lawrence, p. 350.

111 "Mr. McIlvain, one of the greatest . . ." *TocqD*, Pierson, p. 582.

115 "I have previously made the distinction . . ." Lawrence, p. 241.

116 "The U.S. Department of Housing . . ." The issue of the *Louisville Times* referred to is January 19, 1979.

116 "The U.S. Office of Surface Mining . . ." The issue of the *Courier-Journal* referred to is January 10, 1979.

121 "The man you left behind . . ." *TocqD*, Pierson, p. 237.

121 "The time must come . . ." Lawrence, p. 378.

Chapter 9: NASHVILLE AND MEMPHIS

126 "Nothing is more rare . . ." *TocqD*, Pierson, p. 585.

126 "Slavery. We are habituated . . ." *TocqD*, Pierson, p. 586.

126 "We made the acquaintance . . ." *TocqL*, Pierson, p. 581.

127 "The roads, the canals and . . ." *TocqD*, Pierson, pp. 598–599.

127 "As they mingle . . ." Lawrence, p. 352.

129 "We spend our life enduring howling . . ." *TocqL*, to his sister-in-law Alexandrine, New York, June 20, 1831; Pierson, p. 142.

130 "Tocqueville and I laughed like the blessed . . ." *BeauL*, Pierson, p. 150.

130 "The fine arts are here . . ." *BeauL*, Pierson, p. 73.

130 "So far" . . . "America . . ." Lawrence, p. 277.

130 "The style will often be strange . . ." Lawrence, p. 441.

131 "What I say about the Americans . . ." Lawrence, p. 591.

132 "It is their mores . . ." Lawrence, p. 283.

132 "I do not think the intervening ocean . . ." Lawrence, p. 422.

136 "all have a lively faith . . ." Lawrence, p. 343.

Chapter 10: NEW ORLEANS

138 "There is not a white but . . ." *TocqD*, Pierson, p. 631.

138 "You must provide a higher level . . ." The quotation is from the February 8, 1979, edition of the *Times-Picayune*.

139 The city still had two . . . The three-day period referred to is February 6–8, 1979.

142 "The influx of Vietnamese refugees . . ." This quotation appeared in the *States-Item*, February 6, 1979.

143 "New Orleans is a patchwork . . ." *TocqD*, Pierson, pp. 627–628.

143 "Everybody works," Tocqueville wrote home . . . *TocqL*, Pierson, p. 453.

144 "Free, they can hope for nothing . . ." *TocqD*, Pierson, p. 631.

146 "The power of association . . ." Lawrence, p. 487.

148 "Mr. Smith, a very able . . ." *TocqD*, Third Notebook; Pierson, p. 514.

148 On May 17, 1954, the Chief Justice . . . The historic case referred to is *Brown* v. *Board of Education of Topeka*, 1954. An analysis of the case and of the history of black legal rights in America is found in Richard Kluger's *Simple Justice* (Knopf, New York, 1976).

152 ". . . the Constitution of the United States . . ." Lawrence, p. 134.

Chapter 11: MONTGOMERY

153 "I have just made a fascinating . . ." *TocqL*, Pierson, p. 636.

156 "On arriving in Montgomery . . ." *TocqD*, Fourth Notebook; Pierson, p. 642.

156 "There is no one here . . ." *TocqD*, Pierson, p. 640.

159 "How are roads made and repaired . . ." *TocqD*, written January 12–17, 1832, Non-Alph. Notebook III; Pierson, p. 653.

162 "Thus, in the moral world . . ." Lawrence, p. 40.

Chapter 12: BALTIMORE

165   "A Negro having taken the liberty ..." *BeauL*, to his brother, Achille, Philadelphia, November 8, 1831; Pierson, p. 491.

165   "He possesses the most vast domain ..." *TocqD*, Non-Alph. Notebook III; Pierson, pp. 506–507.

171   "There is indeed a manly and legitimate passion ..." Lawrence, pp. 473–476.

171   "All the ways and habits of mind ..." *TocqD*, Pierson, p. 507.

171   "Do you not regret ..." *TocqD*, Pierson, p. 497.

172   "What do you expect from society ..." Lawrence, p. 226.

172   "You mustn't exaggerate the inconveniences ..." *TocqD*, Pierson, p. 497.

Chapter 13: SAGINAW

177   "We bought pillows, a compass ..." *TocqD*, Pierson, pp. 240–241.

178   "The Americans never use ..." Lawrence, p. 278.

182   "Nothing even resembles our villages ..." *TocqD*, pp. 236–237.

183   "Twenty very neat and pretty houses ..." *"Quinze Jours au Désert,"* Pierson, pp. 246–250. *Quinze Jours* was published in part in 1860 and its first full publication was in Pierson's book. Tocqueville apparently decided not to insert it in the appendix of the second volume of *Democracy in America*, so as not to compete with Beaumont's novel about race relations, *Marie, ou l'Esclavage aux États-Unis, Tableau de Moeurs américaines.*

185   "We pursued our way in the woods ..." *"Quinze Jours au Désert,"* Pierson, pp. 252, 258–259.

186   "A wilderness of fifteen leagues ..." *"Quinze Jours au Désert,"* Pierson, pp. 260–261.

187   "Each of these trees rises ..." *"Quinze Jours au Désert,"* Pierson, p. 262.

187   "In a few years these impenetrable forests ..." *"Quinze Jours au Désert,"* Pierson, p. 278.

188   "I am going to describe them here ..." *"Quinze Jours au Désert,"* Pierson, pp. 241–244.

Chapter 14: GREEN BAY

192   "All have a lively faith ..." Lawrence, p. 343.

192   "How Equality Suggests ..." Lawrence, pp. 419–420.

193   "The idea of perfection ..." *TocqL*, First Notebook; Pierson, p. 119.

194 "For people in this frame of mind . . ." Lawrence, p. 429.

195 "These Presbyterians," Father Mullon said . . . *TocqD*, Pierson, pp. 292, 298.

195 "At bottom as intolerant . . ." *TocqL*, New York, June 20, 1831, from the Yale Tocqueville Collection; Pierson, p. 155.

195 "Their sects are without number . . ." *"Quinze Jours au Désert,"* Pierson, p. 283.

195 "We are not afraid of Catholicism . . ." *TocqD*, Boston, September 30, 1831, Sixth Notebook; Pierson, p. 415.

198 Sigmund Freud, the Viennese founder . . . The two quotations appear in Ronald W. Clark's biography, *Freud: The Man and the Cause* (Random House, New York, 1980), pp. 278–279.

199 "In the long run," Tocqueville wrote . . . Lawrence, p. 455.

200 "It's incredible to see . . ." *TocqL*, New York, June 20, 1831, from the Yale Tocqueville Collection; Pierson, p. 155.

201 "Economic man himself has given way . . ." These quotations appear in Lasch's *The Culture of Narcissism* (Norton, New York, 1978), pp. xvi, 13.

201 "Sunday is rigorously observed . . ." *TocqL*, New York, June 20, 1831, from the Yale Tocqueville Collection; Pierson, pp. 153–154.

205 "While the law allows . . ." Lawrence, p. 269.

205 "In ages of faith the final aim . . ." Lawrence, pp. 519–521.

Chapter 15: DETROIT

207 "Walk in the town," Tocqueville wrote . . . *TocqD*, Pierson, p. 224.

207 "I don't believe I've ever experienced . . ." *"Quinze Jours au Désert,"* Pierson, p. 233.

207 "Soon after the shores of Canada . . ." *"Quinze Jours au Désert,"* Pierson, pp. 238, 236.

210 "great social principles" . . . *TocqD*, Pierson, p. 414.

215 "Brandy" said another man . . . *TocqD*, Pierson, p. 235.

220 "If the whites of North America . . ." Lawrence, pp. 328–329.

221 "Is it that the Indians do not . . ." *TocqD*, Pierson, p. 303.

221 "It is obvious," he wrote . . . Lawrence, p. 292.

221 "The Spaniards let their dogs loose . . ." Lawrence, pp. 312–313.

222 "In Kentucky the majority would . . ." *TocqD*, Pierson, p. 583.

222 "The great rankling sore . . ." *TocqD*, Pierson, p. 474.

222 "There are two facts which . . ." *TocqD*, Pierson, p. 418.

223 "The most formidable evil . . ." Lawrence, p. 313.

224 "You can make the Negro free" . . . Lawrence, p. 314.

226 "One would say that the European . . ." *TocqD*, First Notebook, July 6, 1831; Pierson, pp. 191–192.
229 "Once one admits," Tocqueville wrote . . . Lawrence, p. 327.
231 "The absolute sovereignty of the will . . ." Lawrence, pp. 227, 233–234.

Chapter 16: PHILADELPHIA I

237 The next morning, the city's . . . The story ran on June 20, 1979.
237 "They associate in the interests of commerce . . ." *TocqD*, Pierson, p. 381.
238 "Of all that I have seen . . ." *TocqD*, Pierson, pp. 480–481; this citation includes Tocqueville's conversation with Charles Ingersoll.
239 "There is only one party . . ." *BeauL*, Pierson, p. 116.
240 "This form of freedom . . ." Lawrence, p. 494.
242 "In America," . . . "there is no limit . . ." Lawrence, p. 495.
242 "The power of association . . ." *TocqD*, Pierson, p. 482.
246 "manufacturing aristocracy . . ." Lawrence, p. 530.
247 "the victory and the rule . . ." *TocqD*, Pierson, p. 483.
250 "futile pursuit of that . . ." Lawrence, p. 509.
252 "This city of 200,000 souls . . ." *BeauL*, to his father, October 16, 1831; Pierson, p. 457.
252 "Philadelphia is, I believe . . ." *TocqL*, Pierson, p. 458.

Chapter 17: PHILADELPHIA II

253 "The prison is truly a palace . . ." Beaumont and Tocqueville, *On the Penitentiary System* . . . ; Pierson, p. 463.
255 "In its intention . . ." Charles Dickens, *American Notes for General Circulation* (Chapman and Hall, London, 1842), pp. 119–120.
255 "No. 41. This inmate is a young man . . ." Beaumont and Tocqueville, *On the Penitentiary System* . . . ; Pierson, 464–465.
258 "During the whole course . . ." *TocqD*, Pierson, p. 210.
260 "I doubt whether in any other country . . ." Lawrence, p. 86.
262 "The traditional residential . . ." Marvin Wolfgang, "Real and Perceived Changes of Crime and Punishment," *Daedalus*, Vol. 107, No. 1 (Winter 1978).
265 "It would be degrading . . ." *TocqD*, Pierson, p. 512.
266 " 'The people is always right' . . ." *TocqD*, Pierson, p. 515.
266 ". . . in democracies there is nothing . . ." Lawrence, p. 227.

Chapter 18: BOSTON I

270   "Mr. Clay, who appears to have . . ." *TocqD*, Pierson, p. 375.

272   "To clear, cultivate, and transform . . ." Lawrence, p. 597.

274   "The people has the Republic . . ." *TocqD*, Pierson, p. 378.

275   "For fifty years," Tocqueville wrote . . . Lawrence, p. 343.

277   "Reflection: What disturbs us . . ." *TocqD*, Pierson, p. 380.

277   "The effort made in this country . . ." *TocqL*, Pierson, p. 452.

Chapter 19: BOSTON II

289   "Causes of the social condition . . ." *TocqD*, Pierson, p. 453.

290   "I believe that our origin . . ." Lawrence, p. 228.

290   "I here mean the term 'mores' . . ." Lawrence, pp. 264, 282–284.

294   "I cannot express my thoughts better . . ." Lawrence, p. 369.

294   "Although its curriculum . . ." "The Success of a Strategy," by the Board of Directors, Harvard Business School Publication, p. vii.

295   "A decision tree . . ." Peter Cohen, *The Gospel According to Harvard Business School* (Penguin, New York, 1973).

296   "Nowadays the need is to keep men . . ." Lawrence, p. 430–431.

296   "Instead of meeting the challenge . . ." Ryohei Suzuki, "Worldwide Expansion of U.S. Exports—A Japanese View," *Sloan Management Review*, Spring 1979, p. 1.

296   "It's much more difficult . . ." Robert H. Hayes and William J. Abernathy, "Managing Our Way to Economic Decline," *Harvard Business School Review*, July/August 1980, p. 68.

300   "Americans are naturally inclined . . ." Lawrence, pp. 422, 427.

302   "Not a man but may reasonably . . ." *TocqL*, Pierson, p. 130.

Chapter 20: BOSTON TO NEW YORK

304   "Family sentiments have come . . ." "*Quinze Jours au Désert,*" Pierson, pp. 243–245.

304   "In America, a woman loses . . ." Lawrence, p. 568.

305   "I have shown how democracy . . ." Lawrence, p. 576.

305   "And now that I come near . . ." Lawrence, pp. 578–579.

305   "In the United States . . ." Lawrence, p. 222.

307   "The women's movement . . ." Elizabeth Hardwick, "Domestic Manners," *Daedalus*, Vol. 107, No. 1 (Winter 1978), p. 10.

309   "I repeat what I have said before . . ." *TocqD*, Pierson, p. 152.

309   "When a woman marries . . ." *TocqL*, Pierson, p. 144.

311 "Whatever happens to the feminist . . . movement . . ." Sandra
Baxter and Barbara Lansing, *Women and Politics:* The Invisible
Majority (University of Michigan Press, Ann Arbor, 1980), p.
53.

Chapter 21: NEW YORK

315 "We understand that two magistrates . . ." Pierson, p. 58.
315 "To a Frenchman the aspect . . ." *TocqL,* Pierson, p. 67.
316 "Saturday evening," Beaumont wrote . . . *BeauL,* Pierson, p.
73.
317 "Everyone here overwhelms us . . ." *BeauL,* Pierson, p. 59.
317 "I should like to describe it . . ." *TocqL,* Pierson, pp. 90–91.
318 "These people seem to me . . ." *TocqL,* Pierson, p. 68.
319 "Picture to yourself an attractively . . ." *TocqL,* Pierson, p.
493.
322 "What strikes every traveler . . ." *TocqL,* Pierson, p. 161.
325 "This nomad people . . ." *"Quinze Jours au Désert,"* Pierson, p.
244.
331 "I'm the assistant manager of . . ." Daniel Yankelovich, "Work,
Values, and the New Breed," in *Work in America: The Decade
Ahead,* Clark Kerr and Jerome Rosow, eds. (Van Nostrand and
Reinhold, New York, 1979), pp. 3–34.
332 "Choose any American at random . . ." Lawrence, p. 370.
335 "Cities are not permanent . . ." "A National Agenda for the
Eighties," *Report of the President's Commission for a National
Agenda for the Eighties* (Government Printing Office, Washington, D.C., 1980). This report, a product of 13 months of study,
was presented to President Jimmy Carter during his last month
in office.

Chapter 22: WASHINGTON

340 "The American, on sea as on land . . ." *TocqD,* Pierson, p.
645.
341 "Only an ambitious or a foolish man . . ." *TocqD,* Pierson, pp.
659–660.
341 "We find it hard to hold . . ." *TocqL,* Pierson, p. 670.
341 "One hears that generally . . ." *TocqD,* Pierson, p. 645.
342 "Washington," he told his father . . . *TocqL,* Pierson, p. 667.
343 "When one enters the House of Representatives . . ."
Lawrence, p. 185.
343 "He would certainly have lost . . ." Lawrence, p. 360.
343 "Accidental Causes That May Increase . . ." Lawrence, pp.
113–114.
343 "In the half century . . ." Lawrence, p. 205.

345 ". . . as people become more like . . ." Lawrence, p. 539.

345 "The ever increasing number of men . . ." Lawrence, p. 621.

345 "Military revolutions," he wrote . . . Lawrence, p. 624.

352 "What do you expect from society . . ." Lawrence, p. 226.

353 "Bad laws, revolutions, and anarchy . . ." Lawrence, p. 377.

353 "In America," the Frenchman wrote . . . Lawrence, pp. 502–503.

354 "Since in times of equality . . ." Lawrence, p. 648.

354 "Democratic ages are times . . ." Lawrence, p. 648.

354 "Aristocratic nations are by their nature . . ." Lawrence, pp. 419–420.

355 "An Indian woman came up . . ." Lawrence, p. 295.

356 "I hope," he said . . . *TocqL*, Pierson, p. 678.

356 "It is natural to suppose . . ." Lawrence, pp. 678–680.

Bibliography

Abel, Elie, ed., *What's News: The Media in American Society*, Institute for Contemporary Studies, San Francisco, 1981.

Abrahamsen, David, M. D., *Our Violent Society*, Funk and Wagnalls, New York, 1970.

Adler, Richard, ed., *Television as a Cultural Force*, Praeger, New York, 1976.

Anderson, Thornton, *Jacobson's Development of American Political Thought*, Appleton-Century-Crofts, New York, 1961.

Auletta, Ken, *The Streets Were Paved with Gold*, Random House, New York, 1975.

Baltzell, E. Digby, *Puritan Boston and Quaker Philadelphia*, Macmillan/Free Press, New York, 1979.

Barnet, Richard J., *The Lean Years: Politics in the Age of Scarcity*, Simon and Schuster, New York, 1980.

Baskil, Lawrence M., and William A. Strauss, *Chance and Circumstance: The Draft, the War and the Vietnam Generation*, Knopf, New York, 1978.

Baxter, Sandra, and Marjorie Lansing, *Women and Politics: The Invisible Majority*, University of Michigan Press, Ann Arbor, 1980.

Becker, Carl L., *The Declaration of Independence: A Study in the History of Political Ideas*, Vintage, New York, 1958.

Beer, Samuel H., "Federalism, Nationalism, and Democracy in America," Presidential Address, American Political Science Association, 1977. *American Political Science Review*, Vol. 72.

Bezold, Clement, ed., *Anticipatory Democracy*, Vintage, New York, 1978.

Birmingham, Stephen, *"Our Crowd,"* Harper and Row, New York, 1967.

Boorstin, Daniel J., *Democracy and Its Discontents: Reflections on Everyday America*, Random House, New York, 1971.

———, *The Americans: The Democratic Experience*, Random House, New York, 1973.

Brant, Irving, *The Bill of Rights*, Mentor, New York, 1965.

Brogan, D. W., *The American Character*, Knopf, New York, 1944.

Brogan, Hugh, *Tocqueville*, Collins/Fontana, London, 1973.

Bryce, James, *The American Commonwealth*, The Macmillan Company, New York, 1907.

Bushman, Richard L., et al., eds., *Uprooted Americans*, Little, Brown, Boston, 1979.

Cash, W. J., *The Mind of the South*, Knopf, New York, 1960.

Cater, Douglass, ed., *Television as a Social Force*, Praeger, New York, 1975.

Clark, Ronald W., *Freud: The Man and the Cause*, Random House, New York, 1980.

Coffin, Frank M., *The Ways of a Judge*, Houghton Mifflin, Boston, 1980.

Epstein, Joseph, *Ambition*, E. P. Dutton, New York, 1981.

Evans, Eli N., *The Provincials: A Personal History of Jews in the South*, Atheneum, New York, 1974.

Fallows, James, *National Defense*, Random House, New York, 1981.

Farrand, Max, *The Framing of the Constitution of the United States*, Yale University Press, New Haven, Conn., 1913.

Foehl, Harold M., and Irene M. Hargreaves, *The Story of Logging the White Pine in the Saginaw Valley*, Red Keg Press, Bay City, Mich., 1964.

Forster, Arnold, and Benjamin Epstein, *The New Anti-Semitism*, McGraw-Hill, New York, 1974.

Freud, Sigmund, *A General Introduction to Psychoanalysis*, Garden City Publishing, Garden City, N.Y., 1938.

Fried, Charles, *Right and Wrong*, Harvard University Press, Cambridge, Mass., 1978.

Friedan, Betty, *The Second Stage*, Summit Books, New York, 1981.

Fuller, Chet, *I Hear Them Calling My Name: A Journey Through the New South*, Houghton Mifflin, Boston, 1981.

Garreau, Joel, *The Nine Nations of North America*, Houghton Mifflin, Boston, 1981.

Giscard d'Estaing, Valéry, *French Democracy*, Doubleday, New York, 1977.

Glazer, Nathan, *Affirmative Discrimination: Ethnic Inequality and Public Policy*, Basic Books, New York, 1976.

Glazer, Nathan, and Daniel P. Moynihan, *Beyond the Melting Pot*, M.I.T. Press, Cambridge, Mass., 1963.

Graham, Gene, *One Man, One Vote*, Little, Brown, Boston, 1972.

Hadden, Jeffrey K., and Charles E. Swann, *Prime Time Preachers*, Addison-Wesley, Reading, Mass., 1981.

Hale, Nathan G., Jr., *Freud and the Americans*, Oxford University Press, New York, 1971.

Handlin, Oscar, *Race and Nationality in American Life*, Little, Brown, Boston, 1957.

Harris, Leon, *The Merchant Princes*, Harper & Row, New York, 1979.

Henn, Harry G., *Corporations: Cases and Materials*, West Publishing, St. Paul, Minn., 1974.

Hodgson, Godfrey, *America in Our Time*, Doubleday, New York, 1976.

Hoffman, Stanley, *Primacy or World Order: American Foreign Policy Since the Cold War*, McGraw-Hill, New York, 1978.

Hofstadter, Richard, *The Age of Reform*, Vintage, New York, 1955.

Howard, A. E. Dick, "The Law: A Litigation Society?" *Wilson Quarterly*, Vol. 5, No. 3 (Summer 1981).

"How Others See the United States," *Daedalus*, Vol. 101, No. 4 (Fall 1972).

Huer, Jon, *The Dead End: The Psychology and Survival of the American Creed*, Kendall/Hunt, Dubuque, Iowa, 1977.

Isaacs, Stephen D., *Jews and American Politics*, Doubleday, New York, 1974.

Johnson, Paul E., *A Shopkeeper's Millennium: Society and Revivals in Rochester, New York, 1815–1837*, Farrar, Straus & Giroux, New York, 1978.

Journal of Drug Issues, Vol. 9, No. 2 (Spring 1979). Volume Title: "Control Over Intoxicant Use: Pharmacological, Psychological, and Social Considerations," Richard L. Rachin, ed.

Kaiser, Robert G., and Jon Lowell, *Great American Dreams*, Harper & Row, New York, 1979.

Kammen, Michael, *People of Paradox*, Knopf, New York, 1973.

Kennedy, John F., *A Nation of Immigrants*, Harper & Row, New York, 1958.

Kennedy, Robert F., Jr., *Judge Frank M. Johnson, Jr.*, Putnam, New York, 1978.

Kirkpatrick, Jeane J., *Political Woman*, Basic Books, New York, 1974.

Kriegel, Leonard, and Abraham H. Lass, eds., *Stories of the American Experience*, Mentor, New York, 1973.

Lasch, Christopher, *The Culture of Narcissism: American Life in an Age of Diminishing Expectations*, Norton, New York, 1978.

Laski, Harold J., *The American Democracy*, Viking, New York, 1948.

LeBoutillier, John, *Harvard Hates America*, Gateway Editions, South Bend, Ind., 1978.

Lippmann, Walter, *Public Opinion*, Macmillan/Free Press, New York, 1965.

Lipset, Seymour Martin, ed., *The Third Century: America as a Post-Industrial Society*, Hoover Institution Press, Stanford, Calif., 1979.

Malcolm X, *The Autobiography of Malcolm X*, Grove, New York, 1966.

Mandelbaum, Michael, *The Nuclear Revolution*, Cambridge University Press, New York, 1981.

Marshall, Paul W., William J. Abernathy, et al., *Operations Management: Text and Cases*, Richard D. Irwin, Homewood, Ill., 1975.

Maurois, André, *A History of France*, Funk and Wagnalls, New York, 1948.

McCarthy, Eugene J., *America Revisited*, Doubleday, New York, 1978.

McWilliams, Carey, *California: The Great Exception*, Peregrine Smith, Santa Barbara, Calif., 1979.

———, *North from Mexico*, Greenwood Press, Westport, Conn., 1968.

Miller, William Lee, *Of Thee, Nevertheless, I Sing*, Harcourt Brace Jovanovich, New York, 1956.

Muller, Steven, "A New American University?" *Daedalus*, Vol. 107, No. 1 (Winter 1978).

Murphy, William J., Jr., "Alexis de Tocqueville in New York," *New York Historical Society Quarterly*, Vol. 61, Nos. 1/2 (Jan./Apr. 1977).

The Public Interest, No. 41 (Fall 1975).

Rawls, John, *A Theory of Justice*, Harvard University Press, Cambridge, Mass., 1971.

Reich, Charles A., *The Greening of America*, Random House, New York, 1970.

Remini, Robert V., *Andrew Jackson and the Course of American Freedom 1822–1832*, Vol. 2, Harper & Row, New York, 1981.

Report of the National Advisory Commission on Civil Disorders, Bantam, New York, 1968.

Rieff, Philip, *The Triumph of the Therapeutic*, Harper & Row, New York, 1966.

Riesman, David, *Individualism Reconsidered and Other Essays*, Free Press, Glencoe, Ill., 1954.

———, *The Lonely Crowd*, Yale University Press, New Haven, Conn., 1950.

Robinson, Michael J., "Television and American Politics: 1956–1976," *The Public Interest*, No. 48 (Summer 1977).

Schrank, Robert, *Ten Thousand Working Days*, M.I.T. Press, Cambridge, Mass., 1978.

Scott, William G., and David K. Hart, *Organizational America*, Houghton Mifflin, Boston, 1979.

Sennett, Richard, *The Fall of Public Man*, Knopf, New York, 1977.

Sidorsky, David, ed., *The Future of the Jewish Community in America*, Basic Books, New York, 1973.

Stearn, Gerald Emmanuel, ed., *Broken Image: Foreign Critiques of America*, Random House, New York, 1972.

Thurow, Lester C., *The Zero-Sum Society*, Basic Books, New York, 1980.

Toffler, Alvin, *The Third Wave*, William Morrow, New York, 1980.

Tussman, Joseph, *Obligation and the Body Politic*, Oxford University Press, New York, 1960.

Vaillant, George E., *Adaptation to Life*, Little, Brown, Boston, 1977.

Vogel, Ezra F., *Japan as Number One*, Harper/Colophon, New York, 1979.

Wade, Richard C., *The Urban Frontier*, University of Chicago Press, Chicago, 1959.

Weaver, John D., *Warren: The Man, the Court, the Era*, Little, Brown, Boston, 1967.

Weinberg, Louise, "A New Judicial Federalism?" *Daedalus*, Vol. 107, No. 1 (Winter 1978).

Westin, Alan F., and Barry Mahoney, *The Trial of Martin Luther King*, Thomas Y. Crowell, New York, 1974.

Wicklein, John, *Electronic Nightmare: The New Communications and Freedom*, Viking, New York, 1981.

Wills, Garry, *Bare Ruined Choirs*, Doubleday, New York, 1971.

Wiltse, Charles M., *The New Nation*, Hill and Wang, New York, 1961.

Wolfgang, Marvin E., "Real and Perceived Changes of Crime and Punishment," *Daedalus*, Vol. 107, No. 1 (Winter 1978).

Woodford, Frank B., and Arthur M. Woodford, *All Our Yesterdays: A Brief History of Detroit*, Wayne State University Press, Detroit, 1969.

Yankelovich, Daniel, *New Rules: Searching for Self-Fulfillment in a World Turned Upside Down*, Random House, New York, 1981.

Index

About the Author

RICHARD REEVES was born in New York City and grew up in Jersey City, New Jersey. A graduate of Stevens Institute of Technology, he worked as an engineer before becoming the first editor of the weekly Phillipsburg, N.J., *Free Press*. He was a reporter for the Newark, N.J., *Evening News, The New York Herald Tribune*, and *The New York Times*. His syndicated column appear twice weekly in more than 150 newspapers nationwide. His work has appeared in virtually every national magazine, and he has been the political editor of *New York* and the national editor of *Esquire*. He has written and hosted two nationally televised films, one of which, *Lights, Camera . . . Politics*, for ABC News, was the winner of the 1980 Emmy for documentaries. He is the author of five books.